Challenging Global Inequality

Development Theory and Practice in the 21st Century

Alastair Greig, David Hulme and Mark Turner

First published 2007 by
PALGRAVE MACMILLAN

Palgrave Macmillan in the UK is an imprint of Macmillan Publishers Limited, registered in England, company number 785998, of Houndmills, Basingstoke, Hampshire RG21 6XS.

Palgrave Macmillan in the US is a division of St Martin's Press LLC, 175 Fifth Avenue, New York, NY 10010.

Palgrave Macmillan is the global academic imprint of the above companies and has companies and representatives throughout the world.

Palgrave® and Macmillan® are registered trademarks in the United States, the United Kingdom, Europe and other countries.

ISBN-13: 978–1–4039–4823–6   hardback
ISBN-10: 1–4039–4823–2   hardback
ISBN-13: 978–1–4039–4824–3   paperback
ISBN-10: 1–4039–4824–0   paperback

This book is printed on paper suitable for recycling and made from fully managed and sustained forest sources. Logging, pulping and manufacturing processes are expected to conform to the environmental regulations of the country of origin.

A catalogue record for this book is available from the British Library.

Library of Congress Cataloging-in-Publication Data

Greig, Alastair, 1960–
    Challenging global inequality : development theory and practice in the 21st
    century / Alastair Greig, David Hulme, and Mark Turner.
        p. cm.
    Includes bibliographical references and index.
    ISBN-13: 978–1–4039–4823–6 (cloth)
    ISBN-10: 1–4039–4823–2 (cloth)
    ISBN-13: 978–1–4039–4824–3 (paper)
    ISBN-10: 1–4039–4824–0 (paper)
        1. Economic development. 2. Income distribution. 3. Equality. I. Hulme,
    David. II. Turner, Mark, 1949– III. Title.

    HD82.G674 2007
    338.9—dc22   2006049783

10   9   8   7
16   15   14   13   12   11   10

Printed and bound in Great Britain by
CPI Antony Rowe, Chippenham and Eastbourne

Contents

Acronyms and Abbreviations

APEC	Asia-Pacific Economic Cooperation
BCCs	basic Christian communities [Latin America]
CCP	Chinese Communist Party
CDP	Community Development Program [India]
CEO	chief executive officer
CIA	Central Intelligence Agency [USA]
CIS	Commonwealth of Independent States [former Soviet Union]
EU	European Union
FGT	Foster, Greer, Thorbeeke (measures of poverty)
G3	Group of 3 countries (Brazil, India, South Africa)
G8	Group of 8 (industrialized countries) – Canada, France, Germany, Italy, Japan, United Kingdom, United States of America and Russia
G20	Group of 20 poor countries formed to negotiate within the WTO
GATT	General Agreement of Tariffs and Trade
GDP	Gross Domestic Product
GNI	Gross National Income
GNP	Gross National Product
HDI	Human Development Index
HIPCs	heavily indebted poor countries
HIV/AIDS	Human Immunodeficiency Virus/Acquired Immunodeficiency Syndrome
IBRD	International Bank for Reconstruction and Development
ICSID	International Centre for Settlement of Investment Disputes
ICT	information and communication technology
IDA	International Development Association
IFC	International Finanical Corporation
IFI	international financial institution
ILO	International Labour Organization
IMF	International Monetary Fund
IT	information technology
IITs	Indian institutes of technology
MDGs	Millennium Development Goals
MIGA	Multilateral Investment Guarantee Agency
NAFTA	North American Free Trade Agreement
NATO	North Atlantic Treaty Organization

NEGS	National Employment Guarantee Scheme [India]
NGO	non-government organization
NIC	newly industrializing country
NLD	National League for Democracy (Burma)
NRI	non-resident Indian (see Box 6.3)
ODA	Official Development Assistance
OECD	Organization for Economic Co-operation and Development
OPEC	Organization of Petroleum Exporting Countries
PPA	Participatory Poverty Assessment
PPP	purchasing power parity
PRA	Participatory Rural Appraisal
PRIs	*Panchayati Raj* institutions [India]
PRS	Poverty Reduction Strategy
PRGF	Poverty Reduction and Growth Facility Loan
PRSC	Poverty Reduction Strategy Credit
RRA	Rapid Rural Appraisal
SADC	South African Development Community
SAP	Structural Adjustment Programme
TCC	transnational capitalist class
TINA	'there is no alternative' principle
TNCs	transnational corporations
UFC	United Fruit Company (USA)
UNCTAD	United Nations Conference on Trade and Development
UNDP	United Nations Development Programme
UNICEF	United Nations Children's Fund
UNHCR	United Nations High Commissioner for Refugees
VLWs	village-level workers
WB	World Bank
WCS	World Capitalist System
WTO	World Trade Organization

Boxes

Preface and Acknowledgements

This book emerged out of many requests for David Hulme and Mark Turner to produce a second edition of their popular text *Sociology and Development: Theories, Policies and Practices*, originally published in 1990. However, David and Mark's ever-lengthening commitments kept the project at arms length. That original book began through a chance encounter of two Liverpudlians on the shores of the Coral Sea, and this new project received its impetus from another chance encounter of one of those Liverpudlians with a Glaswegian on the shores of Lake Burley Griffin in Canberra, Australia. A mutual friend introduced Mark to Alastair Greig and they soon established a routine of tennis matches followed by football stories over a beer. Alastair was an admirer of *Sociology and Development*, having used it in his development courses, and was delighted when Mark suggested he help substantially revise the book.

Our initial aim was more modest than the final product. At this stage we remained attached to the structure of the original text which began with the methodologies and theories of development before exploring various themes within the field. However, comments from anonymous referees convinced us that the changes within development studies since 1990 – the implosion of the communist bloc, growing global interconnectedness, regional divergences and new developmental initiatives from the world community – justified a more ambitious project. While this book remains inspired by the original text, not one sentence remains. The first three chapters still provide a methodological and contextual introduction to development, but in a very different way than in *Sociology and Development*. The rest of the book departs significantly from its predecessor by providing a more chronological flow, greater interdisciplinary character and increased attention to international political economy.

These emphases on chronology and interdisciplinarity relate to the two key arguments we advance. First, we argue that it is important to historically contextualize contemporary developmental problems in order to assess policy proposals. It is sometimes difficult to appreciate the weight of 60 years of development theory and practice when focusing on immediate practical problems. We have dealt with this history by endeavouring to allow competing views on development to speak for themselves rather than impose our judgement on them. Our aim is to allow readers to reflect on debates and issues and make their own judgements, either through the further readings provided or through discussion with others. This stance that we have adopted resembles the rules that the playwright Harold Pinter (2006: 17) lays down for political theatre: 'Sermonising has to be avoided at all cost . . . The characters must be allowed to breathe their own air. The author cannot confine and restrict them to satisfy his own disposition or prejudice.'

The dialogue focuses on our second and more specific argument – that inequality matters – and we show how this issue of inequality has remained a central feature of development debates from colonial times to the present. As the title of the book suggests, we strongly believe that a just global order must challenge global inequality and this involves inequalities between nations as well as between people and within nations. As a consequence, each chapter explores inequalities from different angles, from neoliberalism to globalization, and from the Millennium Development Goals to political participation. By exploring global inequalities from as many perspectives and through as many issues as possible, we hope to evoke C. Wright Mills' (1973) injunction in *The Sociological Imagination* to allow our mind to become a moving prism, catching light from as many angles as possible.

Jointly authored books pose their own challenges which can threaten the viability of a project, especially if the contributors disagree on particular matters. Fortunately, in this case we found that we were generally singing from the same songsheet and that communication and discussion could resolve any minor differences of opinion. But even where authors are in agreement on the contents of a book, there has to be coordination. This role was assumed by Alastair who was the hub, with spokes extending to Mark, David and Steven Kennedy, the publisher at Palgrave Macmillan. The hub was also mobile with a sabbatical partly spent in the United Kingdom enabling Alastair to meet up directly with both David and Steven. Thus, distance did not prove to be tyrannical. David originally drafted Chapter 2 and Mark drafted Chapter 10. Alastair drafted the remaining chapters. Each chapter received substantial input from the other two authors (especially Mark's contribution to Chapter 3 and David's to Chapter 6) and we therefore take joint responsibility for its final shape.

Alastair would like to thank his colleagues Lawrence Saha, Andrew Hopkins and Maria Hynes as well as the many tutors who have worked with him thoughout the years designing development courses. He is also indebted to the Institute of Development Policy and Management at the University of Manchester where the earliest drafts of this book were written in the most congenial circumstances possible. At the Australian National University, the time to research and write were only made possible through the administrative skills of Helen Felton. Collectively, we would like to thank Steven Kennedy for his patience and his enthusiasm for the project, the anonymous reviewers who provided us with sage advice on the original proposal and the later drafts, Dayle Stubbs for casting her keen student eye over an earlier draft, Lulu Respall-Turner for her copy-editing and for producing the index, Valery Rose for her careful and sensitive editing, David Clark for his generosity and his wonderful *Companion to Development Studies* (2006), and Paul Kringas without whom this collaboration would never have occurred. Our partners, as always, deserve the final thanks.

A website with internet links, update materials and other resources to support this text can be found at http://www.palgrave.com/politics/greig

Chapter 1

Introduction: the Story so Far . . .

Arguing about Inequality

An Overview of Global Inequality
  Inequalities across countries
  Inequalities within countries
  Inequalities across the world's people

The Paradox of Modernity: the Polarization of Opulence and Deprivation

Debating Development in the Twenty-first Century

Arguing about Inequality

In the aftermath of the Second World War, development studies emerged as a discipline concerned with bridging the gap between richer and poorer countries through economic growth. Confidence abounded among Western academics and politicians that this development project could be accomplished. Development was listed high on the priorities of both the wealthier and the poorer nations and the techniques and resources to achieve it were available. Never before had such a constellation of forces for overcoming global inequality come into alignment.

However, a quarter of a century later, the economist Peter Donaldson (1973: 224) considered the 'development gap' between the few rich countries enjoying affluence and the majority of the world's deprived population as '*the* most pressing economic problem of our times' (Donaldson's emphasis). A further quarter of a century later, David Landes (2002: xx) claimed that the 'gap in wealth and health that separates rich and poor' was the 'greatest single problem and danger' confronting the twenty-first century. In 2005, the Commission for Africa (2005: 7) described the contrast between the world's wealthy and the conditions of the poor in Africa as 'the greatest scandal of our age'.

1

Given the persistence of global inequality, it is understandable that many commentators consider the development project to be a failure. This book assesses the history of development theory and practice since the end of the Second World War, draws lessons from this experience and then outlines the key challenges in addressing global inequality in the twenty-first century. In charting this path, the book highlights the fact that global inequality 'trails the career of modern development policy as its dark shadow' (Pieterse 2004: 69). In the early twenty-first century, this shadow of inequality is lengthening and deepening over the world (UNDP 1992: 45; UNDP 2005: Ch. 2). While Chapters 3 and 7 are devoted to the analysis of contemporary data on poverty and inequality, an initial sketch of the key dimensions of inequality and development is an essential starting point for our account.

An Overview of Global Inequality

The United Nations' *Human Development Report 2003* (UNDP 2003: 39) provides a useful classificatory scheme for looking at income inequalities: inequality across countries, inequality within countries, and inequality across the world's people. While income inequality cannot capture the full impact of inequalities along other dimensions of social life (such as gender, ethnicity and region), these indicative economic statistics clearly demonstrate the enormous gulf between rich and poor. They also illustrate the scope and scale of challenging global inequality in the twenty-first century.

Inequalities across nations

By the turn of the new millennium, the richer countries (representing just over one-fifth of the world's population) were producing over four-fifths of the world's measurable production or Gross National Product (GNP). Even the remaining one-fifth of global GNP was disproportionately accounted for by a small number of East Asian countries. Gross National Product per head ranged from US$100 or less in Ethiopia, Democratic Republic of Congo and Burundi through to over US$35,000 in Japan, Norway, Switzerland and Luxembourg.

The per-capita income gap between the richest and poorest countries has progressively increased over the past 200 years from a ratio of 3:1 to between 30:1 or 50:1 (J. Kay 2003: 40; see also Landes 2002: xx; Sachs 2005: 26; UNDP 2003: 39). Even though global per-capita income trebled between 1960 and the mid-1990s, there were over 100 countries whose per-capita income had declined since the 1980s (W. Robinson

2004: 139). For many of these countries, their 'share of world exports had declined, food production per capita had decreased, their infrastructure had deteriorated, and most of them were even more dependent on agricultural-commodity exports than they had been when they started out' (Rapley 2002: 152). Average daily calorie intake in the poorest one-fifth of countries is one-third of that of the richest one-fifth (Easterly 2002: 11).

The wealthiest countries also dominate global trade and have most clout in influential international institutions such as the International Monetary Fund (IMF) and the World Trade Organization (WTO). One of the most contentious issues in global politics in the twenty-first century involves this inequality of power between nations to dictate the rules of global trade (Buckman 2005).

Inequalities within countries

While these statistics suggest growing levels of inequality between nations, they cannot shed light on inequalities within countries. Such evidence indicates that the distribution of national income within countries has become increasingly skewed towards the rich over the past few decades. Assessing data from 73 countries, the United Nations Development Programme (UNDP 2005: 55) estimated that 53 countries (containing 80 per cent of the world's population) experienced rising inequality. A narrowing of inequality occurred in only nine countries (containing 4 per cent of the world's population).

All nations exhibit some degree of inequality and this is often measured using the Gini Index. Using this method, a country with a perfectly even distribution of income is assigned a value of 0 and a country where one person possesses all income is assigned a value of 100. Poorer countries tend to have a more uneven distribution of income. According to the UNDP (2003: 282–5), the world's three most egalitarian countries (with scores under 25) are Japan, Denmark and Hungary. The most unequal (with scores over 60) are Brazil, Nicaragua, Botswana, Swaziland, Central African Republic and Sierra Leone. In egalitarian Japan, the poorest 20 per cent of the population received 10.6 per cent of income, while the richest 20 per cent receive 35.7 per cent. This contrasts with Brazil and Botswana where the poorest 20 per cent receive just over two per cent and the richest 20 per cent account for over 70 per cent of income (UNDP 2005: 56). In Mexico, the richest person commands an income equivalent to the poorest 17 million citizens (Rapley 2004: 87). Wealthier countries have also recently witnessed rising inequalities, suggesting that national wealth does not shield the entire population from poverty (for the USA, see Wade 2004; Yates 2004).

Inequalities across the world's people

The increase in the global movement of goods and services over the past few decades has encouraged researchers to employ more global indicators of inequality. Large transnational corporations now employ far fewer workers from their country of origin than they did 30 years ago. According to Rapley (2004: 88): 'the principal polarity is not between rich and poor countries, but between rich and poor people across the globe'. This globalization of production and trade has raised the salience of inequalities across nations *and* classes. Klein (2001: 390) calculated that in the late 1990s Disney Corporation's CEO earned in one hour the equivalent of 16.8 years wages of one of the company's Haitian clothing workers. Nike's annual advertising budget was equivalent to 19 years' worth of wages for the entire 50,000 workforce at one of its Chinese factories.

The richest 20 per cent of the world's population accounted for 70 per cent of income in 1960. By 1991 this share increased to 85 per cent. Meanwhile the bottom 20 per cent declined from 2.3 per cent to 1.4 per cent. The ratio between the richest and poorest increased from 30:1 to 60:1 (Pieterse 2004: 61). By the end of the millennium, the wealthiest 5 per cent of the world's population earned 114 times as much as the poorest 5 per cent and the top 1 per cent earned the equivalent of the bottom 57 per cent (UNDP 2003: 39). The 200 largest US fortunes exceeded the income of 43 per cent of the world's population, or the entire wealth of over a billion Chinese.

Some futurologists have predicted the emergence of an '80:20 society', where technological efficiency will reduce the gainfully employed to 20 per cent of the world's population, leaving the biggest 'problem' for the world's policy-makers one of determining what to do with the superfluous 80 per cent of humanity (Martin and Schumann 1997: Ch. 1). Others claim that we are already in the midst of a 'two-thirds society' where the bottom third is denied meaningful participation in formal economic activities (Lash and Urry 1994). Regardless of the label, these statistics suggest that the global trend is towards more regressive distribution of income and wealth – or as Easterly (2002: 60) states: 'The rich have grown richer; the poor have stagnated'.

The Paradox of Modernity: the Polarization of Opulence and Deprivation

While the economic data points to the perpetuation, or even extension, of social inequality across the globe, it is equally valid to maintain that the world has never seen so much wealth, innovation and ingenuity (Norberg 2005). It now takes under two weeks for the world to produce the same output as the whole of the year 1900 (George 2004: 47). Even discounting for population growth, this is testimony to the staggering increases in human productive capacity. In many profound ways, the world has progressively become a healthier, wealthier place (Lomberg 2001). Sachs (2005: 49) defends modern economic growth on the grounds that it has brought higher 'living standards than were imaginable two centuries ago, a spread of modern technology to most parts of the world, and a scientific and technological revolution that still gains strength'. Referring to global economic growth in the new millennium, the Economic Counsellor of the IMF, Raghuram Rajan, informed a press gathering in May 2006 that 'it would be fair to say to the world, "You have never had it so good"' (International Monetary Fund 2006).

The evidence in this book suggests that this statement needs substantial qualification. This form of growth 'has also brought phenomenal gaps between the richest and poorest, gaps that were simply impossible when poverty gripped all of the world' (Sachs 2005: 49). Even institutions usually associated with unbridled optimism in modern economic growth, such as the IMF, have acknowledged that over the past few decades one in five of the world's population has gone backward economically. A key challenge for development involves addressing this gap between 'unprecedented opulence' and 'remarkable deprivation' (Sen 2001: xi). This sharpening of inequality represents one of the distinguishing features of contemporary life.

Given the global reach of modern communication systems, there would appear to be much greater scope for cross-cultural benevolence. However, the instantaneous communication systems at the fingertips of most people in high-income countries must be contrasted with the fact that one-third of the poorer world does not even have access to a postal service (Bibby 2003: 10). By the turn of the new millennium, while 50 per cent of US citizens had internet access, the corresponding figure for the continent of Africa was 0.4 per cent (McCormick 2002; Woodall 2000). Hobsbawm (2000: 166–7) identified this 'digital divide' as one of the greatest paradoxes of the new millennium:

> in a world filled with such inequalities, to live in the favoured regions is to be virtually cut off from the experience, let alone the reactions, of people outside those regions. It takes an enormous effort of the imagination, as well as a great deal of knowledge, to break out of our comfortable, protected, and self-absorbed enclaves and enter the uncomfortable and unprotected larger world inhabited by the majority of the human species. We are cut off from this world even if the sum

total of amassed information is everywhere accessible at the click of a mouse, if the images of the remotest parts of the globe reach us at all times of day and night, if more of us travel between civilizations than ever before.

Within the field of development studies there has long been a wide variety of explanations for this paradox of modernity – the existence of extreme poverty in a world of unprecedented wealth. The middle section of this book (Chapters 5 and 6) is devoted to outlining the history of these theoretical approaches. One type of analysis that has remained influential pays attention to endowment factors within poorer countries. By identifying characteristics that a country lacks – or internal forces that inhibit development – this 'endogenous' approach adopts an 'individualistic' perspective on development and social change. Each country is assessed as a self-contained unit where the development policy objectives involve restructuring the cultural, economic and political conditions to lay the foundations for the form of development that previously occurred in the now-developed world. Countries that experience mass deprivation must be lifted up to the status of the wealthier ones.

However, ever since development emerged as a global concern after the Second World War, there have been voices that drew attention to the *interconnected* nature of global inequality. This approach looks to the relationship between different national units of analysis. From this 'structural' perspective, global inequalities are an inherent characteristic of development. A different set of questions emerge from this more 'exogenous' approach. Do powerful actors maintain their dominance by undermining the development of subordinate nations? Is the growth of poorer countries hindered by the presence and/or the strength of more powerful states? If the paradox of modernity is posed in this interconnected manner, then the answers – and solutions – to development would focus on transforming the very structures that link deprivation to opulence, rather than lifting the poorer countries up to the level of the wealthier ones.

If inequality is approached from this structuralist perspective, then the 'problem' of development shifts its focus from one of the 'lack' of development inherent within specific countries to one of how wealth is generated, e.g. who benefits and who pays? As Comeliau (2002: 13, 17) points out, if it is possible to establish a 'link' between global wealth and global poverty then the 'problem' of inequality is no abnormality to be remedied by more economic growth. Researchers would have to accept that inequality is 'the other side of the coin of progress'. This conclusion was drawn by Pope John Paul II when he condemned 'a small number of countries growing exceedingly rich at the cost of the increasing impoverishment of a great number of other countries; as a result the wealthier grow even wealthier while the poor grow even poorer' (quoted in *Asian Times Online*, 7 April 2005). If global wealth and global poverty are interconnected then the object of development studies is refocused. While individualist approaches tend to focus on the material, cultural or psychological attributes of the poor, the more structural approaches target how wealth perpetuates inequalities.

Debating Development in the Twenty-first Century

The development project, which commenced with such optimism after the Second World War, remains far from finished. It is now clearer that these efforts have not brought development to many areas of the world, despite the trillions of aid dollars transferred to the poorer countries (Easterly 2002, 2006). However, perhaps even more challenging is the growing sense of unease associated with the direction of 'progress' and development itself.

This disillusionment with the postwar development project has forced analysts to clarify the aims, means and strategies of development. One response from world leaders was a commitment in 2000 to the Millennium Development Goals (MDGs), which aim to halve global poverty by 2015. The more optimistic argue that this new restatement of the development project demands greater cooperation between rich and poor to meet the targets and that political will can overcome the paradox of increasing wealth amid extreme poverty. The more pessimistic point out that one-third of the way through the MDG project many poor countries are well-off-target.

Pessimism is not confined to the world of the poor. The high-income countries have not been immune to traumatic changes. Earlier postwar approaches to development tended to assume that these countries had attained their goal of development and that the problem of progress was the domain of the 'developing' world. However, over the past few decades, the so-called 'developed world' has experienced profound economic change and social dislocation – industrial restructuring, technological change, growing inequality and insecurity. Their higher productive capacity has not shielded them against sudden shifts in fortune (Wallerstein 2002: 93).

There is also a foreboding that the world might be overshooting its ecological threshold (Meadows, Randers and Meadows 2005). Environmentalists who voice this concern radically revise the question of development – it has become *the* problem rather than an answer to global problems. Increasingly, the capacity of the planet to accommodate a

---

Box 1.1   Questions addressed by chapter

Chapter 2
What is the relationship between poverty and inequality?

Chapter 3
How can international development be measured?

Chapter 4
How did the idea of development emerge and how was it related to inequality?

Chapter 5
What were the dominant ways of understanding development after the Second World War?

Chapter 6
What are the dominant approaches to and forms of development in the 21st century?

Chapter 7
What are the Millennium Development Goals, do they address inequality and how are they related to development theory?

Chapter 8
What is globalization and how is it related to inequality?

Chapter 9
What approaches have emerged that challenge mainstream understandings of development?

Chapter 10
Does development facilitate political equality and higher levels of community participation?

Chapter 11
By the beginning of the 21st century, is it possible to assess the development project as a failure? What are the most useful ways of understanding development?

---

world of 'developed' nations has been questioned by researchers who point to the adverse consequences of modern economic growth; from greenhouse gas emissions, desertification, loss of biodiversity, salinity, water scarcity, air pollution and enhanced risk of disease transmission. In addition, the model of development that has produced such unprecedented material abundance in the West is based on a number of non-renewable resources whose depletion can only accelerate if more countries develop in the same direction as the advanced capitalist world. Thus, global inequalities pose serious moral and political dilemmas for international cooperation on environmental sustainability.

The environmental question is only one of several challenges to the development project. Another important contemporary challenge in development studies is the 'postdevelopment' critique that forms part of a broader postmodern rejection of Western belief in progress. Postdevelopment thought has pointed to the frailty of our theoretical tools and provides a valuable warning that the stories generated about the past – and which are used to help outline the contours of the future – should always be open to reinterpretation and never considered fixed.

These are some of the central challenges that are addressed in the following chapters (see Box 1.1). This book deliberately avoids beginning with a definition of 'development' precisely because its nature has become more contentious as the field of development studies has broadened. To begin with a fixed definition would narrow the debate before assessing the history of development. The following chapters therefore set the conceptual, methodological and theoretical foundations for development studies (Chapters 2–4) before examining the practice of development over the past half century (Chapters 5 and 6) and evaluating the current challenges facing development studies in the foreseeable future (Chapters 7–10). The Conclusion reviews competing definitions of development and concurs with Hobsbawm (2000: 141) that 'inequality of opportunity in the world will be one of the crucial factors in the future of mankind'. The most pressing task facing development practice is to take sustained steps towards reducing social inequalities, for this is the most effective way of liberating the millions of people who live in poverty and giving them a life of greater opportunity, security and dignity.

Chapter 2

The Nature of Inequality and Poverty

The Nature of Inequality

The Nature of Poverty

The Conceptualization of Poverty in Development Theory and Policy

Poverty and Inequality: What are the Interactions?
    Individualist approaches
    Structuralist approaches

Inequality and poverty have long been major concerns within development thinking, but the relative emphasis on them has changed over time. While there are several strands to development debates over these concepts, the central issue has been whether inequality plays a key role in the processes that create and maintain poverty. As the following sections show, although inequality and poverty are closely interrelated – both as concepts and as social experiences – they need to be differentiated. As Lister (2004) points out, the way that an idea – such as poverty or inequality – is conceptualized has profound implications for the identification of its 'causes' and for the forms of public and private action that are claimed to be able to tackle social problems. In the present global context this would encourage us to ask:

- What exactly do development theorists and practitioners mean when they talk about inequality and poverty?
- Is development largely about reducing absolute poverty or should it also be about reducing inequality?
- Can greater equity be achieved through developing countries 'catching up' economically or is redistribution (from rich to poor countries) and levelling down needed?

The Nature of Inequality

Like most ideas, 'inequality' appears initially to have a commonsense meaning that most people can agree on. Surely it is about the differing shares of income or wealth that the people of a particular country have. However, although this is certainly part of it, once the idea is explored more deeply its complexity begins to emerge. It is also about differences in educational levels, access to health services and perhaps the probability of having one's children die. Is inequality also to do with factors that are less easy to quantify, such as power differentials in social relations? For example, a woman in Zambia may feel obliged to sleep with her husband even though she does not want to and suspects he may have HIV/AIDS. Such power differentials can be internalized, so that a *dalit* (untouchable) in a village in Andhra Pradesh in India believes that she is naturally inferior to higher caste villagers and accepts that her family has no right to draw water from the public tubewell on a neighbour's land. She is silent about this unfair treatment because, as a *dalit* and a woman, she has been conditioned since childhood to accept inequality and, should she have consciousness of this injustice, she realizes that if she challenges such social norms she can expect to be punished.

Before the advent of modernity, inequality was often seen as a natural social condition, but during the eighteenth and nineteenth centuries people began to question this assumption (see Chapter 4). The major task taken on by such dissidents was to achieve equal rights for all before the law and in terms of political participation. As these goals were attained, at least in legislation, over the twentieth century the focus moved on to social equality: 'the idea that people should be treated as equals in all institutional spheres that affect their life-chances: in their education, in their work, in their consumption opportunities, in their access to social services, in their domestic relations and so forth' (Miller 1992: 200). Theorists exploring this idea have commonly identified two very different goals that need to be pursued – *equality of opportunity* (Friedman and Friedman 1980; Mill 1859) and *equality of outcome* (Tawney 1931).

Equality of opportunity posits that everyone should have an equal chance to achieve the benefits and rewards a society can offer. None should be privileged or held back because of their social attributes. The outcomes that individuals achieve – income, wealth, marital status, social position, education level – will vary, but this will depend on a person's efforts, abilities and choices. In the politics and policy of the second half of the twentieth century much energy was expended on the capacities of poorer countries to provide citizens with an equal start. Across the world this led to the state provision of 'free' services to children and adolescents – education, basic medical services, dental services and nutrition – so that all could fully develop their physical and cognitive abilities. Proponents of 'rights based' approaches to development have extended the concept from civil rights (political freedom, freedom of expression, equality before the law) to social rights (access to food, education, health services, water, social security) and economic rights (access to a national or global minimum income) (see Gaay Fortman 2006).

Equality of outcome is an altogether more radical concept and has been associated with socialist and communist ideology (Tawney 1931). How radical it is depends on answering the question 'equality of what?' Most commonly this has been envisioned in material terms – income, assets, housing, durable goods, basic services – rather than as complete equality. The latter has been seen as either impossible (for example, it is impossible to ensure that everyone has the same IQ, health status or lifespan) and/or as undesirable (it would mean a homogeneous society in which an individual's right to make choices and express themselves would be curtailed).

Liberal thinkers have usually concluded that the morally justified concept is 'equality of opportunity' and so the World Bank (2005: 4) is content to argue that 'from an equity perspective, the distribution of opportunities matters more than the distribution of outcomes'. In a capitalist world, inequality of outcome is to be expected. Radical conservatives even argue that inequality is essential for human prosperity and that the promotion of equality, and/or policies that seek to reduce inequality, may impact negatively on freedom and welfare (Letwin 1983). By contrast, socialists have been keener to achieve some degree of equality of outcome, but this has and is usually defined in terms of a narrow set of factors rather than complete equality.

But there is a dilemma in the present position that (in)equality has reached in development theory and practice. While most writers and organizations support the concept of equality of opportunity rather than equality of outcome, it is much easier to study and measure outcomes than opportunities (World Bank 2005: 4). Opportunities are potentials for which it is relatively difficult to acquire data. Outcomes are *ex post* achievements on which data can be collected much more easily. For example, look at education. Answers may be shaped by 'adaptive preferences' – disadvantaged people may aspire to lower levels of opportunity because they have lower expectations (Connell 1977). If we wish to measure educational outcomes we can ask people 'what is the highest level of education you achieved?' or 'what academic and professional qualifications do you have?' These are relatively easy questions to answer and they can be checked against the records of schools, universities and examination boards. By contrast, if we are looking at educational opportunity we need to ask people 'what is (or was) the highest level of education that you can (could) achieve if you fully pursue(d) all of the opportunities that are (were) available to you'? This is a much more difficult question to answer and is likely to require complex value judgements about personal circumstances and the nature of social rights to education. As a result, most studies of inequality commence by arguing that equality of opportunity is the main analytical issue but then examine this empirically largely through the use of data on outcomes (for an example, see World Bank 2005).

Empirical work on inequality has in recent times moved beyond a focus purely on 'moneymetrics' such as income inequality or land inequality and is instead examining a much wider set of variables – such as longevity, access to education and health services, and leisure time. This broadening is to be valued not merely because it provides a fuller understanding of the multidimensional experience of inequality, but also because many of these indicators relate to individuals rather than households. Much of the empirical literature on inequality needs to be treated with caution as it focuses on household level measures, income or assets, and assumes that these measures are shared equally across all the members of a household. Such an assumption means that intra-household inequality is totally ignored (see Lister 2004: 56–7).

Conceptually and empirically, research on inequality seems to reach a fork in the road when the issue of power relations – who has the ability to influence other people's lives – is broached. Structuralists argue that rather than looking at the symptoms of inequality (individual opportunities and outcomes), the focus should be the underpinning processes and causes (social structures that foster unequal power relations). Inequalities are not simply carefully constructed measurement scales but complex webs of dynamic social relations that privilege some while constraining the life-chances of others. From a structuralist perspective, poverty and deprivation are not the result of a lack of resources but the maldistribution of resources. The social structural features that mediate inequality include class, gender, race, ethnicity, caste, disability, age and position within the household.

Structuralist analyses of inequality highlight the ways in which everyday social experiences and economic processes maintain and reproduce patterns of inequality. Although such experiences and processes can be challenged through individual agency and collective action, commonly they allow the privileged and powerful to directly or indirectly limit the opportunities of the disadvantaged and powerless. Such processes usually have deep historical roots. A common device is to stigmatize certain individuals or groups so that they feel shamed and humiliated. By making jokes about them in public, giving them dismissive or aggressive looks or challenging their right to participate in social and economic life, specific people (for example, a disabled child) or groups (for example, an ethnic minority) can be encouraged to withdraw from family, community or public life. Such tactics can also undermine self-confidence and identity, reinforcing a self-image of social inferiority. There are also more direct forms of action – the threat of violence, actual violence and public beating and humiliation. Around the world these devices have been and are used to ensure that women are 'under the control' of their husbands and male relatives and that racial and ethnic minorities do not 'get above their station'. Economic practices can also be deployed – making low castes do work that is regarded as socially demeaning, such as sweeping and sanitation, or paying women lower daily rates than men when they are doing the same type of work.

While there are many different ways that everyday social experiences and economic processes interact to reproduce inequality, a particular concern within development has been gender inequality. The evidence indicates not merely that women and girls have fewer opportunities than men and boys but that absolute poverty – be it measured in terms of income, assets, human development or leisure time – is 'feminized' (Lister 2004: 55). The UN Development Programme (1995) has claimed that 70 per cent of the world's poor people are female. Amartya Sen's (1990b) work indicates that the ways in which girls are treated differently than boys leads to there being '100 million missing women' (see also Klasen 2006). Female child mortality is higher because of gender inequality.

There is also much evidence, and a vast and expanding literature, examining racial and ethnic inequality (Bates 2006). In most parts of the world, racial and ethnic minorities are highly overrepresented among the extreme poor. Racial and ethnic discrimination ensures that patterns of inequality are transferred across generations. In India, 60 years after the official abolition of the caste system, processes of stigmatization and discrimination based on caste limit the life-chances of tens of millions of people, and the 'scheduled tribes' remain excluded from the benefits of India's economic growth and rising social indicators (CPRC 2004).

Recently, there has been growing interest in age discrimination in developing countries with concerns focused on the old and the very young. The UN's Summit on Ageing in 2002 and the work of activist NGOs such as HelpAge International (1999) has put ageing on the agenda for development policy. Research has revealed that changes in family and community structures may in some situations increase the likelihood of older people being isolated and having few ways of meeting their material needs and their needs for affection and self-esteem. In other situations, especially Sub-Saharan Africa, older people may find that they have to take responsibility for their grandchildren as the HIV/AIDS pandemic spreads. The ways in which social standing changes with age vary, but a common pattern in many countries is for ageing women to experience diminishing status as their social identity shifts from wife and mother to widow with adult offspring. In a similar fashion, children have been put on the development agenda through the 1990 World Summit for Children, the Convention on the Rights of the Child and UNICEF funded surveys (Gordon et al. 2003; Mehrotra 2006).

Last, but by no means least, is the issue of class relations and inequality in the poorer countries. Analyses of unequal class relations – and their role in economic stagnation, deprivation and poverty – were central to much development theory in the 1970s and early 1980s (Amin 1974; Wallerstein 1976, 1980). But since then, class has become a concept that is much less regularly used (Booth 1985). To a significant degree this stemmed from problems of translating the concept of class across socio-economic and cultural settings and national borders. While class analysis in developing countries has not disappeared (for example see Harriss-White 2002; Huws 2000), it is much less prevalent than 30 years ago. At present, analysis focuses more on individuals and households or collectivities based on gender, race or ethnicity. As an example, the index of Desai and Potter's (2002) *Companion to Development Studies* has 3 references to social class but 19 to gender. Studies of the emerging proletariat in the factories of India and China are more likely to focus on gender relations than on class relations.

To conclude this section, and lay the ground for the next, three points must be observed. First, the concept of inequality is complex and multidimensional. Second, there are conflicting theoretical approaches to understanding the role that inequality plays in maintaining power differentials within society and across different societies. Third, when analysing the relationship between inequality and poverty, this section also suggested that there is a strong evidence, at least from a structuralist perspective, that a shift from examining inequality to analysing poverty can lead to a focus on the symptoms of poverty rather than the causes. As the next section shows, if the focus of development moves to the concept of poverty, researchers tend to turn to the lack of resources and gaps in service delivery rather than the unequal social relations that mediate the allocation of resources and the delivery of services.

The Nature of Poverty

Like inequality, poverty can appear initially to have a commonsense meaning that most people could agree on. Surely it is about people not having enough food and other essential items for basic survival? But, how much food is enough? What are the other essential items – potable water, basic clothing, minimum shelter . . . perhaps primary education and basic health services? Is poverty about not having access to these goods and services or is it about some minimum level of income? Moving on from these pragmatic issues we might ask 'what right have educated, middle-class researchers and policymakers to impose their understanding of poverty on the poor?' Shouldn't the poor themselves have a right to say what they understand poverty to be? So, as becomes evident, the concept of poverty is far from straightforward. There are many competing ideas that must be explored if one is to grasp the debates about what poverty is and how it is produced.

As a starting point it is useful to explore some of the main issues around which differing conceptual positions can be held. These are often presented as dichotomies, but it aids analysis to think of them as continua. Three such continua are narrow or broad conceptions of poverty, absolute and relative poverty, and objective and subjective poverty.

Poverty can be framed in *narrow* or *broad* terms (Lister 2004: 13). A narrow approach has the advantage of being easily comprehensible and measurable. A broader approach has the advantage of more fully exploring the multifaceted nature of poverty and of the processes that create, maintain or reduce poverty. At the *narrow* end of the continuum are meanings such as envisaging poverty as the 'inability to participate [in society] owing to lack of resources' (Nolan and Wheeler 1996: 193; see also Townsend 1979). In perhaps the greatest 'narrowing', the concept is seen as having a per capita income of less than US$1 per day. These unidimensional, money-metric conceptualizations contrast with multidimensional notions that see poverty as a set of material and non-material deprivations – lack of participation in decision-making, experiencing violence, humiliation, lack of respect and powerlessness. While some writers and agencies will argue passionately for a narrow or a broad concept, others use both at the same time.

There are also heated debates on the merits of *absolute* and *relative* poverty. The seminal work of Seebohm Rowntree (1901) has been interpreted as defining poverty in absolute terms. From this perspective poverty occurs when people cannot meet their minimum physical needs because of lack of income. As a consequence an unambiguous poverty line can be identified. In most poorer countries these lines are officially set at the point at which a person is unable to access their minimum nutritional needs for survival and reproduction (Box 2.1) – in most countries this is around 2300 calories per day for an adult (Dercon 2006). Commonly, a less stringent moderate poverty line is also set. This is the value of the extreme poverty line increased by 20 to 30 per cent for other items that are judged to be essential for survival.

Box 2.1 National poverty lines

Developing countries that have set national poverty lines have generally used the food poverty method. These lines indicate the insufficiency of economic resources to meet basic minimum needs in food. There are three approaches to measuring food poverty:

- *Cost-of-basic-needs method.* This approach sets the poverty line at the cost of a basic diet for the main age, gender and activity group, plus a few essential non-food items. A survey then establishes the proportion of people living in households with consumption (or sometimes income) below this line. The basic diet may consist of the least expensive foods needed to meet basic nutritional requirements, the typical adult diet in the lowest consumption quintile or the investigator's notion of a minimum but decent diet. The choice of both food and non-food components included is necessarily arbitrary.

- *Food energy method.* This method focuses on the consumption expenditure at which a person's typical food energy intake is just sufficient to meet a predetermined food energy requirement. Dietary energy intake as the dependent variable is regressed against household consumption per adult equivalent. The poverty line is then set at the level of total consumption per person at which the statistical expectation of dietary energy intake exactly meets average dietary energy requirements. The problem with this method is the *caviar caveat*: groups that choose a costly bundle of foods are rewarded with a higher poverty line than that for more frugal eaters.

- *Food share method.* This method derives the cost of a consumption plan to acquire just sufficient nutrients. If the cost of basic nutrients is a third of total consumption, the poverty line is fixed at three times that cost.

Source: Based on information from (UNDP 1997: 13).

Such a method has great simplicity and measurability and it focuses attention on the paramount human needs. Without sufficient food people cannot function effectively and their health declines. Prolonged dietary inadequacy is permanently detrimental to physical development (and mental development in children) and eventually results in death.

However, the apparent precision of this approach cannot go unchallenged. The first criticism is that there are big differences in the minimum amount of nutrition that people need according to their age and so adult equivalent scales are needed. Second, the unit costs of acquiring food and other essential items decrease as the size of the household increases so further adjustments have to be made. Third, there are large differences in the minimum calorific needs of people depending on their health status and employment. People with malaria or worms (most often poorer people) need additional calories to deal with their ill health. For the authors of this book, driving to work and sitting in front of their computers, 2100 to 2300 calories per day is more than sufficient. However, rickshaw pullers in Bangladesh cycling 8 to 10 hours per day require several thousand more calories if they are to be able to return to such work day after day. Thus, poverty lines assume homogeneity of needs when heterogeneity may be the dominant characteristic within a population.

The fourth criticism of income poverty lines is that such devices treat people as if they are livestock – being reared individually rather than part of a broader society. From this critical perspective comes the argument that as human beings are social actors, poverty needs to be defined in relation to other people in a society. Such arguments have won out in OECD countries where official poverty lines are almost always defined in *relative* rather than *absolute* terms. So in European countries, for example, the poverty line is usually set at 60 per cent of a country's median income (Lister 2004: 42). Thus, as a country's wealth increases so does its official poverty line. A relative poverty line is seen as more appropriate as people experience poverty in relation to their fellow citizens. How could someone in Canada, for example, participate in society if they did not have access to television, radio, telephones, culturally appropriate clothing or were not functionally literate – things that most fellow citizens see as 'normal'?

A related axis of debate among poverty researchers concerns *objective* and *subjective* poverty. Objective definitions and measures of poverty are specified by researchers who collect and analyse data and decide who is poor and non-poor according to these definitions. Such definitions and measures have the advantages of being rigorously specified and permit comparisons to be made over time and space. However, critics would point out that such definitions inevitably involve explicit or implicit value judgements and so the claim to 'objectivity' needs to be scrutinized.

By contrast, subjective definitions and measures (or assessments) of poverty are made by people about their own status and of others in their community or society. They are subjective as the respondents, rather than the external analysts, determine what poverty is and what the acceptable 'minimum levels' of goods, services, well-being or other factors should be. In terms of knowledge creation this has the great advantage of letting those most knowledgable about the experience of poverty (such as the people who live in poor communities) determine what the content of poverty is. It can also be argued to be ethically more justifiable than objective approaches, as it recognizes the right of poor people and poor communities to create and disseminate social knowledge. But it also has disadvantages as people living in different areas may set different criteria and, over time, people may change their definitions and their perceptions. This makes subjective comparisons more difficult than objective ones (Clark and Qizilbash 2003).

In development studies and development policy, subjective approaches to poverty assessment have become *de rigueur* in the last few years. The Poverty Reduction Strategies (PRSs) that poorer countries now have to prepare to access development assistance funds (foreign aid) require that Participatory Poverty Assessments (PPAs) be conducted alongside the conventional statistical analyses of 'objective' data. It is argued that combinations of orthodox, quantitative analysis and participatory subjective assessment produce deeper understandings of the nature and causes of poverty. In this way, more effective poverty reduction policies can be designed. There are debates, however, about whether such differing approaches can be integrated and/or whether PPAs are a mere 'add-on' to 'objective' analyses (see McGee 2004 for a review of these issues in Uganda).

Across the social sciences there are considerable tensions between those who pursue conceptualizations of poverty that facilitate measurement (narrow, means-based, absolute and objective) and those who believe that such simplifications are fundamentally flawed as they avoid the less quantitative, more structural, aspects of poverty that are essential to understanding how poverty is produced and reproduced. The measurement 'camp' is usually occupied by economists, econometricians, quantitative sociologists and social statisticians. Governments, international financial institutions (IFIs such as the World Bank and IMF) and policymakers gravitate towards this camp. In the structuralist 'camp' are critical sociologists, anthropologists, radical political economists and heterodox economists. Their analyses are most often picked up and supported by radical NGOs and civil society groups, trade unionists, environmentalists and left-of-centre political parties.

The clearest and most trenchant criticism of 'measurement' approaches, however, comes from du Toit (2005: 1–2) on the 'poverty measurement blues'. He argues that:

> the difficulties arise out of the domination of development studies and poverty research by . . . the 'econometric imaginary': an approach that frames questions of social understanding as questions of measurement . . . [They] are undermined by their reliance on a mystificatory theoretical metanarrative that tries to imbue poverty judgements with a spurious objectivity, and . . . they direct attention away from *structural* aspects of persistent poverty.

By focusing on what is readily measurable at the individual and household level, these dominant 'measurement' approaches neglect the analysis of culture, identity, agency and social structure that are central to the processes that create wealth and poverty (see Chambers 1983; Bevan 2004). The simplifications that promise to make poverty 'legible' to governments (Scott 1998) are highly problematic as 'this process of abstraction and decontextualization leads not to legibility but to misreading' (du Toit 2005: 18).

The Conceptualization of Poverty in Development Theory and Policy

At different times over the past fifty years the issues discussed in the previous section have shaped the dominant conceptualizations of poverty in development theory and policy in varying ways. In the period immediately after the Second World War, poverty was not a central issue for development. Other concerns – decolonization, national economic planning, agricultural modernization, industrialization and managing the 'Cold War' – held more attention (see Chapter 4). Academics, planners and policymakers were aware of widespread deprivation and suffering in poorer countries but there was an assumption that economic growth would sweep away poverty as incomes rose.

By the 1970s, however, development theory and policy began to look more closely at poverty. Agencies such as the World Bank promised to shift their focus from growth to poverty reduction, while the International Labour Organization (ILO) spearheaded a 'basic needs' approach to development. The ILO's concept of poverty as a multidimensional set of deprivations challenged the neo-classical economists' concept of poverty as a unidimensional income shortfall. This challenge had a technical dimension, concerning the failure of income/consumption measures to capture the complexity of poverty. It also had an ideological dimension. The concept of income poverty favours analyses that see economic growth as the solution to – and market-based strategies as the mechanism for – poverty reduction. By contrast, the basic needs approach favours analyses that see service delivery (food, water, education, health) as the solution and state action as the main mechanism. These skirmishes occupied the late 1970s but in the early 1980s the global ascendancy of neoliberal thinking and policies pushed basic needs off the agenda. Poverty was not central to neoliberalism: it was a residual problem that growth would sweep away as economies liberalized, free markets expanded and the dead hand of the state was minimized (see Chapter 6).

Box 2.2   Measuring the incidence of poverty

- *The incidence of poverty.* Expressed as a headcount ratio, this measurement is simply an estimate of the percentage of people below the poverty line. It does not indicate anything about the depth or severity of poverty and thus does not capture any worsening of the condition of those already in poverty.

- *Depth of poverty.* The depth of poverty can be measured as the average distance below the poverty line, expressed as a proportion of that line. This average is formed over the entire population, poor and non-poor. Because this measure – also called the poverty gap – shows the average distance of the poor from the poverty line, it is able to capture any worsening of their conditions.

- *Severity of poverty.* The severity of poverty can be measured as a weighted average of the squared distance below the poverty line, expressed as a proportion of that line. The weights are given by each individual gap. Again the average is formed over the entire population. Since the weights increase with poverty, this measure is sensitive to inequality among the poor.

Source: Based on information from UNDP (1997: 13).

During the 1980s there were two significant but contrasting theoretical advances that maintained analytical and policy interest in the topic of poverty. The first was in poverty measurement where the Foster, Greer, Thorbecke (FGT) measures of poverty incidence, depth and severity moved thinking beyond simple headcounts. These widely adopted measures assess how deeply a population is experiencing income poverty and the relative distribution of different levels of poverty among the poor (Box 2.2).

The second advance was Amartya Sen's work (1981, 1984, 1990a, 1993, 2001), initially on entitlements and subsequently on capabilities, which laid the foundations for envisioning development as individual human development rather than national economic development. For Sen, development is about people being able to raise their capabilities so that they have greater freedom to achieve the 'functionings' they value (Box 2.3). *Functionings* are the things that people manage to be or to do (for example, living a long and healthy life, being a respected member of a community, raising a family, achieving satisfaction in sports or cultural activities). From this human development perspective people experience

---

Box 2.3   Sen's framework for conceptualizing human development

The conceptual foundations of the capability approach can be found in Sen's critiques of traditional welfare economics, which focuses on resource-(income, commodity command, asset) and utility-(happiness, desire-fulfilment) based concepts of well-being. Sen rejects these frameworks in favour of a more direct approach for measuring human well-being and development, which concerns itself with the full range of human function(ing)s and capabilities people have reason to value. Sen's (2001) framework makes the following distinctions:

- *Functionings.* 'The concept of functionings reflects the various things a person may value doing or being. The valued functionings may vary from elementary ones, such as being adequately nourished and being free from avoidable disease, to very complex activities or personal states, such as being able to take part in the life of the community and having self-respect.'

- *Capability/freedom.* 'A person's capability refers to the alternative combinations of functionings that are feasible for an individual to achieve. Capability is thus a kind of freedom: the substantive freedom to achieve alternative functioning combinations (or, less formally put, the freedom to achieve various life-styles).'

- *Development.* The expansion of freedom is the primary end and principal means of development. Development involves the expansion of human capabilities and the enrichment of human lives.

Source: Adapted from Clark (2006) and Sen (2001: 3 and 75).

---

poverty when they are deprived in terms of a basic capability (Sen 1984, 1993, 2001), such as being able to avoid hunger, achieve literacy, appear in public without shame or take part in social activities.

The most readily identifiable 'foes' of the human development approach are those who focus the discourse on global poverty around two international poverty lines – per capita consumption of US$1 per day (extreme poverty) and US$2 per day (poverty) at 1985 prices. While the $1 and $2 poverty lines have an immediacy that permits the lay public and many policymakers to grasp that these levels of consumption are inadequate ('Gee, how does anyone live on a dollar a day?') this understanding of poverty is overly simplistic. Estimating how many people live below these lines is technically complex and, even more worrying, is based on data of dubious quality (Reddy and Pogge 2003). Wade (2004:

571) has made the case that these estimates 'contain a large margin of error', and this makes it look as though poverty has reduced significantly over the period 1985–2000. Furthermore, it is hard to believe that, purely by coincidence, 'in its first global poverty estimation this procedure [estimating the value of a minimum consumption package] yielded a conveniently understandable US$1 per day for the base year of 1985' (Wade 2004).

Whatever the empirical arguments, there is an important conceptual issue behind concerns about the US$1 per day measure. Although, the Millennium Development Goals cover a wide set of issues (poverty reduction, gender equity, education for all, reduced infant and maternal mortality, sustainability, etc.), Goal 1/Target 1/Indicator 1 is reducing extreme poverty (US$1 per day) by 50 per cent over the period 1990–2015. For target-obsessed policymakers (national and international) this has meant that in an era in which there is widespread agreement that poverty is multidimensional, the overarching concept that shapes policy and debates is narrowly defined income/consumption poverty (White 2006: 387). Analysts who are committed to human development and/or structuralist conceptual frameworks are thus concerned that the insights of their work are pushed to the margins and that the emphasis on economic growth within development theory and practice continues to dominate (see Chapter 7).

Poverty and Inequality: What are the Interactions?

Earlier parts of this chapter have referred to potential cause-and-effect relationships between poverty and inequality. In this section these are explored in more detail with a focus on conceptual and philosophical aspects.

While there are many different ideas about the relationship between poverty and inequality, it is useful for analytical purposes to identify two main theoretical approaches: those focused on the *behaviour of individuals* and those focused on the *operations of social structures*. The relative emphases on these two approaches has waxed and waned over time. Structuralist analyses were most influential in the 1960s and 1970s. In the 1980s and 1990s the shift towards a more neoliberal framework led to individualist approaches increasingly being the analytical focus. Since the late 1990s moderate versions of structuralist frameworks have been making a comeback, as evidenced by the World Bank's *World Development Report 2006*. Both of these approaches have their strengths and weaknesses but the individualistic approaches have benefited from the precision with which they identify their units of analysis (individuals) and their behavioural models (rational choice). Structural analyses find it hard to match such precision and simplicity as they argue that the units of analysis are multiple and overlapping and the behaviours are complex and, at best, only partly predictable.

Individualistic approaches

Neoliberal (or rational choice) frameworks focus on individual human agency and conceptualize social processes as the aggregation of the choices and outcomes that all the individuals in a society take and achieve. From this perspective, human behaviour is derived from conscious, comprehensive, individual computations of the benefits and costs of all available choices and courses of action. People will select the choices that will achieve the goals they are pursuing at the lowest possible investment of resources. Operationalizing such concepts is most readily achieved by valuing benefits and costs in monetary terms. The environments within which such choices are made and outcomes realized are theorized as markets, usually 'perfect markets' (that is, markets with large numbers of buyers and sellers, no buyers and sellers who are so big that they can influence prices, homogeneous goods, freely available information on prices and freedom of entry to the market).

In such theoretical frameworks, inequality is viewed purely in economic terms (income and assets). By assuming that there is equality of opportunity, they lead to the conclusion that inequality of outcomes shapes human behaviour in positive ways. Those who are not getting the things they want (such as a good income) will work harder, revise their choices and use their creativity. High incomes are seen as the reward for taking high risks. This improves efficiency and raises economic growth. The 'invisible hand' of the market then distributes the benefits of economic growth, through employment creation, increased demand and new opportunities. As former British Prime Minister Margaret Thatcher stated, 'it is our job to glory in inequality and see that talents and abilities are given vent and expression for the benefit of us all' (quoted in George and Sabelli 1994). From this perspective poverty is largely a transitory economic phenomenon resulting from bad choices and, perhaps, bad luck. People experiencing poverty (those on low incomes) will rapidly make a set of choices (working longer hours, reducing expenditure, developing new skills, taking new jobs) that will lift them out of poverty. High rates of personal economic mobility mean that no one should be trapped in poverty or permanently caught at the bottom end of income distribution.

This individualistic analysis has links to many powerful ideas about poverty, some with deep historical roots. Golding and Middleton (1982) have shown that from the sixteenth century onwards the poor in Europe were seen as either 'deserving' or 'undeserving'. The deserving poor are theorized as a group of people who are unable to participate in economic activity because of factors beyond their control: disability, accident, elderly, infirm and orphans. They merit social support. By contrast, the undeserving poor are a group of voluntary indigent people who choose to be poor because of their immorality or character defects: laziness, lassitude, work-shirking, drunkenness, promiscuousness and others. Society has no obligation to such people as they choose to live in poverty. Implicitly, such views theorize the undeserving poor as living in an economy that can provide all of them with adequate incomes if they choose to take advantage of the available opportunities. Lack of employment, unemployment, excessively low wages and worker exploitation (debt bondage, slavery, child labour) are not issues for such a model.

These ideas ran through the Victorian era to more recent times (Himmelfarb 1991). Murray (1984, 2001) has argued that the contemporary 'underclass' in the USA is perpetuated through 'welfare dependence'. He used a rational-choice model to argue that, in the short term, social welfare programmes changed the computations of poor people so that they opted for unemployment, illegitimacy and crime. In the long term, such choices became pathological as they led to self-perpetuating bad behaviour that created a morally bankrupt black, urban 'underclass'.

While Murray's work has been heavily criticized for its theoretical and empirical flaws (see O'Connor 2001: 247–50), the power of the image of an undeserving 'underclass' has had a profound impact on public debate and politics throughout the world. Such theories – transmitted through media popularizations (Putnis 2001) – have had much broader international influence because of the power of the USA in terms of both politics and ideas (see Chapter 6). Many of the 750 amendments that John Bolton, US Ambassador to the UN, sought in September 2005 to the UN's review of the MDGs (including efforts to remove the term 'poverty' from the document) can be traced back to the idea that poverty exists because people choose to be poor (*Guardian On-line* 2005).

Structuralist perspectives

Structuralist accounts directly challenge rational choice analyses and ultimately argue that inequality is the cornerstone of processes that create absolute and relative poverty. Its units of analysis are those collectivities referred to earlier – classes, races, genders, ethnic groups – and the focus of structuralist analysis is on the power differentials between such entities. While economic inequality is important to structuralists, they are also concerned with social and political inequalities.

Structuralists highlight the ways in which more powerful groups are able to impose their preferences (low rates of pay, privileged access to resources and services, and so on) on less powerful groups through the exercise of economic, social and political power. These different dimensions of inequality interact in ways that are often reinforcing. For example, those with economic power are able to influence who holds political power. The markets that are emphasized by neoliberals are seen by structuralists as shaped by social structures. As a result they are not 'level playing fields' or perfect markets, as neoclassical economists assume. Unequal social relations influence the opportunities and behaviours of individuals and groups as information is asymmetrically distributed and access to resources (land, water, credit) is differentiated. From such a perspective, inequality is seen as having complex relations with poverty. Most commonly, this structure of inequality helps to produce and reproduce both absolute and relative poverty.

There are many ways that this occurs but childhood experiences and subsequent outcomes of inequality are of great significance. Children born into income-poor households with low social standing and limited political power often fall into vicious circles of capability deprivation. They are underweight at birth and likely to have weakened immune systems as their mothers are also underweight and undernourished. They lack access to adequate prenatal, postnatal and infant care so that they have a lower likelihood of fully developing their capabilities. Higher rates of stunting and greater exposure to deprivations are more likely to curtail their physical and cognitive development (Greig et al. 2003: Chs 2–4). Unequal access to schooling and the need to work for their households mean that they do not fully develop literacy and numeracy skills. Their childhood social networks are largely limited to other disadvantaged people in their neighbourhood so that when they mature the networks they can draw on are constrained.

When they become adults (assuming they survive – the chances of a Malian baby dying in its first year are 18 times greater than a baby in the USA) such people may have limited human capital (such as impaired health and little schooling), are unlikely to inherit land or other physical assets, and may have to take on their parents' debts (debt bondage affects tens of millions of people in south Asia). In markets saturated with unskilled labour they have no choice but to take up low paid, irregular, physically demanding, casual jobs that make it virtually impossible to accumulate productive assets or to fully develop the human capital of their own children through nutritious food, education and health care. In all but the very poorest countries such circumstances are by no means inevitable. Countries have the resources to achieve much higher levels of poverty reduction and human development but reforming the social relations that mediate resources allocation to ensure the redistribution of income, assets and services are not prioritized by many governments. As later chapters will go on to show, similar arguments can be made about international social and economic relations.

Vulnerability further fuels processes of impoverishment and inequality. Poorer people face higher levels of risk than better-off people: they live in areas more likely to be flooded or suffer drought, drink unclean water and lack sanitation (so they have more health problems), face higher threats of violence and have few or no rights to employment. This limits the economic choices they can take. For example, if they have access to land it is wise for them to plant low risk, low value crops rather than higher value crops that would increase the risk they face. When shocks hit them, or stresses become unbearable, their coping strategies tend to reduce their future economic prospects (for example, selling land or tools), transmit poverty to their children (for example, withdrawal from school, poorer diet, child labour), and heighten levels of social and economic inequality (for example, by taking a usurious loan from, or selling future labour or crops at high discounts to, a patron). Wood (2003) provides numerous examples of the phenomenon of 'staying secure, staying poor'.

The structuralist case argues that the outcomes of poverty are rarely the result of indolence, lassitude, immorality or character deficiencies. Many studies have shown that it is common for poor people to work exceptionally hard for excessively long hours (Breman, 1996; Wilson and Ramphele 1989). Rather, it is unequal social relations that permit the poor to be economically exploited, socially subordinated and politically marginalized. Opportunities for their advancement are systematically blocked off by more powerful people while the childhoods of the offspring are blighted so that they can never compete on the 'level playing field' promised by neoliberal economists. Lister (2004: 178) sums up this position:

> Inequalities of power manifest themselves at both the material and the relational/symbolic level. More powerful actors control the wages, benefits, services and opportunities available to people in poverty. They also have the power to construct 'the poor' as other through words, images and deeds.

To quote Tawney's (1931) oft-cited line, 'what thoughtful rich people call the problem of poverty, thoughtful poor people call with equal justice the problem of riches'. For Townsend (2002) 'social polarization' is the key ingredient that creates poverty in an affluent world. Unequal social relations operate at a variety of levels, ranging from the micro-level to the global level (see Box 2.4).

Box 2.4   Bangladesh – the relations between micro- and macro-level inequality

The example of Maymana and Mofizul in Bangladesh (CPRC 2004; Hulme 2004) illustrates the ways in which micro- and macro-levels of inequality interlock.

At the *Local level* Maymana and Mofizul are impoverished by discrimination against widows and the disabled. The labour market is saturated so they can gain only low paid, irregular casual work through patrons. The local and national governments have not delivered on their promises to provide education and health services and social safety nets.

Wider structural factors at the *national level* block off resources and opportunities: a political elite that is corrupt and self-seeking, professions (especially teachers, doctors, and health workers) that absorb public resources but do not provide services to poorer people, and a private sector that pursues profits through political and bureaucratic patronage rather than market-based competition.

And there is also an *international dimension*. Although remote from Maymana and Mofizul these distant strangers impact on their lives; rich governments that use foreign aid to pursue foreign policy goals and not development; businesses that lobby for protection against imports from Bangladesh; pharmaceutical companies that make medicines unaffordable; and fundamentalist Islamic groups who train and finance 'terrorists' in the country.

While hierarchical social relations adversely affect the life-chances of poor people, it would be wrong to see all possible relations in this light. At the micro-level there are individuals and groups – progressive NGOs, altruistic elites, women's groups – that strive to promote countervailing power. At the regional and national levels, human rights groups, lawyers working *pro bono* in public interest litigation, social entrepreneurs and others seek progressive change rather than self-interest. Internationally, agencies (for example, parts of the UN, some NGOs, and some religious groups) and individuals (ranging from Gordon Brown to Muhamad Yunus and from Bob Geldof to protesting youths outside the G8 meetings at Gleneagles in 2005) are striving to find ways of challenging inequality and poverty.

There is the possibility that individualist and structuralist frameworks can be combined to achieve a deeper understanding of poverty and inequality. Such an intellectual position is not easy, however, as attempts to weave the two approaches together can be readily criticized from an individualist perspective (for example, confusing the clarity of behavioural models and introducing elements on which data is not available) and a structuralist perspective (for example, exaggerating the freedom that subordinated groups have to exercise their agency).

The debates about inequality and poverty that have raged since 1945 are driven by ideological, theoretical and policy interests. Over the past 25 years, much of this debate has been polarized between rational choice or individualist concepts (and associated policies of neoliberalism, reduced public expenditure and state minimization) and structuralist concepts (and associated policies of redistribution, social inclusion and an active state). There is a massive divide, on the one hand, between poverty seen as a lack of resources or services for the poorest that needs to be 'caught up', and on the other hand, poverty as a product of unequal social relations that requires a fairer global society. The latter means change for all and redistribution. In policy terms these different frameworks can generate different development strategies.

For neoliberals, inequality (usually assessed in income terms) is often seen as playing a positive role in economic life. It promotes enterprise that increases rates of economic growth, which in turn creates wider social benefits. From this perspective, poverty is largely self-induced so direct state action to reduce poverty will be ineffective or counter-productive. Poor people need to work their way out of poverty, and only policies that create an 'enabling environment' will facilitate this. For structuralists, the analytical stance is quite different. Economic, social and political inequalities interact and underpin processes that make people both relatively and absolutely poor. As a result, direct action is needed by governments and civil societies to redistribute economic resources and social and political power to poorer people. These changes need to occur at local, national and international levels to reduce poverty and promote social justice.

Conceptually, the frontier for development analysis in the twenty-first century is how to effectively integrate individualist and structuralist ideas into a framework that deepens the understanding of inequality and poverty. But concepts do not evolve in isolation, nor do they simply shape policy. Specific historical, ideological and political contexts, and the policy preferences of the powerful, shape development. As Myrdal (1977: 4) reflected: 'For social scientists it is a sobering and useful exercise in self-understanding to attempt to see clearly how the direction of our scientific exertions . . . is conditioned by the society in which we live, and most directly by the political climate.' The following chapters show that this advice is particularly pertinent for exploring the past and present of development studies. The next chapter takes these contexts into consideration when exploring inequalities *between* countries.

Chapter 3

Measuring Development

This chapter examines the scope of development studies and measurements of development. The first part takes up an issue introduced in the previous chapter – the use of statistical indicators to measure development. While the previous chapter focused on the relationship between inequality and poverty within societies, this chapter has a more comparative and global scope. The second issue concerns units of analysis. Historically, the social sciences have tended to emphasize 'national' over 'local' and 'global' units of analysis. The reasons for this are explored and problems with this approach identified. The chapter then moves to the specific focus of development studies – poorer countries – before exploring the historical and contemporary relevance of this unit of analysis.

Developmental Statistics

The previous chapter noted that while many people in richer countries have tended to suffer from 'relative poverty' (a perception that others in their society are better off than they are), a substantial proportion of the people outside these countries suffer from 'absolute poverty' (a lack of the basic material means to sustain life). De Soto (1999: 225) has made a similar distinction between the advanced capitalist countries which contain 'pockets of poverty' and the 'developing' world (including the ex-communist world) that contains 'pockets of wealth' and where poverty is pervasive. Sachs (2005: 20) distinguished between three different forms of poverty that correlate with different levels of development: *extreme poverty* (the incapacity to meet basic needs), *moderate poverty* (where basic needs are just met), and *relative poverty* (where households below the national average income feel deprived when comparing their conditions with wealthier members of their society). Extreme poverty, he claimed, is only found in lower-income countries, whereas relative poverty is a subjective phenomenon found more in 'high-income countries' (see also Sen 2001: 74).

However, classifying countries according to degrees of poverty and inequality requires that these concepts be operationalized. As Comeliau (2002: 77–8) laments, while few deny 'that the sharpening of inequalities is one of the most spectacular recent trends in modernity', debate is hindered by the fact that 'it is not one that is easy to interpret'. Olsen (1983: 96) has noted how modern econometric techniques can 'torture' data sets until they 'confess' the answer the interrogator requires: 'one reason why statistical arguments sometimes fail to persuade is that different statistical methods may produce varying results, and investigators are suspected of choosing the method most favorable to their arguments' (see also Wade 2004).

Alleging such manipulation, Escobar (1995: 213) views statistics as 'techno-representations endowed with complex political and cultural histories' that 'entrench the development discourse'. They represent and identify the 'problem of Third World poverty', which then provide the rationale for intervening and managing its 'helpless' subjects. Statistics, like labels, are implicated in the control over poorer countries by the more powerful. Yet, it is difficult to engage in rigorous debate without such measurement. Statistical representations are indispensable tools for understanding and interpreting the world.

Economy

For the compilers and analysers of development statistics, the economy has always been of central concern. The most commonly cited measures have been Gross Domestic Product (GDP) and Gross National Product (GNP) per capita. The former refers to the money value of all goods and services produced in a country over a year. It is calculated by valuing outputs of goods and services at market prices for a particular country. When income from abroad (such as from property or workers' remittances) is added the measure becomes GNP – or Gross National Income (GNI) as the World Bank now prefers to call it. In order to compare economies it is necessary to divide either the GDP or GNI by the mid-year population, thus producing the GDP or GNI per capita. Local currency must then be converted to US dollars to produce a common measure for all countries. It is then possible to look at the relative economic situations of differing countries. Formerly, the World Bank's annual statistical compilation in the *World Development Report* arranged all tables according to GNP per capita with the lowest-ranked country placed at the top of the league and then working down the page to the richest Western economies. Now, the tables are more diplomatic, listing countries in alphabetical order. They are nevertheless still classified into categories of 'Low Income', 'Lower Middle Income', 'Upper Middle Income', 'High Income OECD' and 'Other High Income'.

GDP and GNP per-capita figures have more than any other been used by analysts and organizations as surrogate terms for 'development'. This derives from the claim that there is a strong positive correlation between these measures and the level of well-being. As Rapley (2002: 10) points out, 'as a rule, there is a correlation between national income and a country's ability to improve the social indicators of its citizenry' (see also Wade 2004: 582; World Bank 2005: 6). Yet apart from the quantification issues discussed in the previous chapter, there are other methodological problems with employing GDP and GNI per capita as measures for development or with awarding them excessive causal significance.

The first problem concerns the comparability of GDP or GNI across countries. The figures do not represent real price levels. Put another way, what you can buy with US$1 in Switzerland or Japan is far less than in Bangladesh or Togo. Thus, statisticians take into account international differences in relative prices to produce a device called purchasing power parity (PPP). The resulting PPP GDP per-capita figures provide a more accurate picture of economic well-being. For poorer countries this generally entails a considerable increase over the raw GDP or GNI per-capita figures. For example, in 2002 Cambodia had a GNI of US$280 per capita but adjusted to PPP the figure rose to US$1590 whereas for Peru the figures were US$2050 and US$4800. But even with the increased figures there is still no disguising the vast differences in wealth between nations. 'Low Income Countries' still only average US$2040 for PPP GNI, well below 'Lower Middle Income Countries' at US$5130 and 'Upper Middle Income Countries' at US$9220 but totally out of touch with 'High Income Countries' at US$27,590.

While the GNI and GDP figures starkly reveal the inequalities between nations they tell us nothing about inequality within nations. For example, the Philippines is a Lower Middle Income country with a GNI per capita almost three times higher than Cambodia and Lao PDR but with almost the same proportion of the population living in poverty (between 37–9 per cent). If the internal distribution of that poverty in the

Philippines is mapped then further contrasts are evident – in the autonomous region of Muslim Mindanao, 60 per cent of the population experience poverty.

A further problem with GNI and GDP per capita is that they principally capture market activity, or goods and services that are bought and sold as commodities. In effect this means that it mainly registers economic activity where money changes hands. Efforts are made by statisticians to incorporate subsistence production and barter but estimating the monetary value of such production and transactions 'remains as much an art as a science, with little known about the physical volume of production in many countries, let alone its financial worth' (Hulme and Turner 1990: 19).

Waring (1989: Ch. 5) has argued that GDP per capita significantly underestimates total economic activity because much unpaid labour is conducted by women, such as domestic work and caring work – tasks often seen as women's 'natural' roles. This is part of a broader phenomenon that feminists have labelled the 'devaluation of women's work' (see Chapter 9). Although more of these 'traditional' gendered roles have been 'contracted-out' by households in wealthier countries as women increase their workforce participation rates, all that has happened is that non-monetized activities have been replaced with monetized activities. The increase in GDP has not measured more economic activity in the domestic sphere but merely a shift from non-monetized to monetized activity. Furthermore, the newly monetized domestic activities (such as cleaning services) may be paid informally, out of view of government calculations.

This alerts us to the fact that GNI and GDP per capita cannot incorporate production and services that are transacted in the 'underground' economy, or economic activity that takes place 'off-the-books' (Mattera 1986). These forms of activity vary in nature, from illicit drug production and distribution that avoid law enforcement, 'sweatshop' production that seeks to avoid labour regulations, and other forms of production and service provision that deliberately avoids taxation authorities. Examples of these activities can be uncovered throughout the world and do not discriminate according to levels of economic development. For example, it has been estimated that illicit narcotics is the fourth largest commodity trade in the world. The UN International Drug Control Program has calculated that illicit drugs account for approximately 8 per cent of world trade (Landes 2002: 563). Most 'underground' money eventually has to be filtered or 'laundered' into the mainstream economy, but the failure to account for the generation and origins of underground activities severely compromises GNI and GDP per capita as accurate indicators of national economic performance. For example, in 2004 the

UN estimated that opium production accounted for the equivalent of over 60 per cent of Afghanistan's GDP and that one in ten Afghans were involved in the industry (UNIS, 18 November 2004).

The illicit drug trade hints at another difficulty with the GNI and GDP per-capita indicators. In an era where transportation and communications has made enterprises more mobile with respect to their choice of production locations, companies have the ability to disarticulate parts of the production process by designing products in one country, manufacturing them in other countries before returning them to the country of origin. Because this occurs within the one enterprise, the prices of the imported in-house components can be fixed by firms to minimize taxes. This 'transfer pricing' gives a distorted global picture of where value is being added (Jawara and Kwa 2003: 243).

While the underground economy operates throughout the world, de Soto has argued that this 'extralegal phenomenon' places a greater burden on poorer countries, including the ex-communist world. Half of all Russian economic activity occurs outside the official market, and the corresponding figure for Georgia is 62 per cent. Since 1990 it has been estimated that more than 8 out of 10 new jobs in Latin America have been 'off-the-books', while 9 out of 10 Zambians who work are employed illegally. It is estimated that there are three million Chinese operating in illegal workshops around Beijing. A study in the late 1980s estimated that Mexico's underground economy was equivalent to somewhere between 28 per cent and 39 per cent of official GDP (de Soto 1999: 69–75). During the 1990s official and anecdotal reports indicated that illegal 'sweatshop' activities were increasing in the heartlands of so-called post-industrial service economies, such as the USA, Europe and Australia (Greig 2002; Rowbottom 1993).

There are other non-technical criticisms levelled against the use of GNI and GDP that are derived from ethical issues. For example, GDP per capita can place socially destructive activities on the positive side of the financial ledger. Environmental degradation is an example increasingly offered by critics of 'economic growth' (Hamilton 1994: Ch. 3). A nation that enforces strict environmental codes concerning the transportation of hazardous substances would probably make its citizens feel more secure. However, this 'non-event' does not generate any activity, apart from that of the regulating authority. On the other hand, a large oil slick can cause incalculable environmental devastation, while the clean-up can contribute significantly to GDP. An ethical question-mark might be placed over an indicator that 'valued' such an environmental catastrophe. Some forms of growth are actually indicators of social maladjustment rather than increasing well-being, such as 'prison construction, reconstructive surgery, cancer treatments, anti-theft devices in automobiles, reconstruction after terrorist attacks and wars' (George 2004: 50). Most economic indicators are not sensitive enough to calibrate ethical concerns over 'good' and 'bad' economic behaviour or over useful and worthless economic activity.

Society

Although they may dominate, economic statistics do not monopolize development accounting. There is a vast array of other measures that represent a range of phenomena in society and can be marshalled to analyse inequality. Demographic, educational and health indicators have been employed for many years while newer 'cross-cutting' indicators of gender and environment have been added to an ever-increasing number of statistical representations of development presented by governments and multilateral financial institutions.

Population growth statistics reveal that the lower-income nations have generally experienced higher levels of growth than higher-income countries. Many low-income countries in Africa saw their populations increase by 2.3–3.3 per cent per year between 1975 and 2002, compared with the wealthier countries, which recorded growth rates of only 0.2–1.3 per cent per year. Thus, the countries most in need of investment in education, infrastructure, health and other developmental needs were having to cope with rapidly increasing populations and were thus least able to afford such investments. A growth rate of 2.77 per cent leads to a doubling of the population in 25 years (Hull and Hull 1992: 1). Western Europe and the USA, along with other industrializing nations, all experienced a 'demographic transition' as development progressed from high birth-rates and high mortality through to low birth-rates and low mortality. Indeed, when fertility rates are examined (the number of children born per women living to the end of their childbearing years) there is an observable difference, with the tendency for fertility rates to be significantly higher in poorer countries, from 1.8 in China and 1.9 in Thailand to 6.1 in Ethiopia and 6.7 in the Democratic Republic of Congo. The differences between Asia and Africa are also striking, with the former experiencing much lower and declining fertility rates. Projections for population growth between 2002 and 2015 do, however, indicate a reduction of fertility in many poorer countries and a lowering of population growth. But, in 2002, 19 out of 20 births were still from the poorer countries.

Life expectancy is lower in almost all poorer countries, although marked differences exist between them, from over 70 years in countries such as Mexico, Malaysia, Sri Lanka and China, down to a range of 42–8 years in Ethiopia, Democratic Republic of Congo, Tanzania, Kenya,

Cote d'Ivore and South Africa. Sub-Saharan Africa has witnessed an alarming decline in life expectancy over the past two decades, dropping seven years, mainly due to HIV/AIDS (Ramonet, 2004: 132). The former Soviet Union has also experienced a decline in life expectancy, especially for men, since the end of communist rule. By contrast, in richer countries the leading demographic issue is that of ageing populations with life expectancy rising to between 77 and 82 years.

Education, like health, has long been seen as an essential component of human development, and education systems across the world have generated numerous statistics for decades. These include enrolments, school attendance, drop-out rates, teacher–pupil ratios, public spending, adult literacy, gender comparisons, and many more. The most used education statistic, and the one which is a target of the MDGs, is the achievement of universal primary education. This has long been achieved in richer countries while many poorer countries have more recently attained the target or have made significant progress towards it. However, there are still millions of children who fail to complete primary education. In India, 24 per cent of the relevant age group in 2001 fell into this category, while in Pakistan the figure was 41 per cent. Meanwhile, the ratio of female to male enrolments was only 3:5 (World Bank 2003: 255). In general, poorer countries lag behind the richer ones in enrolments, especially in the later years of the education system. Investments in education are also considerably less in the poorer countries. Lack of funds adversely affects the quality of education and this is reflected in indicators such as pupils without books, schools with insufficient teachers, and buildings which are in urgent need of repair.

The statistics on urbanization are also illustrative of international differences. Broadly speaking, lower-income countries have lower rates of urbanization than higher-income countries. Yet, geographically, there are significant differences among the poorer countries. In Latin America, over 90 per cent of the populations of Argentina, Uruguay and Chile live in urban areas, while in Brazil the figure is only marginally lower at 88 per cent. Such levels of urbanization are higher than those in many rich countries and certainly far above those found in many Asian and African nations where the majority remain rural dwellers. Urbanization is often linked in development studies with increasing agricultural productivity, which allows growing numbers of rural dwellers to leave the agricultural sector and move into urban areas and industrial activity. However, land pressure, rural poverty, armed conflict and environmental degradation are also 'push factors' out of rural areas and drivers of urbanization in many poorer countries. When further disaggregated, statistics reveal other inequalities. For instance, greater poverty can be generally found in rural areas than urban areas. Rural areas tend to suffer worse malnutrition and have worse health and educational facilities and poorer quality shelter and communications infrastructure than urban areas.

Overall, even though statistics must be treated with caution, rich country/poor country comparisons reveal a pattern of marked inequality. Yet, it is only as we dig deeper, disaggregate the figures and – to return to Olsen's analogy – interrogate the data from as many angles as possible, that we are able to shed more light on the shadowy figures.

Composite measures of development

Using GDP or GNI per capita to measure development has been likened to flying an aircraft using only the speedometer. The complexity and the quality of developmental processes clearly cannot be gauged using a single instrument. GNI per capita does not provide adequate information on levels of poverty, inequality or general welfare (such as malnutrition, health, employment, literacy and personal security), nor personal and collective happiness. During the 1970s, the economist Peter Donaldson (1988[1973]: 229) emphatically rejected 'the nonsense of equating growth with progress' (see also Comeliau 2002: 158, 164; Inkeles and Smith 1993: 159–60; Passe Smith 1993), and more recently Hamilton (2003: 23) concluded that 'there is now a large body of evidence that casts serious doubt on the dual assumptions that more economic growth improves social well-being and that more income improves individual well-being'.

This rejection of monocausal indicators of development has led to a growing recognition that the process of development can be understood and assessed more adequately through monitoring a wider range of socio-economic and political gauges. Over the past couple of decades this has led to a range of 'composite' indicators of development and progress (see Hulme and Turner 1990: 20–1). The Human Development Index (HDI) has become the leading composite index since it was introduced by the UN Development Programme in 1990. It represents an attempt to put a 'human face' on development through operationalizing other indicators, such as well-being, governance and participation (Green 2002: 58). The fact that *human* development had to be stressed gives some indication of the extent to which many commentators felt that 'development' had become detached from 'well-being'. By including variables such as education, life expectancy and literacy, the index is able to 'throw systematic light on the actual lives people lead, especially by the relatively deprived' (Sen 2001: 73). Perhaps more importantly, however, the HDI also sheds more light on how different governments prioritize development aims (Green 2002: 59). Calculated on a scale from 0 to 1, in 2001

Table 3.1 *Selected development statistics for various countries*

Country (Low, Medium and High human development), 2002	GDP per capita (PPP US$), 2002	Annual population growth, 1975–2002	Life expectancy at birth (years), 2002	Adult literacy rate (% ages 15 years and above), 2002	Urban population (% of total), 2002	GDP per capita rank minus HDI rank
Low income						
Bangladesh (M)	1700	2.4	61.1	41.1	23.9	1
Tajikistan (M)	980	2.2	68.6	99.5	25.0	45
Haiti (L)	2200	1.9	49.4	51.9	36.9	–25
Nigeria (L)	860	2.9	51.6	66.8	45.9	15
Lower middle income						
Thailand (M)	7010	1.5	69.1	92.6	31.6	–9
Tunisia (M)	6760	2.0	72.7	73.2	63.4	–23
Peru (M)	5010	2.1	69.7	85.0	73.5	7
Upper middle income						
Malaysia (M)	9120	2.5	73.0	88.7	63.3	–2
Chile (H)	9820	1.5	76.0	95.7	86.6	11
Botswana (M)	8170	2.8	41.4	78.9	51.1	–67
High income OECD						
USA (H)	35,750	1.0	77.0	99.0	79.8	–4
Japan (H)	26,940	0.5	81.5	99.0	65.3	6
Spain	21,460	0.5	79.2	97.7	76.4	5

Source: Data from UNDP (2004b).

Norway's score of 0.944 placed it as the country with the highest level of human development while Sierra Leone registered the lowest Human Development Index value (0. 275) of the 175 countries included in the data. The UN Development Programme uses the HDI scores to classify countries into 'High', 'Medium' and 'Low' human development. The 'High' category embraces all rich OECD countries but also includes some states from Eastern Europe, Latin America and the Caribbean. The 'Medium' category comprises countries from many regions while the 'Low' group is dominated by the Sub-Saharan countries of Africa (31 out of the 35 countries included in this category).

Table 3.1 compares the 2003 HDI rankings with GDP per capita. It suggests (as does the UNDP) that there *is* a positive, though by no means exact, correlation between PPP GDP per capita and the HDI. Anomalies include Equatorial Guinea, whose HDI ranking is 103 places below its PPP GDP per-capita rank, and Cuba whose HDI is 39 places above its PPP GDP per capita rank. Despite these and other examples it would still be unreasonable to suggest that economic growth is of minor importance in development. Regardless of how we measure growth, its presence is important for the *possibility* of social resource redistribution. Composite indicators such as the HDI do not banish economic growth from our calculations. Rather, they add to our understanding of development by emphasizing its complex multidimensional nature and alert us to the fact that economic growth is not synonymous with human well-being and the eradication of inequality.

Units of Analysis

The nation-state as a unit of analysis

The ways in which statistics are employed also depend on the units of analysis to which they refer. For most of the history of development studies, the principal unit of analysis has been the nation-state. By the time the modern social sciences were established in the nineteenth century, European international relations had come to be dominated by this nation-state centrality. The Treaty of Westphalia in 1648 had established that nation-states possessed sovereign authority within their own borders, with all the military, economic and legal protection that this entailed. The nation-state then became a logical and convenient entity with which to study modern social change (Sutor 2000: 13–5). Thus, few questioned why the late-eighteenth-century political economist Adam Smith wrote about the 'wealth of nations'. Malthus also defined the object of political economy as the study of the wealth and poverty of nations. By the early nineteenth century, the boundaries of nation-states had become firmly fixed in the European intellectual imagination as 'natural' units of spatial differentiation.

The social sciences reinforced this age of nationalism. The discipline of history was dominated by attempts to establish national histories and 'imagined communities' (Anderson 1991; Hall 2005; Wallerstein 2004: 4–7; E. Weber 1976). Likewise, the discipline of political science concentrated on the political and legal structures that constituted the nation-state. Within the field of international relations theory, the world community was understood as a 'society of states' (Hoogvelt 1997: 7). Scholte (2000: 56–8) has referred to this state-centred approach within the social sciences as 'methodological territorialism'.

Classical sociology also accepted this methodological territorialism and it remained unchallenged until very recently. Sociology originated primarily as an attempt to interpret the dynamics of change within a small number of societies that were in the process of becoming modern (Etzioni-Halevy 1980). Even though its object was the study of modernity, like other social sciences the sociological focus remained fixed on these coherent nation-state entities with definite physical dimensions and boundaries, even if they were experiencing internal conflict and pressures for secession.

Prior to the Second World War, the study of the non-Western world tended to be reserved for anthropologists, who examined the pre-modern and 'static' structures of colonial domains (Hulme and Turner 1990: 33; Myrdal 1977: 3). After 1945, as the newly independent territories achieved nationhood, other social scientists became interested in tracking their path to modernity. This comparative national methodology became central to development studies (see Box 3.1), contrasting the more 'developed' nations that had reached modernity with the 'less developed' nations that were assumed to be travelling to this same destination (see Chapter 4).

Later chapters will reveal why this methodological territorialism, focusing on the nation-state, increasingly came under challenge after the 1970s. But briefly, social scientists began to look for answers to why the postwar development project had produced such disappointing results in many poorer countries. In addition, more social scientists began to reconsider the 'developed' nature of the Western capitalist world, and became more preoccupied with unanticipated 'postmodern' developmental problems, such as growing poverty, inequality, unemployment and industrial restructuring (see Chapter 8). The question that a growing number of social theorists have therefore been posing over the past decade is whether it is still appropriate to analyse and comprehend the processes of development by focusing on the study of nation-states or

Box 3.1   Comparative analysis

There are two forms of comparative methodology that perform an important role in the analysis of development – comparisons of individual societies across time and comparisons between different societies. Each comparative choice made by a researcher is informed by the hypotheses and theories that guide research. No comparative choice is arbitrary.

Historical comparison is the very essence of development studies. From the eighteenth-century Enlightenment onwards, researchers began to apply the tools of reason not only to the inanimate world but also the process of history (see Chapter 4). The aim was to understand, influence and predict the course of change within a society from one condition to another over time. After the Second World War, this comparative historical methodology was adapted to the study of the postcolonial world. Prior to this, these regions were mostly seen as existing outside history. The nineteenth-century historian Thomas Macaulay placed them in 'the waiting room of history' (quoted in Hall 2005: 21). They were now on the tracks of modernity. As they were entering the modern world of nation-states, it was now necessary to chart their progress. Thus, comparisons across time could assist development researchers in determining the extent to which poorer countries had travelled from their 'original' state.

This form of historical comparison required another measuring stick to help gauge the depth of this process of modernization and social change. This is where comparative analysis between different societies entered the framework. It was assumed that the newly independent poorer countries were roughly heading along the same path to modernity that the more industrially developed capitalist nations previously traversed. These more advanced nations could then act as the yardstick for the less developed nations and a range of measurements were designed using the historical template of the now developed forerunners. As we shall see in Chapter 5, these concepts included industrialization, urbanization, individualization, secularization, democratization, rationalization, universalization, mass literacy and an achievement ethic (Inkeles and Smith 1993). The measurement of development therefore depended on a comparative methodology whereby one set of nations followed the path of predecessors.

even their interaction. From a more global perspective, methodological territorialism is too *atomistic* an approach to account for the transnational traffic in information, goods and culture. The social sciences, it has been argued, requires a more *holistic* unit of analysis and the most appropriate focus is the 'global system', a unit greater than the sum of individual nation-states (Bergesen 1980 and 1990; Robertson 1990; Robinson 2004). As Chapters 5, 6 and 8 show, this remains one of the most contentious issues in contemporary development studies. However, it

---

Box 3.2   Behind the label

No label has been able to proclaim universal acceptance in the area of development studies, including the term 'development' itself (see Chapter 11). The lexicon of development studies is a linguistic and political minefield. Its terminology opens a window onto different commentators' attitudes towards the world and the assumptions they draw about social processes.

- Third World (Smith 1996)
- traditional world (Rostow 1960)
- emerging countries (George 2004: Hertz 2004: Spulber 1964)
- colonial, postcolonial and neocolonial world (Goldthorpe 1996; Hoogvelt 1997)
- backward countries (Banfield 1958; Baran 1970; Lewis 1969)
- modernizing world (Apter 1967)
- developing world (Alavi and Shanin 1982; Payne and Nasser 2006)
- less developed countries (Lerner 1972)
- non-industrialized countries (Price 2003)
- underdeveloped countries (Bauer 1976; Benham 1961)
- pre-capitalist modes of production (Hindess and Hirst 1975)
- poorer countries (Yates 2004)
- low-income countries (World Bank 1989)
- unfortunate countries (Huxley 1958)
- underprivileged nations (Moussa 1962)
- aid-dependent countries (van de Walle 2005)
- the periphery (Wallerstein 1974)
- the satellites (Frank 1970)
- the South or Global South (ICIDI 1980; Wade 2006)
- the tropics (Easterly 2002)
- marginalized countries (World Bank 2001)
- subordinate countries (Hardt and Negri 2001)
- the new states (Tucker 1977)
- transitional societies (Lerner 1972)
- the Majority world (Elworthy and Rogers 2001)
- developmentally challenged (Bali 2002)

would have been impossible to make sense of the statistical evidence presented in the previous section without taking for granted territorial state boundaries.

Development studies emerged as a postwar challenge to help poorer countries catch up with richer countries. The dominant approach to development has been to classify all poorer countries as a single category for analysis, diagnosis and intervention. The principal objective of the following section is to examine the validity of this category – the 'poorer countries'. How analytically useful is a collective noun for poorer countries?

In everyday speech and in intellectual circles, collective nouns abound to describe the poorer countries as a whole. Most people would be able to conjure up some image when confronted with terms such as the 'developing world', the 'under-developed world', the 'backward countries', the 'Third World', the 'South' or the 'emerging countries' (see Box 3.2). However, in the same way that the centrality of nation-states has been challenged, there are many critics who question the way poorer countries have been classified and labelled.

The problem with a collective identity

Critics of a collective label question whether the majority of the world that is labelled the 'poorer countries' can be embraced adequately in a single category. Any collective noun chosen would have to include around 190 countries and territories spanning the globe from Africa, Asia, the Middle East and Latin America, the Caribbean and the Pacific. The population would encompass some 4 billion people – in other words, 75 per cent of the world's population. The territory would cover some 70 per cent of the world's land mass (Smith 1996: 3). The dimensions are truly global.

The idea that the collective noun over-generalizes experience and under-emphasizes difference has been a perennial criticism of development thinking. Power (2003: 105) has claimed that such terms persist in encouraging 'a homogenized understanding of a considerable part of the globe'. This refers to the difficulty of incorporating such a diverse range of cultures, politics and ideologies into one all-encompassing label. Such an approach fails to capture the uniqueness of different histories and cultures.

These criticisms cut across the political spectrum. The conservative Peter Bauer (1981) lamented the tendency to envisage the poorer world as 'an undifferentiated, passive entity, helplessly at the mercy of its environment and of the powerful West'. Likewise, Naipaul (1988: 31) bemoaned the modern trend of viewing people as representatives of some abstract concept or shadowy relationship, rather than 'seeing them as they really are'. Collective nouns such as 'Third World' (originally coined to distinguish the advanced capitalist and communist 'worlds' from the rest of the world) might have a certain 'congenial simplicity' but ultimately they fail to 'adequately sum up the human condition of three-quarters of mankind' (Naipaul 1988: 38–9). From a more radical perspective, Mark Berger (1993) interpreted the tendency to speak of the 'generalized other' as a strategy used by more powerful interests to effectively manage the poorer countries through controlling the perception of their 'problems'.

A related objection to the collective approach refers to the enormous disparities between the nations that are classified as 'poor'. The experiences of poorer countries since the Second World War have been highly variable with some countries faring much better than others. Any label that embraces the industrial transformation of East Asia along with the economic stagnation of most of Sub-Saharan Africa stretches the credibility of classification. As the development indicators listed earlier in this chapter reveal, disparities within the poorer countries manifest themselves on a wide range of socio-economic, demographic and political indicators (Smith 1996: 25).

A further problem with collective identification is the danger of glossing over some spectacular inequalities *within* poorer countries. Not all social groups within the 'poorer countries' suffer equally. Under Papa Doc and Baby Doc from the 1950s to the 1980s Haiti might have been one of the poorest of the poor nations, but these dictators built fantastic fortunes at the expense of the population. The same phenomenon was experienced in Nicaragua under the Somoza dynasty between the 1930s and the 1970s, and Mobutu in Zaire from the 1960s to the 1990s.

As the data on income inequalities within nations presented in the introductory chapter showed, on any measurement scale there are classes in the poorer countries that enjoy immensely more wealth and power than most of their fellow citizens. The living standards and consumption patterns of such elites – international travel, BMWs, plastic surgery, Gucci shoes – rival those of Western elites. Some of the richest people on earth are citizens of the so-called poorer countries. Three of the five top names on *Forbes*' 'World's Richest People' list hail from India, Mexico and Saudi Arabia. The 691 billionaires identified are spread across 47 different countries (Krol and Goldman 2005). Given this observation, there is a danger that any collective noun for the poorer countries might divert our attention away from internal status differentials within poorer countries.

The same logic holds for wealthier countries – labelling a country 'rich' does not preclude the existence of significant poverty. In 'high income' countries, poverty and inequality not only exist – many studies argue they are increasing (Saunders 2005; Yates 2004). Becoming 'more like the west' does not ensure that social inequality is declining. As the appallingly low rates of life expectancy among Indigenous Australians demonstrate, 'poorer country' conditions prevail within many advanced industrial countries (Jolly 2000). The life expectancy of an African-American male in Harlem, New York, is less than that of the average Bangladeshi male (Pieterse 2004: 128; Sen 2001). To speak of 'rich' and 'poor' countries might also gloss over the fact that the wealthy of the poorer countries feel a greater sense of affinity with the wealthy of the richer world than the poor of their own country (Smith 1996: 29). Indeed, as shown time and again, they often treat poorer fellow citizens with brutality and contempt. A classification of global stratification based on national units of analysis is open to the charge of under-emphasising internal social stratification and internal inequalities of wealth and power.

Finally, other critics have questioned whether the disparities in wealth, resources and conditions between poor countries preclude any genuine solidarity among this amorphous group. Comeliau (2002: 2) has argued that the poorer countries now possess few common characteristics and therefore there is 'little scope for united political action'. Ramonet (2004: 8) likewise believes that the 'third world has ceased to exist as a political entity' (see also Berger 2004; Escobar 2004). Even if a common set of characteristics could be agreed on that adequately defined the poorer countries, this would not guarantee that such an entity would be free of the 'divisiveness and mutual betrayal' that has plagued the more developed world (Tucker 1977: 89).

The value of a collective identity

Despite these objections, there are many commentators who continue to adopt a collective term to understand development processes. In order to justify using the collective noun as a unit of analysis, it is necessary to demonstrate that these nations perceive themselves subjectively as a collectivity, or are bound by ties of solidarity, or possess enough objective similarities to place them in the same category.

Evidence for subjective identification requires some historical background. As the process of decolonization proceeded after the Second World War, the newly independent countries became an arena of contestation between the Cold War superpowers (see Chapter 4). However, there emerged a hope among many of the new regimes that the post-colonial world could become a 'third force', independent of the power blocs of the USA and the USSR. This search for diplomatic and military independence among various nations in the face of the superpowers became the cornerstone of the Non-Aligned Movement (Power 2003: 103–4).

The political objective of non-alignment was to demonstrate that the 'new nations' had nothing to gain from associating themselves with military superpowers. The Non-Aligned Movement sought to remain politically and diplomatically independent from the ideological war between the USA and the USSR. Non-aligned leaders such as Nehru in India, Nkrumah in Ghana, Tito in Yugoslavia and Sukarno in Indonesia argued that the Cold War was detrimental to the interests of less powerful nations – despite US rhetoric that it sought to save vulnerable nations from communism, and despite Soviet rhetoric that it would liberate the exploited from imperialist slavery. Non-alignment stated: neither Washington, nor Moscow, but Third World autonomy.

This hope that the newly independent countries could act as a third force was enhanced by claims that the historical legacy of exploitation and their current economic predicament made them distinct from both the capitalist and Soviet blocs. The Non-Aligned Movement proclaimed that the poorer countries possessed a material and ideological basis for collective action in defence of common interests. This argument has continued to manifest itself in various campaigns over the years, such as the call during the 1970s for a new international economic order (where various poorer countries acted in unison in an effort to use the United Nations Conference on Trade and Development [UNCTAD] to secure a more favourable and fairer international trading system). More recently, there have been collective efforts within the World Trade Organization to secure greater access to advanced technology patented within the wealthier countries (see *New Internationalist*, May 2001). Various nations have also banded together to seek reforms on issues as diverse as resource cartelization, greenhouse gas emissions and a moratorium on foreign debt. At Cancun in Mexico during September 2003, a Group of 20 poor countries, led by Brazil, brought the WTO 'Doha' Development Round of negotiations to a halt by refusing to accept the demands of various high-income countries.

By 2004, despite decades in which its demise has been predicted, the Non-Aligned Movement contained 116 members and remained a forum for discussing issues of development. At its August 2004 Summit in Durban, South Africa, the host nation's President Mbeki emphasized the importance of using the forum to challenge global inequality. He stated that 'developing countries should not allow powerful nations to dictate the world on their own terms', and he called for the 'transfer of resources to poor countries by the West' through efforts to tackle debt, First World protectionism and movement towards meeting the UN's Millennium Development Goals (*BBC News* 2004).

Claims that poorer-nation solidarity is moribund are made so frequently that they begin to sound more like wishful thinking than acute observation. Few doubt the collective importance of the G8 group of high-income nations despite the significant differences within its membership. Even though large poorer countries such as Brazil, India and China also face difficulties working together in international forums, the denial that poorer countries are capable of acting in unison could be interpreted as the product of rich-country condescension.

Some observers claim that the actions of groups such as the G8 have marginalized the developmental efforts of the poorer countries, and therefore argue that the poorer world must 'draw its own agenda, including its plans for development' (Rapley 2002: 162). Sachs (2005: 365) has also called for more collective action from the poorer countries:

> The poor cannot wait for the rich to issue the call to justice. The G8 will never champion the end of poverty if the poor themselves are silent. It is time for the world's democracies in the poor world – Brazil, India, Nigeria, Senegal, South Africa, and dozens of others – to unite to issue the call to action. The poor are starting to find their voice, in the G3 (Brazil, India, South Africa), the G20 (a trade grouping that negotiates within the WTO), and elsewhere. The world needs to hear more.

The collective image of the poorer countries can therefore be justified on the grounds that throughout the past few decades a variety of nations and leaders have called for solidarity among such countries, and occasionally have acted upon this perception of a world divided into rich and poor countries in terms of both wealth and power. Perceptions of solidarity regularly lead to collective action that attempts to influence the balance of global power relations.

Underlying the argument that the poorer world should be considered a collective entity is the observation that their human development status remains significantly below that of the richer countries. Mittelman (1988) claimed that a collective identity is warranted on three other grounds: *geographic* concentration in Latin America, Africa and Asia; *historical* status as former colonies of the Western powers; and the present predicament of *economic* weakness (see also Hobsbawm 1994: 357; Muni 1979: 128; Todaro 1980: 20–1).

Although each individual country has its own specific characteristics, Rapley (2002: 10) has identified the following ones as constituting the collective identity of poorer countries:

- relatively low average per-capita income
- relatively poorer health outcomes

- relatively poorer educational outcomes
- relatively higher population growth rates
- relatively higher proportion of population engaged in agricultural pursuits
- relatively lower proportion of the population engaged in industrial pursuits
- an export portfolio focused on a limited number of primary products
- an introduction to modernity through colonization by a foreign power.

This section has examined whether there is sufficient justification for adopting a collective term to describe those nations that are relatively poorer than others. While acknowledging the problem of overgeneralization and recognizing the porosity of national boundaries, it is still possible to show that differences between the poorer countries pale into insignificance when compared with the wealthier countries. The development statistics presented earlier in the chapter support this comparative argument.

The Language of Development

Even if a collective identity for the poorer countries is accepted, problems do not end there. There remains an issue of deciding *which* label most accurately defines the problems besetting this category of nations. A variety of labels has been attached to the countries that have been the subject of development studies (see Box 3.2). The labels not only reflect features about the designated countries, but also provide insight into the theories adopted to make sense of their historical origins, their dynamics of change and their likely futures. This is another way of saying that each descriptive label in the field of development studies is contested and politically loaded (Worsley 1979: 100). Drawing on our discussion of different approaches to inequality in Chapter 2, terms such as 'backward countries', 'developing countries', 'less-developed world', 'agrarian countries' and 'non-industrial world' emphasize *individual* attributes that characterize specific countries, while terms such as 'periphery', 'satellites', 'marginalized countries' and 'subordinate countries' hint at more *structural relationships* that determine a country's status. Each one of these labels is also burdened with historical context (see Box 3.3).

Social constructionists have argued that labelling serves a range of purposes. First, it identifies 'outsiders' as 'others' while bonding and giving a sense of identity to 'insiders'. It provides a sense of 'us and them' or – translated into the language of development – a sense of who has achieved the goal of modernity and who 'needs help' (Power 2003: 99–101). As Chapter 2 pointed out, labels and stigmatization can assume a self-fulfilling function, influencing the way in which actors behave towards one another. Social constructionists argue that labelling by powerful global actors helps to define global realities and it constrains the choices of action available to subordinate groups and nations (Berger 1993; Said 1979). According to Escobar (1995: 30), as soon as the poorer countries achieved independence, they were 'infantalized' by Western academic and political discourse. This provided the pretext for the West to come to their 'salvation' through approaching them as a 'child in need of adult guidance'. Peter Berger (1985b: 21) also used development discourse to illustrate how language reflects perceptions which, in turn, shape realities. Much of the language of development, he felt, was pejorative: backwardness suggested 'mental retardation' while 'underdevelopment' suggested a 'physical lag'. The term 'development' itself hinted at ' "growth" as a child catches up with an adult'.

This 'linguistic turn' in development theory serves as an important reminder of the power of language not only to represent reality but also to guide it. The use and abuse of language became a familiar cry as the twentieth century unfolded. The abuses of language by totalitarian regimes in the service of mass mobilization have been attacked by writers as diverse as the novelist George Orwell (1946) and the economic philosopher Frederick von Hayek (1944: 148–9). The former alerted readers to how euphemisms can be deployed to make the unthinkable seem innocuous and that latter warned of the 'complete perversion of language, the change of meaning of the words by which the ideals of new regimes are expressed'. However, if dialogue is to take place within theoretical frameworks and between competing paradigms, it is necessary for analysts to know what words describe. It is telling that even critics of collective terms in development studies often find themselves returning to them for the convenience of communication, even if they do place inverted commas around the label or insert the prefix 'so-called' (see Escobar 1995; Power 2003). Labelling performs a range of functions: from classifying, evoking a set of images, providing a comparative schema, through to a ranking device. Labels are a necessary feature of communication and as long there is an awareness that they remain a shorthand means to help make sense of the world, then their discursive power – just like statistics – can be acknowledged more reflexively as being both convenient and potentially misleading (Hulme and Turner 1990: 33).

Language and communication require that we compare, contrast and

---

Box 3.3   Historical shifts in the language of development

The following chapters explore in greater depth some of the main theoretical approaches to development practice since the Second World War. However, as a lead into these chapters, this box examines how the language of development has altered over time. It illustrates many of the points made in this chapter: the terms employed in development studies reflect authors' broader political and philosophical understandings of social change and also reflect the historical circumstances under which they write.

- *Third World* as a development term emerged in the 1950s to suggest that in the wake of the Cold War certain countries were rejecting the limited options of either being under the shield of the Western capitalist powers, led by the USA (First World) or the USSR-led communist bloc (Second World). There was a 'third way' that would present itself on the international stage as 'non-aligned'. The initial sense of the Third World as a category within international relations gradually gave way in the 1970s to the sense of the Third World as a socio-economic phenomenon – those nations whose developmental potential had been adversely shaped by the structure of colonial relations and more recently by the international trading system.

    Nevertheless, as the communist Second World crumbled and global politics became more 'unipolar' in the 1990s the term lost much of its meaning. The political hopes of Third Worldism have never been realized and, as Terry Eagleton (2004: 10) notes, as early as the late-1970s, 'Third Worldism' began to give way to 'postcolonialism'.

- *Post-colonial society*: this term was often used descriptively to describe the nations that had achieved or received independent nationhood status from the colonial powers after the Second World War. However, by the 1960s and 1970s many radical development theorists came to consider the term to be overly conservative, suggesting a more

→

---

form links between individuals and categories, self and other. The deconstruction of language can perform an important role in raising self-awareness about our logic, but language necessarily needs to be reconstituted if research is to shed any light on its subject. It would take a brave person to state that they had uncovered a 'pure' set of concepts to define the reality of development. As Box 3.3 demonstrated, language is not only captive to theoretical frameworks – it is also a prisoner of history.

This awareness that our theoretical models are prisoners of history

→ decisive break from colonial structures than was warranted. Many felt that the newly independent states remained 'neo-colonial' rather than postcolonial due to the political, economic and cultural influence that the former colonial powers held over the nations.

By the 1980s, the term began to take on a new meaning, associated with the growing popularity of postmodern studies and the emergence of literary trends that dealt with the hybrid cross-cultural experiences associated with global migration. Postcolonial voices challenged Western discourses within development studies and called for a greater recognition of marginalized or 'subaltern' voices, both in the West and in the former colonial nations. This 'decentring' of development studies allowed postcolonialism to re-emerge as a more all-embracing label for the global phenomena discussed in the introductory chapter and at the beginning of this chapter, as it avoided the problem of methodological territorialism.

- *South* or *Global South* was another term adopted to overcome problems with the label 'Third World'. It refers to the geographic observation that most rich countries are in the northern hemisphere whereas poorer ones are in the south. By the mid-1970s, as a period of détente between the superpowers revived hopes of global peaceful coexistence rather than global nuclear obliteration, some development thinkers argued that the 'East–West' division that had captured the attention of most postwar analysts placed focus on the wrong axis of the problem of world poverty. The term 'Third World' remained embedded in a discourse that emphasized this political divide. The more important divide was between the rich world and the poor world, regardless of ideological persuasion and our language should therefore reflect this binary division. 'North–South' was the title of the Brandt Report (1980) and, for a period during the 1980s, South was used as a more acceptable term than Third World. It remains the preferred collective noun for writers such as George (2004) and perhaps surprisingly organizations such as Third World Network and their magazine *Third World Resurgence*.

does not diminish development studies. It makes it a reflexive subject, reconstituting the world at the same time that it is shaped by that world. Similarly, the presence of competing models or frameworks – and their often combative stance over the language of development – presents an opportunity to understand the world through a variety of lenses, and to be able to look at the world 'with new eyes' (Game and Metcalfe 2003: 63; Mills 1973: 235–6). The following three chapters deal with the historical development of these lenses on development.

Box 3.4   Why we adopted the term 'poorer countries'

As academics or development practitioners we use labels to construct and describe the world with which we are engaging. As such, we acknowledge that labels can be powerful instruments in determining development policies, programmes and projects, and they can produce unintended consequences (Institute of Development Studies 2006). Throughout this book, we have decided to adopt the term 'poorer countries' to define those nation-states that have been the focus of analysis within most development studies. As the following discussion shows, development language has gone through various fashions and thus it is important for us to state here that we are not arguing that others should adopt the term 'poorer countries'. Nor are we saying that it is the 'latest' term. Although it is a term commonly used within the literature, there are many other terms that continue to be popular (see Box 3.3).

We decided to employ the term because it fits the context of our focus on inequality and poverty. It is therefore a useful shorthand term for the differences in national wealth generation and accumulation within those units of analysis called 'nation-states'. Terms also reflect the persuasion of authors, and we feel that as a relative term 'poorer countries' allows us to take into account many of the structural factors that are given inadequate acknowledgement in some development analysis (see Chapters 1 and 2). Furthermore, our approach in this book ruled out certain terms. For instance, 'developing countries' was ruled out as we resisted the temptation of providing a fixed definition of the term 'development' at the beginning of the book, recognizing that the term has meant many different things to different development theorists throughout the history of postwar development (see Chapter 1). We wanted to avoid defining countries by using the very term we are trying to problematize.

We are therefore not necessarily wedded to the term 'poorer countries' and we would use other terms in different contexts. We also recognize that the term could result in misleading impressions if not qualified. For example, there are wealthy and powerful people who live in 'poorer countries' while there are deep pockets of poverty in 'wealthy countries'. These facts were highlighted in Chapter 1.

Chapter 4

The Roots of the Development Project

Progress and Modernity

Colonialism and Inequality

The Setting for Development Practice after 1945

The previous chapters have examined a range of themes that have remained contentious throughout the history of development studies. This chapter begins by stepping back into history to explore how the process of social change has been understood since the Enlightenment. The chapter then examines key issues that continue to resonate in analyses of global inequality: the relationship between poorer countries and the legacy of colonialism; the relationship between developmental pacesetters and late-comers; and the associated relationship between endogenous and exogenous forces in the process of development. These issues will reappear in different settings throughout the remainder of the book.

Progress and Modernity

Progress and modernity are twin concepts underpinning development studies. Derived from the Enlightenment, and adopted by classical sociology, they refer respectively to the path along which, and the goal towards which, all civilizations are assumed to head. More recently, the nature of progress and modernity has been placed under more critical scrutiny within the social sciences and this has reverberated through development studies (see Chapter 9). Despite this, the centrality of these concepts in the history of modern thought cannot be disputed (Wright 2005: 3–4).

Since the eighteenth century, Western civilization has tended to revere the 'modern' and debase the 'traditional'. This contrasts with medieval Europe, when the modern was considered unworthy of serious attention

(Kumar 1993: Ch. 4; Rist 1999). For modern 'dwarfs' perched on the shoulders of ancient 'giants', antiquity represented the authentic intellectual and social order, whereas modern times were dismissed as trivial and superficial. One twelfth-century poem lamented: 'Whatever changes, loses its value' (Kumar, 1993: 72). Classical texts were regarded as sacred.

This approach to knowledge and social change was reinforced by religious dogma. Religious texts determined how the material world was observed and understood. Until the late Middle Ages in Europe, people continued to have faith in a stable geocentric order, and supernatural forces were used to explain unforeseen events (Lines 1992: 16). Few questioned the self-evident and God-given order of nature. This approach to the natural world also held for the social order. In both the social and the physical realms, people were drawn back to ancient texts such as the Bible for answers to metaphysical and existential problems. For the Muslim world as much as the Christian, the Garden of Eden had been lost and people now lived in *lesser* worlds.

It is only with the beginning of the modern era that these self-evident truths were more widely questioned (Bock 1979: 47–50; Rist 1999: Ch. 2). In 1661, the English clergyman Joseph Glanvill proposed that 'scientists should try to explain the physical world by doing experiments, rather than deferring to what the ancients believed' (quoted in Margolis 2000: 27). Descartes – the grand sceptic who questioned everything except the existence of an omnipotent God – turned the relationship between ancients and moderns on its head with the logical point that his modern times were more ancient than the earlier times because the 'world is older now than before and we have greater experience of things' (quoted in Rist 1999: 35). The modern dwarfs began to gain confidence that their accumulated height – derived from standing on the shoulders of the giants – gave them greater vision that their predecessors (see also Olsen 1982). This led to the Enlightenment approach to knowledge as a progressive, cumulative process, 'an inherited body of generalized understanding [as] the jumping-off point for the development of more' (Babbie 1983). This could be contrasted with 'traditionality', where culture is pervaded with 'the recognized value of the already-said, by the recurrence of discourse, by the "citational" practice under the seal of age and authority' (Foucault 2000: 273–4; Habermas 1971: 95).

As secularization advanced in the eighteenth century, scientists increasingly rejected the proposition that the natural order and the social order were laid down by God. The French writer Louis Sebastien Mercier speculated in 1770 that if Newton 'could explain the physical world then some rational law of social motion must be at work in human history . . . and that must mean that with reason and hard work and the understanding of such laws of social science, human society would be set on an ever-improving upward curve' (quoted in van Krieken et al. 2000: 30). In this way, the concept of 'development' took root as a critique of the feudal life-world (Larrain 1989: 1).

Two other revolutionary changes of the late-eighteenth century acted as catalysts for modernity – the French Revolution and the Industrial Revolution (Giddens 1997, 6–7). The Industrial Revolution loosened rigid traditional relationships and transformed the countryside through agricultural and technological innovation. It brought forth new social relationships, shifted populations across the land, fuelled urbanization, transformed family relationships and promoted Enlightenment ideas based on experimentation and science.

The French Revolution of 1789 under the banner of 'Liberty, Equality and Fraternity' shook the European social order that had been held together by the fixed estates of monarchy, aristocracy and clergy. The possibility of mass democracy excited many and horrified others but almost all agreed that there was no return to the past. Under conditions of unprecedented social change, people scrutinized the contours of this emerging order to imagine the outcome of these transformations. French sociologists such as Saint Simon and August Comte were devoted to observing the dynamics of social change and understanding these upheavals in social life. They were confident that a more rational society could be constructed through applying the tools of science, observation, experimentation and measurement. For Comte, progress was the unfolding of social order inherent within the historical process. Thus, the emergence of this modern era that unleashed unprecedented political, economic and social transformations was associated with a series of critical questions about the nature of existing social arrangements and the dynamics of social change.

Karl Marx was also in awe of the revolutionary transformations that modern capitalism brought in its wake, transforming cultures, dissolving superstition and drawing pre-capitalist cultures into the orbit of modernity. In the following passage he highlighted the victory of the moderns over the ancients, and the forces of modernity over tradition:

> Constant revolutionizing of production, uninterrupted disturbance of all social conditions, uncertainty and agitation distinguish the bourgeois epoch from all earlier ones. All fixed, fast-frozen relations, with their train of ancient and venerable prejudices and opinions, are swept away, all new formed ones become antiquated, before they can ossify. All that is solid melts into air, all that is holy is profaned. (Marx and Engels 1969: 5–6)

Other social scientists emphasized the significant shifts in Western European sensibility that modernity brought in its wake (Roxborough

Box 4.1   Prototypes and emulators

The reflexive nature of human beings ensures that an awareness of past events and processes influences the options open to later social actors. In this sense, even though development theory has always been concerned with the general process of modernity, no two social developments across time can ever be alike and each experience of social change will contain its own historical and cultural idiosyncrasies (Chang and Grabel 2004: 44). Furthermore, as Carr (1976a: 53) pointed out: 'One reason why history so rarely repeats itself is that the *dramatis personae* at the second performance have prior knowledge of the denouement.' Despite this, one of the most persistent themes encountered in the history of development thought is the assumption that history contains 'proto-types' and 'emulators'. *Prototypes* refer to societies that first embark on a path of development; *emulators* refer to societies that attempt to follow these trailblazers.

The presence of prototypes and emulators was evident in classical soci-ological thinkers. Marx saw the industrial nations as simply further along the same monorail as the more backward nations. The following chapter will show that after the Second World War this 'original' transition to modernity was the yardstick by which development researchers measured the development of 'emergent' countries. These approaches postulated that the historical trajectory of the more 'advanced' capitalist nations could be emulated by the poorer countries. According to Lerner (1972: 387), the less developed country has the opportunity to see 'pictures' of 'more developed societies and decides, as a matter of high priority for its own policy planning, which of them constitutes the preferred picture of its own future'.

This developmental model assumed that the 'West' plants its pioneering feet and that the 'rest' only have to follow in its footsteps. Like Good King Wenceslas assisting his faithful page, the West has laid down the path

→

1979: Ch. 1; Webster 1984: 44–9). Max Weber (1978) traced the rise of capitalism and the effects of calculative rationality on all aspects of every-day life, from work through to the organization of public affairs. Emile Durkheim (1964) examined the growing division of labour as a key vari-able that led to the breakdown of more static, traditional, agrarian-based communities and the rise of modern and dynamic urban associations between people. Georg Simmel (1964) observed that under modern urban conditions, people began to adopt a more blasé attitude towards social change. Herbert Spencer (1982) reinterpreted Darwin and applauded the modern emphasis on competitive behaviour, ensuring that the best equipped would be elevated to the apex of the social order (though Darwin himself found Spencer 'pompous but gifted' [Browne 1995: 354]).

→

along which the rest can follow. Such is the opportunity that nations of 'wealth and rank' have to 'bless the poor'. This 'linearism' continues to be widely accepted in the twenty-first century: 'It is an integral part of the faith in progress that has replaced religion in most of the advanced industrial societies, and the basis of development programmes throughout the world' (Gray 2004: 58). De Soto (1999: 71), for example, remains optimistic that poverty and inequality will eventually be overcome in the poorer world because these countries 'are experiencing nearly the same industrial revolution that arrived in the West more than two centuries ago'. The novelty of the process experienced by today's emulators is that their process 'is roaring ahead much faster'.

Despite this penchant for prototypes and emulators within development theories, there is a growing recognition of the diversity of paths to modernity and even a questioning of the very generalisability of modernity itself. George (2004: 164) has demanded that the specificity of the present be acknowledged more, 'without trying to make it conform artificially to past models'. Likewise, Comeliau (2002: 164) argues that modernity 'has shown itself to be non-generalizable, thereby transforming the hope of development into a false promise except perhaps for a privileged minority'. It is misleading to speak of 'the modern world' when a more accurate description suggests a few pockets of modernity coexisting with a majority world marginalized from modernity's benefits. If modernity is non-generalizable, then development truly has been one of the greater frauds of the past half century, by building prototypes that are not replicable (see Chapter 9).

However, it is important to learn from the lessons of history. As Chang and Grabel (2004: 147) point out, past 'success stories' can assist our understanding of developmental processes. Reflexivity holds out the hope that poorer countries can learn from the past even if this 'heuristic device' loses its utility when 'blindly followed' or adopted as a 'template'.

Although these theorists viewed development in different ways, all were inspired by the spirit of progress. Their approach can be described as 'linear': the idea that history progresses along a single path and that all societies can be located somewhere along this historical trail of development. Societies were understood to be at different *stages* of development, in the same way that a human child inevitably grows into an adult human, or an acorn into an oak tree. Biological metaphors abounded in nineteenth-century social sciences and many came to labelled 'evolutionary' or 'neo-evolutionary' perspectives on development. This linearism was expressed in Karl Marx's (1976: 91) claim in the 'Preface' to *Capital*, volume 1 that 'the country that is more developed industrially only shows, to the less developed, the image of its own future' (see Box 4.1).

The focus of these theorists was the 'more developed industrially'. There were important exceptions, such as Weber (1947), who studied Chinese and Indian society, and Durkheim (1965) who discussed Indigenous Australian societies. Yet even in these cases, the 'other' was used as a yardstick to measure the progress of European modernity. The primary aim was to explain the path from feudalism to modern rational capitalistic industrial society in Western Europe (Eisenstadt 1973: 7–8).

Only at the end of the colonial era after 1945 were the classical socio-logical theories adapted to provide an explanation for postcolonial development, using generalizations from the history of the more advanced industrial societies to predict the future of 'developing' coun-tries. For this reason, postwar development thought can be seen as 'the continuation of the Enlightenment and the West European Industrial Revolution' (Comeliau 2002: 138).

Yet, this search for greater certainty and more perfect knowledge engendered by modernity coexisted uneasily with the 'scepticism' that lay at the heart of the scientific method (Toulmin 1990). On the one hand, there was a belief that accumulated knowledge would enable humanity to control its destiny through fully understanding the truth of material and social existence. On the other hand, there was a rejection of any 'single privileged truth' as prejudicial to scientific analysis and observa-tion (see Lehman 2003: 178–9). In other words, modernity has always contained an inbuilt tension between certainty and uncertainty.

Most classical sociologists possessed this blend of certainty and uncer-tainty in their work. At times, the transition to modernity appeared as a positive step for humanity, while in other places it is viewed as alienating, anomic and dehumanising. This represented another defining paradox of modernity (see Chapter 1). For Marx, the awesome power that modern society had generated for the creation of social wealth had to be offset against problems such as the growing concentration of capital, the polar-ization of wealth and alienation of producers from their products. Weber contrasted the instrumental rational efficiency of modern life with the tendency to turn individuals into 'little cogs' encased in a regulatory 'iron cage' of their own making. Durkheim observed how the freedom from traditional constraints could lead to 'anomie', a condition where individ-uals lost their sense of place within changing social structures (Coser 1971; Giddens 1978).

Chapter 5 will show how a *cult* of progress came to dominate many postwar social theories of development. The more sceptical and pessimistic side of classical sociological thought was marginalized, leaving a more optimistic and unidimensional approach to developmental processes. For this reason, Gray (2004: 3) has claimed that 'belief in progress is the Prozac of the thinking classes', while Wright (2005: 4) has defined progress as a modern 'secular religion'. For the moment, it is sufficient to stress the multifaceted approach that the classical sociologists took to modernity and modernization. As Comeliau warns (2002: 1): 'Unless our eyes and ears are closed to the world around us, these transformations appear both as a source of collective satisfaction and pride, and as the object of gloom, unease and profound disarray.' This relationship between developmental advance and human costs is nowhere more contentious than in the study of colonialism and inequality.

Colonialism and Inequality

Chapter 3 referred to the experience of colonialism as a potential source of collective identity among poorer countries. As the previous section pointed out, the colonial world was present as a 'generalized other' in the modern social sciences, which were concerned mainly with the pan-European world. The modern idea of the 'West', however, could only be constituted out of an awareness of those who were *unlike* Europeans (Power 2003: 100). More importantly, however, this 'New World' was also the object of European imperial desire.

Modern European colonial expansion began with the conquest of the 'New World' by the Spanish in the late fifteenth century, and by 1800 the Western powers (principally Britain, Holland, France, Spain and Portugal) controlled 35 per cent of the earth's surface. By 1878 these powers held 65 per cent, although the influence of the Iberian Peninsula had waned (Smith 1996: 36). The years between 1878 and the outbreak of the First World War in 1914 witnessed the 'scramble' for the rest of the world, especially African territory, among the colonial powers (Betts 1972; Wright 1976). Only a small number of non-European societies escaped the experience of direct colonial rule by the beginning of the twentieth century, such as Thailand, Abyssinia and Japan. Most of the former Spanish and Portuguese colonies of Latin America had gained their independence early in the nineteenth century.

The European powers justified their possession and control over these territories in a number of ways. Within the space of 100 years after 1492 almost all of Latin America became part of either the Spanish or Portuguese empires. Colonialism was motivated by the search for precious minerals to bolster the coffers of the feudal Iberian crowns (Thomas 2003). However, the autobiographies of early conquistadors such as Bernal Diaz also reveal the religious zeal that motivated these men. In the process of plundering the Americas, the Spanish and Portuguese were intent on saving heathen souls or exterminating them if they persisted in life without Christ the Saviour. Here and elsewhere there was theological controversy over whether indigenous peoples possessed souls (Reynolds 1989: Ch. 4).

As the belief in progress began to prevail in modernizing Europe, other justifications for colonialism emerged. Non-European societies were considered 'backward', 'pre-civilized' and closer to the original state of nature. As Said (1994: 96) noted: 'Almost all colonial schemes begin with an assumption of native backwardness and general inadequacy to be independent, "equal", and "fit"'. The nature of such savages, noble or otherwise, became a subject of intense debate in eighteenth-century Europe but by the nineteenth century the dominant discourse within Western social sciences regarded the colonial societies to be 'childlike'. They therefore required either protection or tutelage, before they assumed their place at the civilized table of sovereign nation-states (Tucker 1977: 9; Wallerstein 2004: 56).

Colonialism was an early example of the modern tendency for the more powerful to see themselves as a template out of which the colonies could be shaped. Ignatieff (2003, 42, 121) interprets it as a 'narcissistic enterprise' driven by a 'desire to imprint our values, civilization and achievements on the souls, bodies and institutions of another people'. How else, he reasons, can we understand this 'belief that all the variety of the world's peoples aspired to nothing else but to be a version of themselves'?

During the nineteenth century, racism emerged as a 'scientific' justification for the inequalities between nations. Phrenology, and later eugenics, purported to demonstrate that inequality between peoples was a natural phenomenon manifesting itself in the racial superiority of certain peoples over others. These were supplemented by theories asserting that ethnic characteristics determined the level of development. Environmental determinism was also used to explain the higher level of civilization achieved in Europe over other parts of the world, emphasizing the factor endowments of different areas. While each of these theories sought to explain inequalities between peoples, their arguments tended to be circular, spurious, ahistorical and ethnocentric or were encumbered with so many counterfactuals that they appeared as ideological props for imperial domination (Galbraith 1987: Ch. 1; see also Olsen 1982). For these reasons, Galbraith (1987: 28) concluded that 'until the Second World War, there was relatively little serious discussion of the causes of mass poverty, and likewise very little of its remedy'.

European colonial expansion was also defended on grounds that colonies expanded trade through providing markets for domestic products, and thereby expanding employment opportunities for European workers. Imperial rivalry also helped strengthen nationalistic sentiments and feelings of 'imagined community' within European countries.

Regardless of the justifications that were used for colonialism, they ultimately amounted to different voices singing the same tune. By the late-
nineteenth century, 'the white man had worked himself into a high state
of self-conceit' (Kiernan 1972; see also Ferguson 2003).

The 'age of empire' reached its zenith in the 30 years prior to the First
World War (Hobsbawm 1987). The European powers had colonized 85
per cent of the earth's land mass and imposed a global matrix of inequality, involving a configuration of ideological and institutional forces that
accelerated international trade and facilitated the movement of populations where that was deemed beneficial for economic expansion (such as
the movement of Tamils to Sri Lanka and Malaysia). By 1914, the world
had become a globally integrated network of socio-economic and political relationships (Friedan 2006: Chapters 1–5).

However, in the aftermath of the First World War, a range of factors
made the maintenance of imperial rule less tenable and more unpopular.
First, colonial power provoked rebellion in the form of independence
struggles. Anti-colonial movements resisted the exploitation of local
resources for the benefit of external administrators. This exploitation sat
uneasily with colonial justifications that the relationship was a necessary
stage of modern tutelage. Furthermore, many anti-colonial movements
were organized by students sent to the colonial metropolis who later
returned with greater awareness of the exploitative nature of the ties that
bound their land to empire. The more aware people became of their place
in the global economy, the more they demanded self-determination, equal
status, political freedom and material improvement (Baran 1970: 287).

The 1917 Bolshevik Revolution in Russia provided anti-colonial
movements with another illustration of anti-imperial possibilities. The
Russian Communists sponsored anti-colonial forums where the impending crisis of capitalist imperialism was debated, tactics for anti-colonial
struggles were discussed and a future federated world of equal states was
envisaged (Carr 1976b: Chapter 32).

During both World Wars, the colonies and dominions were enlisted to
fight on the side of their colonial powers, but this often required some
inducement of greater self-determination, especially when the colonial
power claimed to fight for the future of freedom and democracy. The
colonial powers also had to ensure that the colonial rebels would not
take the opportunity to receive assistance from an enemy that promised
immediate independence. The experience of Japan was also instructive.
Not only had that country shown how a politically independent non-
Western country could successfully modernize, it also provided examples
of the vulnerability of the European powers, defeating Russia at the
beginning of the century and humiliating the British at Singapore in
1942.

There were also strong liberal sentiments within Europe and the USA after the First World War claiming that the conflagration had been caused by imperialist rivalries. This suspicion was reinforced by the expansionist behaviour of the fascist powers during the 1930s. Under these circumstances, 'a deepening commitment to democracy and equality at home was bound to prove increasingly difficult to reconcile with the assertion of the right of one people to impose its rule on another, even when this rule was justified by the purpose of enabling subject peoples to rule themselves eventually' (Tucker 1977: 29–30).

The anti-colonial movement proved irresistible in the wake of the defeat of the fascist axis in 1945. In some cases colonial powers attempted to reclaim their right to rule, but for the most part the war had weakened their will and their capacity to maintain their empire. The independence struggles on the Indian subcontinent and in Indonesia and Vietnam inspired other anti-colonial struggles. Between 1954 and 1969, 54 states achieved their independence, leaving few colonial possessions in European hands (see Box 4.2). The politics of independence will be discussed in greater detail in Chapter 10.

The legacy of the colonial era continues to generate controversy. This historical point was emphasized by later structuralist theorists who argued that modern history cannot be understood outside of this colonial context which burdened poorer countries with technological, financial and trading disadvantages *vis-à-vis* former colonial powers (see Chapter 5). In addition, many former colonies have experienced, and continue to experience, civil conflict that appears to have colonial roots.

This claim that the colonial legacy distorted the socio-economic development of postcolonial societies has not gone unchallenged. Others argue that, on balance, colonial contact had positive effects and that the relationship between the colonizers and colonized facilitated progress, or that it was 'a Good Thing' (Berger 1985a; 11; Ferguson 2003). Drawing up a balance sheet of colonialism, d'Souza (2002) argues that while colonial institutions left much to be desired, their consequences were ultimately beneficial for the colonized. People in the postcolonial world 'are better off than they would have been had colonialism never happened'. For instance, British colonialism disseminated attitudes that allowed the colonial subjects to adapt to technological change as well as scientific and liberal humanist education. Colonialism 'was the transmission belt that brought to Asia, Africa, and South America the blessings of Western civilization'. Under these circumstances, d'Souza calculates that 'two cheers' are due to colonialism. Windschuttle (2000) offers the full three cheers, at least as far as the British legacy is concerned, arguing that 'the uncivilized conditions in which many people in the old imperial realm now live is evidence that

Box 4.2 Colonialism and independence in Papua New Guinea

Unbeknown to the overwhelming majority of indigenous inhabitants of the area now known as Papua New Guinea, in the late nineteenth century the Germans claimed the north while the British declared the remaining 223,000 square kilometres in the south to be their 'protectorate'. After a brief skirmish that constituted the First World War in Papua New Guinea, it was Australia that emerged as the colonial overlord of both territories. But it was a rather indifferent colonialism. Capitalism experienced stunted growth, Australia being content to maintain the territory as an 'inert shield' against potential threats from the north. Colonial administration was described by Lord Hailey of the Permanent Mandates Commission of the League of Nations as 'a benevolent type of police rule' with the indigenous inhabitants being regarded as either needing paternalist protection or being a subspecies of humanity.

Both portrayals justified indigenous exclusion from decision-making positions. A small white caste of public servants and planters undertook these roles. But for much of the colonial period many inhabitants lay outside of Australian control or were only partially and intermittently affected. For example, the first white men only arrived in the densely populated Highlands in the 1930s almost four decades after the territory had been claimed by either Britain or Germany. In other areas such as along the Sepik River and its tributaries, where there had been negligible capitalist development, the official government patrols were infrequent and brief. Infrastructure was poor or non-existent in many parts of the country so that many people continued to be governed in large part by the rules that had evolved in their own particular cultures over previous centuries. And there were many cultures. Estimates place the number of languages as over 800. Paternalism continued in the postwar era although the pace of change quickened and in the 1960s Papua New Guineans were actually recruited to new local government councils and a national House of Assembly as democratic socialization for a distant independence.

However, that distance was considerably reduced by the Australian Labor Party urging decolonization rather than by any nationalist movement in Papua New Guinea and in 1975 Papua New Guinea became an independent country. A liberal democratic parliamentary system of government was adopted and the behaviour of Westminster mingled with those derived from inter- and intra-tribal politics stretching back generations.

Source: Griffin et al. (1979); May (1997); Turner (1990).

Box 4.3   Endogenous and exogenous factors of development

Ongoing debates concerning the impact of colonialism form part of a wider theoretical and practical debate on the role that 'endogenous' and 'exogenous' forces perform in the process of development. Endogenous forces refer to factors that are internal to a social structure, while exogenous forces refer to those that impact from outside (or which are external to) that structure.

This distinction will emerge in various guises in the following chapters, but here it is applied to the debate over the balance sheet of colonialism. In order to examine contemporary global inequalities between nations, some analysts have considered colonialism and its legacy as an exogenous force with negative implications for social well-being and economic growth. In other words, colonialism is identified as the external force that impoverished the colonialized areas. The title of Walter Rodney's (1972) book, *How Europe Underdeveloped Africa*, clearly implicates colonialism as the exogenous cause of the problem.

Those who defend the legacy of colonialism look to other causes for the existence of inequalities between nations. Many writers point to endogenous forces that have acted as a 'break' on the development of poorer countries (Harrison and Huntington 2000; de Soto 1999). From this perspective, the maintenance of traditional social structures and values remain the principal causes of global inequalities. According to Berger (1985a: 12), most developmental problems in the poorer countries stem from 'internal' causes, such as 'economic systems that stultify growth and impede productivity; political corruption; oppression of people to the point where they cease to be economically active; persecution of economically productive minorities (such as the Asians in eastern Africa and the Chinese in southeast Asia); and, in some cases, indigenous

→

---

the world would be a better place today if some parts of it were still ruled by the British empire'. The claim that throughout history imperialism has coincided with political stability, peace and socio-economic improvement has also been advanced by Lal (2004) in his book *In Praise of Empire*. Each of these writers views colonialism as a positive 'exogenous' force that fostered development (see Box 4.3).

Critics of colonialism such as Amartya Sen (2006a) point out that large-scale famines were a feature of British colonial rule up until the 1940s. Since independence, India has avoided such catastrophes. Other critics argue that positive assessments of colonialism dismiss too lightly many of the ethical complexities of the developmental process. Before a balance sheet is settled, other questions need to be addressed: to what

→

social patterns and cultural values that are not conducive to economic activity'.

Bauer (1981: 4) also adopts this endogenous-oriented position on the problems of development, arguing that 'the causes of backwardness are domestic' and that 'external commercial contacts are beneficial'. He challenges the anti-colonial thesis, arguing that colonial contact was positively correlated with economic development and social progress in the post-colonial world: 'Far from the West having caused the poverty in the Third World, contact with the West has been the principal agent of material progress there' (Bauer 1981: 2; see also Bauer 1976: Ch. 3). According to Bauer, the anti-colonial argument places guilt at the feet of external forces and thereby allows the governments of poorer countries to abrogate any responsibility for their actions (see also Berger 1985a: 12). A focus on exogenous forces generates 'victimhood'. On the other hand, anti-colonialists reply that an emphasis on endogenous forces 'blames the victims' for their poverty. Thus, the weight attached of exogenous and endogenous forces in development depends on the author's political or ethical persuasion.

This distinction between exogenous and endogenous factors sheds light on the key themes of Chapter 2 – the individual and structural underpinnings of inequality. Those who focus on exogenous forces argue that the generation of global wealth among the former colonial powers has been built on the impoverishment of former colonies (A. Smith 1983: 18). On the other hand, those who focus on endogenous forces would tend to emphasize that global wealth and global poverty are not necessarily interrelated. The generation of wealth in one society is the result of factors inherent within that society through the discovery or application of ingredients conducive for modern sustainable growth (d'Souza 2002). All societies can achieve this growth if they follow the correct policy options and adapt to the necessary internal cultural and social changes.

extent should the inequalities and poverty suffered by one generation be seen as the necessary sacrifice for future sustainable growth? Is it better to be exploited by imperialism rather than not be exploited at all? What duties and moral obligations do people in wealthier countries have towards those suffering in other parts of the world?

The answers provided to these questions are themselves dependent on the lenses through which we perceive and understand the world. This requires us to return to the question addressed in the introductory chapter: are global wealth and poverty interconnected? Is global inequality a consequence of structures that hold the world together as an economic unit or, alternatively, are poorer nations simply at an 'earlier' stage of development? The debate on colonialism is one part of a larger theoretical controversy related to the nature of inequality that continues to challenge development theorists in the twenty-first century.

These questions will be addressed in the following two chapters, which deal with the theory and practice of postwar development. Before entering that field, however, it is necessary to look deeper into the intellectual milieu out of which development studies emerged in the wake of the Second World War.

The Setting for Development Practice after 1945

Between 1945 and 1981, UN membership rose from 51 to 156 nation-states. This was a momentous shift in the international structure of nation-states. Colonial administrators were replaced by local civil servants and a new band of Western experts ready to assist the newly independent states. These experts and political leaders devoted unprecedented attention to poorer countries. As Mabogunje (1980: 13) notes, 'at no time in human history has so much intellectual energy and humanitarian concern been directed towards understanding the basis for such poverty and evolving strategies for its eradication' (see also Easterly 2003: 30; Galbraith 1987: 32). A constellation of forces came into alignment to create 'development' as an intellectual and practical project. These included Western responses to the experiences of economic depression and global conflict, the emergence of postcolonial independent states, the onset of the Cold War and the structure of the postwar global economy.

In hindsight, the era between 1945 and 1970 is often referred to as 'the long economic boom' – a 'golden age' of capitalist growth and Western prosperity (Harvey 1989; Hobsbawm 1994). However, at the beginning of the postwar era, there were grave concerns among Western economists and politicians that peace would return the world to the recessionary conditions that had visited the decade prior to the war. The twin experiences of depression and war had left a profound mark on the temperament of most policymakers as well as social scientists. The expansionary economic policies introduced by President Roosevelt during the mid-1930s and the use of state powers to command the war economy had suggested a means of levelling out the cycles of booms and slumps that had so characterized the prewar capitalist economy. Economic theories associated with English economist John Maynard Keynes were on the rise. If the levers of state power could be employed to such effective use for prosecuting the war effort, then they could also be used to facilitate postwar reconstruction. States could use their fiscal clout as a means to maintain high levels of employment, generate local demand, deliver social services and steer the economy away from recession (Myrdal 1951).

A dominant view emerged that the market mechanism had failed to meet the needs of the poor. Prewar *laissez faire* economic approaches had generated growing poverty and inequality. Throughout most of the Western world, postwar education, health, housing and other services came to be seen as social goods that required either state provision or state regulation in order to ensure greater access for the deserving poor (Greig 1995: Ch. 1; Minogue 2002: 133–4). Only a small number of dissident voices were prepared to challenge this Keynesian consensus (see Box 4.3).

This atmosphere of intellectual confidence in the powers of state regulation and economic management encouraged Western policymakers and social scientists to broaden their concerns to the non-Western world. Now that the modern industrialized countries had solved their prewar economic problems, it was possible to examine the dilemmas of poverty in the poorer countries. Economists and other social scientists could now embark of the practical challenge of replicating the form of development achieved in the West (however, see Box 4.4 for a dissenting voice).

There were other factors that gave rise to this 'development project' (McMichael 2004: Ch. 1). Among the Western powers there was a growing acceptance that the colonial era was drawing to a close, and the most pressing issue was whether its demise would occur peacefully or through bloodshed. An associated question therefore involved the future prospects of postcolonial societies. Western leaders regularly presented their concern for postcolonial development in the guise of 'enlightened self-interest'. If poor countries remained in a state of general impoverishment, then those living in the more affluent countries could never feel safe.

US President Truman, for instance, based his hopes for the security of the postwar world on three developmental drives: a belief in progress, the beneficial effects of exogenous assistance, and the possibility of emulating the developmental trajectory of the United States:

> More than half the people of the world are living in conditions approaching misery. For the first time in history humanity possesses the knowledge and the skill to relieve the suffering of these people. . . . I believe that we should make available to peace-loving peoples the benefits of our store of technical knowledge in order to help them realize their aspirations for a better life. . . . What we envisage is a program of development based on the concepts of democratic fair dealing. . . . Greater production is the key to prosperity and peace, and the key to greater production is a wider and more vigorous application of modern scientific and technical knowledge. (quoted in Escobar 1995: 3)

Box 4.4   A voice from the wilderness – Hayek against state regulation

This acceptance of economic planning and state regulation rose from the direct experiences of the 1930s and 1940s. However, there remained a minority view that drew other lessons from the trend towards state control. Economic libertarians saw the iron hand of totalitarianism within the welfare state's velvet glove. According to Hayek, these developments had led to the rise of fascism in Germany and communist oppression in Russia. He feared that postwar free Europe was heading in the same direction, ironically after defeating the forces of fascism. In his book *The Road to Serfdom* (1944: 10 and 12), he warned that:

> There exists now in this country [UK] certainly the same determination that the organization of the nation we have achieved for purposes of defence shall be retained for the purposes of creation. There is the same contempt for nineteenth-century liberalism, the same spurious 'realism' and even cynicism, the same fatalistic acceptance of 'inevitable trends' (as one found in interwar Germany). . . . The important point is that, if we take the people whose views influence developments, they are now in this country in some measure all socialists. The wartime reliance on the state might have been a temporarily expedient, but it should not be considered a permanent blanket over the market.   (Hayek 1944: 189–90)

However, Hayek's defence of the market and his warnings about state interference would remain a cry from the wilderness during the long post-war boom (see Galbraith 1962: 42–3). The Western economy appeared to flourish and, however much criticism was levelled at the postwar social-democratic state, it hardly assumed the guise of totalitarianism. Nor did it drive the population towards serfdom, as Hayek had warned.

For the moment, the planners held the high ground in the battle for postwar reconstruction and socio-economic development. However, Hayek had 'planted the seed for the future blossoming of economic liberalism' (Cockett 1994: 99). As Chapter 7 will show, Hayek's views gained ground during the 1970s as the postwar welfare state consensus unravelled and state-led development faltered.

Western experts would perform a catalytic role in this development project as exogenous bearers of technological know-how, administrative efficiency and economic enterprise (Valenzuela and Valenzuela 1978: 538–9).

The Cold War was another reason why President Truman was intent on ensuring that poorer countries emulated the developmental trajectory of the USA. By mid-century, the capitalist world no longer monopolized the road to progress. Their former anti-fascist ally, the USSR, had presented itself as an alternative route to development (see Box 4.5). By the 1950s, these two models were in 'irreconcilable conflict' over global hegemony (Ambrose 1979: Ch. 8). The victory of the Chinese communists in 1949 meant that one-sixth of the world lived under communist

Box 4.5   Russia – the Soviet model of development

When the Bolsheviks took power in Russia in 1917, they believed that their revolution would herald the beginning of an international class struggle leading to world socialism. When this didn't materialize, the Bolsheviks were left ruling a country that had been devastated by the First World War and the following Civil War (1918–21). Industry and agriculture had collapsed, the rest of the world refused to lend more money (the Bolsheviks had defaulted on the debts accrued by the old regime) and foreign capitalists were reticent to invest in Russia.

The problem of how to fund development (or 'primitive socialist accumulation' [Preobrazhensky 1967]) preoccupied the Russian Bolsheviks during the 1920s. Some economic historians have argued that they invented 'development economics' under these difficult circumstances (Nove 1980; see also Spulber 1964: 59).

The development path adopted by Josef Stalin from the 1930s onwards involved a combination of exploiting the peasantry and industrial working class, politically emasculating civil society and erecting high economic and military defensive walls against the technologically stronger world capitalist system. This system of development came to be known by a range of labels, such as 'Stalinism', 'state communism', 'the soviet system', 'mono-organizational society', 'state capitalism' or a 'bureaucratically degenerated workers state' (Rigby 1977; Shachtman 1962; Spulber 1964: 54; Trotsky 1980).

Regardless of the label, this was the system that the post-Second World War USA was engaged in mortal combat with during the Cold War for the hearts and minds of the poorer countries. It was presented by friends and foe alike as an 'alternative' model of development (Hobsbawm 1994: 203). Though this form of state structure and social organization was rejected by many as contrary to the modern goals of liberty, it attracted many developmental thinkers and policy-makers who saw it as a prototype for rapid economic development (Spulber 1964: 127). The 'successes' of the Soviet Union during the 1930s – where it appears to have achieved extraordinary rates of economic growth at a time when the capitalist world stumbled through the Great Depression – fuelled the argument that the Soviet model was a prototype for the postcolonial world.

The feature of this model that captured most attention among the newly independent nations was state planning. From afar, it seemed that the results of the Soviet five-year plans combined science with production targets to achieve rapid economic growth. This planning principle was adopted by many non-communist countries, such as India.

regimes. As the two postwar superpowers manoeuvred for position throughout the world, the fear of communist expansion made the future development of poorer countries a higher priority for US foreign policy.

The initial Cold War concerns for the USA centred on the security of Western Europe, where countries such as France and Italy contained large Communist parties. The USA assisted their postwar reconstruction through supplying material, technical and financial aid in the form of the Marshall Plan (Ambrose 1979: Ch. 5). The concern over poorer countries expressed by successive US presidents occurred within this geopolitical milieu. President Kennedy, in one of his most memorable statements, warned that 'those who make peaceful revolution impossible will make violent revolution inevitable' (LeFeber 1983: 154). The USSR cast a totalitarian shadow over the future of the 'free world' and the postwar struggles for national liberation within the poorer countries suddenly took on new meaning and new urgency. This concern was heightened by the acknowledgement that independence struggles had often been inspired by socialist ideology. The poorer countries therefore became a major battleground for Cold Warriors.

From the perspective of US strategists, the newly independent states had to be protected from the seductive promises of communism. The most effective means of accomplishing this was to assist poorer countries to become more like the West. The sooner this could be achieved, then the quicker the threat of communism could be overcome, because mass poverty was seen as a breeding ground for communism – and nowhere was poverty more widespread than in the former colonies of the European powers. This geopolitical crusade of saving the world from communism therefore elevated the importance of overcoming poverty in the poorer countries (Valenzuela and Valenzuela 1978: 535).

Many poorer countries were able to exploit this geopolitical position to negotiate concessions from the superpowers. All territory was considered strategic in the nuclear age. Aid became a weapon in the Cold War, and the US (in combination with their NATO allies) held the advantage of possessing more resources to bestow on the poorer countries. The Cold War was more than a military stand-off – it was a struggle over different paths to development, and development aid figured prominently in the calculations of the superpowers. While poorer countries possessed some leverage, their options entailed high risks. Any search for alternative paths to development could prompt foreign intervention from highly strung superpowers that saw the hand of the enemy in any development plans that strayed from the hegemons' chosen paths (Horowitz 1967; Kolko 1988).

To fully appreciate the environment that generated the postwar developmental project, it is also necessary to understand the growing global economic reach of the USA. The USA began its journey to global dominance as early as the 1820s, when the Monroe Doctrine proclaimed that no external interference should take place in its hemisphere without the agreement of the USA. By the mid-twentieth century, US economic, organizational and military power had made it the beacon of capitalist modernity (Ferguson 2004). After 1945 – unlike the rest of the capitalist world – it was not faced with a massive reconstruction programme. Indeed, it possessed the capital and technical support to aid the postwar recovery of Europe. When attention began to turn to the poorer countries in the late 1940s, the problems of mass poverty came to be framed around lack of capital, inadequate technical competence and insufficient entrepreneurship. There was supreme confidence that Western technologies could be applied with modifications to the problems of poorer countries. The postwar developmental project emerged from this confluence of the intellectual confidence that the problems of Western economies had been solved along with the availability of the physical and material means to affect postcolonial development (Galbraith 1987: 40–1).

A new governance framework was required to coordinate the substantial flows of capital and expertise. The United Nations would perform the role of maintaining a more harmonious political world, while the Bretton Woods conference (held in New Hampshire, USA, in July 1944) drew up the blueprint for the postwar international trading system. Reflecting on the experiences of the 1930s depression and the rise of ultra-nationalism, these architects of the postwar economic order concluded that many of the prewar conflicts between nations had been exacerbated by the collapse of international trade and the growth of economic isolationism.

The General Agreement of Tariffs and Trade (GATT), the International Monetary Fund (IMF) and the World Bank (WB) were founded as international institutions to facilitate postwar international economic stability. The IMF would provide short-term loans for nations experiencing balance of payments difficulties, and these loans were dependent on the borrower taking economic adjustment measures to correct these problems. This would reduce the temptation for nations to adopt policies that adversely affected other countries, such as protectionism or currency devaluations. The voting structure of the IMF was proportionate to the capital subscribed by each country, and therefore the USA along with the other European powers controlled the Fund.

Control over the World Bank operated in the same way. The initial function of the World Bank was to provide finance for the reconstruction of Europe, but once that was under way its mandate was expanded to provide loans to poorer countries to pay for large-scale investments in basic productive infrastructure (such as dams, railways, roads and power plants). These development projects would act as an inducement to private foreign investment. Loans were 'concessional', usually for specific purposes and offered at artificially low interest rates. The Bretton Woods agreement underpinned the global reach of the US government and US capital. As the major subscriber to the IMF and the World Bank, and with its currency acting as an international medium of exchange, the US's hegemonic role throughout the capitalist world was secured (Tanzer 1995: 8; Tucker 1977: 32).

Although the Bretton Woods system aimed to alleviate problems associated with international monetary flows, this issue later resurfaced in the form of 'unequal terms of trade' created by the relationship between the industrialized world and the non-industrialized world. As the following chapter will show, there were structuralist economists who argued that there was an imbalance in the world trading system whereby countries that exported primary commodities were faced with declining prices relative to the industrial goods they imported (Preston 1996: Ch. 10). They claimed that the 'poverty' of capital and technology and hence the 'backwardness' of poorer countries was a consequence of the way in which global trade was structured.

The importance of this issue will be explored in the following chapter, but at this stage it is sufficient to note that the dilemma of development has consistently turned on this axis – namely, is overcoming inequality a matter of time, whereby the deficiencies found in individual poorer countries will be overcome by following the path of the more advanced 'prototype' countries and thereby 'catching up' with them? Or are the economic differences built into the structure of an unequal system of nation-states within the global economy? As we will see later in the book, these questions remain central to development debates in the twenty-first century. The following chapter explores two influential intellectual approaches to these questions. The first (modernization theory) understands the relationship between rich and poor nations as 'generally beneficial' whereas the second (dependency theory) argues that the relationship is 'generally harmful' (So 1990: 107).

Chapter 5

The Postwar Development Project

Modernization and Equality through Catch-up
  Critiques of modernization theory

Combined and Unequal Development
  Imperialism and development
  Dependency and world-systems analysis
  Critiques of dependency theory and world-systems analysis

The previous chapter explored how the social sciences and policymakers embraced postwar development as an intellectual and practical challenge in the wake of decolonization. The key issue in this chapter concerns how poorer countries were expected to become more modern. Competing perspectives attempted to explain the problems of underdevelopment, inequality and poverty and they designed policies to build modern nation-states, increase general prosperity and bridge the gap between the richer and poorer countries. Two approaches that dominated postwar development studies until the 1980s were *modernization theory* and *dependency theory*. Much of their analysis remains germane to the way in which global inequalities are understood in the twenty-first century.

Modernization and Equality through Catch-up

The dominant approach to development theory and practice within the social sciences in the aftermath of the Second World War drew on classical sociological frameworks and the concept of universal progress. Development involved facilitating the postcolonial world along this path of progress towards modernity. The route from traditional society to modern society was named the 'process of modernization' and scholars embracing this framework were labelled 'modernization theorists' (see Box 5.1 for a summary). 'Modernization' was defined as 'the process of social change whereby less developed societies acquire characteristics common to more developed societies' (Lerner 1972: 386).

Box 5.1   The key characteristics of modernization theory

Modernization theory encapsulated the theoretical confidence of postwar modern thought:

- *first,* progress involved breaking the chains of traditional society and moving towards the enlightened space of modernity, where individuals increasingly took control of their social and physical environment through an ever-expanding appreciation of science and experienced high levels of material affluence;
- *second,* this process could be observed and measured in a scientific manner now that social scientists had a historical model – the modernization of the West – which acted as a successful prototype that the object of enquiry – the poorer world – could emulate;
- *third,* while the 'original transition' to modernity was mainly seen as a result of endogenous forces, the existence of the prototype could help promote development and modernization through exogenous assistance;
- *fourth,* methodologically, this framework presented a 'dualist' model of history that measured the change from 'ideal type' poles of tradition and modernity and compared and contrasted the contemporary reality of poorer countries with the history of the western industrialized world. As Rapley (2002: 15) notes, this methodology required the researcher to 'identify the conditions that had given rise to development in the first world, and specify where and why these were lacking in the third world'.

The practical advantage of this model was that by comparing poorer countries with the Western model, the attributes that a society 'lacked' could be determined. Policies could then be derived that removed 'obstacles' that lay in the path of historical development. Whereas Weber used the comparative method to identify the *unique* additional forces that propelled the West towards modernity compared with other civilizations, modernization theorists used historical comparison to discover the *missing* ingredients that were necessary for all countries to achieve future modernity.

The existence of an 'ideal-type' or prototype also gave modernization theory a highly technical flavour. Hoogvelt (1997: 35) speaks of it as a 'how to develop' manual for poorer countries, and for Hirschman (1981) 'the underdeveloped countries were expected to perform as wind-up toys'. Prime Minister Nehru of India typified this modernism: '[planning] and development have become a sort of mathematical problem that can be worked out scientifically . . . [men] of science, planners, experts . . . agree broadly that given certain preconditions of development, industrialization and all that, certain exact conclusions follow almost as a matter of course'. These observations on the mechanical nature of the development process hint at the importance of exogenous forces. Lerner (1972: 286) observed that the process could be 'activated' by either 'international or inter-social' forces. Modern societies might apply the initial force to poorer countries, but the key was to work out how this propulsion could unlock the forces of self-generating economic growth.

In many ways modernization theory marked an advance over classical sociological models of social change. Durkheim and Toennies, for instance, also used the polarities between tradition and modernity as an explanatory framework for social change, but neither provided much insight into the transition from one pole to another. By contrast, modernization theory emphasized the dynamics of social change *between* these polarities. The classical theorists analysed an entity that had already *become* modern, whereas modernization theorists were faced with the more practical challenge of *achieving* modernity. Its research agenda forced it to fill in the gaps between the traditional and modern polar opposites while simultaneously measuring the timing and the pace of the process of modernization (see Box 5.2 and Eisenstadt 1973: Ch. 1).

Modernization sociologists argued that development demanded more than an injection of capital and technology. Rejecting economic reductionism, they emphasized the need to 'make men modern' (Inkeles and Smith 1993). The principal issue for development became how different institutions function to maintain social cohesion, and the consequences for social equilibrium when changes are introduced into the social structure (Eisenstadt 1973). This might have sounded like abstract sociological theory, but it dealt with a highly practical issue: the possibility that under prevailing Cold War conditions, any social conflict associated with social change or 'disequilibrium' could be seized on by opportunistic discontents to sow seeds of rebellion and revolution. The social sciences were therefore seen as central to planning programmes that would allow the process of modernization to occur as smoothly as possible, taking into consideration the delicate institutional and attitudinal equilibrium that maintained social, political and economic cohesion. Rapid change was required without generating conflict (see Horowitz 1974: Part 5).

Modernization theory offered an approach to development that acknowledged the complex interaction between social, cultural, political and economic life (Lerner 1972: 388–9). It stressed how changes in one part of a social structure had repercussions for other parts. Additional capital or modern technology could not in itself be sufficient to spark the process of modernization into life. The transformation

---

Box 5.2   Measuring time and speed: staging development

One of the most influential texts on modernization theory was written by W. W. Rostow (1960). His book *The Stages of Economic Growth* captures the spirit of modernization theory. According to Rostow: 'it is possible to identify all societies, in their economic dimensions, as lying within one of five categories: (1) traditional society; (2) the preconditions for take-off; (3) the take-off; (4) the drive to maturity; (5) the age of high consumption' (Rostow 1960: 4).

These universal stages could be read into the past and future of all societies. The first stage assumed a pre-modern social formation in which life hardly changed from generation to generation. In the second stage, social, economic and technological initiative by enterprising sectors of society 'jump-start' a process of transformation. This facilitator can also be an exogenous force, particularly for late-comers. The third, or 'take-off', stage involves 'the great watershed in the lives of modern societies' where modern values begin to permeate society. The fourth stage witnesses the growing diversification of the economy, and the final stage – the age of high consumption – represents the maturation of modernity and the further diversification of employment into service and welfare sectors.

The 'take-off' metaphor has proven to be long-standing and pervasive within development thinking, suggesting that modernization entails a sharp break between the more stable or static social relations of traditional society and the more fluid and uncertain conditions of modern society (see Sachs 2005; UNDP 2003).

---

required simultaneous attention to political structures, technologies, cultural institutions and individual behaviour.

The search for a model that dealt with this 'correspondence' between the different elements of transitional societies coincided with the dominance within US academic sociology of 'structural functionalism'. Talcott Parsons reinterpreted Weber's complex contours of the process of rationalization in Western Europe to form the basis of an evolutionary scheme centred on the ideal types of tradition and modernity. He identified different sets of social relations and role behaviour that characterized traditional society and modern society. These 'pattern variables' were polarities used to explain changes in individuals' attitudes as modernity unfolded (see Box 5.3; see also Etzioni-Halevy 1981: 37–8; Parsons 1964: 58–67).

This combination of historical observation and prediction provided modernization theorists with the conceptual tools to understand the transition to modernity. Modernization could be measured 'by assessing

Box 5.3   Pattern variables

Parsons' sociology operated at a rarefied level of abstraction (see Mills 1973: Ch. 2; Craib 1984), but development theorists such as Germani (1973) and Inkeles and Smith (1993) adapted the pattern variables to the transition to modernity.

Traditional		Modern
ascription	v	achievement
functional diffuseness	v	functional specificity
particularism	v	universalism
affectivity	v	affective neutrality
collectivism	v	individualism

From these pattern variables, sets of polarities could be identified that characterized the transformation from traditional to modern society:

change as abnormal and rare	change as the norm
undifferentiated social institutions	specialized institutions
simple division of labour	complex division of labour
predominance of primary group	predominance of more impersonal relations and secondary groups
gemeinschaft	*gesellschaft*
high birth and high mortality rates	low birth and low mortality rates
prescriptive norms and behaviour	elective norms and behaviour
religious beliefs	secular beliefs
inequalities based on ascription	inequalities based on achievement
personal authority	rational and bureaucratic norms
authoritarian	democratic and participative

As these polarities suggest, there was an assumption within modernization theory that societies became more democratic, meritocratic and egalitarian as the stage of modernity approached.

Source: See Etzioni-Halevy (1980); Germani (1973); Larrain (1989: 85–98).

the spread and proliferation of modernising roles' (Apter 1967: v). Social scientists could then report on the extent to which the process of modernization was progressing and identify any 'breakdowns' in areas of the social structure that were impeding development.

Modernization theory explained the prevalence of extreme poverty in poorer countries primarily as a consequence of endogenous forces. Traditional social structures lacked certain ingredients – or change agents – that had propelled the process of modernization forward in the West. Traditional societies had evolved as internally coherent social organisms whose institutions functioned in a coordinated manner to maintain social stability. However, the impact of colonialism had already introduced these societies to modernity, and once this had gained a foothold within the society traditional values and institutions were helpless to restrain its diffusion. Through time, the darkness of the traditional society would retreat and modernity would emerge from the shadows.

There were unique factors that would influence postwar development projects in ways uncharted by the more developed nations. These took the form of advantages and disadvantages for postwar emulators (Easterly 2002: Ch. 9). The first disadvantage emerged from an apparent advantage. Modern medical advances led to lower mortality rates and higher population growth. This could create higher unemployment and poverty unless poorer countries attracted higher investment rates than the more advanced countries during their transitional phase. The absence of significant surplus capital in traditional societies made it attendant on the West to assist the transition through supplementing foreign capital where it did not exist locally. This was one of the terms of reference of the World Bank (see Chapter 4).

A second disadvantage experienced by postwar modernizing states was the Cold War. As noted in Chapter 4, all developing countries were affected by this geopolitical struggle and found themselves distracted by military and political considerations, diverting valuable energy away from the more fundamental tasks of economic and institutional development. However, these military considerations were important because modernization theorists saw communism as a 'virus' that was attracted to the problems which developing countries confront at the earlier stages of development. Therefore, greater effort would have to be devoted to security concerns in the transitional phase, especially as social discontent was most likely during the 'preconditions-for-take-off' stage (Kuznets 1952; Rostow 1960). During this stage, traditional social structures were dissolving but modern structures and attitudes had yet to fully congeal.

There were also advantages that postwar transitional societies could seize that were not available to the earlier prototypes. First, they could procure the latest technology developed in the west. In other words, they did not have to go through as lengthy a process of innovation. Gerschenkron (1962) referred to this as 'the technological advantages of economic backwardness'. 'Late developers', or 'emulators', could avoid reinventing the technological wheel of modern industry.

The second advantage was that the west could provide international aid and technological assistance to ease the growing pains of transition. This was not available to the west at its preconditions-for-take-off stage. Modernization theorists assumed that the earlier prototypes relied on their internal resources to fund the transition – conveniently ignoring the wealth previously generated by European colonialism. As we will see later in this chapter, that claim was challenged by dependency theorists. Furthermore, it was in the enlightened self-interest of the free world to provide this aid and assistance to transitional societies. The threat of communist expansion could be reduced by accelerating the pace of growth through the preconditions-for-take-off stage.

These advantages would produce one major difference between the western prototype and the postwar emulators – time would be 'telescoped'. The transitional societies would have to climb a steeper gradient to the pinnacle of modernity, but this would entail a shorter path. Fortunately the journey had been navigated before and there were spare resources available for followers to rely on. Despite the tense global geopolitical climate, modernization theory was optimistic about the prospects for overcoming global poverty and inequality.

The process of modernization would overcome the inequality gap between the richer and poorer countries through the latter *catching up* with the former. Modernization also involved a progress of global *homogenization* as the poorer countries adopted the values that earlier developers had found consistent with modernity. Furthermore, the relations between the richer and poorer countries were understood to be *reciprocal and beneficial*.

Critiques of modernization theory

In its pioneering work, modernization theory encountered a range of methodological, theoretical and ideological criticisms. There were doubts concerning the extent to which past observations relating to western culture could be used to predict future developments in other cultures. This assumption meant that modernization looked like *westernization* – the model could be thus tainted with ethnocentrism. The variables that modernization theory relied on contained certain value judgements about the desired ends of development. As a result, modernization theory, like much social theory, falls between social policy and science, keeping one eye on society 'as it really is' and another on society 'as it should be' (Stretton 1987: Ch. 13). Critics claimed that its assumptions were premised on a normative framework that accorded with what some western academics and policymakers wanted to happen. Accordingly, the pattern variables were nothing more than a wish list of developmental objectives that confused what was happening with how researchers felt poorer countries should develop.

Some critics questioned the extent to which the pattern variables and the polarities between traditional and modern society accurately depicted western history. Modernization theorists tended to present western capitalism as a relatively conflict-free, classless, democratic, egalitarian arrangement (see Box 5.3). At the traditional pole negative values predominate (such as absolutism, authoritarianism, rigid social stratification), whereas positive values are emphasized at the pole of modernity (such as meritocracy, democracy and reason). Some critics suggested that the model shed more light on how these theorists saw their own modern identity rather than the reality of poorer countries. Burke (1980: 93) noted how 'people so often interpret the other as the opposite of themselves'. Poorer countries were being used as a yardstick to measure the rise of western civilization. Hall (1992: 221) has also contended that 'the west' was the implicit focus of attention in much development studies:

> Without the Rest, the West would not have been able to recognise and represent itself as the summit of human history. The figure of 'the Other' banished to the edge of the conceptual world and constructed as the absolute opposite, the negation of everything the West stood for, reappeared at the very centre of the discourse of civilization, refinement, modernity and development in the West. 'The Other' was the 'dark' side – forgotten, repressed and denied: the reverse image of enlightenment and modernity.

This suggests that modernization theory offered a big ideological hooray for postwar capitalism in the midst of its 'golden age'. It also avoided some serious challenges still facing developed countries. For instance, in the 1960s President Johnson's domestic 'war on poverty' and racial segregation reminded 'modern' USA that it had not yet overcome inequalities based on ascribed characteristics. Indeed, one striking difference between modernization theorists and the classic sociological tradition they drew on was that modernization theorists presented the modern world through more rose-tinted glasses than Weber and Durkheim, who gave a more balanced judgement of the modern condition. Under modernization theory, the Janus-faced nature of modernity gave way to a more unidimensional approach.

There were clearly contributing circumstances to this blurring of theory, ideology and policy. As the previous chapter emphasized, the Cold War permeated all considerations within developmental policy. In the postwar era, the USA had assumed the leadership of the 'free world' and if the theories of modernization looked like prescriptions for rapid capitalist economic growth, then that could partly be attributed to the fear of communist expansion. One proponent of modernization theory stated explicitly that modernization placed the United States 'in the marketplace of ideas and ideologies' (Apter 1967: 1–2). If modernization theory rarely criticized US foreign policy in the poorer countries – even when this policy supported brutal dictatorial regimes (see Box 5.4) – this was justified under the rationale that right-wing authoritarian dictatorships were better than communist totalitarian regimes. The former could act as catalysts of the developmental process and therefore promote the social forces that worked for democratic reform. The latter did not possess this saving grace (see Kirkpatrick 1979 for an exposition of this view, even though she was also highly critical of modernization theory).

Other critics regarded modernization theory as an ideological screen for postwar neocolonial dominance:

> If it had not been for the scholarly proliferation of *bona fide* structural-functionalist theories of modernization, students of development would have more readily seen through the true nature of the western philosophy of development. For structural-functionalist theories of modernization have in fact very usefully served as an ideological mask camouflaging the imperialist nature of western capitalism . . . the success of its expansion depends largely on its ability to reproduce, wherever it reaches out to, the structural conditions under which it operates at home. Thus westernization becomes a tool of imperialism.   (Hoogvelt 1978: 48; see also Escobar 1995: 84; Frank 1969)

Other critics were concerned that the path from tradition to modernity was not as straightforward as modernization theorists suggested. The process had been presented as a smooth transition from take-off, with perhaps some inevitable social turbulence along the way. Yet, observation of the process suggested in many cases that social conflict was endemic and pervasive and that inequalities between and within countries were sharpening (Donaldson 1973; Wertheim 1974: 317; Morawetz 1977). Modernization theory underplayed issues of power inequalities within and between societies (Webster 1984: 55–63).

Some development thinkers began to suspect that the cure proposed

Box 5.4   Guatemala: from democracy to dictatorship

In 1944, a popular uprising overthrew the brutal dictatorship of Jorge Ubico in Guatemala. The new Arevalo government promised free elections, a progressive labour code, improved welfare services and agrarian reform. His successor, Jacobo Arbenz (1950–4) maintained this reformist zeal, aiming to 'modernize and to democratize Guatemala in order to overcome traditional barriers' and to 'convert Guatemala from a . . . feudal economy to a modern, capitalist one'. The main beneficiaries of these reforms were the poorest section of the population, the Mayan majority.

The goals corresponded with the stated aims of modernization theory. However, the government's relations with the country's largest firm – the US-based United Fruit Company (UFC) – soon deteriorated due to the implementation of the Labour Code and agrarian reform. The UFC and the US government accused Arbenz of harbouring communists and expressed concern that Guatemala was a Soviet beachhead in the hemisphere.

The CIA sponsored a mercenary army headed by a disaffected general named Castillo Armas and succeeded in overthrowing the democratically elected government. A dictatorship was established, land was returned to the UFC, repressive labour conditions were reimposed and many opponents of the regime 'disappeared'. The US government hailed the new dictatorship as a loyal ally and the embargos imposed by the USA against Guatemala during the Arbenz regime were removed.

While US policy ostensibly sought the gradual and orderly transition to capitalism and liberal democracy within poorer countries, they were also acutely concerned that these countries were impatient for reform, and that communists could easily arouse sentiments for more radical change. One difficulty that the USA encountered during this period was distinguishing between the nationalist sentiments of the local reformists for modernization and external revolutionary internationalist communist conspiracies emanating from Moscow. All too often, successive US administrations saw evidence of exogenous communist subversion in the most moderate attempts to modernize and reform conditions within the Latin American region – and all too often the only reliable local allies were reactionaries and dictators, whose only support base rested on traditional oligarchs and foreign interests. This severely compromised the prospects for a just and peaceful path to modernization.

Source: Black (1984); Immerman (1982); Schlesinger and Kinger (1982).

by modernization theorists for alleviating extreme poverty was actually the disease vector itself. While there was agreement that capitalist values had propelled the transformations that led Europe out of feudalism and into the modern era, perhaps capitalism in the non-western world was acting as a far more pernicious force. Its presence was clearly reconfiguring the postcolonial world, but it was much less certain that it was moving towards modernity. Perhaps the very existence of a developmental prototype inhibited the chances of emulation. Wertheim (1974: 317), for example, hinted at a more structuralist approach to understanding global inequality, believing that the main deficiency of modernization theory lay in its 'neglect of the international environment and power structure in which the new nations are forced to operate'. The inattention to the concept of power is a characteristic feature of modernization theory. This critique was taken up by more radical development theorists who questioned the tendency of modernization theory to see the persistence of extreme poverty as a problem generated by forces endogenous to individual poorer countries. In order to understand the origins of this more structural perspective, it is necessary to examine how Marxist views of development evolved.

Combined and Unequal Development

Imperialism and development

The general schema of development outlined by modernization theory appears consistent with classical Marxism. As Chapter 4 noted, Marx had stated that the more advanced nations held out a mirror to the poorer countries, showing them 'an image of their own future'. The key difference between modernization theory and Marxism was that whereas the former viewed the age of high mass consumption as the pinnacle of history, for Marx the prehistory of humankind would only come to an end once the contradictions of capitalism had been transcended through a subsequent proletarian revolution leading eventually to communism.

Marx was conscious of the double-edged nature of capitalist development. For him, it brought progress as well as misery, but these contradictions were the motive force of social transformation. Although capitalism destroyed traditional cultures and brought uncertainty and exploitation to the producing masses, it was also progressive in the sense that it signalled a higher stage of technological and organizational development and also generated the social conditions for collective organization and solidarity that would herald the end of capitalism (Marx and Engels 1969).

Marx and Engels tended to dismiss premodern and non-European cultures as primitive, historically insignificant, obscurantist and static, whereas they saw the west as possessing rationality, enlightenment and dynamism. These ancient social formations were inevitably doomed as the waves of capitalist expansion crashed upon them. They were described as stagnant and prehistorical, without a catalyst for transformative social change (Larrain 1989: 45–52). Capitalism would be the exogenous force rudely awakening poorer countries from their ancient slumber and placing them on the historical tracks of progress (Avineri 1976, ch. 23). Indeed, Engels regarded the French colonization of Algeria as 'an important and fortunate fact for the progress of civilization', while Marx rejoiced that 'California was snatched from the lazy Mexicans, who did not know what to do with it'. Marx and Engels could sometimes sound like politically incorrect modernization theorists (see Larrain 1989: 57–60).

It is clear, however, that Marx's views on the progressive role of capitalism in the 'less developed' world altered over time. His earlier denigrating comments on peasants and traditional societies were tempered by economic developments in places such as Ireland and India (Larrain 1989: 61–2; Shanin 1984). According to Wada (quoted in Shanin, 1984: 18), Marx began to appreciate that there was a 'structure unique to backward or colonial capitalism'. In other words, he began to question his earlier generalized application of the inexorable laws of capitalist development. The more developed nations might not show the less developed nations the image of their own future. As he became involved in practical political questions over whether Marxists in Russia should support the bourgeoisie or peasant-based 'populist' socialism, he rejected readings of history (including interpretations of his own work) based on linear determinism and offered the following methodological advice:

> events that are strikingly analogous, but taking place in different historical milieu, lead to totally disparate results. By studying each of these developments separately, and then comparing them, one can easily discover the key to this phenomenon, but one will never arrive there with the master key of a historico-philosophical theory whose supreme virtue consists in being suprahistorical.   (quoted in Alavi and Shanin 1982: 110; see also Rubel 1969: 388–91; Walicki 1979: 406–8)

He also came to question whether colonialism would act as the bearer of universal progress. Capitalism planted in colonial soil reacted differently from the capitalism which thrived in European soil. His earlier optimism about the diffusion of technology was tempered by the time he wrote Volume 3 of *Capital*, recognizing that a 'new and international division of labour, a division suited to the requirements of the chief centres of modern industry springs up, and converts one part of the globe into a chiefly agricultural field of production, for supplying the other part which remains a chiefly industrial field' (Marx 1967: vol. 3, ch. 13). This was a structural insight that postwar critics of modernization theory would draw on.

From this new perspective, colonialism could act as a barrier in the path of historical development. While modernization theory would later see 'tradition' as a blockage to capitalist development, Marx had observed that capitalism itself might divert the development of traditional society away from the modern capitalist path. Melotti (1981: 25–7) argues that the idea that there could be 'multilinear' paths to development becomes more pronounced in Marx's later work. Furthermore, the notion of a 'new and international division of labour' suggests a need for concepts that account for the interconnected relationships between nations that move beyond 'methodological territorialism' (see Chapter 3).

This 'combined and uneven' nature of capitalist development reappeared in many later Marxist analyses, from Leon Trotsky's (1959: 2–4) vivid introductory chapter to his *History of the Russian Revolution* through to attempts to assess the nature of 'imperialism'. Ronald Hilferding, Rosa Luxemburg and Nikolai Bukharin all rejected linear conceptions of development and questioned the progressive impact of colonialism and imperialism (see Brewer 1989). Bukharin (1976: 164), for example, argued that colonial policies allowed the bourgeoisie to placate the industrial working class through using its colonial 'super-profits' to raise proletarian wages 'at the expense of the exploited colonial savages and conquered peoples'. Lenin reintroduced a higher level of linearism by suggesting that 'imperialism' *as a system* was the final stage of capitalism and that this stage produced divergent effects on different parts of the world (Harding 1983: vol. 2, ch. 3).

While these early twentieth-century Marxists explored the economic processes that linked the colonizer to the colonized, their specific focus remained the implications of imperialism for the more advanced capitalist countries rather than those subjugated by imperialism. There lay the hope for world proletarian revolution. After the Second World War, other theorists began to focus on the unique class structures of poorer countries and the economic processes that perpetuated extreme poverty (see Larrain 1989: 80). Paul Baran (1973: 267–8) summed up the postwar development problem in a manner that challenged the optimistic premises of modernization theory:

The question that immediately arises is, why is it that in the backward capitalist countries there has been no advance along the lines of capitalist development that are familiar from the history of other capitalist countries, and why is it that forward movement there has either been slow or altogether absent? A correct answer to this question is of foremost importance. It is indeed indispensable if one is to grasp what at the present time stands in the way of economic and social progress in underdeveloped countries, and if one is to understand the direction and the form which their future development is likely to assume.

This line of reasoning broke with the assumption that capitalism is automatically associated with development, or that the presence of capitalist relations guarantees economic growth. Progress under capitalism had been 'not only spotty in time but most unevenly distributed in space' (Baran 1970: 285). For Baran, 'backwardness' was not the result of the lack of capitalist development, as modernization theorists proposed. Postcolonial poverty was the reverse side of capitalist expansion – the form that capitalism assumed under specific relations of domination. Through this process of combined and uneven development, capitalism caused *under*development rather than development in particular circumstances.

Unlike the west, the economic surplus that was produced in the underdeveloped countries was not reinvested into the local economy. Under colonial rule part of this surplus was extracted through colonial taxation and plunder. In the postcolonial era, this extraction continued to take place because the most profitable sectors of the economy continued to be controlled by outside interests, and profits were siphoned back to the west rather than reinvested in the poorer country. Another part of the surplus was consumed by local elites through the conspicuous consumption of luxury goods imported from the more advanced countries to emulate western lifestyles. This surplus was also used to purchase rent-bearing land and other speculative ventures, or invested abroad and held as insurance in case of social and political upheavals (Baran 1970). Modernization theorists placed strong emphasis on these local 'entrepreneurs' as catalysts of change (Roxborough 1979: 16). However, Baran identified them as part of the reason why poorer countries failed to develop in the same way as the earlier industrializers. These classes acted as a 'lumpenbourgeoisie' (Frank 1974), or a 'comprador' class that sold out local interests and acted as agents of foreign firms exploiting local resources. These political and economic elites were incapable of performing the same developmental role that the bourgeoisie performed in the western transition to capitalism. One important consequence of this behaviour was to maintain the inequality gap between the richer and poorer countries and the unequal power relations within poorer countries.

The introduction of capitalism and modernity in colonial and post-colonial societies therefore produced a different effect than the earlier experience in western Europe. The development of these regions was deflected away from balanced economic growth and their economies were made to serve the needs of western interests. Thus, while imperialism laid down some of the preconditions for capitalist development through destroying precapitalist agrarian social structures, it performed only the destructive role that capitalism performed in the west. It did not initiate the creative impulse of capitalist development. Indeed, it blocked this by extracting the economic surplus, facilitating foreign exploitation of local resources and destroying any local industries which might become competitors to western industries (Rhodes 1970; Rodney 1972).

The history of colonization and the behaviour of local elites were only two factors that perpetuated the gap between the rich and poorer countries. Throughout the postwar period, there were other critics that emphasized how the structure of global trade operated against the poorer countries. These critics came to be known collectively as dependency theorists or world-systems analysts.

Dependency and world-systems analysis

According to classical political economists such as David Ricardo, general wealth would be optimized if each nation focused on producing and trading commodities in which they possessed a 'comparative advantage'. Transposed onto the postwar world, the USA and western Europe should concentrate on exporting industrial goods to the rest of the world while the postcolonial world should focus on trading its primary commodities. However, over time there was a tendency for the price of primary products to decline relative to the higher value-added industrial products. This left poorer countries exporting more, simply to purchase the same quantity of industrial goods (Kiely 1998: 8; Preston 1996: ch. 10). In effect, this transferred capital out of the non-industrial world into the industrial world. One global consequence of these declining terms of trade was that regions relying on primary exports would fail to 'catch up' with the wealthier industrial west. The structure of the global market thus promoted growing international inequalities rather than the promised convergence of 'development'.

For poorer countries, one policy option to emerge from this observation was for the state to regulate the impact of the global market through promoting and protecting local industries. This came to be known as 'import substitution' (see Kiely 1998: Ch. 6). This measure required greater reliance on an active 'developmental state' to reduce the inequalities between the industrial and non-industrial worlds created by the 'late-comer' status of the former colonial world and its postwar role in the international division of labour (Cammack 2002: 161).

It should be noted that these policy prescriptions did not necessarily conflict with the prescriptions of modernization theory. Although some modernization theorists might question the negative impact of state-facilitated development on dampening private entrepreneurship, the goals of import substitution coincided with the ideals of modernization theory. The main difference between the two perspectives was that modernization theory viewed exogenous forces (such as the role of foreign capital and trade) as facilitating the developmental process, while proponents of import substitution considered them as more malignant. The policy prescription of import-substitution suggested that poorer countries would have to rely more heavily on endogenous forces in order to bridge the developmental gap (see Rapley 2002: 16).

A more direct challenge to modernization theory emerged in the 1960s and 1970s in the form of dependency theory and world-systems analysis. These argued that linear approaches to history failed to account for the interconnected development that Baran had shown constituted modern capitalism since the discovery of the Americas (Frank 1971). Capitalism was not an economic phenomenon injected into individual states to promote modernity. Capitalism was born as a world system of unequal states. To understand why a nation was poor, it was futile to examine the values and attitudes endogenous to an individual society. It was more pertinent to explore the role a nation performed within the world capitalist system. This marked a shift towards a more structural understanding of the problem of global poverty and inequality (see Chapter 2). The developmental status of individual nations could be more fully understood within the framework of a broader unit of analysis, namely an international division of labour.

Drawing on the notion of inequality between the industrial nations and the non-industrial world, dependency theorists referred to the former as the 'core' and the latter as the 'periphery'. Wallerstein (1982: 41–2) later added a 'semi-peripheral' category to explain the structural stability and conjunctural movement within this international order of stratified states. Contrary to modernization theory, these dependency theorists and world-systems analysts viewed development from the perspective of the impact of exogenous forces on the periphery.

These differences led to radically different readings of inequality. In the dependency model, capitalism was understood as a world system that contains an inherent core-periphery duality, determining the developmental potentialities of different countries. Dependency was defined as a 'situation in which a certain number of countries have their economy conditioned by the development and expansion of another' (Dos Santos quoted in Valenzuela and Valenzuela 1978: 544). The possibility of development was determined by the relationship of exploitation that existed between core and periphery.

This framework turned modernization theory on its head. Modernization theory assumed that any relationship between traditional and modern societies would result in mutual gain or reciprocity. For dependency theory, the possibility of peripheral development is hindered by this relationship. According to Frank, pre-Columbus America might have been *un*developed but it was never *under*developed (Frank 1970: 5). In other words, postwar underdevelopment needs to be distinguished from 'lack' of development. Modernization theorists assumed that the state of underdevelopment was a *traditional* condition that the colonial world had experienced since time immemorial. Dependency theorists posited it as a modern phenomenon created by contact with modern colonial powers.

What appeared to be 'traditional' (such as the predominance of agriculture and a peasant labour force) was in reality the consequence of underdevelopment and the penetration of capitalism where production was destined for the world capitalist market. This was the function that was imposed on the colonized world by the international capitalist division of labour. Even the tri-continental slave trade introduced into Africa and America by the Europeans was not precapitalist, because the relationship of the indigenous people and the colonizers from the very beginning involved what Marx labelled the 'cash nexus' (selling commodities on the market with the view of making a profit). It served a broader triangle of trade and production between the three continents (primary commodities and precious metals from the Americas to Europe; manufactured products and liquid assets from Europe to Africa; and slaves from Africa to the Americas) that was essential for capital accumulation (Williams 1987). Slavery and forced labour were the means by which the periphery was integrated into the world capitalist system from its origins in the sixteenth century onwards (Buckman 2005: ch. 1; Rodney 1972).

This world capitalist system was characterized as a chain of exploitation and dependency that ran from the most industrialized sections of western economies through to the commercial and urban sector of the periphery and through to rural 'hinterlands'. Frank (1970: 8) illustrated how the poorest and most remote parts of contemporary Latin America had been historically linked to the world capitalist system and how this contact between tradition and modernity invariably led to 'underdevelopment'. The same historical process of capitalism that generated western European development was directly associated with the creation of generalized poverty in poorer countries (see Box 5.5). While modernization

---

Box 5.5   The development of the World Capitalist System

Stage One: Early Mercantilism (stabilized by 1640)
North-west Europe established as the core, specializing in high-skill agriculture and wage labour in this period before the Industrial revolution.

The Mediterranean (Spain, Italian city-states) established as the semi-periphery, specializing in high-cost artisan products, credit and trade.

Eastern Europe and America established as the periphery, producing grain, gold, cotton, sugar, cash crops using slave labour.

Stage Two: Later Mercantilism (1650–1730)
Britain ousted Holland and France as the principal core state.

The world system was still principally at a mercantilist stage, whereby capital was accumulated through trade and commerce – and plunder and looting – rather than directly through core production. Transportation, shipping and strong naval fleets were the key to British global dominance.

Stage Three: Industrialization (1750–1914)
Industry and manufacturing comprised a growing part of world trade and world surplus. The world capitalist system now encompassed the entire globe.

The core remained Britain – the 'workshop of the world'.

Semi-periphery expanded to include Russia and the emerging powers of Japan, Germany and the United States.

→

---

theory viewed the developed world and the underdeveloped world as opposite poles in a linear spectrum, dependency theorists considered them as two interrelated elements of a mutually reinforcing system of exploitative exchange.

Frank questioned modernization theory's premise that contact with capitalism diffuses the process of modernity throughout the contact society. On the contrary, the weaker the ties between the core and the periphery, the more possibility there was for autonomous development. Drawing on the history of Latin America, he observed that during periods where the ties that bound the periphery to the core were weakened (for example, during times when Europe was preoccupied with internal problems, such as the Napoleonic Wars, depressions and the World Wars), the peripheral economies experienced their most rapid and balanced growth. Manufacturing expanded, living conditions improved and exports diversified (Frank 1970: 10–11).

The dependency stance located the dynamics of exploitation in the

→

The periphery included Latin America and colonized Asia and Africa. This stage also witnessed the emergence of the anti-systemic movements that will eventually challenge the world capitalist system – the organized proletariat, with its union movement and socialist parties.

Stage Four: the Rise of Pax-Americana and the Cold War (1914–1970s)
This stage witnessed two key developments. First, out of the First World War, the Russian Revolution changed the balance of global power. Previously a downwardly mobile semi-peripheral state, Russia challenges for full core status after the Second World War. Second, capitalist Europe lost ground during the interwar years to the USA. After the Second World War the USA clearly emerges as the most powerful core nation in the World Capitalist System. It expanded its markets in the wake of the Second World War through: (a) helping in the reconstruction of Europe; (b) consolidating its dominant position in Latin America; (c) promoting Asian and African decolonization, in order to open up the rest of the poorer world for the more competitive US products.

Wallerstein argued that by the 1970s it had become increasingly difficult to speak of core nations, because growing global trade means that capitalist enterprises in the form of multinational corporations are able to outmanoeuvre states and government bureaucracies. This hinted at a complete shift away from 'methodological territorialism'.

Source: Wallerstein (1974, 2002, 2004).

transfer of the periphery's resources to the core through a process of *unequal exchange* on the international market (Emmanuel 1972). The core accumulated its resources for modern development through exploiting countries that consequently *underdevelop*. Throughout the twentieth century the dynamics of core–periphery exploitation moved away from the extraction of direct tribute (colonial taxation or plunder) towards unequal exchange through international market forces (neocolonialism). These initial colonial relationships left an indelible mark upon the former colonized countries. Increasingly throughout the twentieth century, terms of trade moved against primary products in favour of technologically more sophisticated goods. This unequal exchange acted as a further drain on the surpluses of the periphery and inhibited the process of capital accumulation. Later commentators extended this analysis, arguing that the core also monopolized the patents for sophisticated technology and possessed the crucial technological know-how needed to stimulate modernity (ILO 2004, para. 30).

The dependency approach was also consistent with the earlier Marxist theories of imperialism that focused on how the exploitation of the colonial labour force reduced the costs of commodities, thereby cheapening the cost of reproducing the working class in the advanced countries, as well as keeping the core working class politically more pliant (Larrain 1989: 118). The logical consequence was that exploited classes in the periphery would have to rely primarily on their own resources to overthrow the oppressive state structure that tied them to the world capitalist system. Only then could the exploitative links that chained them to the world system be severed and progressive policies implemented for the benefit of national development and popular demand (Frank 1974: ch. 9; Amin 1985).

The class relations that emerged from this chain of exploitation not only weakened the peripheral state in its relations with the core, but also undermined the foundations for democratic government. The same developmental process that facilitated liberal democracy in the core also set in train authoritarianism and dictatorship in the periphery.

Critiques of dependency theory and world-systems analysis

Like modernization theory, dependency theory and world-systems analysis have been criticized for methodological territorialism. Even though the latter sought to analyse nation-states within a broader context of a world capitalist system, they still explained an international system of *state stratification*. This holistic model, in other words, remained rooted in a state-centred outlook that studied unequal exchange between geographically framed units (Kiely 1998: 66; Robinson 2004: 93). However, the emphasis that dependency theories placed on the holistic nature of development (whereby the wealth generated at the core was linked to the poverty of the periphery) distinguished them from modernization theory (see So 1990: 107).

Dependency theory and world-systems analysis were often accused of presenting the global economy as a zero-sum or negative-sum game whereby the gains of the core came at the expense of the periphery (see Hoogvelt 1997: 4). This insight is valid on the level of *individual* nation-states, where Wallerstein would agree that the 'upward mobility' of some states within the world capitalist system inevitably takes place at the expense of other states that become relatively less competitive and suffer downward mobility. However, capitalism *as a world system* is not necessarily a zero-sum game, because the expansion of the system along with increasing productivity allows for nations to grow even though their relative position might decline.

While parallels can be drawn between world-systems analysis and modernization theory (see Kiely 1995: 57; So 1990), there were major differences in their use of prototypes and emulators. Modernization theory identified western prototypes and then calculated how poorer nations could reach that level of modernity. World-systems analysis left the future practice of development more open to speculation. The notion that global equality between nations could be achieved within the confines of capitalist relations was undermined by the structural inequalities inherent within the world capitalist system. Wallerstein (2004: 18) has also claimed that world-systems analysis became more sceptical of the inevitability of progress, viewing it merely as a possibility.

The logic of this system also suggested that if the exploitative links between the core and the periphery caused global inequality, then this might be alleviated through breaking the chains of unequal exchange, or 'delinking' from the system (Amin 1985). Wallerstein (1974) also suggested this possibility when he regarded 'mercantilist withdrawal' as a strategy adopted by states to achieve upward mobility within the confines of the world capitalist system. Experience seemed to indicate that strong semi-peripheral states – such as nineteenth-century USA, Germany and post-Meiji Restoration Japan – could strengthen their position within the world system. A strong state structure allowed these nations to erect protective barriers to shield infant industries against more competitive core products, militarily defend themselves against core interests and mobilize sufficient cross-class support to extract endogenous resources and quell any domestic unrest. Chase-Dunn (1980) also believed that the Soviet Union was able to achieve its core position in the twentieth century through such 'withdrawal' from the world capitalist system – a developmental approach also attempted by China during the Cultural Revolution. However, the list of morally appealing autarchic regimes during the twentieth century fills a very slim volume, and policies of 'closure' or 'autarchy' gave twentieth-century socialism a bad name, thanks to models in Burma Albania, North Korea and the Kampuchean model (Brenner 1982; Kiely 1995: 52–3).

Another issue raised by more 'orthodox' Marxists concerned the premise that capitalism causes underdevelopment in poorer countries. If this was valid, then the logical policy response for poor countries was to abandon capitalism. This effectively called for a socialist revolution in an underdeveloped country (Frank 1974). This appeared to contradict Marx and Engels (1976), who believed that socialism could only be established on an advanced technological base where general want could be overcome. Even Lenin premised the Russian Revolution on the understanding that Russia was the weakest link in a chain of imperialist states and that the Russian Revolution would herald the beginning of the socialist revolution throughout more advanced Europe. Otherwise, he argued, socialist Russia would be overwhelmed (see Box 4.5; Liebman 1975). The practical dilemma facing dependency theory was that capitalism might cause underdevelopment, but socialism might prove incapable of overcoming underdevelopment in peripheral conditions. Whereas Marx had envisaged socialism on the basis of a relatively advanced technological base (McMurtry 1978), dependency theory appeared to see socialism as a policy prescription for overcoming relatively primitive forces of production. Could a socialist regime in poorer countries simultaneously offer economic growth and equality? Again, the experience of the twentieth century did not hold out many positive examples (Christian 1992; Weaver and Berger 1984: 55).

One resolution to this dilemma has been to discuss the end of global inequality in terms of cycles of 'anti-systemic movements'. World-systems analysts have argued that each stage of the world capitalist system produces its own unique form of emancipatory anti-systemic political mobilization (Arrighi et al. 1989). Despite their diversity, the aim of such movements is to struggle over the surplus value created by capital. Thus, the past 150 years has seen the industrial workers' movement fight with industrial capital, and Third World socialism and national liberation movements struggle against imperialism. The anti-corporate globalization movement which will be discussed in Chapter 9 is sometimes portrayed as the latest challenge to the power of global capital (Robinson 2004; Wallerstein 2002, 2003).

Ultimately, however, dependency theory and world-systems analysis drew more pessimistic conclusions than modernization theory about the possibility of peaceful and evolutionary development. As Wallerstein (2004: 10) noted, modernization theory suggested 'that the "most developed" state could offer itself as a model for the "less developed" states, urging the latter to engage in a sort of mimicry, and promising a higher standard of living and a more liberal government structure ("political development") at the end of the rainbow'. Various peripheral countries *did* find the metaphorical pot of gold, and dependency theories have been criticized for inadequately accounting for unexpected capitalist successes in the periphery. If capitalism caused peripheral underdevelopment, then dependency and world-systems theorists had to explain the spectacular success of industrialization and economic growth that the Newly Industrializing Countries (NICs such as South Korea, Taiwan, Singapore, Hong Kong) experienced during the 1970s and 1980s (Harris 1987; Lipietz 1988: 16). In these circumstances exogenous links with core capitalism (especially with the USA) did not produce standard peripheral underdevelopment.

The NICs are often portrayed as 'economic miracles'. However, Frank (1984) has argued that practical policy options cannot follow miracles. The NICs, according to Frank, were 'exceptional cases', and historical and geopolitical reasons could explain the unique nature of their development. However, 'exceptions' assume that there is a 'normal' path of capitalist development. A detailed investigation of every successful road to modernity would reveal that each transition was exceptional – Britain in its golden age, Germany under Bismark, Japan under the Meiji Restoration, Russia after 1890, the NICs in the 1970s and 1980s, and China in the 1990s (Meiksins Wood 1999: 7–8). As the exceptional nature of so many exceptional cases is clarified, the status of 'normality' becomes simultaneously more opaque (Kiely 1995: 52). Dependency theory operated on the assumption that if the periphery was left alone, then it too could undertake the 'normal' path to capitalist development that the core embarked on previously. In this sense, Frank's duality between core and periphery appears much closer to the polar opposites in modernization theory, tradition and modernity. The shimmer of the 'original transition' hovers over both theories. This presence poses a danger that concrete historical cases of development are viewed through a distorted lens clouded by the experience of the European prototype.

Box 5.6   Summary of world-systems analysis

Strengths	Weaknesses
Its insistence on understanding the modern world historically	Its tendency towards teleology and reification
Its employment of modes of historical analysis that encompass very long periods of time	Its overemphasis on exogenous forces at the expense of endogenous ones
Its highly interdisciplinary nature	Its misrepresentation, in its classical form, of the effect of foreign investment on the periphery
Its rigorous materialism	Its underestimation of the developmental prospects of the periphery
A conception of capitalism that is broader and more useful than the traditional Marxist conception	Its relative helplessness in understanding the nature and collapse of state socialist societies
Its situation of the current phase of globalization in its proper historical context	Its relative helplessness in understanding the future prospects of socialism

Source: information from Sanderson (2005).

Box 5.7   A synthetic model of development

While most observers tended to present modernization theory and dependency theory as competing paradigms in development studies, there have been attempts to synthesize the models. Etzioni-Halevy (1980) believed that 'both theories brought to light some crucial factors in development and modernization, but neither paradigm is complete; and the variables which each has neglected are precisely the ones that have been best analysed by the other'.

Etzioni-Halevy argued that modernization theory and dependency theory were 'complementary and should be utilized in conjunction with each other for a better understanding of modernization and development'.

Stage 1: 1500–1800
  The Mercantilist Phase
• Exploitation was mainly carried out through trade
• Core (north-west Europe, Holland and Britain)
• Semi-periphery (the Mediterranean, Spain, Portugal, Italy)
• Periphery (Eastern Europe, the Americas – and anywhere else that could be found)

Stage 2: 1800–1950
  The Colonial Phase
• Political domination of the periphery by the core fully established
• Exploitation occurs mainly through colonial taxation, the organization of production, marketing and distribution of colonial products, the creation of preferential markets, and the creation of colonial monocultures serving the needs of core markets

→

The structural model of development offered by dependency and world-systems theory also contains another theoretical trap. Critics from both the left and the right have pointed out that 'imperialism' appears as 'the root of all evil' (d'Souza 2002) or 'the beast of the apocalypse' (Lipietz 1988: 17) or a 'monodiabolism' (Olsen 1982: 177). In this model the periphery is constructed as a passive respondent to forces centred elsewhere and this restricts its options and its room to manoeuvre. It denies peripheral countries agency, allowing scope for a 'victim mentality' to emerge, while 'fostering a morbid propensity to find fault with everyone but oneself' (Landes 2002: 328). Bauer (1981: 6; see also Bauer 1976: 161–3) believed that this emphasis on the malignant nature of exogenous forces also leads to western 'guilt-peddling' rather than rigorous economic analysis:

→
- Core (USA and north-west Europe)
- Semi-periphery (Mediterranean, Hapsburg Empire, Italy, Russia, Japan)
- Periphery (the rest of the world, including Australia, New Zealand and Canada)

Stage 3: 1950–1980s
   The Neo-colonial Phase
- This stage differs from Stage 2 in the sense that the form of exploitation is carried out by multinational firms, rather than through colonial political ties
- Core (USA, Japan, Italy, Australia, Canada, north-west Europe)
- Semi-periphery (Soviet-style economies, OPEC, Brazil, Argentina, Turkey, India)
- Periphery (Africa, Asia, Latin America)

The key feature which makes Etzioni-Halevy's model notable is that even though she accepts the historical approach of world-systems analysis, over time more nations have been achieving core and semi-peripheral status. The periphery is slowly shrinking. Both models, it appears, focus on different aspects of social reality. Exploitation continues to generate inequalities on a global scale, but capitalism, bureaucratization, rationalization, and modern values are increasingly penetrating the periphery. In other words, the world is converging, and it is becoming more homogenous, as modernization theorists predicted (and as neoliberal triumphalists would proclaim in the 1990s).

The allegations that external contacts damage the Third World are plainly condescending. They clearly imply that Third World people do not know what is good for them, nor even what they want. The image of the Third World as a uniform stagnant mass devoid of distinctive character is another aspect of this condescension. . . . Time and again the guilt merchants envisage the Third World as an undifferentiated, passive entity, helplessly at the mercy of its environment and of the powerful West. . . . The exponents of Western guilt further patronize the Third World by suggesting that its economic fortunes past, present and prospective, are determined by the West. . . . According to this set of ideas, whatever happens to the Third World is largely our doing. Such ideas make us feel superior even while we beat our breasts.

As a consequence, some critics have warned against assuming that the only agents of change in the world system are core countries, while viewing the periphery as pliable material in the hands of the all-powerful imperialist nations (Kiely 1995: 51). It is possible to accept the conditioning influence of exogenous forces (such as powerful core states) while simultaneously recognizing the importance of endogenous relations (such as internal relations of production, internal class struggle, status conflict, culture, geography) as critical elements that determine how external influences operate and are internally negotiated. This tendency to view imperialism as some global maestro led Baudrillard to ponder why, if the 'West' had created the 'Third World problem', it wasn't right for it to reap the rewards (see Horrocks 1999: 44–6).

As this chapter has shown, dependency theory links global inequalities with relationships between rich countries and poor countries. However, critics such as John Kay (2004: 277) are more circumspect: 'we who live in rich states are not rich because those who live in poor states are poor. It is simply not true that the market economy and the world trading system are structured in ways in which the rich gain at the expense of the poor.' Kay also suggests that exogenous forces do not necessarily act as underdeveloping agents. In this sense, social scientists can do worse than to return to the classical sociological emphasis on the Janus-faced nature of capitalist modernity (see chapters 1 and 4). Indeed, following Marx more closely (as well as the economist Joan Robinson) Geoffrey Kay (1975: 4) remarked that 'capital created underdevelopment not because it exploited the underdeveloped world, but because it did not exploit it enough'.

A choice between modernization theory and dependency theory ultimately comes down to the question raised in earlier chapters concerning whether the economic and social circumstances of poorer countries are due to their relationship with the richer world, or from the lack of such a relationship. These issues are more than historical curiosities. As the remaining chapters will show, they are central to understanding global inequalities in the twenty-first century. Modernization and dependency theories merely drew them in stark relief.

Both dependency theory and modernization theory assigned a significant role to planning and co-ordinated assistance in the development project. Only a few dissidents such as Hayek argued that unbridled market forces could achieve a state of universal welfare and bridge the gap between the richer and poorer countries. These dissenting voices increased during the 1970s and by the 1980s neoliberal thinkers and practitioners challenged the principles of state-led economic development and the vision of the state as a social leveller. This neoliberal challenge drew on significant socio-economic problems that the wealthier countries began to experience, such as growing unemployment, high inflation and deindustrialization. The idea of modernity as a well-defined goal became less tenable as greater uncertainty began to pervade modern societies.

As this chapter has shown, modernization theory had always emphasized that being modern meant accepting change as normal. However, over the past 20 years the pace of social and economic change has accelerated, resulting in what has been called 'hypermodernity' or 'postmodernization' (Crook, Waters and Pakulski 1992), a condition in which nothing seems to congeal into a stable relationship. Modernity is characterized as a state of 'flux' or 'liquidity' (Bauman 2000; Gleick 1999). However, if there is one consistent pattern or any solidity, then it is that the richer countries and the poorer countries remain 'world's apart' (Donaldson 1973). The following chapters examine how development practitioners have responded to the challenge over the past two decades.

Chapter 6

The Framework of Early 21st-Century Development

Neoliberalism and Market-oriented Development

The American Century

The Financial Architecture of Neoliberal Development
    International financial institutions: the IMF and the World Bank
    The WTO

State-centred models of development had lost much of their allure by the 1980s. The end of the Cold War encouraged a 'triumphalist' sentiment within the USA that proclaimed that the new century would be controlled by its benevolent hand in coordination with the invisible hand of the market. This chapter assesses this neoliberal approach to development before describing the global financial architecture of the post-Cold War order. The values underpinning this neoliberal approach placed a stronger emphasis on market-oriented growth, although many critics argued that this new order exacerbated inequalities between and within countries.

The end of the Cold War was symbolized by the demise of the Soviet Union, the fall of the Berlin Wall and the popular uprisings throughout eastern European communist states in the late 1980s and early 1990s. Despite the nuclear threat that the Cold War presented to global survival, it was one of the few certainties of international relations. As Korany (1994: 7) recalled, since the end of the Second World War, this atmosphere 'defined our world mental map and honed our conceptual lenses', determining how 'we could arrange intellectual categories and establish their linkages to make sense of our international environment'.

Most socialists had long since abandoned any illusions concerning the liberating potential of Soviet power (Blackburn 1991; Callinicos 1991). To all but a hard core of nostalgic Stalinists, the Soviet Union and its satellite states represented a new form of oppression that coexisted uneasily with western capitalist states. World-systems analysts argued that the 'really existing socialist states' had proven too weak to be able to transcend the structural strength of the world capitalist system and that they remained tied to the logic of capitalism through economic and military competition (Chase Dunn 1980). These social formations therefore could not deliver on their promise of world equality.

The consequences of the end of the Cold War were also felt in poorer nations. Despite the apocalyptic dangers of superpower nuclear conflict, it had allowed certain regimes to play one superpower off against the other. As Egypt's President Nasser had shown in the 1950s, aid and assistance could be obtained by poorer countries simply through the fear that their territory might fall into the hands of one or other of the superpowers. Many unsavory dictatorships – such as the long-standing Somoza dynasty in Nicaragua – persistently played the anti-communist card in order to obtain part of the USA's stake in the fight against Soviet expansion (Morley 2002: ch. 2).

Therefore, the 'periphery' assumed an importance that it might not otherwise have possessed (Myrdal 1977: 4–5; Tucker 1977: 45). The end of the Cold War changed this status. As Harries (2003: 1) recalled, suddenly actors were deprived of their role and their script: 'The Cold War had represented a remarkably simple and unambiguous state of affairs, with a clearly designated enemy, longstanding allies, fixed strategies, and a well-rehearsed rhetoric.' The attention that had been devoted to the poorer nations was withdrawn. It is for this reason that George (2001) argued that 'Northern concern with the South was largely a Cold War phenomenon', and Arnold (1993: 1) predicted 'the disappearance of any independent capacity to bargain on the part of the Third World on the one hand, and a growth of neo-colonial controls exercized by the North on the other'. These controls (administered by IFIs such as the IMF and the WTO) will be examined later in this chapter.

Another consequence of the end of the Cold War was that development studies and international relations turned their attention more to scrutinizing the face of the victorious US superpower, its global role as sole hegemon, and the nature of the social system it represented. The following two sections deal with the neoliberal philosophy that claimed victory over statism before examining differing perspectives on the role of the victorious developmental prototype, the USA. On the one hand, its supporters were optimistic that unimpeded capitalist growth would result in the spread of global wealth, the reduction of poverty and inequality and the extension of democratic institutions. On the other hand, many critics accused the USA of assuming the mantle of a new emperor intent on asserting its global dominance regardless of the consequences for global inequality.

Neoliberalism and Market-oriented Development

Given that the USSR came to be associated with statism, its demise understandably was heralded as a political victory for the USA as well as an economic victory for market-oriented development. Witnesses from the less travelled Soviet path told stories full of disillusionment with state-sponsored development. By the 1990s, the developmental path promoted by the USA was touted not as a *possible* path leading to greater quality and freedom, but as the *only* path pointing in that direction. This came to be known as the 'TINA principle', after British Prime Minister Margaret Thatcher had proclaimed that 'there is no alternative' but to follow her monetarist reform path. According to de Soto (1999: 1), the capitalist system 'stands alone as the only feasible way rationally to organize a modern economy'.

Peter Berger's intellectual journey exemplified this discovery that there was no acceptable alternative to the capitalist path of development. In the early 1970s, Berger's book *Pyramids of Sacrifice* had criticized both the capitalist and the socialist roads to development. The former path led to profound economic inequalities and the latter to abuses of human rights and lack of individual freedom. However, by the early 1980s Berger's views had altered considerably. He admitted being 'much less evenhanded' in his judgement and had 'become much more emphatically pro-capitalist' (Berger 1985b: 23). The Asian NIC experiences had impressed Berger, but the most significant influence on his shift of thinking had been the negative consequences of statist experiments under socialism. Countries that had fallen under the allure of statism registered an almost uniformly disastrous record of social development and individual freedom:

> socialism is not good for economic growth, and also it shows a disturbing propensity toward totalitarianism (with its customary accompaniment of terror). What has become clearer is that socialism even fails to deliver on its own egalitarian promises. . . . In country after country, socialist equality has meant a leveling down of most of the population, which is then lorded over by a highly privileged and by no means leveled elite.   (Berger 1985b: 26)

These regimes undermined the initiative of 'real' agents of development – the innovative entrepreneurial classes capable of generating the transformation from feudalism to modern capitalism. Socialism possessed the 'intrinsic genius' of reproducing nothing more than 'modern facsimiles of feudalism', with its attendant traditional forms of inequalities (Berger 1985b: 26).

According to Berger (1985a: 19–20), the only real revolution occurring in the postwar poorer countries was democratic capitalism and its standard bearer – or prototype – was the USA. The USA therefore had a responsibility to use its status to promote its political and economic virtues through offering the advice that development 'should emphasize the private sector and private entrepreneurship wherever possible' (Berger 1985a: 16). Thus, capitalist triumphalism preceded the end of the Cold War. To many supporters of the free market, the history of postwar development had been a road to nowhere, led by statist postindependence regimes spellbound by hollow socialist promises of greater equality. All they delivered was growing global inequalities.

Chapter 4 described how the enthusiasm for economic planning in both the wealthier and the poorer countries had been forged by the experiences of the 1930s depression and the Second World War. The early modernization theorists might have been vehemently opposed to Soviet socialism, but the majority never questioned the important role that planning performed for development. Some of the most vocal supporters of development planning were economists, such as W. Arthur Lewis (1969). The warnings delivered by Hayek towards the end of the Second World War remained unheeded among the majority of theorists and practitioners until the 1970s, but when economic liberalism began to resurface it pointed to empirical evidence demonstrating that the revered planning principle had proven to be a false god. By that time, a network of small but highly influential think tanks had been established (for instance, the Institute of Economic Affairs and the Adam Smith Institute in the UK, and the American Enterprise Institute and the Heritage Foundation in the USA) to serve as the intellectual artillery for the neoliberal shift that was about to sweep the world.

State socialism was only one example of the failure of state-planned development. In Latin America, import-substitution industrialization also began to experience difficulties as early as the 1960s, manifested in inefficient production, balance of payments deficits, growing unemployment, sectoral imbalances and inflation (Kiely 1998: 95; Norberg 2003: 163–8). When stagflation enveloped the wealthier capitalist nations in the 1970s, the foundations of postwar state intervention were looking decidedly shaky (Mandel 1980). Economic liberalism was rejuvenated in the wealthier nations as supporters of the welfare state lost ground to 'Reaganomics' and 'Thatcherism'.

By the 1980s, then, the world had come round full circle: 'Where neoclassical theory had once been a dissenting school, and Keynesianism and structural economics the orthodoxy, in both academic and policy circles, neoclassical theory was the new orthodoxy' (Rapley 2002: 70). The main principles of neoliberalism have been defined as 'self-interest rules, market fundamentalism, the minimal state, low taxation' (Kay 2003: 308). One of the consequences this entailed was a shift away from explicit concerns with inequality towards more explicit concerns with economic freedom and growth. Equality would follow in the wake of liberalization. Drawing on Hayek (1944: 70), economic liberals argued that market freedoms were positively correlated with the other key ingredient of modernization – political freedom (Friedman 2000; Norberg 2003: 40).

This shift in orthodoxy had its counterpart in the attack on statism and planning within development studies. The very idea of 'development economics' or development theory, came under attack from neoliberal economics, which approached development using more abstract, universal criteria (Cammack 2002: 159; World Bank 1993). Development everywhere – north, south, east or west – would be enhanced through removing the distortions that governments, special interest groups and rent-seekers imposed on the operation of market forces. According to Olsen (1982: 65), these 'distributional coalitions slow down a society's capacity to adopt new technologies and to reallocate resources in response to changing conditions, and thereby reduce the rate of economic growth'. Development was synonymous with sending the right signals to the market through the deregulation of national economies and international trade. The policy implications were 'freer trade and fewer impediments to the free movement of factors of production and of firms' (Olsen 1982: 141). After all, it was claimed, the economic successes of the NICs proved that 'an open free-enterprise economy' was the '*sine qua non* of development' (Norberg 2003: 103; World Bank 1993; see also Kiely 1995: ch. 5 for a critique).

Many economic liberals acknowledged that the free market, left to itself, could not overcome inequalities. As earlier chapters have shown, the relationship between inequality and growth has often been portrayed as a trade-off. Kuznets' (1952) 'inverted U-curve' suggested that the process of modern economic growth is initially accompanied by higher levels of inequality. However, levels of inequality diminish as an economy diversifies, the accumulation of physical and human capital expands and as economic growth becomes more sustained. Modernization theorists such as Rostow accepted this series of causation. The shift from traditional society to the take-off stage required capital to gravitate towards risk-taking entrepreneurial sectors with a far-sighted approach to investment. Tackling inequalities was only possible once society had accomplished the task of meeting basic needs.

During the first few decades of postwar development, economic liberals accepted that the state performed an important role in alleviating poverty and restricting inequalities. Even Hayek (1944) dismissed *laissez-faire* approaches as damaging to the reputation of economic liberalism. Olsen (1982: 147) also argued that:

> Since the alleviation of poverty on a society-wide basis is a public good, efforts to redistribute income to the poor as a group require governmental action. In this respect, it is true that governments in some societies do mitigate inequalities. Since both the taxes and the transfers have adverse effects on incentives, it is also true that there are trade-offs between equality and efficiency.

However, during the 1980s, the demise of state-led development policies, the decline of the Soviet Union and the resurgence of market ideology all strengthened the belief that free-market policies would deliver not only higher levels of economic growth but also greater levels of poverty reduction, as well as liberty, compared to any other social system. Neoliberalism retained the historico-philosophical premises of modernization theory, with the key difference being the reduced role of the state and the enhanced role of the market – or more specifically, the state was 'reoriented in order to underpin and support market-friendly policies' (Cammack 2002: 166).

According to de Soto (1999), the key to unlocking the wealth that lies dormant within any social structure is the creation of a formal system of property titles and property rights. This happened at the advent of modernity in Europe and on the United States frontier only 150 years ago. The reason why capitalism has yet to deliver its promised bounty of affluence in poorer countries has less to do with the cultural traits within poorer nations, or racial inferiority, and even less to do with any inherent tendencies towards inequality within the capitalist system. What are missing are the legal keys that unlock successful capitalist development:

> The poor inhabitants of these nations – the overwhelming majority – do have things, but they lack the process to represent their property and create capital. They have houses but not titles; crops but not deeds; businesses but not statutes of incorporation. It is the unavailability of these essential representations that explains why people who have adapted every other Western invention, from the paper clip to the nuclear reactor, have not been able to produce sufficient capital to make their domestic capitalism work. This is the mystery of capital.   (de Soto 1999: 7)

According to de Soto, the persistence of extreme poverty and inequality is due primarily to the inability or unwillingness of poorer countries to build the political and legal structures that allow people to transform their possessions into capital and thereby generate more wealth. The problems that ensue when capitalism is promoted without the legal protection for capital are manifest across the non-western world from Latin America to the former Soviet republics, where there exists 'glaring inequality, underground economies, pervasive mafias, political instability, capital flight, flagrant disregard for the law' (de Soto 1999: 9–10). In this picture, poorer countries needed to unleash the process of wealth creation through offering secure title to people's property, which they could then use as collateral for engaging in legal economic activities without bureaucratic corruption and inertia blocking their initiative.

De Soto retains the universal optimism of modernization theory, arguing that all humanity possesses the same potential and that all individuals possess the same rational decision-making powers. The inequalities that persist are due mainly to different conditions under which capitalism operates. Depending on the underlying property framework, capitalism can either generate equality and wealth or perpetuate inequality and poverty. De Soto's developmental programme also mirrors modernization theory in identifying the same western prototypes that the poorer nations can emulate. The main difference is that the activator of development has shifted from culture to property law. According to one critic, de Soto retains a 'single magic-bullet solution' to development, and, like neoliberals, remains 'seduced by the beauty of how the market is supposed to operate, and loses track of how it does' (*New Internationalist* May 2006).

By the beginning of the twenty-first century, neoliberal solutions prevailed across the globe, as a result of a confluence of factors ranging from disillusionment with postwar welfare state policies, the fall of Soviet-styled economies and the failure of state-induced development strategies in poorer nations. Neoliberal policy prescriptions rested on less government regulation, greater economic openness and the unleashing the entrepreneurial spirit inherent in every social formation.

One of the main criticisms levelled against neoliberalism is that the focus on economic growth overshadowed a concern with growing inequality. Although neoliberals have argued that growth assists the poor as much as the rich (Norberg 2003: 79; Wolf 2005: ch. 9), Chang and Grabel (2004: 19–20) concluded that the approach promoted 'international unevenness and inequality rather than widespread growth', with the gap between the richest and poorest 20 per cent doubling during the last decades of the twentieth century (see also Pieterse 2004: 76). Hobsbawm (2000: 69) has also questioned whether the distribution of wealth under neoliberalism is socially optimal, even though he acknowledges that this economic system 'produces a higher rate of growth than any other system' (see also Christian 1992).

While some neoliberals claim that absolute poverty has declined over the past two decades, other supporters maintain that even if inequalities have widened, then this 'should not be seen as negative' so long as the system provides more for everyone (World Bank 2000; see also Norberg 2003: 54). Galbraith (quoted in Wright 2005: 127) has satirized neoliberalism – or 'trickle-down theory' – as a prediction that if 'you let the horses guzzle enough oats, something will go through for the sparrows'.

Chang and Grabel (2004: 22–3) also challenge neoliberal development by arguing that poverty alleviation in the poorer countries has rested largely on the recent strong growth rates in two large countries, China and India. Neither, however, chose the neoliberal developmental path (see also Kiely 1998: ch. 8, for South Korea and Taiwan). Wade (2004) concludes that many such countries have reaped the benefits of increased international trade without adopting 'liberal trade policies'. Critics of neoliberalism also query the positive correlation between democracy and free markets, pointing out that open markets are compatible with regimes across the political spectrum, from authoritarian to libertarian. Sachs (2005: 219) has also questioned the 'magic thinking' implicit within neoliberal policy prescriptions for the poorer world that asserts the developmental equivalent of the TINA principle – there is only one developmental road.

This neoliberal economic framework for development in the twenty-first century owes its dominant position not only to its intellectual strength and empirical evidence, but also to support from influential global institutions and powerful governments. There remains a wide gap in the ability of different nations to influence global politics, and the USA in particular has used its strength to reshape the global economy in its own neoliberal image – when it suits its interests (Soros 2004: 3).

The American Century

Modernization theory has been accused of being the ideological handmaiden of US Cold War geopolitical aims (see Chapter 5). While modernization did appear to enjoin newly independent states to emulate the western capitalist path of development, there are also reasons to qualify an instrumental relationship between mainstream development theory and US foreign policy during the Cold War. First, modernization theory had deeper roots than postwar geopolitics. As Chapter 4 showed, these roots can be traced back to the late-eighteenth-century Enlightenment ideas of progress. Secondly, the poorer world had a legitimate aspiration to standards of living characteristic of the more affluent world. Modernization theory mapped out an optimistic path to follow. Even if

US policy did not promote modernization theory in practice, it held out the promise of poverty alleviation to newly independent states. The end of the Cold War realigned debates over the relationship between development theory and global hegemony. With the 'death of communism', the world was now more ideologically unipolar. This immediately begged the question of the developmental responsibilities of the world's remaining superpower.

The most optimistic response came from Fukuyama (1989, 1992), who reiterated the underlying message of modernization theory – that the spread of political liberty marched triumphantly alongside economic liberalism. Now that communism was ideologically moribund, the USA was in a better position to pursue its enlightened self-interest on the global stage, free of the blemishes that had occasionally tarnished its actions during the Cold War (see Minogue 2002: 122).

According to Fukuyama (1989), the triumph of liberalism over communism was the historical culmination of the world's search for a universal social model that could deliver global harmony. For this reason, he believed that humanity had reached the 'end of history', not just the end of the Cold War. This signalled 'the end point of mankind's ideological evolution and the universalization of Western liberal democracy as the final form of human government'.

From this perspective, the history of humankind was interpreted as the quest for an ideal form of social order and eventually – through the struggle of competing models – victory had been delivered to liberal democracy. Like Peter Berger, Fukuyama saw the USA as its most advanced example. The collapse of communism suggested that the world was now ready to progress towards a more homogeneous and harmonious future based on the universal extension of liberal sentiments, western democratic institutions and market forces. After all, as Condoleeza Rice asserted, 'American values are universal' (quoted in Pieterse 2004: 42). Global convergence would explicitly remove political inequalities between countries and it was implicitly assumed that market liberalization would alleviate poverty.

Fukuyama admitted that periodic conflict would remain, particularly in the 'vast bulk of the Third World [that] remains very much mired in history' (Fukuyama 1992). However, this would pose no threat to the ongoing spread of liberal democracy as no global alternative was visible on history's horizon. While Rostow gave primacy to economic variables in the process of development, Fukuyama substituted political ideals. Furthermore, he rejuvenated the Enlightenment belief that history was 'directional, meaningful, progressive'. He therefore presented a contemporary variation on modernization theory modified to meet the challenges of a new world order, retaining an underlying optimism that universal equality could be achieved through following westernization. Under these circumstances, the impending new century would be – in the words of a famous manifesto signed by Fukuyama – 'the American century' (PNAC in Soros 2004: 5–7; see also Pieterse 2004: 21).

However, before the century was over, it was clear that the range of post-Cold War conflicts were no less problematic than many of the more 'historical' versions. International relations continued to be fraught with serious conflict, such as nationalist independence struggles, territorial incursions by one state into another, border disputes and ethnic cleansing (UNDP 2003: 45). In this new world order, the international community – spearheaded by the UN – was forced to, or asked to, intervene more effectively in tackling human rights abuses (Ignatieff 2003). The end of communism had unleashed a Pandora's box of new conflicts along religious, racial, ethnic and nationalist lines. Analysts of conflict hypothesized that the end of the Cold War had ushered in a shift from conventional wars of state against state, to vast numbers of 'small wars' and complex 'political emergencies' for which it was difficult to identify clear 'sides'. Foreign aid budgets shifted resources from development to humanitarian relief as the promised 'peace dividend' at the end of the Cold War failed to emerge. By the mid-1990s, the US military budget was larger than the combined total of all the other military powers and its military strength was deployed in a wide range of global theatres.

The idea that humanity had reached the 'end of history' was also criticized by commentators who approached the future with a greater sense of openness. The phrase seemed to limit political choices and act as a political counterpart to the neoliberal claim that 'there is no alternative' other than to accept the logic of the market (Kay 2003: 192). World-systems analysts saw Fukuyama's *end* of history as the *continuation* of fundamental global divisions. The end of the Cold War left untouched the nature of global inequality and unequal exchange. Wallerstein (2004: 84) argued that even though global economic growth was strong during the 1990s, 'the gap between core and periphery had become greater than ever'. Derrida (1994: 85) also questioned why Fukuyama's 'neo-evangelistic' rhetoric was gaining ground at a time when 'never have violence, inequality, exclusion, famine, and thus economic oppression affected as many human beings in the history of the earth'.

Other critics reflected that the east–west confrontation had always been a diversion from the more fundamental global conflict between North and South, or the inequalities between the global rich and the global poor. This argument provided space for the Non-Aligned Movement to reassert its relevance into the twenty-first century, despite its historically ill-fitting name. Structuralist critics therefore saw the 'end of history' as only the continuation of existing power relations and relations of inequality (Ramonet 2004: 140–1).

Other critics saw a geopolitical affinity between Fukuyama's thesis and US foreign policy interests. According to Hamilton (2003: 103), Fukuyama was the prisoner of his own historical time, offering a benevolent picture of the role of the USA as the harbinger of peace and security:

> Ultimately, Fukuyama's thesis turns out to be no more than a pseudo-philosophical variation on modernization theory. Science, technology, market growth – these forces must take over the world and lead to homogenization of societies, political systems, consumption patterns and tastes. And on which model does the world converge? That of the United States, of course.

Fukuyama's triumphalism and vision of global homogeneity did not have a monopoly within US policy circles. One influential challenge to his thesis emerged from Samuel Huntington (1993). Being more sceptical that the west provided a path for the poorer world to emulate, Huntington rejected Fukuyama's optimistic claims that western liberalism was now free to march unhindered into the darkest corners of the globe and awaken peoples from their traditional slumber.

Setting more store on the cultural *differences* between world views, Huntington dismissed Fukuyama's narrative as too universalizing. Indeed, he considered Fukuyama's notion of a universal civilization to be a 'Western idea' (Huntington 1993: 41; see also Gray 2004: 176). In what appears as a momentary lapse of postmodernism, Huntington dismissed any overarching narrative of human progress that explains all historical, social and political development in favour of less unitary and more distinct histories of different cultures, which grow, stabilize, decline and clash according to their own systemic logic and laws of development. He did, however, retain a 'stages of development' approach that outlined the history of global conflict since the advent of modernity (see Box 6.1).

According to Huntington (1993: 25), the approaching new century would be characterized by 'civilization politics' where people would identify themselves with their own cultural group rather than class, ideology or nation. These new faultlines would be the key markers of social identity and social action: 'Civilization identity will be increasingly important in the future, and the world will be shaped in large measure by the interactions among seven or eight major civilizations.' One of the key divisions within this emerging civilization conflict was the rise of poorer countries that were previously the objects of history and the pawns of the western colonial powers. These cultures will emerge more and more as 'movers and shapers of history'. As non-western civilizations flexed their muscles on the world stage, the principal conflict alignment would be 'the west versus the rest' (Huntington 1993: 39–41).

This scenario represented a sharp break from postwar modernization theory as well as Fukuyama's more contemporary version. Huntington suggested that liberal democracy might be culturally unsuitable for other civilizations. Furthermore, he rejected the key defining feature of modernization theory: that all societies will inevitably converge as they industrialize and pass through ascending stages of growth. Huntington believed that the emerging world order would heighten cultural diversity rather than encourage growing homogeneity. A revitalized form of tradition could emerge as a means of constructing identity and making sense of the world, generating a potential source of tension between civilizations. Huntington (2004) was also concerned that multiculturalism within western countries could result in an 'internal' clash of civilizations. Countries containing large groups of people from different civilizations were 'candidates for dismemberment' (Huntington 1993: 42). While Fukuyama remained confident that global inequalities could be reduced through the adoption of political and economic liberalism, Huntington's approach relegated issues associated with global equality and promoted those associated with 'identity politics'. For Huntington, the focus is firmly placed on *differences* rather than inequalities.

Huntington did follow earlier modernization theorists in treating the west and the rest as polar opposites that possess 'good' and 'bad' civilizational attributes respectively. Critics of Huntington have pointed to the rise of fundamentalism and anti-liberal views in the heartland of the west, including the rise of the religious right. Huntington also underestimated the extent to which 'the rest' have adopted the techniques of modern technology, communications, science and rationality. As Robertson (quoted in Chase Dunn 1999) has observed, growing global interconnectedness has for the first time in human history resulted in a 'near-convergence between subjective cosmology and objective networks', pointing to global homogeneity as much as heterogeneity (see Shahidullah 1996: 124–5 for other critical points).

Furthermore, Huntington tended to portray civilizations as seamless entities free of internal inconsistencies. Following modernization theory, he approached 'western culture' as a relatively harmonious and conflict-free set of values. Some critics suggest that it is more appropriate to speak of 'clashes within each civilization'. Adopting a social constructivist approach, Zizek (2004: 41) argues that specific characteristics are not 'inscribed into' civilizations, but can be better understood as 'the outcome of modern socio-political conditions'. Huntington's global civilizations are presented as if they are billiard balls ricocheting off each other and incapable of absorbing influences from outside. Zizek (2004:

Box 6.1   Huntington and the 'clash of civilizations'

Huntington identified four periods in modernity, distinguished by the nature of conflict:

- In the **first period**, prior to the French Revolution, conflict and wars were fought between princes and their principalities. This was an era of powerful individuals who legitimized their authority over territory through mandates from God.

- The **second period**, from the French Revolution until the end of the First World War, was characterized by wars between nation-states. This was the age of nationalism and colonialism.

- In the **third period** the rise of communism and the growing strength of the Soviet Union provoked global conflicts in ideological dressing, as the ideas of liberalism fought on the world stage, including the Third World stage, against the ideological forces of communism. In this era, the poorer nations emerged as a territory of dispute between these ideological forces of liberalism and communism, democracy and totalitarianism, market versus planned economy, and the individual versus the state.

- In the **fourth period**, the end of communism and the end of the Cold War in the late 1980s have signalled a shift to a new, fourth era of global confict. In this fourth era, the main fault-lines will not be ideological because we have reached the end of ideology.

  According to Huntington, the 'great divisions' in the future 'among humankind will be cultural' (Huntington 1993: 22). Nation-states will remain the most powerful actors in world affairs, but principal conflicts of global politics will occur between nations and groups of different civilizations. The clash of civilizations will dominate global politics. The contenders included 'Western, Confucian, Japanese, Islamic, Hindu, Slavic Orthodox, Latin American and possibly African civilizations'.

→

110) interprets Huntington's thesis as a search for a new post-Cold War nemesis, rather than an intellectual attempt to outline the contours of future international relations (see also Wright 2005: 49):

> After 1990, and the collapse of the Communist states which provided the figure of the Cold War enemy, the Western power of imagination entered a decade of confusion and inefficiency, looking for suitable 'schematizations' for the figure of the enemy, sliding from narco-cartel bosses to a succession of warlords of so-called 'rogue states' (Saddam,

→

These different civilizations have the potential to clash for a number of reasons (Huntington 1993: 25–7):

- Each civilization has basic cultural and moral standards which lead to different understandings of political participation, good government, human rights, freedom and social control, which can lead to potential conflict in the realms of international politics.

- As the world becomes smaller, cultures interact more and more, and this heightens an awareness of their basic differences. Familiarity with different cultures can lead to tolerance, but it can also exacerbate difference and animosity.

- The rise of fundamentalism, or the 'unsecularization of the world', in various civilizations tends to transcend national boundaries, and tends to create identity along the lines of culture, or civilizations.

- The dominance of the west over the rest has led many of the rest to respond by looking back to their traditional social and political practices as a means of challenging the west. The rest are asserting their right to reorganize the world in a non-western way. In many cases, this reassertion of tradition is a response to modernity and the forces of modernization.

- These cultural differences, being more basic than political or economic differences, make civilizational conflict more difficult to resolve.

- It is more accurate to define contemporary processes as regionalization, rather than globalization, and this regionalization 'reinforces civilization-consciousness'.

Source: Summarised from Huntington (1993).

Noriega, Aidid, Milosevic . . .) without stabilizing itself in one central image; only with September 11 did this imagination regain its power by constructing the image of Osama bin Laden, the Islamic fundamentalist par excellence, and al-Qaeda, his invisible network.

The attacks of 11 September 2001 provide an opportunity to compare Fukuyama's future-as-homogeneity and Huntington's future-as-polarization. At first glance it appeared that events validated Huntington's analysis. He had warned that:

Box 6.2   The USA – an empire of liberty?

Chapter 4 pointed out that renewed attention has been devoted to reassessing the values of empire in the new millennium. For instance, Lal (2004) has made historical links between global peace, wealth generation and rule by great empires, such as pax-Britannica in the nineteenth century. Since the end of the Cold War, he argued, the USA has been an imperium in all but name. By denying this role, successive US governments have not served global prosperity or stability (see also Ferguson 2003: 365–81; Ferguson 2004). For Lal, the task that the new US empire must embrace involves facilitating the extension of economic liberty while leaving 'people's cosmological beliefs, including their political habits, alone' (Lal 2004: 212). This strategy would hopefully avoid Huntington's 'clash of civilizations'.

Ignatieff (2003) has also argued that an imperial burden remains a moral responsibility of wealthier countries. Reflecting on the many flashpoints that have demanded international intervention since the end of the Cold War, he believes that external assistance in 'nation-building' continues to feed the need for imperialism:

> 'Imperialism doesn't stop being necessary just because it becomes politically incorrect. . . . Nation-building is the kind of imperialism you get in a human rights era, a time when great powers believe simultaneously in the right of small nations to govern themselves and in their own right to rule the world. Nation-building lite is supposed to reconcile these principles'.   (Ignatieff 2003: 106)

→

The underlying problem for the West is not Islamic fundamentalism. It is Islam, a different civilization whose people are convinced of the superiority of their culture and are obsessed with the inferiority of their power. The problem for Islam is not the CIA or the US Department of Defence. It is the West, a different civilization whose people are convinced of the universality of their culture and believe that their superior, if declining, power imposes on them the obligation to extend that culture throughout the world. These are the basic ingredients that fuel conflict between Islam and the West.   (Huntington 1993: 218)

Drawing on an alternative stance that cultures are not hermetically sealed, value-consensual and conflict-free harmonious orders, Tariq Ali (2002) preferred to understand the subsequent 'war on terror' not as a clash *between* civilizations but rather a more specific 'clash of fundamentalisms' emanating from *within* Islam and the west. The Indian writer Arundhati Roy (2002) also pointed out that Huntington's analysis

→

US President George W. Bush also believes that his country was placed in a position of responsibility to spread freedom and democracy across the globe (as well as to defend the 'civilized world' from terrorists). Bush claimed on the eve of the Iraq war in February 2003 that part of the history of the civilized world might have been 'written by others', but 'the rest will be written by us'. One of his closest strategists, Richard Perle (Frum and Perle 2003: 278–9), reinforced this exogenous role that the US was ready to perform in global development –defined as 'a world of peace, a world governed by law; a world in which all peoples are free to find their own destinies'. These values and conditions could be achieved from 'outside', using 'American armed might'. Fukuyama (2004) agreed that: 'Our "empire" may be a transitional one grounded in democracy and human rights, but our interests dictate that we learn how better to teach other people to govern themselves'. This undertaking was a logical extension to the fall of communism, according to Pieterse (2004). He argued that strategists within the US administration were working to develop a 'new narrative of America's role in the world that can serve as the successor to the Cold War narrative'. Employing a phrase first adopted by Thomas Jefferson, he labels this the 'empire of liberty' (see also Ferguson 2004: 2).

However, after the Iraq war began, Fukuyama increasingly distanced himself from the neoconservatism of the Bush administration, claiming that the 'secret to development . . . is that outsiders are almost never the ones who drive the process forward' (Fukuyama 2006: 185).

forced people to choose 'between a malevolent Mickey Mouse and the Mad Mullahs'. Neither, she implied, should be viewed as representative of their civilizations.

Fukuyama (2001, 2002) also rose to Huntington's challenge and admitted that the events of 11 September had demanded that he account for his prediction of the 'end of history'. After all, 'September 11 would seem to qualify, *prima facie*, as an historical event, and the fact that it was perpetrated by a group of Islamic terrorists who reject virtually all aspects of the modern Western world, lends credence, at least on the surface, to Samuel Huntington's "clash of civilizations" hypothesis' (Fukuyama 2002: 1). His response was that even though radical Islamism was a challenge to western liberal democracy – indeed, its tactics and ideas provided a 'sharper' threat than communism did – it would not force a detour off the path of history because there remains 'such a thing as a single, coherent modernization process', and he reiterated that there remained no alternative future other than western liberalism and the free market. All societies, including Islam, would eventually be 'dragged' in the train of modernization. In the longer run of history, groups such as the Taliban or Al Qaeda were merely desperate reactionaries fighting a 'rearguard action' against the onward march of modernity (Fukuyama 2002: 1).

From Fukuyama's (2002) perspective, 'modernization and globalization will remain the central structuring principles of world politics', a position consistent with the support for the process of global neoliberal expansion analysed earlier in this chapter (Fukuyama 2006: 53–7). In the early twenty-first century, US policy rediscovered the positive role of exogenous forces in the process of development, redefined as 'nation-building' (Fukuyama 2004; see also Box 6.2).

The concluding section of this chapter therefore outlines the institutional setting for neoliberal global governance. While supporters of this 'Washington Consensus' argue that it inscribes equality in its very aims by encouraging all countries to compete on a 'level playing field', its critics point to the very different positions from which richer and poorer countries start in the development process.

The Financial Architecture of Neoliberal Development

Chapter 4 described how the Bretton Woods conference reshaped global financial relations at the end of the Second World War. Lasting institutional outcomes of this conference included the International Monetary Fund, the World Bank and the GATT. This section outlines the evolution of these institutions and the role they have performed in global financial governance. Some commentators argue that they are necessary to stabilize the global financial system through ensuring that all nations participate on an equal footing (or an 'even playing field'). Others, such as the 'Fifty Years is Enough' campaigners of the 1990s, view these institutions as handmaidens of neoliberal interests, aggravating global inequality and keeping poor people poor.

International financial institutions: the IMF and the World Bank

The IMF and the World Bank occupy adjacent office blocks in the centre of Washington, DC, and are commonly called the international financial institutions (IFIs). While some critics treat them as virtually a single organization they have distinct roles and, as vividly illustrated by Stiglitz (2002), different analyses and interests. Although the World Bank is the larger organization, with 9000 staff compared to the IMF's 3000 staff, and has a global network of country and regional offices it often has to play second fiddle to the IMF. The 'Bank' can only lend to countries that are IMF members and, when the IMF and a government are in dispute, it can only make new loans once the problem is resolved to the IMF's satisfaction.

The IMF's main role, since its inception, is the stabilization of national economies and more broadly ensuring the stability of the global finance system. As part of this role it has, since the 1980s, become increasingly involved in providing advice to governments to make the recovery of their economies from financial imbalances 'sustainable'. The World Bank, or more accurately the World Bank Group, has had a more dynamic trajectory taking on new roles and creating new units over the years. It started as the International Bank for Reconstruction and Development (IBRD) mandated to finance post-Second World War reconstruction in Europe and Japan and development in low-income countries. Later the International Development Association (IDA) was added to the Group to provide concessional loans to low-income countries, the International Finanical Corporation (IFC) to make commercial loans to the private sector in developing countries, the Multilateral Investment Guarantee Agency (MIGA) and the International Centre for the Settlement of Investment Disputes (ICSID). Most analyses and advocacy about the World Bank is focused on the IBRD and IDA which work closely and share the same staff.

The Bank's global significance is not merely because of the scale of finance it controls but also because of its role as a 'knowledge bank'. Ranis (1997) argues the World Bank Group has four main roles:

- it is the dominant non-private lender to developing countries;
- it is a highly influential generator of research and ideas about development – commonly debates about development are framed as 'pro' or 'anti' the World Bank position;
- it is the main provider of technical advice to developing countries – originally this was economic and financial but now it covers the environment, social development and governance; and
- an informal 'rating' agency' for many bilateral donors who follow its leads and often co-finance its projects and programmes.

An important internal feature of the Bank, ignored by some of its critics, is the breadth of the debates within it. The Bank is not monolithic and, whatever policies it is formally promoting there will be Bank staff internally criticizing and challenging those policies.

During the first quarter century of their existence, the IMF and World Bank were portrayed by modernization theorists as catalysts for development, providing capital and policy support for poorer nations coping with the stresses associated with the 'preconditions for take-off'. Both encouraged large-scale infrastructural projects that private capital might find unprofitable and lent capital (at both concessional and commercial rates) to countries with short-term balance-of-payments problems. Dependency theorists, on the other hand, argued that these institutions tightened the bonds of peripheral exploitation by the core. Unequal exchange fuelled peripheral debt, which then led to a vicious cycle of repayments, external trade difficulties and further debt burdens. Radical critics accused the IMF and World Bank of 'leveraging' or imposing 'financial discipline' on poorer recipient countries (Hayter 1971; Payer 1974), while conservative critics questioned the circular logic whereby foreign 'aid' was used to assist poorer countries to 'service the subsidized loans (concessionary finance) under earlier foreign aid arrangements' (Bauer 1976: 127).

Despite these criticisms debt remained a 'peripheral' concern until the 1970s. It attracted little attention from development commentators due partly to strong global growth during the long boom (1950–70). The poorer countries might have been unable to overcome mass poverty, but at least the economic indicators suggested that their economies were growing, even if the gap between richer and poorer nations was widening (Donaldson 1973: 13). As long as interest rates remained low and growth was maintained, debt was viewed as an effective means of generating the resources that a modernizing nation required for development, even if the lender had to be compensated with interest.

However, by the late 1960s the Bretton Woods system – with the US dollar as the fixed international currency – began to unravel due to growing US trade deficits, growing budgetary problems and the financing of the Vietnam war. This was exacerbated in 1973 when the Organization of Petroleum Exporting Countries (OPEC) increased the price of oil significantly, affecting the entire basis of the global petro-chemical based production system (Buckman 2005: 23–6; Hertz 2004: 108).

From a dependency perspective, it might appear that the success of the OPEC cartel signalled a victory for peripheral solidarity and the revenge of primary commodity producers against the beneficiaries of global unequal exchange. Equality between nations might be attained through the cartelization of commodity producers, rather than through the creation of a new international economic order. However, the consequences of higher oil prices hit non-oil producing poorer nations harder than wealthier non-oil producers.

The massive surpluses amassed by the oil-producing OPEC countries found their way back into the large private banks in the USA, Europe and Japan that were then faced with the problem of recycling the money. Some of these funds were lent out to the non-oil producing poorer nations who were exposed to higher fuel bills, rising import costs and growing balance-of-payments deficits. Banks also encouraged poorer nations to undertake large-scale developmental projects, such as the building of dams and other infrastructure. The world was awash with petrodollars and western banks were content to offer general purpose loans to all takers. As a result, many of the projects were ill-conceived or used to benefit the consumption patterns of the wealthy elite. The money was also spent by repressive regimes on military hardware, with some being siphoned off by corrupt elites and reinvested back into Swiss bank accounts. Mobutu, Zaire's notorious dictator, had 11 bailouts from the IMF during his rule despite detailed reports by IMF and World Bank staff of the way he was stealing the money (Easterly 2006: 149). His was not an isolated case. As a consequence, a good deal of the money recycled through the western banks into the poorer nations ended up back in the west with interest (George 1990; George 2004: 55–7) and Mobutu's pro-western vote at the UN could be counted on.

To compound matters, during the 1970s higher interest rates, inflation, the slowing down of the world economy and a second 'oil shock' in 1979 deepened the problems of non-oil producing poorer countries. Suddenly the world awoke to the fact that many poorer nations were unable to service even the interest on their loans. In 1970, the debt of the poorer world totalled $68 billion. By 1982, it had soared to well over $600 billion. In the early 1980s, after Mexico and Argentina defaulted on their debt repayments, a growing chorus of commentators began to call for a debt moratorium. Cuban President Fidel Castro (1985) urged that the debt be cancelled. The 'Third World debt crisis' – a headline story in the western press – was not principally about the indebtedness of the poorer nations. Rather, it was a crisis of the western banking system, which had lent its money unwisely and as a consequence become overburdened with too many bad debts. Many private financial institutions began to look vulnerable (Hertz 2004: 73).

The IFIs stepped in to deal with this problem of runaway debt. Not only did the problem pose a threat to the development of poorer indebted countries, it also had potentially damaging repercussions for world trade and financial confidence. During the 1980s, the IMF went beyond its mandate of helping adjust balance of payments 'to addressing structural economic crises in third world countries . . . and increasingly became the vehicle for imposing a type of conditionality, in exchange for loans, that incorporated global capital's concerns' (Panitch and Gindin 2003: 16). The IMF and World Bank collaborated with the indebted poorer countries and the western banks to coordinate the handling of the debt (Lal 2004: 131–2).

The IFIs were in a better position than the private banks to help restructure the economies of the poorer nations and undertake the inter-related tasks of meeting debt obligations, liberalizing economies and encouraging greater openness to international trade (Wachtel 1986: 125). Their policy advice aimed to generate 'high-quality growth', defined as sustained growth that laid the foundations for future develop-ment. As time moved on, their mission extended so that by the early 1990s they were encouraging growth that protected the environment and by the late 1990s growth that 'attempted to reduce poverty and improve the equality of opportunity' (IMF 1998: 1). The leverage the IFIs used to achieve compliance from the poorer indebted countries involved with-holding future loans until the appropriate policy medicine was adminis-tered. Such a sanction had important ramifications. Generally, once the IMF decided a country was ineligible for loans then multilateral agencies, such as the World Bank, and most bilateral aid donors would stop new loans and grants. Similarly, most major commercial banks avoid new loans to countries that do not have IMF approval. The prescription offered by the IMF came to be known as Structural Adjustment Programs (SAPs), stipulating tighter fiscal control and liberal economic reform within poorer countries. These reforms were another nail in the coffin of postwar state-led development (Rapley 2002). They were also consistent with the neoliberal framework outlined earlier in this chapter.

SAPs also remained true to the prototype/emulator model of develop-ment. As Gray (2004: 87) described it, there was 'only one route to modernity, and the seers who ruled the IMF were resolved that it be followed everywhere' (see also Hertz 2004: 112; Sen 2001b: 126–7). The prototype/emulator relationship inherent within this model has also been noted by Sachs (2005: 81): 'Be like us (or what we imagine ourselves to be – free market oriented, entrepreneurial, fiscally responsible) and you, too, can enjoy the riches of private sector-led economic development.'

Emulation required the pursuit of the 'Washington Consensus' model focused on the following policies:

- controlling inflation through wage controls;
- privatization of publicly owned enterprises;
- balancing state budgets through reducing government expenditure;
- eliminating or reducing state subsidies on basic goods;
- generation of foreign exchange through export-oriented industries rather than support for import substitution; and
- elimination of controls on foreign capital.

The IFI reforms have had some success. First, the net transfer of money out of the indebted world has continued to increase since the 1980s and poorer countries have demonstrated their ability to meet repayments and therefore be worthy of further loans. Secondly, the approach has managed to shift most of the debt burden from private banks to multi-lateral donors. The debt accumulated by the poorer countries therefore does not generate as much newspaper copy today in the wealthier world compared to the early 1980s. Thirdly, increased liberalization of the economies of the poorer indebted nations forced them to participate more openly in the world economy. Even some critics agree that economic reforms were necessary, while questioning the way SAPs were introduced (ILO 2004: 58; Rapley 2002). Over 70 poorer and former socialist nations have swallowed 566 SAPs that encouraged a 'shift from production for domestic markets to production for the world market' (Robinson 2004: 79, 124).

Whether the IFI policies are considered a success or failure depends on one's vantage point (Pieterse 2004: 12). Despite acknowledging some mistakes, the IFIs (and especially the IMF) retain confidence that their prescriptions remain the best hope for poorer nations to alleviate their poverty, catch up with the wealthier nations and bridge the inequality gap (IMF 1998). They also stress that the SAPs cannot be held responsible for the conditions that most indebted nations subsequently found themselves in, because few signatories to SAPs had the courage to fully implement their policy prescriptions (Bhagwati 2004: chs 16 and 18). Once SAP conditionalities were agreed, complex cat-and-mouse games were played between Ministries of Finance and the IMF about how to measure structural change and renegotiate conditions (Easterly 2002: ch. 6).

Most critics of the IFIs have focused attention on the impact that their prescriptions have upon inequalities between countries and within countries. If global inequality was labelled a problem of 'unequal exchange' prior to the 1980s, in the new millennium this has been compounded by 'debt-peonage' (Hoogvelt 1997: 50). This form of control over poorer countries has the advantage that it does not require direct administration – only arms-length control through 'market discipline' and 'conditionality' (George 2004: 57; Hertz 2004: 41; Kothari 2002: 33). Minogue (2002: 122) suspects that demands for 'good governance' mark 'a new phase of surveillance and control on the part of international capital'.

It has been argued that the IMF's enthusiasm for bailing out countries whose currency collapses encourages global speculators to throw capital at opportunities without considering the costs. During the 1997 Asian financial crisis, Tanner (1999) accused the IMF of underwriting the 'risks of global speculators', then tightening fiscal conditions on poorer nations at the least appropriate moment. In this climate, the poor lose out while the wealthy cannot lose (see ILO 2004: 39). Stiglitz (2002), chief economist at the World Bank, felt that the IMF advice caused more harm than good, but he had to resign his position when he broke ranks, went public on this and angered the US Treasury's Secretary of State.

This issue of 'who pays' for the SAPs has generated growing global attention over the past two decades. Critics claim that state withdrawal from the economy and the marketization of social services has overwhelmingly disadvantaged the poor, deepening poverty and widening the gulf between rich and poor. In order to repay the debts of past governments, citizens within poorer countries must forgo educational resources, health and hygiene services and must suffer the consequences of poorer quality or privatized water and power. The adoption of fiscal restraint in countries with acute social problems has been seen as inappropriate by many critics (Chang and Grabel 2003: 202; Sachs 2005: 78–80). One of the most glaring inequalities facing the global community today, critics argue, is that the world's poor are denied basic services that many in wealthier countries take for granted in order to repay debts incurred by regimes that used the loans to maintain the oppression of the poor (Hertz 2004: 113–14, 173–4). The poor received no benefit from loans, yet ultimately pay the price. Ironically, the part of the world that has received the most extensive SAP lending and expert advice – Africa – is where economic growth has been most problematic and poverty has remained entrenched (Easterly 2006).

Since the late 1990s two potentially significant changes have occurred at the IMF and World Bank. The first relates to their statements about shifting to a 'post-Washington Consensus' approach that recognizes the need for state action as well as market forces, avoids the 'one size fits all' naivety of the structural adjustment era and seeks to ensure that reforms are 'owned' by recipient countries and not just the IFIs. The second concerns the declared prioritization of poverty-reduction by both organizations. The main instrument of the IMF is now the Poverty Reduction and Growth Facility Loan (PRGF) while that of the World Bank is the Poverty Reduction Strategy Credit (PRSC). Both require that governments prepare national poverty reduction strategies (PRSs) in consultation with their civil societies before loans can be granted. These shifts can be interpreted as a genuine refocusing of policy or as the presentation of structural adjustment in a more user-friendly guise or, more cynically, as a recognition by the IFIs that with the growing volume of private finance flowing to developing countries they need to demonstrate what market gap they are filling. The IFIs interpret poverty reduction in absolute terms (Chapter 2) so that they are generally ambivalent about the effects of their policies on inequality.

Finally, in this section, it must be noted that although the IFIs are mandated to be apolitical they operate in a highly politicized environment. In particular, the US government and other political forces in the

USA have considerable influence over them (Cohn 2005: 363–407). Unlike other UN agencies with 'one member, one vote' governance structures, the IFI voting is weighted in terms of capital subscriptions based on national GNP. This makes the USA the most powerful member, with around 17 per cent of total votes (Payne 2005: 109 and 114). As changes in the Articles of Association require 85 per cent member approval, this gives the USA an effective veto. But US influence goes well beyond these simple numbers (Cohn 2005: 373–5) as the USA can persuade other countries to vote alongside it. In addition, the official language of the IFIs is English (unlike other UN agencies that are multilingual) and a high proportion of IFI staff, and particularly their economists, has US postgraduate training. Arguably, the key staff of the IFIs are part of an epistemic community that uses neo-classical economic frameworks and rational actor models to understand the world. This leads to a preference for market-based solutions.

Being based in the USA makes the IFIs accessible to both broader ideological influences (a concern about welfare dependency and a suspicion of government) and the lobbying of US-based NGOs and interest groups. The power that the USA has over the IFIs is evidenced by their politically skewed allocation of loans (Harrigan et al. 2006) and the pushing out of senior staff, such as Ravi Kanbur and Joseph Stiglitz, when their analyses did not agree with the US Secretary of State (Wade 2001a).

The WTO

World trade in goods was 22 times greater in 2000 than it was in 1950. The body assigned by the Bretton Woods framework to promote this global trade was the General Agreement on Tariffs and Trade (GATT). After the Second World War, GATT became the principal forum for negotiating lower tariffs and quotas on goods in order to grease the wheels of international commerce. This effort was conducted through a loosely structured series of negotiations among the trading nations of the world.

During the Uruguay Round between 1986 and 1994, GATT began to expand its mandate into services – such as telecommunications, finance, banking, health and transport – and also began to examine 'non-tariff' barriers such as environmental regulations that impeded trade along with other forms of government regulation (Buckman 2005: 40–6). To deal more effectively with these issues, in 1994 it was agreed to transform the GATT into a more formal organization that would legally bind countries to global commercial codes and administer sanctions against those that failed to comply with these new trading rules. This shift from GATT's promotion of global trade in goods to the investigation of other 'trade-related issues' meant intervening more directly in the domestic laws of sovereign states. The argument made by proponents of the formalization of GATT was that environmental legislation, higher labour standards, food safety laws, product standards and investment laws can be used by governments to maintain disguised forms of protection for domestic industries and services.

This entailed GATT being reconfigured into the World Trade Organization, its supporters claiming that 'the result is a more prosperous, peaceful and accountable economic world' (WTO 2002). According to Thomas Friedman (2000: 101–11), the WTO is a 'golden straitjacket', which might appear to limit individual freedom but ultimately ensures greater wealth for all. It is a new global social contract, whereby a portion of national liberty is forfeited in order to partake in the benefits of global harmony and trade. The WTO provides an international legal framework that guarantees formal equality between nations and it aims to ensure that all nations and private corporations are treated equally in the competitive market.

What the WTO cannot ensure is that all nations and firms compete from an equal footing. Its critics doubt whether the WTO treats rich and poor fairly (ILO 2004: 52). Many poorer countries, global social movements and even UN organizations have claimed that the WTO focuses on eliminating barriers erected by poorer nations while ignoring the more damaging protectionism practised by affluent countries (UN Millennium Project 2005). While the WTO demands that poorer countries lower their levels of protection and facilitate global competition, richer countries maintain high levels of protection on the agricultural and industrial products for which poorer countries have a competitive advantage. Bello (in Constantini 2001) has complained that the WTO has misused its power and become 'the blueprint for the global hegemony of Corporate America'. After street battles forced the premature end to the 1999 WTO meeting in Seattle (see Chapter 9), the WTO engaged in a publicity drive to enhance its reputation for fairness and equity between nations and to reverse the impression that it was a 'rich man's club'. Thus, the professed aim of the WTO's 'Doha Development Agenda' (2001–6) was to open up the markets of the wealthier countries to the products of poorer countries.

Politically, the WTO appears to function in a more egalitarian manner than the IMF and the World Bank, where the rich countries with 15 per cent of the world's population control approximately 60 per cent of the votes (ILO 2004: 116). In the WTO, each of the 149 member states has an equal vote and decisions are taken on a consensus basis. However, in practice, this democracy is openly flaunted. Most decisions have been negotiated away from the gaze of full-board membership by the wealthiest countries that set the agenda and direction of the WTO (Jawara and Kwa 2003: 133). Robinson (2004: 88, 117) views the WTO – along with the IMF and the World Bank – as part of an emerging transnational capitalist class structure with the WTO as 'perhaps the archetypal transnational institution of the new epoch' due to the fact that it is 'the first supranational institution with an enforcement capacity embedded not in any particular nation-state but rather directly in transnational functionaries and the transnational corporate elite'. Again, while the rules of the WTO proclaim the formal equality of nations, substantively the poorer countries find it more difficult to exercise that equality due to differences in economic and political clout (ILO 2004: 76; see also *New Internationalist* 2001). There are also simple practical limitations. At the December 2005 WTO negotiations in Hong Kong, many poorer countries could support only one delegate. This makes it difficult for them to compete with the hundreds of delegates that the EU and the USA field at such meetings.

The neoliberal framework adopted by the WTO and the IMF creates a blindspot to the issue of inequality (Wade 2001a). Bello (2003) even suggests that the WTO's rules 'institutionalize the current system of global economic inequality'. WTO assumptions rest on economic growth providing more job opportunities and eventually alleviating poverty. It maintains that policies that redistribute resources without sustained economic growth merely generalize poverty in poorer countries. Growth therefore provides a win/win trade scenario. However, this positive-sum prediction obscures the possibility that modern economic growth has its losers and can generate new inequalities (Kay 2003: 7). Others have questioned whether recent economic success stories can be attributed to the policies advocated by the Washington Consensus (see Box 6.3).

Critics claim that the WTO allows considerations of market efficiency and free trade to override all other values, such as working conditions, environmental concerns, bio-diversity, human rights, consumer safety and public health (Singer 2002; see also Sen 1999: 263). For example, WTO rules prohibit trade restrictions on the basis of how a product is produced. This 'process/product distinction' tends to turn global regulation into an amoral realm (Tabb 2001). Thus, goods manufactured by exploited child labour cannot be banned in favour of goods manufactured under conditions where workers receive a liveable wage. Or, a country cannot discriminate in favour of environmentally friendly products over products whose processes degrade the environment. Japan and the EU were successful in repealing laws in the state of Massachusetts that discouraged procurement from firms that conducted business with the Burmese dictatorship. Under these conditions, the International

---

Box 6.3   India – growth, poverty reduction and inequality

Economists used to write of the 'Hindu equilibrium', a situation which viewed India as a shackled economic giant fated to slow growth and deep poverty through an historic legacy of traditional institutions and state intervention. Since the early 1990s that image has been shaken off as India has increasingly engaged with the global economy and gradually liberalized its economic policies.

Between 1990 and 2001, the country's average rate of economic growth was 4 per cent per annum. Since 2000 the growth rate has surged. This has been achieved through growth in the agricultural, manufacturing and service sectors. The development of an ICT-based service industry has been especially important in southern states, such as Karnataka and Andhra Pradesh, with massive expansions in computer software development, data processing and call-centres. Much of this growth has its roots in India's state-supported education system that produces thousands of world-leading IT specialists from its Indian Institutes of Technology (IITs) each year, and hundreds of thousands of highly literate and numerate people from its colleges who can staff service centres.

India's large corporations, most notably the Tata conglomerate, and its diaspora have played major roles in the growth process. Emigrants from India, officially called non-resident Indians (NRIs), are encouraged to invest in and bring their knowledge and skills back to the country. The high proportion of NRIs in California's Silicon Valley means that India can attract a vast share of the global market for IT outsourcing.

This growth has been associated with a significant decline in poverty in India, although exactly how much has been a subject of heated debate and technical nuances (Sundaram and Tendulkar 2003). There is widespread

→

Labour Organization (2004: 7) claims that global trade operates in a 'moral vacuum'.

WTO rules also contradict the 'precautionary principle' adopted at the 1992 Rio Earth Summit, which approved the maxim that 'it is better to be safe than sorry' when it comes to the environmental impact of introducing new processes or products. In the past, corporations were required to furnish proof to governments that new products or processes were safe. Now governments must 'scientifically demonstrate that something is dangerous before it can be regulated' (Working Group on the WTO/MAI 1999: 12). For instance, when the European Union refused to accept hormone-fed beef from the USA, the USA took the EU to the WTO, claiming that the product was not a threat to humans. Even though the EU did not discriminate between nations on this issue – by

→

agreement that the reductions in income poverty have not been matched by equivalent improvements in social indicators and, for example, 47 per cent of Indian children under 5 are reported as underweight (UNDP 2003: 199).

The debates around the Indian data mean that authoritative statements about inequality are difficult to make. Nevertheless, almost everyone in India talks of growing inequality. This has two important dimensions. The first is regional inequality, as India's economic growth and income poverty reduction is concentrated in the states of the south and the west. In the northern 'poverty belt', states such as Bihar, Orissa, Uttar Pradesh and Assam have seen few changes in economic or social indicators. Problems of governance in these states – corrupt politicians, collapsed public service delivery, the breakdown of law and order, militias controlled by 'big men' – are seen as major obstacles to development. The second is individual inequality. While the number of dollar millionaires in India steadily increases the contrasting millions of landless and destitute people remain a striking feature of everyday life.

While the IFIs and proponents of structural adjustment and neoliberal policies enthusiastically use accounts about India to point to the benefits of their policies it must be noted that India, like China, has never taken the medicine of the Washington Consensus. Its economic liberalization has been determined by domestic political forces, has been gradual and recognizes a continued major role for the state. While the pursuit of growth is central to the Indian strategy there are also major welfare initiatives, such as the National Employment Guarantee Scheme (NEGS), to directly alleviate poverty and reduce inequality.

Source: Sundaram and Tendulkar (2003); UNDP (2003).

also banning hormone-fed beef from EU farmers – the WTO ruled against the EU (Ellwood 2000: 36–7).

Along with the IMF, the WTO has helped governments reinforce pressures to reduce social spending and attack the power of labour organizations though their demands for more flexible labour markets. For these reasons, the WTO has been a target of global anti-systemic movements. These new social movements are demanding a world where greater equality coexists with diversity. Even Fukuyama (2006: 109) has acknowledged that the disappointing results of pro-market policies over the 1990s had discredited neoliberalism in many poorer countries by the turn of the new millennium. Chapter 9 discusses the growth of global social movements over the past few decades that brought together a wide variety of forms of resistance to the practices and consequences of neoliberalism outlined in this chapter.

In the years preceding the 50th anniversary of the IMF, a global push was initiated through the 'Jubilee' campaign to restructure or forgive the indebtedness of poorer nations. Among the Jubilee demands that remain relevant in the new millennium are:

- make the IMF and the World Bank completely open and accountable;
- support development programmes that are equitable, sustainable and participatory;
- end all environmentally destructive lending;
- scale back the Washington Consensus and redirect financial resources into a variety of development assistance alternatives;
- cancel all outstanding debt owed to the IMF and the World Bank by the world's poorest countries.

Although these demands remain unmet, the past decade has witnessed many coordinated global campaigns to acknowledge the unfairness of much debt. This has forced wealthy nations, private banks, and IFIs to engage in dialogue on the problem. In 2005, the campaign culminated in the Live 8 music concerts held in various countries whose leaders were attending a G8 meeting at Gleneagles, Scotland. The concerts were designed to raise awareness of three interrelated development demands: 'drop the debt', 'make trade fair' and 'make poverty history'. These demands are echoed in the Millennium Development Goals, agreed to by the world's leaders at the UN in 2000. This campaign will be explored in the following chapter, but Hertz (2004: 206) makes a direct link between the MDGs and the IMF by claiming that unless the poorest nations are unburdened from their debt obligations 'to free up resources to address their citizens' basic needs . . . there is no chance in hell that the Millennium Development Goals will be met'. Furthermore, while Easterly (2002: 136) makes the behavioural point that debt relief would be pointless if the forgiven governments continued to mismanage the economy, it is also important to acknowledge the structural point that cancelling debt in itself would have only a limited impact on global poverty and inequality if the global financial system that generated the debt in the first place remains unreformed (see Wade 2006).

Chapter 7

The Millennium Development Challenge

The past half-century has been both the best and worst of times, depending on how the evidence is assessed (UNDP 2003: 40). The postwar period can be viewed as an era of remarkable achievement in human progress, in which technological innovation flourished, global commerce expanded significantly and a lower proportion of the world's population than ever before lived in poverty. Others, however, have claimed that global development has been a failure. Almost everyone would agree, however, that overcoming global poverty and multiple inequalities remain key challenges for the new millennium. This chapter examines the latest response by the world community to this quest. It also provides an opportunity to review the local, regional and global outcomes of postwar development.

Setting Development Goals for a New Millennium

At the United Nations' Millennium Summit in September 2000, the largest ever assembly of world leaders committed their governments to a goal-oriented programme named the Millennium Development Goals (MDGs). It was designed to: reduce extreme global poverty by half; increase participation in basic education; improve child and maternal

---

Box 7.1   The Millennium Development Goals and Targets

Goal 1   Eradicate extreme poverty and hunger
- *Target 1*: halve, between 1990 and 2015, the proportion of people whose income is less than $1 a day.
- *Target 2*: halve, between 1990 and 2015, the proportion of people who suffer from hunger.

Goal 2   Achieve universal primary education
- *Target 3*: ensure that, by 2015, children everywhere, boys and girls alike, will be able to complete a full course of primary schooling.

Goal 3   Promote gender equality and empower women
- *Target 4*: eliminate gender disparity in primary and secondary education, preferably by 2005, and in all levels of education no later than 2015.

Goal 4   Reduce child mortality
- *Target 5*: reduce by two-thirds, between 1990 and 2015, the under-five mortality rate.

Goal 5   Improve maternal health
- *Target 6*: reduce by three-quarters, between 1990 and 2015, the maternal mortality ratio.

Goal 6   Combat HIV/AIDS, malaria and other diseases
- *Target 7*: have halted by 2015 and begun to reverse the spread of HIV/AIDS.
- *Target 8*: have halted by 2015 and begun to reverse the incidence of malaria and other major diseases.

Goals 7   Ensure environmental sustainability
- *Target 9*: integrate the principles of sustainable development into country policies and programmes and reverse the loss of environmental resources.

→

---

health; achieve gender equality; control and reduce transmittable, air-borne and water-borne diseases; accelerate agricultural productivity in the poorest nations; provide neglected areas with safe water and improved sanitation; meet these goals in an environmentally sustainable manner; and establish a global partnership for development (see Box 7.1). The UN Millennium Project (2005b: 2, 12 and 263) – an independent advisory body established by the UN Secretary General – hailed

→

- *Target 10*: halve, by 2015, the proportion of people without sustainable access to safe drinking water and basic sanitation.
- *Target 11*: have achieved by 2020 a significant improvement in the lives of at least 100 million slum dwellers.

Goal 8   Develop a global partnership for development
- *Target 12*: develop further an open, rule-based, predictable, non-discriminatory trading and financial system (including a commitment to good governance, development, and poverty reduction, both nationally and internationally).
- *Target 13*: address the special needs of the Least Developed Countries (including tariff- and quota-free access for least developed Countries' exports, enhanced programme of debt relief for heavily indebted poor countries (HIPCs) and cancellation of official bilateral debt, and more generous official development assistance for countries committed to poverty reduction).
- *Target 14*: address the special needs of landlocked developing countries and small island developing states (through the Program of Action for the Sustainable Development of Small Island Developing States and 22nd General Assembly provisions).
- *Target 15*: deal comprehensively with the debt problems of developing countries through national and international measures in order to make debt sustainable in the long term

Some of the indicators listed below are monitored separately for the least developed countries, Africa, landlocked developing countries, and small island developing states.

- *Target 16*: in cooperation with developing countries, develop and implement strategies for decent and productive work for youth.
- *Target 17*: in cooperation with pharmaceutical companies, provide access to affordable essential drugs in developing countries.
- *Target 18*: in cooperation with the private sector, make available the benefits of new technologies, especially information and communications technologies.

these goals as 'the most broadly supported, comprehensive and specific poverty reduction targets the world has ever established', 'the fulcrum on which development policy is based', a 'linchpin to the quest for a more secure and peaceful world', and a 'mid-station en route to ending poverty within a generation'. In 2005, UN General Secretary Kofi Annan referred to the MDGs as a 'seminal event' in the history of the UN (UNMP 2005b: 3).

This is far from the first occasion that the UN has proclaimed an ambitious scheme for tackling global poverty. The 1960s, 1970s and 1980s were each labelled a 'Decade for Development'. These interventionist declarations had lost much of their credibility by the 1990s due to their failure to meet declared targets. Furthermore, as neoliberal policy preferences spread, goal-oriented indicators of development came to be regarded with greater distrust.

Given its past record and the prevailing intellectual climate, the Millennium Declaration was a bold move by the United Nations (Sachs 2005: 210–14). It went beyond previous schemes that set vague developmental aspirations and committed the world's richest and poorest nations to work in harmony to meet a set of quantifiable targets by the year 2015. Never before had the world community accepted such accountability, measurability and responsibility for global development. Earlier 'developmental decades tended to focus on the narrower indicator of economic growth' whereas emphasis was now placed on 'human well-being and poverty reduction' (UNDP 2003: 27).

The MDG partnership between the richer and poorer countries is referred to as a 'compact'. The poorer countries are responsible for providing the appropriate policy context for development (including good governance, sound economic decision-making, transparency, accountability, rule of law, respect for human rights and civil liberties and local participation). The richer countries will commit themselves to meeting its aid obligations in a timely, generous and coordinated manner while simultaneously renegotiating debt relief and abolishing discriminatory trade restrictions against the poorer world. Kofi Annan (2005b) referred to the MDGs as a 'manifesto for newly enfranchised poor people throughout the world'.

The emphasis on *goals* suggested a shift away from the more market-oriented policies that the IMF and the World Bank had favoured during the previous two decades. The IFI's growth strategies began with calculations of what was achievable under existing fiscal, physical capital and human capital possibilities and assumed that development would be achieved at a pace dictated by prevailing constraints. However, the MDGs overcame these constraints by adopting a more teleological (or goal-oriented) approach to planning the development process (UNDP 2003: 25). The UNDP (2003: 5, 21) demands that: 'Governments of poor and rich countries, as well as international institutions, should start by asking what resources are needed to meet the Goals, rather than allowing the pace of development to be set by the limited resources currently allocated' (see also Sachs 2005: 271).

The UN Millennium Project (2005a: 59, 61) explicitly acknowledges that this goal-oriented approach 'differs starkly from the prevailing practice in developing countries, which is to formulate investment strategies after the macroeconomic framework, official development assistance, and overall budgetary ceilings have been set independent of needs'. Under the MDGs, the pace of development would be dictated by measurable goals. These targets for the year 2015 would determine what needed to be accomplished now in order for the goals to be achieved. The gap between the existing resources and development needs became the moral responsibility of the wealthier world, through 'increased donor assistance, expanded market access, swifter debt relief and greater technology transfer' (UNMP 2005a: 21). Middle-income countries (such as Brazil, Malaysia, Mauritius and Mexico) would also perform an important role in raising the developmental performance of the poorest countries, given their more recent experience of sustained growth.

The MDGs could be accepted by both the optimists who believed that global development was within reach and pessimists who claimed that development has failed. On the one hand, it accepts that world development was 'off track', in the sense that it is in danger of leaving behind at least one-fifth of world's population as the majority stride ahead. On the other hand, it does not view this state of affairs as an inherent trend within the structure of global interconnectedness. The past 50 years provide a rich repository of positive experiences from which to draw. The recent past has seen astonishing economic growth and human development in regions that had previously been among the world's poorest. What draws optimistic and more pessimistic assessments towards the Millennium Project is the urgency through which the moral imperative of development is expressed, and the clear definition of measurable targets, stated deadlines, required inputs and expected outputs. By setting the clocks ticking and translating time into lives saved, the world community is enjoined to engage in a global partnership for development.

The MDGs are based not only on the vast scale of the problem of poverty and inequality facing the world in the new millennium, but also on a recognition of the significant improvements in the living conditions of hundreds of millions of people over the past few decades. Between 1981 and 2001, the proportion of the world's population living in extreme poverty (US$1 a day or less) almost halved to 21 per cent (UNMP 2005a: 2; see also ILO 2004: 44). The average income of the poorest 20 per cent of the world's population rose from US$551 to US$1137 between 1965 and 1998 (Norberg 2003: 25; see also Sachs 2005: 165; Lomborg 2001), and the proportion of people suffering hunger dropped from 37 per cent to under 18 per cent between 1960 and the end of the century (Norberg 2003: 31). Indeed, the progress achieved in the fields of health and education by many poorer countries over the past half century had taken over two centuries to achieve in the wealthier countries. Progress is not only visible – it has been telescoped.

Telecommunication connectivity has also grown rapidly over the past 15 years in all regions of the world, although from a much lower base in poorer countries (UNMP 2005a: 26–7). Many now believe that the key problem that the world faces is not increased production to meet a growing world population, but distributing the proceeds to eliminate disadvantage and poverty (see Hobsbawm 2000: 87–8).

Average life expectancy in the poorer countries has risen dramatically from 30 years in 1900, to 46 by 1960, to 65 years at the end of the 1990s (Norberg 2003: 28). In the last two decades of the twentieth century, overall life expectancy rose by 8 years. By the beginning of the new millennium, over 124 of the 173 countries that had a life expectancy below 60 years in 1980 had reached or surpassed this threshold (UNDP 2003: 31). Advances in human development have been most spectacular in a small number of large countries in Asia. During the 1990s alone, the proportion living in extreme poverty in East Asia was almost halved (UNDP 2003: 2; see also Box 7.2).

The poorer countries now produce three times as much food compared with 1970 and the real price of staple foods has dropped. Undernourishment in poorer countries declined by 3 per cent during the 1990s and under-five mortality declined by 15 deaths per thousand to 88 per thousand. Eight per cent more people had access to safe water and almost twice as many to improved sanitation (UNMP 2005a: 13–4).

The UN Millennium Project points out that growing global trade has contributed to impressive improvements in development outcomes, and this translates into better life chances for hundreds of millions of people. In the 30 years prior to 2000, the share of the poorer countries in global industrial production rose from 7 per cent to 20 per cent, although this industrial activity was highly concentrated in a select number of mainly East Asian and Latin American nations. Total foreign direct investment in the poorer countries has increased significantly over the past few decades, although 85 per cent of this investment is concentrated in only 12 countries and China takes a very large share of this investment (UNMP 2005a: 47; Wade 2006).

Despite these benefits and achievements, the MDG framework draws attention to the fact that growth is 'bypassing hundreds of millions of the world's poorest people' (UNDP 2003: 15; Sachs 2005: 19). If the world is divided into High, Medium and Low human development countries (as classified by the UNDP – see Chapter 3), each category increased its trade in goods and services considerably between 1990 and 2001 (by 52 per cent, 49 per cent and 67 per cent respectively). However, the lowest

Box 7.2 China: growth with inequality

China's economic growth over the past two decades has been unprecedented, transforming the country from an inward-looking agrarian economy transfixed by achieving food self-sufficiency to become the world's factory. Between 1975 and 2003 the economy rolled on at an impressive average annual growth rate of 8.2 per cent and shows no signs of letting up. During the past 20 years more than 400 million people have been lifted above the US$1 per day poverty line, life expectancy at birth has improved from 63.2 years in 1970–5 to 71.5 years in 2000–5, and adult literacy in 2005 had risen to 90.9 per cent as against 63 per cent in 1978.

The welfare gains are substantial but they hide profound inequalities. Growth has been concentrated in the East, focusing on hubs such as Shanghai and the hinterland of Hong Kong in Guangdong province. But move west into the provinces of Anhui or Hunan and GDP per person plummets from US$4000 to under US$1499 per capita (*The Economist*, 25 March 2006).

Some recent evidence does indicate that foreign and domestic companies are moving into the lower-cost cities of the west and north in an effort to make savings on wages, land and utilities (Chan and Qingyang 2006). But within provinces there can be an even bigger divide, that between rural and urban populations. Rural incomes have certainly been rising following the abolition of various government fees but urban incomes have consistently risen much faster creating a widening rural–urban income gap.

Furthermore, many local governments are unable to pay for basic services such as health and education as too little money is transferred from central government. Township and village governments' debts may be as much as US$125 billion, over 5 per cent of GDP (*The Economist*, 25 March 2006). But the major bone of rural contention is land. Peasants cannot sell their land or use it as collateral for loans unlike in urban areas. Local governments also seize land to attract industry or to sell to property developers especially on urban fringes. This has prompted numerous, sometimes violent protests in villages across China. When the ousted villagers migrate to the cities they often lack residency permits and work for below minimum wages, lack access to basic services and may suffer from harsh treatment by the police.

The challenge for China's leaders is how to ensure its future growth – still officially predicted to be at least 7.5 per cent for the 2000–10 economic plan – is more equitably distributed than has been the case so far.

countries were coming off a base so low that even by 2001 their trade amounted to only US$61 billion compared to US$7602 billion in the high human development countries (UNDP 2003: 154). Thus, despite advances, the poorer nations continue to lag behind.

Developmental successes also place global poverty in starker relief,

especially the coexistence of 'extensive hunger in a world of unprecedented prosperity' (Sen 2001: 204). Kofi Annan has emphasized the
moral obligation imposed on the richer part of the world community:

> Sixty years of peace and economic growth in the industrial world have
> also given the human race today, for the first time, the economic and
> technical power to overcome poverty and its attendant ills. . . . There
> is no longer an excuse for leaving well over a billion of our fellow
> human beings in abject misery.   (2005b: 2)

The UN Development Programme (2003: 50) also concluded that
there is 'no doubt' that all countries can achieve the MDGs, given past
performance and given the fact that experience has demonstrated that
progress is possible 'without incurring higher inequalities'. This is
supported by the UN Millennium Project (2005: 64), which draws the
lesson from the history of postwar development practice that 'the world
has the practical knowledge, tools, and means to reach the MDGs' (see
also Sachs 2005: 3, 51). This would involve kick-starting economic
growth through forms of public spending that will encourage private
investment and simultaneously increase human development. The
MDG strategy therefore appears to bring the state back onto the centre
of the developmental stage after twenty years on the wings (see Chapter
6).

At first glance, it appears that the MDGs are *poverty*-focused, and
they are explicitly expressed in this way. However, they also demand an
attack on widening inequalities. The UN Millennium Declaration not
only committed the world community to eradicating poverty, but also to
promote 'human dignity, equality, and achieve peace, democracy and
environmental sustainability'. These principles were reaffirmed in 2003
as part of the world community's 'collective responsibility' (quoted in
UNDP 2003: 1, 27), and as 'the world's time-bound and quantified
targets for addressing extreme poverty' (UNMP 2005a: 1). In another
declaration, the values guiding the MDGs are identified as 'freedom,
equality, tolerance, respect for nature and shared responsibility'. In his
preface to the 2005 *UN Report on the World Social Situation* (2005: iii),
Kofi Annan proclaimed that 'we cannot advance the development
agenda without addressing the challenges of inequality within and
between countries'.

The UN Millennium Project also emphasizes the relationship between
poverty and inequality through identifying two different sets of problems
countries face in moving towards the MDGs. The first set consists of
'countries that combine low human development and poor performance
towards the Goals'. Global inequalities between nations will continue to

increase unless these countries receive priority assistance. The second set consists of countries where progress is being made towards the Goals, yet 'deep pockets of poor people are being left behind'. The MDGs therefore acknowledge that inequalities within nations can threaten the global targets to alleviate poverty, even though per-capita GNP is growing (UNDP 2003: 3, 33). Women, rural inhabitants and ethnic minorities are overrepresented among the poor within this set of countries. The UNDP (2003: 3, 34, 47) recommends that the global community look beyond national averages and warns that some countries might be tempted to aim for 'false progress' (or 'ruthless growth') through 'improving the circumstances of people already better off' while 'leaving behind many poor people' (UNDP 2003: 67). To avoid this, the MDGs return to a 'basic needs' approach, emphasizing sustainability, inclusiveness, participation, equity and 'those most in need of support' (UNDP 2003: 27).

Past experience shows that political resources in the poorer world (as in the rich) tend to be captured by the wealthiest (see Chapter 10). This influences how developmental resources are distributed. Thus, inequality affects poverty in another more direct political manner. Under conditions of widespread inequality 'rich people often control the political system and simply neglect poor people, forestalling broadly based development' (UNDP 2003, 16). There is an explicit acknowledgement here of the structuralist argument outlined in Chapter 2 that focuses on how resource and power inequalities rob poorer people of capacity to improve their life-chances.

The cost of meeting the MDGs is clearly within the reach of the world community, considering the spectacular growth in global income and technological innovation over the past few decades. Indeed, Jeffrey Sachs (2005: 289–304, 346) – the US economist who heads the Millennium Project – believes that the effort is 'modest' compared to what would have been needed in the past. For instance, while the increase proposed in Official Development Assistance (ODA) to US$195 billion by 2015 might seem considerable, it still only represents a small proportion of the US$1.118 trillion devoted to global military expenditure in 2005 (SIPRI 2006: Ch. 8). Meeting the MDG targets should also reduce the geopolitical insecurity that fuels arms expenditure. The increased ODA needed to meet the targets represents only 0.5 per cent of the rich nations' GDP (UNMP 2005a: 263).

The following section begins with an examination of three elements of well-being central to the MDGs – income, education and health – before exploring regional disparities. Gender inequality, environmental sustainability and participatory development will be dealt with separately in Chapters 9 and 10.

The MDG Challenges

There are additional methodological challenges associated with achieving teleological goals such as the MDGs. They not only require accurate measurements of existing social well-being indicators, but also a detailed projection of future needs. Furthermore, in order to analyse complex patterns of poverty and inequality it is essential that countries present 'disaggregated reporting' that allows comparison between different social groups and geographical regions. However, high-priority MDG countries are invariably those least likely to be able to provide an accurate statistical picture of current needs, due to limited data-gathering capacity or consistent trend data (UN Millennium Project 2005a: 185; Easterly 2002: 65). There are 19 African countries that have failed to hold a national census in the past decade and many of these are MDG-target countries. Even where such censuses are conducted, the quality is compromised by the fact that between 70 to 80 per cent of non-agricultural private actors in Sub-Saharan Africa operate outside the formal sector (UNMP 2005a: 134).

These practical challenges do not change the fact that accurate statistics can be a tool of empowerment for the disadvantaged and progressive development agencies, providing valuable information on government performance. This problem was acknowledged in the Marrakesh Action Plan for Statistics (2004). Statistical indicators of inequality demonstrate the gap between the rich and poor and vividly illustrate the lack of access to services that people in wealthier countries take for granted. The need for statistical representations of inequality will only abate once the basic needs of the poor are fulfilled. The UN Development Programme (UNDP 2003: 134) was clearly addressing the wealthier world when it described the dreams of people in the poorer world: 'a school nearby with teachers who show up to work and with books and pens for students . . . a hand pump that provides safe water and that women and children can walk to easily . . . a local health clinic supplied with drugs and staffed by a doctor and nurse'. The MDGs place responsibilities on the shoulders of the wealthier countries to ensure that these dreams are transformed into reality.

Improving well-being

As mentioned in the previous section, much of the success in poverty alleviation over the past 20 years has been mainly due to the striking developmental successes of China and India, with a combined population of 2.3 billion, or 38 per cent of the world's population. However, these two very large cases cannot be the foundation of progress if many other countries have either regressed or stagnated (Wade 2004). Over the 1990s, poverty increased by eight million people in Latin America and the Caribbean, 14 million in Europe and Central Asia and 82 million in Sub-Saharan Africa (ILO 2004: 44). Despite declining poverty rates, Asia still contains the largest mass – some two-thirds – of the world's poor.

In the last decade of the twentieth century, per capita income fell in 54 countries (UN HDR 2003: 3) and in 21 of those countries a higher percentage of the population was experiencing hunger. Even more alarmingly, in 34 countries life expectancy fell. The Human Development Index (HDI) of 21 countries fell during this period. Falling incomes and HIV/AIDs were among the principal causes behind declining HDI scores (UNDP 2003: 2, 34 and 40).

Among the countries where per capita income fell, 37 per cent were in Sub-Saharan Africa, 31 per cent were in Eastern Europe and the CIS, while the remainder was spread evenly between Latin America and the Caribbean, East Asia and the Pacific and the Arab States. Throughout the world, over 1.2 billion people – 20 per cent of humanity – survive on less than US$1 a day and over 40 per cent on less that US$2 per day. Even the declining proportion of people living in extreme income poverty needs to be tempered by the recognition that world population continued to expand during the 1990s.

Excluding China, more people were hungry at the end of the 1990s than at the beginning, with South Asia and Sub-Saharan Asia possessing the largest proportions of hungry people. In poorer countries, some 800 million people live in persistent hunger and 75 per cent of these people live in rural areas (UNDP 2003: 88). To exacerbate matters, the average size of farms has been declining over the past few decades.

Access to electricity – a service everyone in wealthier countries has come to perceive as essential – is still only provided to two-thirds of the world's population. Rural areas are disproportionately represented among those communities without access to electricity. Even so, over two out of every five inhabitants in the cities of the poorer world live in slums, where access to electricity is often unavailable, irregular or illicit (UN Habitat 2004: 107; see also Davis 2006). The proportion of urban people living in slums rises to over seven out of ten in Sub-Saharan Africa, compared to one in 20 in the richer countries, one in 10 in the CIS and Eastern Europe and one in three in Latin America. Approximately 900 million people live in slums. Globally, the number of people living in cities is estimated to rise to over 60 per cent by the year 2030, irrespective of productivity increases in agriculture and this will add pressure to creaking urban infrastructure in poorer countries (UN Habitat 2004: 108). It has been estimated that some 200 million rural migrants will enter Chinese cities in the decade up to 2010 and it is expected that the population of Chinese cities will increase by an extra 300 million residents during the same decade (*Far Eastern Economic Review* 2003: 24). Raising rural *and* urban incomes among the poorest are therefore priority targets for the MDGs.

Over 75 per cent of children in the poorer world are now enrolled in primary school (ILO 2004: 47). During the 1990s, primary education completion rates increased in the Middle East and North Africa, West Asia and Latin America and the Caribbean, even though they remained low by global standards. On the other hand, primary school completion rates remained stagnant in East Asia and the CIS, although they began at relatively high levels (UNMP 2005a: 23). Enrolments remain lowest in Sub-Saharan Africa and South Asia. Some 115 million still do not attend primary school, and 60 per cent of these are girls. Furthermore, only slightly more than half of those enrolled complete primary school, while the Sub-Saharan African rate drops to one third (ILO 2004: 47; UNDP 2003: 92). For example, two out of every three rural Ghanaians do not have the resources to send their children to school (UNDP 2003: 115). There is much evidence in Africa and South Asia that progress in raising school enrolment figures has been offset by a lowering of the quality of education. In Bangladesh, some educationalists talk of 'schooling without learning' (Rahmen 2000). Between 15 and 25 per cent of the world's adult population is illiterate (UNDP 2003: 92).

International financial institutions such as the IMF and the World Bank that previously supported user fees for educational services during the 1990s are reconsidering their position and recognizing the inequalities that result from user-pay models of educational provision. When budgetary constraints forced the Tanzanian government to cut its education spending, net primary school enrolments declined from 80 per cent to under 60 per cent (UNMP 2005a: 85). The UNDP (2003: 115) noted that 'children have flooded into schools' in cases where countries drop school fees, as has happened in Kenya and Uganda. Despite this, many poor countries do not prioritize education. For example, while Angola allocated 2.7 per cent of its 2001 budget to education, military expenditure consumed 3.1 per cent. The corresponding figures for Sierra Leone were 1 per cent and 3.6 per cent (UNDP 2003: 93). Furthermore, the wealthiest 20 per cent of population within the poorer countries capture far more than their fair share of the education budget (UNDP 2003: 7). Thus, to compound educational inequalities, secondary and higher education receives disproportionately more money per student than primary education, even though the primary sector benefits poorer people more (see also Goldthorpe 1996).

Health outcomes have a flow-on effect to education, income and general economic development. Improved health is a core indicator of human development. It is also a key investment in economic development, increasing workforce productivity and encouraging foreign direct investment (FDI). For instance, during 1998, Zambia lost 1300 teachers to HIV/AIDS, an equivalent of 67 per cent of those trained as teachers that year. Yet 'inequalities in health status and in access to healthcare are pervasive and growing, both among and within countries' (UNMP 2005a: 77).

Some 10 million children die every year from easily preventable illnesses – 30,000 every day (UNDP 2003: 8). Only North Africa, Latin America and the Caribbean and South East Asia are likely to reach the MDG child-mortality targets by 2015 on current trends. During the 1990s, more children died of diarrhoea and sanitation-related disease than all the people who died in armed conflict since 1945 (UNDP 2003: 104). Tuberculosis and malaria between them kill another 3 million people every year. Around 1.1 billion of the world's population make do without safe water and 2.4 billion lack access to improved sanitation (UNDP 2003: 9, 103). Some 42 per cent of Africans do not have access to safe water and three in five lacks basic sanitation (Commission for Africa 2005: 68). During the 1990s, rising levels of urbanization contributed to almost 62 million more urban dwellers lacking access to safe water (UNDP 2003: 104).

There are 42 million people living with HIV/AIDS, 97.6 per cent of whom live in the poorer world. In 2002, there were more people in Sub-Saharan Africa with HIV/AIDS than there were *global* cases six years before. On current predictions for HIV/AIDS prevalence, by the year 2025 Chinese life expectancy will be reduced by 8 years, while the corresponding figures for India and Russia are 13 years and 16 years (UNDP 2003: 43).

Even though people in poorer countries experience worse health than those in wealthier countries, their governments only spend approximately half as much on health expenditure as a percentage of GDP. This translates on a per capita basis to US$1356 in high-income countries, US$125 in upper-middle income countries, US$13 in low-income countries, and US$6 in the poorest (UNDP 2003: 8). Furthermore, less than 10 per cent of medical research is targeted at the diseases that affect the poorest 90 per cent of the world's population (George 2004: 22). While tropical diseases and tuberculosis together account for 11 per cent of the global disease burden, only 1 per cent of new drugs are targeted at these problems. Large pharmaceutical firms do not target the poor, preferring to devote their best medical resources into efforts that are peripheral to the MDGs, such as obesity, baldness and impotence (Rapley 2004: 68; Sachs 2005: 63). The poorer countries make up less than 2 per cent of their total sales (UNDP 2003: 158; see also UNMP 2005a: 229).

Box 7. 3   The African mosaic: a tale of two countries (Uganda and Malawi)

Sub-Saharan Africa is deeply troubled and aggregate data shows worsening poverty and slow growth or no growth. Orthodox economists explain this in terms of the continent's failure to liberalize and seize the advantages of international trade, alongside problems of corruption and governance. Such sweeping generalizations make good bullet-point presentations for policy advocates but they run the danger of disguising the range of processes and experience occurring in different countries and the complex factors that underpin changes in growth, poverty and inequality. A short comparison of two landlocked Anglophone countries – Uganda and Malawi – helps to reveal the diversity of development in Africa.

Back in the mid-1980s both Uganda and Malawi had failed to deliver on their postcolonial promise and had uncertain futures. Malawi was ruled by the dictator Hastings Banda, who controlled the economy and liquidated any political opposition. Civil war in neighbouring Mozambique had cut off its transport link to the sea and driven millions of refugees into the country. Uganda was in chaos; the violence of the Amin years had been followed by the Obote II regime which had not brought stability. But over the late 1980s and early 1990s the two countries' prospects began to look up. In Uganda, Museveni's military victory brought peace to most of the country and promised better governance, but not democracy. In Malawi the Banda regime began to collapse in the early 1990s and in 1994 the country returned to democracy. In both Uganda and Malawi, aid donors and the IFIs promised to finance the development with substantial grants and loans.

However during the 1990s the prospects for the two countries began to diverge. Uganda has experienced relatively high rates of economic growth, averaging out at 3.6 per cent per annum over 1990–2001. By 2001 GNP per capita had reached $1490 (PPP) and income poverty had declined from 56 per cent in 1992 to 35 per cent in 1999. Advances in education and health services and an effective HIV/AIDS prevention campaign fostered social gains and the country's human development index (HDI) rose over the 1990s. The Malawian figures provide a stark contrast. Growth ran at only 1.5 per cent per annum (1990–2001) and stagnated in some of the early years of the new millennium. GNP per capita in 2001 was only $570 (PPP), less than 40 per cent of Uganda's level. The country's HDI dropped in the second half of the 1990s reflecting massive increases in HIV infection and AIDS sufferers and weakening public services.

While economists at the World Bank explained Uganda's success as its 'taking the medicine' of neoliberal economic policies, the reality has been

→

→

much more complex. Liberalizing markets did indeed help to attract some Asian businessmen and industrialists back into the country and boosted agricultural production. However, much of the economic achievement of the 1990s was generated by the high price of coffee beans in the mid-1990s. With the collapse of world coffee prices in more recent years – partly due to the World Bank supporting Vietnam to move 'from a virtual non-producer to become the world's second largest exporter of coffee . . . in 2002' (Kaplinsky 2005: 64) – growth has slowed dramatically and many rural people report a slide back into poverty. On balance Uganda has probably benefited from its greater engagement with the global economy but the well-being of many of its people is vulnerable to coffee price fluctuations and many Ugandans are waiting for development to arrive.

The optimism with which Malawians welcomed democracy and the possibility of policy reform has proved unfounded. By 2004, when President Muluzi stepped down after 10 years in office, corruption, poor public management and drought meant that more then 65 per cent of the population were reported as being poor. Dependence on aid was high, reaching 40 pr cent of GNP in some years and the country had experienced a 'small famine'. Inequality was at high levels – the income of the wealthiest 10 per cent of the population was 22.7 times higher than the poorest 10 per cent. (In Uganda the figure is a more modest 9.9). While it can be argued that the Malawian government has failed to seize the opportunities that globalization presents, it would be quite wrong to argue that Malawi is not participating in globalization. Malawian nurses are migrating to the UK in their hundreds to get jobs with the National Health Service. The extraordinary differences – one might say inequalities – between health sector pay in the UK and Malawi mean that more nurses move to the UK each year than graduate from Malawian nursing colleges. Malawian-trained and financed nurses help to raise life expectancy in the UK while 'back home' hospitals report major staff shortages, and as a result life expectancy reduces each year. Perhaps remittances provide a partial compensation for this new wave of 'brain drain' but they flow to specific families and not to public services that would benefit the population more widely.

This comparison provides only a small illustration of the African mosaic – the different development processes and outcomes that are shaping and reshaping African countries and regions within countries. As Ravallion (2001) advises, when looking at growth, inequality and poverty, we need to 'look beyond averages' and see what is happening to specific groups of people in specific countries.

Source: Ravallion (2001); Government of Malawi (2002); CPRC (2004); Kaplinsky (2005).

The UNDP (2003: 101) has recommended greater emphasis on egalitarianism in health spending, arguing that there is a strong correlation between improved mortality rates and higher public spending on primary health care for the poorest sectors of the population. Yet, in many poor countries, benefit incidence studies consistently reveal that the top two income quintiles of the population – those who can afford private services – receive a much greater share of public expenditure on health than the bottom two quintiles. Furthermore, large health budgets are often necessitated by the failure to control preventative diseases. For example, one out of every two beds in the world's hospitals are occupied by people with water-borne diseases (UNDP 2003: 104). As noted in the previous chapter, the conditionalities imposed by IFIs can pose serious problems for poor countries' health goals (Hertz 2004: 162). The UN Millennium Project (2005a: 201) notes with irony that 'many African countries too poor to invest in AIDS treatment and prevention have been congratulated for successes in macroeconomic stabilization – while life expectancies have turned steeply downward' (see Box 7.3).

Half a million women throughout the world die through complications in pregnancy or childbirth – one every minute – and women in Sub-Saharan Africa are 100 times more likely than women in the wealthier world to die in these circumstances (UNDP 2003: 8). Most of the world remains 'off-track' with respect to maternal mortality goals, and in every poor region maternal mortality remains 'shockingly high' (UNMP 2005a: 2, 24). Chapter 9 will indicate how social relations generate gender inequalities and affect women's well-being.

Health inequalities are also observable across regions, reflecting 'skewed development' (UNDP 2003: 49). For example, in Cambodia, although 83 per cent of the population live in rural areas, only 13 per cent of health workers live rurally (UNDP 2003: 8). Finally, conflict also threatens human development and economic growth. Between 1990 and 2001 – in other words, after the Cold War – an estimated 3.6 million people died as a result of armed conflict, with 90 per cent of casualties listed as civilians, and at least 50 per cent were children (UNDP 2003: 45, 48).

Regional perspectives

The brief regional summaries outlined below illustrate the diversity of developmental experiences across poorer countries. Unless otherwise indicated, all data has been sourced from the *UN Human Development Report 2003* (UNDP 2003) and *Investing in Development* (UNMP 2005a).

East Asia and the Pacific

East Asia has been promoted as the success story of recent global development, despite experiencing a traumatic financial crisis during 1997–9. Economic growth averaged 6 per cent over the 1990s and the percentage of people living below US$1 a day declined from 58 per cent in 1981 to 30.5 per cent in 1990, with a further decrease to 15.6 per cent in 2000 (Sachs 2005: 21). Hunger declined over the 1990s by 6 per cent, leaving just over one in ten suffering hunger. Rural poverty also declined in East Asia between 1990 and 2001 from 30 per cent to 11 per cent. Primary education levels are reaching OECD levels and child mortality continues to fall.

The region's strong development is influenced by China's size and high levels of economic growth. Accounting for 70 per cent of the region's population, it achieved growth rates during the 1990s of 9 per cent per annum, described by the UN Millennium Project as 'nothing short of spectacular'. However, China's form of development coincided with higher incidence of urban poverty, rising from less than 1 per cent in 1984 to 3.4 per cent in 2000. In some rural areas infant mortality has increased, while urban–rural intraregional inequalities have widened (see Box 7.2; Sachs 2005: 165). There are enormous disparities in China. Incomes and social indicators in Shanghai Province are similar to those of Portugal and Greece. By contrast, income and living standards in the western provinces are closer to those of the poorest parts of South Asia.

Poverty in Thailand declined significantly, from 27.2 per cent in 1990 to 9.8 per cent in 2002 and child hunger also declined. These performances, among others, helped eclipse some less impressive economic and human development performances in the region, including the Philippines, Brunei Darussalam, Myanmar, Mongolia and Cambodia. The poorest MDG performances have been in the Pacific Islands – Sub-Saharan Africa is the only region more off-track to meet the MGDs. (For more details, see Beeson 2004; Breslin 2004; Patnaik 1999).

South Asia

South Asia experienced marked progress across most HDI indicators over the past few decades, although some countries (Bangladesh and Bhutan) experienced faster growth and others slower growth (Pakistan). Regardless, the region contains more poor people (430 million) than any other on earth.

Indian development varied by state, with some growing much faster than others, and nationally the proportion living in poverty dropped from 42 per cent to 35 per cent in just eight years up to 2001. However the gap in living standards between rural and urban areas widened (Sachs

2005: 184). Presenting average figures for a large country such as India can give a false impression of what is happening in the country. Some states (for instance, Andra Pradesh, Maharastra, Kamataka and Kerala) have made tremendous economic and social progress, while others (for example, Uttar Pradesh, Bihar and Orissa) are economically stagnant and face fundamental problems of governance (CPRC 2004). A similar situation was found in Nepal where life expectancy can vary by more than 12 years depending on caste status. Sri Lanka has made progress towards the MDGs, especially through high levels of primary school enrolment, low child mortality rates, low maternal mortality rates and improved water and sanitation.

Overall throughout the region, the percentage of people living on US$1 a day fell from 45 per cent to 36.6 per cent during the 1990s. However, one in three live in poverty and lack access to better sanitation; one in four go hungry, one in five children do not attend primary school, and nearly one in ten die before the age of five. It is estimated that only 5 per cent subscribe to telephone services, even though certain South Asian regions – such as Bangalore in India – are central to global telecommunications networks. (For more details, see Wyatt 2004.)

Sub-Saharan Africa

The Sub-Saharan region as a whole has experienced stagnation over the past 20 years, both in terms of economic growth and human development. The UN Department of Economic and Social Affairs (2005) estimates that it is probably *the* most unequal continent, and the UN Millennium Project (2005a: 2) predicts that most of the region is 'on a trajectory to miss most or all of the Goals'. The region's share of world trade has declined from 6 per cent in 1980 to under 2 per cent by the new millennium (Commission for Africa 2005: 21). Life expectancy rates have declined in some countries, with HIV/AIDS taking a particularly heavy toll. Overall, during the 1990s the number of people living below US$1 a day increased from 47.4 per cent to 49 per cent, and 77 per cent survive on less than US$2 a day (UN Department of Economic and Social Affairs 2005). The informal economy absorbs four out of every five non-agricultural workers. One person in three lives in hunger, while one in six dies before the age of five, mostly from treatable diseases such as malaria. Lack of access to medicines and prevention measures remains a barrier to improved health outcomes. Violence accounts for as many African deaths as disease (Commission for Africa 2005: 49, 65). On average, Africans can expect to live only to the age of 46, and that figure is dropping.

The UN and aid donors can point to a number of success stories, such as Ghana, Mozambique and Benin, which have been able to improve health and/or education indicators. Total numbers of primary school enrolments across Africa almost doubled. Improved governance has also been noted in a few instances but, in itself, has been insufficient to alleviate poverty and meet developmental objectives (UNMP 2005a: 146). Poverty interacts with other problems – such as climate, environmental degradation, violence, export-price volatility, skilled out-migration and a weak formal economy – to create a vicious poverty circle. The Commission for Africa (2005: 7) considers the disparity between life in the wealthier countries and the conditions of Africa's poor as the most unacceptable feature of the new millennium. Sub-Saharan Africa has come to symbolize the impoverished face of global inequality. (For more details, see Harrison 2004; Saul and Leys 1999.)

Latin America and the Caribbean

Over the past few decades, Latin America has been able to achieve HDI indicators that approach those of the OECD nations and it boasts the highest average per capita incomes in the poorer world. Despite this high base level, the 1990s were characterized by sluggish economic performance. The region continues to rely on primary commodity exports that face declining long-term relative prices and its manufacturing export successes are concentrated in a limited number of countries, mainly Mexico and Brazil.

During the 1990s, the percentage of people living on less than US$1 a day remained stable, increasing marginally by 0.1 per cent to 11 per cent. During the decade, East Asia outperformed Latin America despite a lower starting point. Unemployment rose from 6.9 per cent in 1993 to 9 per cent in 2002 (UN Department of Economic and Social Affairs 2005). Progress varied considerably by country, with some experiencing greater hunger (such as Cuba) and others reduced hunger (such as Peru) and reduced child mortality (Bolivia and Ecuador). Overall, Central America and the Andean countries are furthest behind the MDG targets, with one in two Nicaraguans living in poverty and almost one in three Salvadoreans. Poverty, and especially severe poverty, is heavily concentrated among Amerindian and indigenous social groups (CPRC 2004). (For more details, see Petras and Veltmeyer 1999; Phillips 2004.)

Central and Eastern Europe, including the CIS

Most post-communist states have failed to turn around the crisis associated with the fall of the centrally planned economies in the 1980s and early 1990s. The transition to market economies has inflicted pain on many, with regional poverty tripling to include one in four people. The number of people living on less than US$1 a day jumped markedly from 6.8 per cent to 20.3 per cent. The region has experienced an increase in

---

Box 7.4   Geographic obstacles facing least developed countries

It is no coincidence that some countries find it difficult to escape their poor status. These are the 'Least Developed Countries', defined as having per capita incomes of less than $US750, and invariably they possess the lowest human development indicators (UNDP 2003: 67). The UN Millennium Project (2005a: 74) identifies a range of structural and geographic factors that inhibit self-sustaining economic development in such cases.

Vulnerabilities take many shapes:

- *Landlocked countries* must rely on the transport infrastructure, port facilities and political stability of neighbouring countries. Among the 30 landlocked countries are also some high-altitude countries that are further disadvantaged by poor transportation and communication systems. The UN Millennium Project (2005: Chapter 15), the UNDP and the ILO all support regionalism as a means of alleviating these difficulties.

- *Small nations* (defined as a population of less than 0.4 million) and small island nations also tend to be disproportionately poor. They are disadvantaged by their small internal markets and high transportation costs. They are also highly exposed to the impacts of global climate change. According to the UNDP (2003: 84) 'countries with larger populations and/or with coastal areas achieved higher economic growth than countries with small populations and/or were inland'.

- *Soil, climate and disease* also discourage economic growth. Farmers in poorer countries must work with depleted soils and can less afford

→

---

child mortality, and life expectancy has dropped in certain countries, including Russia. Regional variation is notable, with the eastern European countries experiencing higher levels of economic and human development, partly assisted by proximity to western European markets. Countries such as Armenia, Azerbaijan, Kyrgyzstan, Moldova and Uzbekistan have moved towards global least-developed country status. Low fertility and regional out-migration is leading to population decline. (For more details, see Menshikov 1999; N. Robinson 2004.)

The Middle East and North Africa
Many Arab countries have been placed in a unique development category due to their high levels of dependence on oil, which remains a high-demand commodity in the global economy. However, control over this resource by a few wealthy families creates disparities in income and human development progress unique in global statistics. The share of

→

chemical fertilizers and nutrient supplements. Indeed, the farm-door price of fertilizers in poorer countries is much higher than in wealthier countries. This further lowers agricultural productivity. Many poorer countries are equatorial and suffer higher tropical disease burdens (see Landes 2002: Chapter 1).

- People in poorer countries are four times more likely to die from *natural disasters* than those in wealthier countries. The Caribbean, Central America, Oceania, south east Asia and south and east Africa tend to be more disaster-prone than other regions and many lack the capacity to deal effectively with emergencies. Throughout the world, regardless of location, the poor suffer disproportionately more from natural disasters (Easterly 2002: 197).

- *Violence* also interacts with environmental degradation, making scarce resources a matter of life and death. Two-thirds of the countries furthest from meeting MDG targets have recently been conflict zones: 'Many of the poorest people in the world live in fragile states where ethnic or geopolitical tensions and vulnerability to conflict or regular natural disasters undermine efforts to achieve the MDGs' (see also UNMP 2005a: 41, 171, 183).

The UN Millennium Project (2005a) stresses that 'geography is not destiny' – geophysical obstacles are not insurmountable. The challenge demands that special assistance, in the form of Official Development Assistance (ODA), be provided to assist poorer countries meet the MDGs.

people in Arab states living on less than US$1 a day rose marginally by 0.1 per cent to 2.2 per cent.

Performance varied throughout the region with some countries (such as Lebanon, and Tunisia) experiencing sustained economic growth while many stagnated. Some countries (such as Kuwait) reduced their proportion of hungry children while others (for example, Yemen) witnessed an increase. Others experienced dramatically higher child mortality rates (such as Iraq) while others achieved a reduction (for example, Egypt). On the whole, however, child mortality rates worsened compared to the richer countries. (For more details, see Bromley 2004.)

* * *

The MDGs recognize the importance of supporting political and governance reforms to help lift each of these regions to basic thresholds in the areas of education and health. However, the UN Millennium Project

(2005a) argues that progress in human development cannot be expected to occur endogenously. Many countries face obstacles that require international cooperation and external support (see Box 7.4). To meet the MDGs, the poorest nations will require assistance to link them to the global economy, in the form of infrastructural aid and access to world markets. Without this outside assistance, the poorest countries will remain within a 'poverty trap' (UNMP 2005a: 29).

Assessing the MDGs as a Developmental Strategy

The principles behind the MDGs have developmental predecessors. However, the way in which they draw on and even synthesize past theory and practice (and apply this to the changing global economic and political environment) all suggest that the developmental challenge has entered a new era. Indeed, the MDGs moved quickly onto 'the centre of the international development agenda' (Vandemoortele 2005: 6) and became 'part of the dominant development discourse' (Shetty 2005: 28).

Criticisms of the MDGs have been varied. Kothari and Minogue (2002: 12) point out that the MDGs themselves signify the 'past failure' of development-as-modernization. On the one hand, the MDGs have been seen by some as lacking ambition, especially in their primary aim to halve global poverty when over a billion people currently survive on less than US$1 per day. Others have argued that the targets will generate 'unrealistic expectations' and oversell the 'efficacy of aid' (Clemens et al., 2004: 4–5). Others focus on the narrow range of indicators used to measure poverty reduction, especially their failure to focus on the creation of decent work, a crucial component of people's participation in social activity and security. Harcourt (2005: 2) also claims that the MDGs' emphasis on quantitative targets reveal a 'technocratic . . . approach to an infinitely complex world'. The danger with a top-down, bureaucratic approach is that important MGDs – such as health – become disconnected from the broader social and political contexts within which they are embedded, including 'globalization, human security, equity, human rights and poverty reduction' (Freedman 2005: 20). Another problem with the technocratic nature of the MDGs is that they can become another form of 'conditionality' imposed by wealthy donor countries onto recipient countries (Sadasivam 2005: 31).

Structuralist critics, such as Paluzzi and Farmer (2005: 12), claim that the MDGs still tend to focus on the 'well-known litany of predictable failings and barriers that exist within any profoundly impoverished country', rather than the 'failed international policies that have perpetuated and contributed to the inequalities from which these problems have emerged'. For example, no poor country can be expected to meet their MDG targets if they continue to be hamstrung by IMF conditionalities, such as social spending restrictions (Sadasivam 2005: 33). The MDGs continue to present poverty as a 'deficit', while structuralists demand that it be seen in the context of how it is experienced – as 'exclusion and voicelessness' as well as 'marginalization' (Freedman 2005: 23). Others compare the vagueness of the performance demanded from the rich world with the precision of the targets for poorer countries, viewing this as a reflection of 'the unequal nature of the global partnership' (White 2006: 382).

More conservative critics consider the MGDs unrealistic and/or question whether the UN can escape from its inconsistent past record of executing developmental plans. Inevitable failure will merely generate more scepticism about international motivation and capability to address global poverty (Easterly 2005). Other sceptics claim that aid provision perpetuates poverty and low levels of economic growth, rather than providing a boost to development. From this perspective, foreign aid remains a 'hand-out' rather than a 'hand-up' (see Box 7.5). Retaining greater faith in neoliberalism, these critics argue that 'trade, not aid' is the panacea for development. Following de Soto (see Chapter 6), still others have argued that the MDGs neglect the vital ingredient that would promote trade among the world's poorest, namely financial and physical capital as well as access to credit (Prosterman 2005: 44).

Easterly (2002: 36–44) has also questioned the teleology inherent in the MDGs, whereby the needs of a country are assessed, the existing resources calculated and the international community supplies the difference (or the 'financing gap'): 'Rather than worrying about how much investment is "needed" to sustain a given growth rate, we should concentrate on strengthening incentives to invest in the future and let the various forms of investment play out as they may.' The 'aid-financed investment fetish' that lies behind the motivation of the international donor community has done more to distort poor economies than improve them and this has also led to the perverse consequence that the worse a country performs, the more help it can expect.

Defenders of the MDGs consider them an 'important frame of reference' for building a more 'decent' and 'fairer' world (ILO 2004: 106; Sachs 2005: 210–15). Any development challenge requires an 'overarching framework' to coordinate international energy (Shetty 2005: 28). To quote Cocks (2003: 293): 'If you don't know where you are going, it does not matter which bus you catch.' Furthermore, the MDGs' quantitative targets can be interpreted as one of their key strengths, allowing their achievements (or lack of) to be monitored more rigorously (Shetty

---

Box 7.5   ODA: problem or panacea?

The UN Millennium Project lists ten 'central problems' with the current operation of Official Development Assistance (ODA):

(1)   lack of consistency with MDGs;
(2)   uncoordinated approach to poor countries' development needs;
(3)   failure to design projects using a long-term horizon;
(4)   lack of technical support to integrate different development projects;
(5)   lack of coordination between donor agencies leading to developmental blindspots, such as enhancing regional cooperation;
(6)   tendency to set goals in line with donor preferences, often leading to the least developed countries receiving a disproportionately low level of ODA;
(7)   inadequate consideration of the MDGs within debt-relief plans;
(8)   poor quality of development finance with consequent cynicism that aid doesn't work;
(9)   failure to consider key MDG goals with positive synergistic effects on development;
(10)   contradictory donor government policies on development and trade.

Source: information from UNMP (2005a: 193–9)

2005: 27; Vandemoortele 2005). They also stress that the MDGs 'must be country owned' and participative, rather than externally managed (UNDP 2003: 30).

Responding to more conservative critics of the MDGs who advance a link between poor governance, corruption and poverty (Easterly 2002: Chapter 12; Kasper 2006), the UN Millennium Project explicitly states that the poor countries themselves are responsible for achieving the MDGs and that the richer countries need to base their support for target countries 'more on performance'. Vandemoortele (2005) has also questioned the emphasis that neoliberals place on trade-led development, arguing that the historical record shows that improved trading performance tends to follow human development rather than spur it on.

An important part of the MDG framework is the responsibility of richer countries to improve the level and quality of Official Development Assistance. ODA refers to grants and concessional loans for the promotion of economic development and welfare for poorer countries from governments of richer countries. It declined over the decade 1990–2001 from an average 0.33 per cent of rich country GNP to 0.22 per cent

(UNDP 2003: 146). This is well short of the 0.7 per cent agreed to in a 1970 UN General Assembly Resolution. Only a handful of European nations have reached this target, including Norway, Sweden, Luxemburg and the Netherlands. Total ODA for 2002 was only around one-quarter of what the world spent on tobacco. To compound matters, the least developed countries experienced the most marked reduction among all ODA recipients, adding weight to the argument that ODA is poorly targeted (UNMP 2005a: 252). The Commission for Africa (2005: 9) also points out that aid sometimes appears to assist the interests of the wealthy countries and large companies as much as it assists poorer countries (see also Hertz 2004: 43–59). Defenders of the MDGs and critics of 'foreign aid skeptics' (see Sachs 2006; Sen 2006a) argue that the purpose of ODA should be to raise infrastructural investment and other human development indicators (or 'merit goods') above the threshold required for self-sustaining development. They believe that existing ODA is uncoordinated and lacking in coherence. Given this, the MDGs provide an opportunity to better harness the world's resources to meet the basic needs of the world's poor. It asks that the standards of governance wealthy donors demand of poorer recipient countries be applied to the quality of donor assistance provided by the wealthy world (see also ILO 2004: 102; Sachs 2005: 276).

The MDGs and neoliberalism

It is instructive to assess the MDGs in the context of the neoliberal developmental trends described in the previous chapter. These efforts focused on promoting economic stability in the poorer world, encouraging fiscal discipline, improving and strengthening governance, while embracing the values of social justice and democratic participation. As noted earlier in this chapter, there is an impressive catalogue of recent success stories and the UNDP (2003: 16) acknowledged that these policies and values are essential for human development. However, the same report also observes that 'this optimistic vision has proven hugely inadequate for hundreds of millions of poor people'. The patchy nature of poverty alleviation also suggests that achieving the MDGs will require more than implementing policies of liberalization. It will involve recognizing that 'structural constraints' exist that 'impede economic growth and human development' (UNDP 2003: 1).

In the context of neoliberal ideas that have shaped so much recent thinking on development, the MDG framework also considers the relationship between private and public investment. The 'mixed economy' model of development that thrived in the early postwar period was superseded during the 1980s with a more entrepreneurial model that discouraged state interference in the economy and the provision of social services. This move coincided with reduced government funding, deteriorating state services and external pressure from IFIs to liberalize economies (UNDP 2003: 116).

While encouraging private investment, the MDG framework also recognizes that countries that cannot reach the poverty threshold will fail to attract foreign capital. The UN Millennium Project (2005a: 31, 46) maintains that sustained growth demands public spending in social services and infrastructure, research, housing, information technologies and environmental regulation. These investments are seen as complementary to private investment rather than competitive. According to the UN Millennium Project (2005a), governments must be responsible for promoting entrepreneurship, through encouraging rule of law, improving infrastructure and providing a stable microeconomic environment. It considers that an efficient market economy is underpinned by strong and effective government support.

The UNDP (2003) also distances itself from the neoliberal suggestion that economic growth will automatically provide the platform for progress in human development. MDG supporters claim that some forms of private economic activities can benefit individuals while imposing high social costs (or externalities). For instance, contrary to the neoliberal claim that environmental consciousness follows economic growth (see Lomborg 2003), the UN Development Programme (2003: 127) claims that 'environmental improvements cannot be deferred until rising incomes make more resources available for environmental protection'. As a result, it calls for selective use of 'regulation and corrective taxation . . . to align private and public incentives with the need for environmental protection' (UNDP 2003: 129).

The UN Millennium Project also points out that the market mechanism is not designed to cater for the needs of the poor, but rather to maximize returns on investment. Public intervention and subsidies are needed to lift poor communities out of poverty and strengthen their participation in the market. This position bears a strong resemblance to the policy reforms that dominated western countries in the wake of the Second World War. The UN Millennium Project returns to the idea of a global welfare state designed to promote full global citizenship (see UNMP 2005a: 141).

Directly responding to the 'trade, not aid' criticism of the MDGs, the UN Millennium Project (UNMP 2005a: 211) accepts that global trade can act as a catalyst for development, but considers the slogan as 'misguided'. The UN Development Programme (UNDP 2003: 156) also acknowledges the advantages of more open markets, while retaining the urgent need for a global developmental strategy:

Though estimates vary of the benefits to poor countries from trade liberalization in rich countries, most show huge gains. Just the static effects – those taking the present economic structure of poor countries – would be about the same as current levels of foreign aid. This does not mean that trade liberalization could or should be substituted for aid. For the top and high priority countries, aid is critical for immediate tackling the structural constraints to achieving the MDGs. For them the gains from trade will take more time to realize as they develop the capacity to respond to new opportunities.

The Millennium Project recommends that poor countries adopt a triple-pronged approach to trade and development: actively pursue international trade opportunities, demand access to rich country markets, while simultaneously demanding more effective aid to help alleviate internal supply-side production blockages.

The MDGs therefore retain a strong commitment to development-as-economic-growth, which is seen as the most effective means of 'pulling poor people above the income poverty line' (UNDP 2003: 68). However, in line with more strident criticism levelled at the architects of global liberalization, the UN Development Programme (UNDP 2003: 24) also argues that the rising tide of economic growth does not *automatically* 'raise all boats'. The attack on global poverty must be 'multi-pronged'.

The UN Millennium Project (2005a: 6, 28) argues that sole reliance on market forces will not 'rescue the village'. As a consequence, it promotes human development *and* economic growth and argues that it is misleading to emphasize 'the level of economic growth needed to achieve the Goals in a country'. Reflecting on the experiences of fiscal constraint imposed by the IMF in poorer countries over the past two decades, the UN Development Programme (UNDP 2003: 107–8) notes that efforts to tackle budget deficits have often occurred at the expense of public spending, rather than 'mobilising tax and non-tax revenues'. Budget cuts affect the poor more than the wealthy. Even where structural obstacles to development are either absent or have been dismantled, experience from recent high-growth countries such as China and Brazil has shown that growth can have a differential regional impact and can increase inequalities between different social categories. To minimize such gaps, the UN Millennium Project (UNMP 2005a: 43) advises that major infrastructural, social and government investments 'get channeled to lagging regions, including slums, and to social groups excluded from the political process and economic benefits'.

The MDGs and modernization theory

If the principles underlying the MDGs reject the more extreme policies of neoliberalism, they can also be interpreted as a millennial reassertion of modernization theory. The UN Millennium Project (2005a: 139) refers to development as a 'ladder' and one of the key purposes of the MDGs is to raise the poorest countries onto the 'first rung' (see also Sachs 2005: 24). Exogenous actors can perform a crucial role in this process through diffusing modernity. According to the UN Millennium Project, the entry of multinational firms into poorer countries helps to establish local 'business ecosystems' through encouraging local supply chains. This 'networking' helps spread 'technologies and skills, bringing local firms into the formal economy, and increasing market opportunities for local suppliers'. Yet the MDG framework also acknowledges that these exogenous forces will only arrive once the basic infrastructural and human capital is established. ODA remains crucial for this early step. Sachs (2005: 366–7) argues that if the conditions for self-sustaining growth are to be universalized, then poorer countries require this exogenous assistance:

> It is not surprising . . . that the rich get richer in a continuing cycle of endogenous growth, whereas the poorest of the poor are often left outside of this virtuous circle. When their needs are specific by virtue of particular diseases, or crops, or ecological conditions their problems are bypassed by global science. Therefore, a special effort of world science, led by global scientific research centers of governments, academia, and industry, must commit specifically to addressing the unmet challenges of the poor.

The UN Development Programme (UNDP 2003: 18) also claims that poverty alleviation involves reaching critical thresholds of human and economic development – reminiscent of Rostow's 'preconditions for take-off'. These thresholds – 'of health, education, infrastructure and governance' generate the momentum 'to achieve take-off to sustained economic growth'. It identifies six 'policy clusters' to raise countries to this take-off stage: helping small farmers to improve agricultural productivity; investment in infrastructure to open market opportunities; investment in industrial development to spur non-traditional private activity; promoting human rights and social equity in order to overcome discriminatory and anti-development values; promoting environmental sustainability; and support from exogenous donors. The report reiterates that improved public health and education are 'important for a later take-off in private activities', while donor assistance is also 'pivotal' to reach the 'take-off threshold' for infrastructure. It also warns that unless gender and ethnic equality is practised from the beginning, then these groups will fail to benefit when 'growth begins to take-off' (UNDP 2003: 19). Donor assistance and foreign investment are seen within the MDG framework as essential components of reversing the vicious circle through providing 'the financing for economic take-off'. Echoing Rostow's optimism, the UN Development Programme (2003: 178) believes that 'take-off can be achieved within a generation'. The metaphorical ladders and 'take-off' suggest a predetermined course set by earlier prototypes.

The UN Millennium Project (2005a: 25) also draws on earlier modernization sociologists in their discussion of 'integrated development', where human, economic and political variables are inserted into the developmental equation at the beginning of the process in order to 'achieve a take-off to sustained economic growth and development'. The MDGs are not only goals – they are also means of effective and human-centred development. Or, in the words of the UN Millennium Project (UNMP 2005a: 29, 50), they are 'capital inputs' into the developmental process, while simultaneously being 'ends in themselves'. A wide range of development goals need to be implemented simultaneously rather than sequentially, from gender equality through to environmental sustainability (UNDP 2003: 78, 125). The language of development articulated by the UN Development Programme builds on the optimism of the 'dynamic equilibrium' that modernization theory outlined whereby developments in one social field can help generate or diffuse change in other areas.

Following Sen (2001), the MDGs are designed as constitutive parts of the successful development process *as well as* development outcomes. A virtuous circle can be generated when human development boosts economic development, which in turn feeds back into resources for further human development. Alternatively, a vicious circle can develop when low levels of well-being translate into investment withdrawal and reduced resources for human development, such as low savings, reduced tax revenue, difficulty attracting outside investment, social and armed conflict, outmigration of skilled labour, high birth rates, high mortality rates and poor environmental conditions. This vicious circle is responsible for much of the stalled regional development described in the previous section. Furthermore, as the links between health and education suggest, these elements of human development are synergistic. For example, gender equality and improved sexual and reproductive health contribute to advancing all the MDGs (UNMP 2005a: 82–3, 93–4).

The nature of the circle is influenced by what the UN Development Programme (UNDP 2003: 69) calls 'agency and equity'. The UN Millennium Project (UNMP 2005a: 99) claims that good governance, transparency and public-sector management have suffered over the past couple of decades in poorer countries as a result of severe financial constraints. The MDGs require rebuilding the capacity of the poorer states, which in turn promotes greater cooperation and dialogue with civil society. This issue of participation is one which the UN Millennium Project (UNMP 2005a: 100) claims most development theories have failed to emphasize. As the UN Development Programme (UNDP 2003: 69) points out, armed with political and civil rights, the poor 'can be more effective in pressing for policies that create social and economic opportunities' (see Chapter 10).

The MDGs and dependency theory

While the language of the UN Millennium Project closely resembles modernization theory, elements of the dependency critique are also present. This is most apparent in the discussion of 'structural constraints' as well as the recognition that the most affluent parts of the world continue to enrich themselves while the poorest parts are becoming poorer. In addition, there is clear recognition that at least some of the developmental problems of the poorer countries have exogenous roots. For instance, the UN Millennium Project (UNMP 2005a: 113–14) recognizes that past development projects were compromised by the geopolitical and strategic interests of powerful donors where funds were often placed in the hands of 'kleptocracies' friendly to rich countries: 'Public officials and the broader public tend to forget the role their countries played in supporting truly corrupt politicians and political structures, while at the same time criticising the developing countries of today for not having developed better institutions.'

One of the structural constraints that the MDG framework recognizes is that most of the poorest nations are heavily reliant on exporting a small range of primary commodities. Since the end of the Cold War, these poorest countries have continued to experience a steady decline in the relative or absolute price of their principal commodities. This feature of the global division of labour was an important platform of dependency theory, which argued that international terms of trade have generally worked against the periphery. Of the 17 Sub-Saharan nations identified as top and high priority MDG nations, 14 remain heavily reliant on primary commodities for exports (UNDP 2003: 45). Echoing earlier dependency criticism, the UN Millennium Project (2005a: 212) concedes that the international trading system has historically 'served the interests of developed counties' and that the poorer countries have had little input into its institutional design.

Rejecting any simple correlation between international trade and economic growth, the UN Development Programme (UNDP 2003: 70) acknowledges the complex structural relations embedded within trading relations: 'Some forms of globalization help produce economic growth, but some do not. Success or failure is related less to a country's initial income than to the structure of its exports.' Drawing on data from the period 1980–98 for a set of non-oil-producing developing countries, it reported that 24 relied on exported manufactured goods while 61 mainly exported primary commodities (UNDP 2003: 70–1, 83). Significantly, only one of the manufacturing developing nations experienced negative growth, compared with over half (32 countries) of the primary commodity producers (see also UNMP 2005a: 221).

However, the policy prescriptions of the MDG strategy clearly reject the economic isolationist implications of earlier dependency theorists. The road to the market cannot be avoided if poorer countries aspire to sustained economic development. This requires assistance from wealthier donor nations combined with policy reforms initiated by the wealthier countries, including expanding trade with the poorer world, renegotiating or cancelling the debt of highly indebted poor countries (HIPCs) and increasing poor-country access to leading-edge technologies. This would involve a reversal of recent trends in the relationship between the rich and poor countries which have been characterized by lower levels of ODA from the wealthier to the poorer countries, continuing debt overhang and high trade barriers against poorer countries' products.

The UN Development Programme (UNDP 2003: 12, 155) admonishes the OECD countries for continuing to place tariffs on manufactured goods from the poorer countries at four times the level of those from other wealthy countries. Rich-country protectionism continues to discriminate against the product sectors in which poorer countries have a competitive advantage, such as agriculture and labour-intensive manufacturing (UNDP 2003: 154). Agricultural subsidies in the OECD countries are six times greater than the amount of official aid they supply to the poorer world, amounting to US$311 billion in 2002 (2003: 12, 92). The combined value of rich-country agricultural subsidies (US$311 billion) is US$10 billion higher than the GDP of the whole of Sub-Saharan Africa. Indeed, each EU cow in 2000 received US$913 worth of subsidies compared to US$8 for each Sub-Saharan human being. Japan's equivalent bovine–human ratio was US$2700 to US$1.47 (Commission for Africa 2005: 6–7; UNDP 2003: 155).

The export subsidies of the wealthier countries not only protect internal markets, but have also had a devastating impact on the industries of poor countries, destroying efficient cotton, dairy, fruit and sugar industries through flooding their markets. Furthermore, most subsidies benefit the wealthiest producers in the rich countries (UNDP 2003: 156). The

MDG framework suggests that much of the history of relations between the richer and the poorer countries has involved hindering development rather than assistance. Where the framework departs from more radical dependency theories is in its rejection of the claim that exploitation is inherent within the process of capitalist development.

The UN Development Programme (UNDP 2003: 145) comes closest to a dependency perspective when it acknowledges that 'poor countries face constraints that can only be eased through policy changes in rich countries'. Even when 'developing', as noted earlier, their structural position operates against catching up with the wealthiest nations, especially as the market rewards the most efficient:

> Today's highly competitive global markets make export diversification difficult for countries with low human development. With open markets, capital, technological and human resource requirements have increased. International buyers of commodities demand high reliability and quality from suppliers in developing countries. These trends place a great premium on knowledge, skills and flexibility. They also put pressure on the poorest countries – which have the least skills, savings and capacity to adapt to changing environments.   (UNDP 2003: 154; see also UNMP 2005a: 221)

Compounding the technological and skills gap between the wealthier and the poorer world is the 'brain drain', whereby skilled people in short supply in poorer countries migrate to the wealthier countries. The UN Millennium Project (UNMP 2005a: 102) has warned that 'rich countries have a responsibility not to fill their human resource gaps by draining the professional work forces of developing countries through aggressive recruiting' (see also ILO 2004). Some 70,000 skilled Africans migrate to the wealthier world each year (Commission for Africa 2005: 20, 40) and there are more Sierra Leonean doctors in Chicago than in Sierra Leone.

Overall – to return to our discussion in Chapter 2 – these structural constraints allow the UN Millennium Project to view the poorer countries as the 'deserving poor' and they therefore merit global assistance. The MDG framework provides hope for a development policy that combines 'growth with redistribution'. For example, the UN Development Programme (UNDP 2003: 17) acknowledges that 'economic growth reduces income poverty most when initial income inequality is narrow'. Unless 'persistent income inequality is dealt with, it may limit the benefits of economic growth for poverty reduction' and it recommends that 'policies should focus on closing the wealth divides within countries' (UNDP 2003: 49; see also UNDP 2005: Ch. 2). The link between higher growth and reduced poverty is strongly influenced by structural and geographic factors, but it is also mediated by policy choice. For instance, the Indian state of Kerala boasts health status roughly equivalent to that of the USA, despite the former having a GNP per capita of one per cent of the latter. Infant mortality rates in Cuba mirror those of the USA, despite Cuba's much lower GNP per capita and a less liberal economic system. The MDG challenge involves harnessing investment in physical infrastructure, human capital and human rights with market-oriented policies that encourage exogenous capital and technological transfer.

Drawing on the experience of the past 20 years of mixed development results around the globe, the MDGs emphasize 'human development' rather than economic growth, while at the same time placing a 'spotlight' on the objectives of the 'elimination of poverty, the provision of employment, the reduction of inequality and the progressive realization and guarantee of human rights' (UNDP 2003: 143). To tackle poverty and inequality, the range of simultaneous interventions needed is broad, and the targeting of specific needs of the poorest is crucial (see also Commission for Africa 2005: 21).

Given the previous practices of wealthier nations, and their current ODA practices, it is understandable that the UN Millennium Project (UNMP 2005a: 202) still could consider in 2005 that 'the notion of taking the Goals seriously remains highly unorthodox among development practitioners'. To remedy this, development principles must be more needs-based and teleological, ensuring that development efforts 'start with the MDG targets and work back from them, asking what needs to be done by 2015 and what constraints need to be overcome' (UNMP 2005a: 207). Returning to the earlier developmental motivator of enlightened self-interest, the UN Millennium Project warns that the 'danger of inaction are tremendous, not only in lives lost and opportunities foregone, but also in threatening the security of everyone' (UNMP 2005a: 258, 263). Historians of development theory and practice might complain that they have heard it all before, but they cannot deny the scale of the problem still facing the development challenge. To quote the ILO (2004: 133), it is the 'abiding challenge of the twenty-first century' – an abiding challenge inherited from the twentieth century.

Chapter 8

Globalization and Inequality

The Components of Globalization

Global Visions

Globalization and the State

Mapping Globalization

During the 1990s, the concept of globalization became ubiquitous. It elicited the widest variety of responses, from those who hailed it as the harbinger of universal fortune to those who thought it forewarned the four horsemen of the Apocalypse. It cut across left/right boundaries and lent its name to the largest anti-systemic mass movement of the contemporary era. It remains a 'defining issue' for the the twenty-first century (Bhagwati 2005: 3). This chapter begins by defining the constituent features of globalization; before going on to examine how various writers understand its significance. It then explores the impact of globalization on cultural practices and on the state, before attempting to 'map' different approaches to globalization.

The Components of Globalization

Whether the assembly of the component parts of globalization was a result of design or happenstance remains a matter of some controversy, but most commentators acknowledge that globalization has introduced new questions into the field of development studies. These components came together at the same time as the long postwar economic boom was coming to an end in the early 1970s. In wealthier countries profit rates were declining, inflation and unemployment levels were rising and the interventionist state was experiencing a growing fiscal crisis (Brenner 1998; Mandel 1980).

A series of *micro-electronic-related technological innovations* also began to transform production, distribution and communication processes. Nowhere was this technological shift more apparent than in the expanded power and capacity of computers. In the late 1940s, IBM's chief had predicted that there was a world market for perhaps *five* computers (Margolis 2000). From the 1970s onwards, computers and robotics were beginning to made deep inroads into industrial processes, allowing firms to increase productivity and shed labour. Drawing on organizational developments from Japan, manufacturing firms increasingly looked at how these new technologies could restructure their business operations (Lipietz 1987).

In addition, the use of information technology to access records and control information on workers, clients and citizens began to alter the way business services operated, from payroll calculation to benefit payments and from banking services to telephony. By the end of the 1980s, personal computers were beginning to move into domestic residences and during the 1990s the internet expanded exponentially. For those connected to this global virtual web, the world suddenly became much smaller.

For enterprises, information technology enhanced sales monitoring and service capacity, enabling firms to track production-to-customer chains more accurately and relay orders almost instantaneously. As soon as the fax machine had become an essential tool for conducting business, it was superseded by on-line ordering systems developed by large corporate customers. Organizational technologies – such as just-in-time management systems – could be combined with computerized machinery to create 'leaner' and more flexible production processes (Piore and Sabel 1984).

The relationship between technological change and globalization was mediated by policy changes, including *financial deregulation*. Chapter 5 pointed out that during the early postwar period, national governments used the fiscal powers of the state to stabilize national economies and encourage high levels of local employment. However, by the 1970s, faith in the ability of the state to stimulate the economy was undermined by growing inflation and unemployment. Central banks started to deregulate their currencies and financial systems, opening up local markets to global trade in currencies and stocks (ILO 2004: 27; Reich 1992; Tabb 2004).

International financial transactions have multiplied as financial capital has become increasingly mobile. Micro-electronic innovations have turned national financial markets into components of a global network, allowing firms to speculate 24 hours a day on currency, stock and bond movements. This 'paper' capital might appear to be detached from productive activity, except that capital flight can have adverse consequences for local economies, as the 1997 Asian financial crisis demonstrated. In addition, currency traders often boast that their speculative activity is equivalent to a plebiscite on the performance of national governments. As one US banking CEO declared:

> global capital markets can have a big say in determining how long before a poorly performing government is forced to reform or is turned from office. Institutional investors in global capital markets conduct a constant plebiscite on political and economic policies and developments in the numerous nation-states of the world.   (Jordan 1999)

The very threat of capital withdrawal can send fear through local markets and affect the credit rating of governments (Held and McGrew 2002: 23; Martin and Schumann 1997).

The *heightened mobility of production capital* has been another constituent part of globalization. Technological innovations improved workers' productivity but more importantly they also opened up the option of transferring production facilities to more profitable locations. During the 1970s, large corporations began to shift their labour-intensive activities to a select group of poorer countries where local governments held wages low enough to compensate for higher transportation costs (Lipietz 1987). This 'new international division of labour' lifted the economic status of the NICs while also posing a new definitional challenge for those who defined the 'core' as the *industrialized* world (Frank 1984; Harris 1987).

By the beginning of the twenty-first century, it had become increasingly difficult to determine the country of origin of many products. Firms can now source, assemble and distribute components and products from a variety of countries. This global activity has been enhanced by the work of IFIs (discussed in Chapter 6), which has encouraged growing trade liberalization. To foster local industry, employment and other development objectives, national governments previously relied on protection measures – such as tariffs and quotas. Under the more deregulated global environment promoted by the WTO, the global market dictates where goods are produced. Governments are now more restricted in designing industry and development policy, and must endeavour to create a more hospitable environment for attracting foreign direct investment.

Another important component of the process of globalization is the *growth of transnational corporations* (TNCs). By the beginning of the twenty-first century, TNCs accounted for two-thirds of world trade and now constitute half of the 100 largest economic entities in the world (ILO 2004: 32). Their company boards determine where capital momentarily rests. Global-sourcing firms predate the contemporary era

– organizations such as the Dutch East India Company even character-ized the early modern mercantile capitalist era. However, physical and regulatory restrictions usually made these firms *multi*national, in the sense that it was more convenient to establish a local plant, engage in local production and then either distribute products locally or export to different parts of the world.

After the Second World War, multinational firms continued to operate plants around the world, but source, assemble and market locally. However, improvements in transportation, communication, trade and financial liberalization now allow these firms to source their various components from around the globe, assemble at the most convenient location and market the products globally. William Robinson (2004: 54, 55) distinguishes between the older process of 'internationalization' and the contemporary global phase of 'transnationalization', where 'national capitals fuse with other internationalizing national capitals in a process of cross-border interpenetration that disembeds them from their nations and locates them in new supranational space opening up under the global economy'. TNCs embody these new transnationalized chains of production through their coordinating role in global commerce.

Many commentators argue that this process of globalization is primarily the geographic expansion of capitalist relations rather than a qualitatively new 'global' epoch. For example, Panitch and Gindin (2004: 3) define globalization as 'the spread of capitalist social rela-tions to every corner of the world', while William Robinson (2004: 2, 6) also sees globalization as 'the near culmination of a centuries-long process of the spread of capitalist production around the world'. Comeliau (2002: 126) is more cautious on whether globalization involves the ongoing systemic stability of capitalism or a structural shift, suggesting that it represents both the 'acceleration of an already existing logic' and an 'entirely new phenomenon in the history of humanity'. This circumspection illustrates the theoretical dilemmas researchers face when coming to grips with the concept of globalization.

Others link this geographic expansion with the deepening of capitalist relations, whereby the system not only conquers more physical space, but also colonizes more areas of everyday life. This can refer to such varied phenomena as the privatization of social services (from public transport, education and healthcare) through to the commodification of personal services that were previously conducted outside the market sphere. From this perspective, neoliberalism has increasingly colonized our dreams and desires, forcing people to consume more in order to identify themselves with images that can only be realized through ever-expanding income or personal debt (Hamilton and Denniss 2005).

Adopting this expansionist approach to globalization, Wallerstein

(2002: 170–1) has argued that it will eventually encounter ecological, economic and political limits. The 'deruralization' of the world will inevitably increase the cost of labour while ecological exhaustion will increase the cost of inputs. Demands for social services will increase the tax burden on the economic system to a point where there will be 'a massive long-term structural squeeze on profits from production'. Following Marx, Wallerstein views globalization as a process of ongoing expansion, followed by collapse due to internal social, economic, ecological and psychological pressures.

An alternative stance on globalization focuses on the differential access that people have to markets, rather than inequalities and contradictions generated by capitalist expansion and exploitation. Norberg (2003: 154), for example, argues that global inequalities are engendered by the *failure* to access the global market. Any lingering inequalities in the world today are caused by the failure of some countries to adopt capitalism. Unequal distribution of wealth 'is due to the uneven distribution of capitalism'. Capitalism does cause inequality, but mainly through blessing those who accept its market discipline. Overcoming inequality therefore involves expanding the scope of market forces and liberal regimes.

Against the dominant interpretation of globalization as an expansionary logic, Hoogvelt (1997: 67) has agued that while the developmental project of the postwar era was marked by outward growth, this new era signals the 'implosion' of the system. If the relationship between the core and the periphery during the earlier era was characterized by 'structural exploitation', globalization has now made certain parts of the world 'structurally irrelevant': 'Rather than being an *expansive* process, the present process of globalization appears to be an *imploding* or *shrinking* one' (Hoogvelt 1997: xiv). Trends in capital flows provide evidence for this implosion. Before the Second World War, the poorer countries accounted for some four-fifths of all foreign direct investment. By the 1980s, most FDI took place between the wealthier countries (Robinson 2004: 57).

The marginalized might still be found overwhelmingly in the regions of Asia, Africa and Latin America, but they are not restricted to specific geographic spaces (ILO 2004: 25–7, 35). For example, in his examination of the socio-economic transformation of Los Angeles since the 1960s, Soja (1989: 215) refers to the growing poverty amid extravagant wealth within the city as the 'peripheralization of the core'. Many social groups within the wealthier countries are also faced with structural irrelevance. The high-income countries are experiencing a 'thickening' or deepening of market relations, but these same forces of consumerism touch more lightly poorer people within the richer world as well as poorer countries.

This poses a different set of questions about global inequality, premised on *access to markets* rather than *exploitation by capitalism*. A new 'periphery' is characterized more by marginalization rather than exploitation. Is it the case, Hoogvelt asks, that 'in the turmoil of the present crisis a new stage of capitalism is fermenting in the core of the system, one in which the geographic core–periphery polarization is being replaced by a core–periphery polarization that cuts across territorial boundaries and geographic regions?' (Hoogvelt 1997: 66). Castells (1998) answers in the affirmative, labelling this social location the 'Fourth World', while Hirst and Thompson (1996) refer to it as the 'written off'. George (2004: 5–6) also notes the tendency for entire populations to become 'superfluous' and laments that whereas 'progressives used to rail against "exploitation", today it's almost a privilege to be exploited – at least you still have a job and a wage'.

The process of globalization reinforces the argument against development as a linear process. Capital can arrive and withdraw from a location, set up or close shop, build communities or have them written off the map. This is not inconsistent with Marx's insight into capitalist development as 'combined and uneven' and Schumpeter's (1975: 82–5) description of 'the perennial gale of creative destruction'. However, combined and even development poses a further question concerning whether the current state of marginalization described by Hoogvelt is itself a temporary phenomenon that will be overcome as capitalist competition encourages capital to move towards today's marginalized areas. Relationships of inequality are neither fixed nor frozen – cores and peripheries become increasingly unstable, and this affects the way people experience their position in the world.

Global Visions

When our idea of rapid transportation was a wind-powered sailing vessel travelling at a maximum of 15 kilometres per hour, the circumference of the globe was rather difficult for the mind to capture. Once mass air-travel could reduce a trip half-way across the world to under 24 hours, not only did a person have a greater chance of directly experiencing the world in all its cultural and physical diversity, it also became possible to understand 'the world-as-a-whole' (Harvey 1989; Robertson 1990). This idea of the world-as-a-whole was boosted enormously by satellite images of Planet Earth. The space race – another arena of military struggle between the Cold War rivals – ironically fostered the realization that humanity inhabited *one* world, rather than a capitalist or communist or third world.

Innovations in transportation and communication have resulted in the 'annihilation of space through time' (Harvey 1989). Yet, if globalization is defined by a series of leaps in technological innovation where our consciousness of the world-as-a-whole gradually expands, then it is hardly a new phenomenon. Indeed, Petras (1996: 59) has stated that 'globalization began in 1492', referring to the conquest of the New World and more pointedly to its connection with European colonialism. Other observers have noted that the extent of foreign capital investment and the global movement of immigration were actually higher in the immediate pre-First World War period than at the beginning of the twentieth-first century (Weiss 1998).

The writers of the European Enlightenment spoke of an emerging global consciousness with great confidence. For example, Turgot (1727–81), in his *Philosophical Review of the Successive Advances of the Human Mind* (1750), calculated that progress was measured in the advance of a global civilization:

> the human race, considered over the period since its origin, appears to the eye of a philosopher as a vast whole, which itself, like each individual, has its infancy and advancement . . . [Imperceptibly] manners are softened, the human mind becomes more enlightened, and separate nations are brought closer to one another. Finally commercial and political ties unite all parts of the globe, and the whole human race, through alternate periods of rest and unrest, of weal and woe, goes on advancing, although at a slow pace, towards greater perfection. (quoted in Rist 1999: 37)

Less than a hundred years later, Karl Marx described his age in a way that was consistent with Turgot, although he identified the capitalist class as the unwitting bearers of global consciousness:

> The bourgeoisie has, through its exploitation of the world market, given a cosmopolitan character to production and consumption in every country. . . . All old-established national industries have been destroyed or are daily being destroyed. They are dislodged by new industries, whose introduction becomes a life and death question for all civilized nations, by industries that no longer work up indigenous raw material, but raw material drawn from the remotest zones; industries whose products are consumed, not only at home, but in every quarter of the globe. In place of the old local and national seclusion and self-sufficiency, we have . . . universal inter-dependence of nations. (Marx and Engels 1969)

For Marx, the dynamics of the capitalist system created this consciousness of the world-as-a-whole. In his vision, all that remained was for the 'universal proletariat' to remove the exploitative shell of this social system and remake the world after its own image. This was why the worldwide workers' movement was named the 'Internationale'.

Fast-forwarding another hundred years – an expression only a technological contemporary could understand – to the mid-twentieth century, modernization theorists also generated their own unique take on globalization, charting social change as the process whereby all societies moved from a traditional phase to a modern phase. In this prediction, there is a universalizing tendency inherent in the process of modernization, as all nations emulate the United States of America. Dependency theorists also argued that the most appropriate way to understand modern capitalism was to analyse 'accumulation on a world scale' (Amin 1974).

Each of these theoretical frameworks hints at the emergence of a global consciousness. However, there are two senses in which the contemporary awareness is unique. First, these historical statements were predictions and, for all their remarkable insight, the process of global connectedness did not unfold in the manner anticipated. Commentators at the beginning of the twenty-first century, like Minerva's owl, have the luxury of interpreting the landscape of history in all its light. With hindsight, it is possible to know more about how globalization actually proceeded compared to early speculation (see Rist 1999: 211). Yet despite this hindsight, our uncertainty over future development seems greater now than ever before.

If the ability to envisage globalization is not new, and if global processes are a constituent part of the process of modernity, then what is unique is a more reflexive awareness of the world as an interconnected network. Robertson (1992: 8) defines globalization as not only a 'compression of the world', but also 'the intensification of the consciousness of the world as a whole'. In other words, globalization has 'moved to the level of consciousness' (Hoogvelt 1997: 117). This marks a new stage in the ongoing process of globalization, claims Hoogvelt (1997: 121). There is a greater appreciation of how global processes affect local possibilities. As an example of this shift in global consciousness, Hoogvelt (1997: 124) points to increasingly mobile productive capital. Once firms are able move their facilities across the globe – looking to settle lightly in an environment with the lowest costs before taking off to more competitive climes – this very possibility forces a global 'discipline' on workers, whose will is bent by the TINA principle into accepting that it is 'natural' that a firm would choose to move to more congenial regions.

Hoogvelt (1997: 125) concludes that 'while global competition has created the structural conditions for the emergence of a global market discipline, it is time–space compression that creates the shared phenomenal world that supports and reproduces this discipline on a daily basis'. This captures how the reflexivity of individuals becomes a constituent part of the reproduction of global socio-economic relations. What is unique about the contemporary age is the extent to which this global reflexivity has become a mass phenomenon. From the perspective of development studies, it distinguishes between the older political economy that is 'driven by the logic of capitalism' and the contemporary era where the consciousness of this logic steers the system. When people are aware that global production, consumption and distributive flows affect their own fortunes, this 'shared phenomenal world' impacts on the way they see themselves as well as shaping their responses.

In the late-twentieth century, satellites were linked to other technological innovations to produce a media-saturated environment. This allowed people to remain in one locality and yet have an experience of the world's diversity beamed into their living rooms through television or internet access. The global consciousness of the contemporary mind 'is provided by a technology originally associated with top–down surveillance and a Cold War military history of the space race and satellite development' (Little 2004: 3). Yet, ironically this global reach also threatens the very diversity that people can now appreciate. This 'shared phenomenon' world raises questions about the relationship between culture and globalization. Has globalization resulted in a convergence of cultures and does this promote greater equality? Holton (2000) has identified three distinct approaches to the cultural impact of globalization: homogenization, polarization and hybridization.

There are optimistic and pessimistic versions of the *homogenization* thesis. The optimistic version states that the technological innovations generated by capitalist competition have had beneficial results wherever modern culture has taken hold (Friedman 2006). Following modernization theory, it argues that inequality is a result of being marginalized from these processes and the best means to overcome poverty and close the inequality gap is to ensure that as many people as possible have access to the modern capitalist market (Norberg 2003). As societies adopt modern methods, their culture inevitably adapts to the changes and therefore cultural homogenization proceeds through emulating modern (western) values.

Homogenization by definition promotes an equality of sorts. It can be viewed as a move towards equalizing life-chances and improving opportunities regardless of origin. However, it is possible to regard this monocultural equality as a form of discrimination against those who practise other cultural belief systems (see Thompson 1993). Supporters of homogenous equality tend to regard multiculturalism with suspicion, opposing it on the grounds that it perpetuates a 'culture of poverty' among those outside the mainstream culture and limits opportunities for advancement. Fukuyama (2002) also presents an optimistic version of the homogenization thesis, arguing that western liberalism is the only cultural form that can meet the challenge of universal development. Drawing inspiration from modernization theory, he predicts that the spread of western liberal capitalism will create a more homogenous world in the image of the USA. This position is not necessarily inconsistent with the claim that global markets are beneficial through offering expanded consumer choices (Cowen 2002).

The more pessimistic homogenization thesis has been labelled the 'McDonaldization' thesis. This perspective regards homogenization as a contemporary form of cultural imperialism, rather than a promoter of equality. The symbols and products of transnational corporations (mainly US companies) extend their reach across the world and crowd out local cultural symbols (Hertz 2002; Klein 2001; Ritzer 1993). McDonaldization destroys local businesses and local culture, replacing them with an idealized promise of western lifestyles (Barnet and Cavanagh 1995: 13–22). However, this promise often remains unfulfilled. As TNCs move across the globe, lengthening their production chains in search of cheaper labour, the discounted wages and the 'McJobs' they offer prevent workers from realizing their aspirations. They participate in the global economy as global producers but not global consumers (Klein 2001; Ross 1997). Landes (2002: 194–5) has argued that globalization has always created 'multiple worlds'. This was the impact of nineteenth-century industrialization, which economically 'brought the world closer together' while at the same time 'fragmenting' it between winners and losers. Economic integration can coincide with cultural polarization (Roy 2004: 99).

It would appear then that while a global consciousness touches every region of the world, the economically marginalized suffer less from *cultural* imperialism than the McDonaldization thesis suggests. This is reinforced if capitalism has 'written off' much of the poorer world and has little interest in weaving the complex web of market relations among the neglected areas that remain outside of the 'thickening' web of relations in the wealthier world. The cultural and technological trends that promote homogeneity could provoke a 'backlash' from the 'world's variety' – from both those who resent and those who demand the Big Mac (Hobsbawm 2000: 66).

Another variant of this *polarization* thesis is associated with Huntington's 'clash of civilization' thesis. Huntington, as shown in

Box 8.1   Globalization and the 'civilizing process'

The broadening of horizons that globalization affords can affect people's consciousness in many ways. Huntington has warned that heightened cultural interaction can lead to a 'clash of civilizations'.

However, the work of Norbert Elias (1982) provides an alternative approach. In his study of the history of manners throughout Europe, Elias charted changes in people's behaviour from the Middle Ages onwards, showing how people came to show greater 'consideration for each other'. This emerged out of European court life and was later diffused throughout society. He labelled this element of the modernization of Europe the 'civilizing process' and this concept has been employed to trace the history of social interactions as diverse as table manners and football hooliganism.

Underlying the civilizing process is a growing awareness of the underlying humanity in others who are different from us, either in the sense of culture, race, ethnicity or class. Once people become conscious of the fact that others are, in fact, a version of themselves, they develop a higher capacity to sympathize and empathize with their plight. The assumption here is that barbarity and neglect requires treating the other as subhuman.

There are many examples that suggest that globalization promotes a deepening of the civilizing process. A global consciousness that we live in 'one world' has been enhanced by modern communications, environmental awareness and cultural interaction. This idea that a shrinking world could lead to 'a new concern over the fate of the world's people' was pointed out by Gunnar Myrdal (1977) in the late 1960s, well before commentators had begun using the term 'globalization'. Indeed, Worsley (1973: 10) claimed that one of the most important roles that imperialism performed was to help humankind acquire the 'knowledge that they were part of a single social world' and in this way 'human society . . . came to exist subjectively'.

This consciousness has become part of what Elias called our social figuration: 'the patterns in which people are bound together in groups, states, societies – patterns of interdependence which encompass every form of cooperation and conflict' (Mennell 1985: 15–6).

The MDGs can also be interpreted as part of this figuration. There has been a much greater effort by the UN to promote the MDGs than figurations in previous developmental decades. This global consciousness has also been promoted in western popular culture, with large-scale spectacles such as Band Aid and Live 8 promoting global awareness of the issues, such as global poverty, debt relief and fair trade (see Chapters 6 and 7.

A clash of civilizations is not inevitable, and philosophers such as Singer (2002) have argued that it is not only enlightened self-interest but moral duty that should dictate our actions towards the world's poor.

Chapter 6, possesses less optimism than Fukuyama that western liberalism will emerge victorious in the new millennium. The progress of modernization is not inevitable and a global culture appears only a distant hope. This also means that 'global difference' rather than 'global inequality' will be a more appropriate focus of attention, as cultural comparisons can lead to inappropriate scales of measurement. Increasingly these global cultures or world religions have spilled over national boundaries and have become global themselves. This, however, has not fuelled Huntington's optimism, as he believes that this cultural mixture is likely to lead to intensified conflict rather than tolerance (Huntington 2004; for a more optimistic 'civilizational' approach see Box 8.1).

The *hybridization* thesis is most often associated with the postcolonial and postmodern schools of thought. It takes as its starting point the cross-fertilization of culture. It argues that there is more to global contact than the subjection of 'subaltern' peoples to core imperialist culture. The influence of the colonized has reverberated back through the core in a multitude of ways, from cuisine to literature, art and design. Indeed, some writers claim that the west appropriated much scientific knowledge from other cultures and later constructed a myth around the west as 'the cradle of civilization' (Escobar 1995). Immigration into the core from the former colonies has given greater strength to the hybridization or 'creolization' of global culture. This awareness of the interpenetration of cultural forms, along with studies that have emphasized the socially constructed nature of modern nationalisms, has made it increasingly difficult to define 'authentic' or 'traditional' culture. While the symbols of US culture can be found from Beijing to Barcelona, it is also true that there is a global market for an ever-expanding variety of cultural products and tastes (Bhagwati 2004: 111). An important consequence that emerges from this hybridization approach is that the concept of culture remains in just as much a state of flux as the concept of globalization (Hogan 2002). This uncertainty over key concepts in development studies has led to much discussion over the *impasse* in the field and also extends to contemporary debates over the role of the state.

Globalization and the State

Many commentators claim that globalization has rendered state-centred approaches to development obsolete. The 'decline of the state' argument can be found in a variety of political shades and these will be examined in this section (Falk and Camilieri 1992; Hoogvelt 1997; Ohmae 2000;

William Robinson 2004). It also points out that the 'declinist' thesis has its critics (Harman 1996; Hirst and Thompson 1996; Ruigrok and van Tulder 1995; Weiss 1998).

This 'declinist' debate reverberates through contemporary development studies in another sense. As noted in Chapter 3, many theorists now reject statism as a form of 'methodological territorialism'. Chapter 5 also pointed out that there was an assumption during most of the postwar era that the state would act as a catalyst for the development project – whether in its modernization or dependency guise (Rapley 2002). The claim that the era of state sovereignty is passing raises important questions concerning the agency for development in the new millennium (Wallerstein 2004: 86). Chapter 6 showed how the decline of the state is viewed as a positive development among neoliberal commentators, signalling the liberation of market forces. However, other 'declinists' view the erosion of state power more darkly and are sceptical that the market can reverse trends towards growing inequality and poverty (ILO 2004: 14).

Among neoliberals, Ohmae (2000) has focused on the way in which new technologies and innovations in financial markets have created the modern virtual networked economy. The new economic world bears little relationship to past physical borders. The new reality consists of an 'invisible continent':

> The economy of this [borderless] dimension is not tied to nation-states at all. It is driven by consumers and financial investors who care not at all for national stability, who avoid taxes wherever possible. . . . Similarly, the expectations of wealth generated by the invisible continent have generated a massive cross-border migration of capital. . . . The sheer magnitude of money involved in the invisible continent, and the cross-border and cross-currency nature of these large multiples and their derivatives, make the invisible continent a terrifyingly slippery entity for governments, businesses and even speculators to deal with.

Declinism often appears in the form of a 'global imperative', suggesting the need for the state to accommodate to global economic forces. This gives capital enormous economic and political power without necessarily taking greater social responsibility. National governments can also evade moral responsibility by drawing on this TINA principle.

Martin and Schumann (1997: 40) take a dimmer view of the decline of the state, arguing that it takes power out of the hands of democratically organized electorates and places it into the hands of unaccountable global financiers. Currency and security dealers 'acting on a world scale direct an ever-growing flow of footloose investment capital and can therefore decide on the weal and woe of entire nations, and do so largely free of state control'. Hertz (2002) has labelled this the 'silent takeover', whereby global capital has undermined local decision-making processes and generated a 'democratic deficit' (see also ILO 2004: 3–4).

A 'weaker' version of the declinist thesis is presented by commentators who oppose 'methodological territorialism', such as William Robinson (2004) and Sklair (2001). Robinson (2004, 36) observes that the traditional focus of radical political economy has always been that 'class formation is conditioned by the history, politics, and culture of respective national societies'. While this state-centred perspective might have served to represent reality in previous eras, 'globalization has rendered it inadequate'. This new reality demands investigating class relations from a global perspective. According to this 'global capitalist' thesis there exists a global ruling class – a transnational capitalist class (TCC) – that controls transnational capital (see also Sklair 2001). The proper unit of analysis is the global system rather than the nation-state, because the latter is 'no longer the organizing principle of capitalism and the institutional "container" of class development and social life' (Robinson 2004: 39–40).

According to Robinson, the underlying dynamics of this global system have evolved from *national* circuits to *international* circuits of capital. As noted earlier, postwar developmental and welfare states performed a coordinating role in regulating capital movements and wage growth, arbitrating a class compromise between labour and capital and protecting the economic conditions for local development. The state bolstered its regulatory authority through tight control over fiscal matters and foreign trade while performing an interventionist role in the provision of public services. This tended to encourage capital to operate within nationally bounded entities. William Robinson (2004: 102–3) argues that it was the ability of popular classes to use the democratic structures of the state for egalitarian and progressive purposes that 'drove capital to transnationalization in the first instance'. Redistributive policies delivered by democratic welfare states might have performed an important role in stabilising mass demand for products, but by the 1970s this threatened capital accumulation.

The process of liberalization or deregulation has weakened the ability or willingness of the state to perform these functions, while encouraging a more footloose form of capitalism. According to William Robinson (2004: 11):

In the emerging global economy this globalization of the production process breaks down and functionally integrates what were previously national circuits into new global circuits of accumulation. The determining distinction between a world economy and a global economy is the globalization of the production process itself, or the rise of globalized circuits of production and accumulation.

This has imposed a new set of rules and competitive conditions which are increasingly generalized and homogenized across the world as a whole. These new rules have been given a whole host of labels, from monetarism, deregulation, economic rationalism, laissez faire, supply-side economics, structural adjustment and neoliberalism (Castells 1991: 3–4). However, they all represent the removal of the wide range of nationally regulated structures that underpinned the postwar compromise between capital and labour during the period of unprecedented growth between 1945 and 1970. Capital no longer relies on the expanding demand of a local workforce that was guaranteed by the welfarist, redistributive logic of the postwar state. The dismantling of this structure has encouraged capital to look upon its relationship with labour as one of 'naked commodification' in which the market becomes the arbiter of relations and fortunes (Probert 1993).

Previously, geographically constrained capital remained hostage to local labour forces. Under these circumstances, minimizing labour costs can only be achieved through large-scale unemployment, a large local reserve army of labour, increased productivity per worker, or repression. However, the ability to move production facilities opens up attractive options that allow a firm to play one state or region off against another. TNCs therefore engage in a less appealing form of equality – 'downward levelling' or a 'race to the bottom' (Brecher and Costello 1994) – whereby the workers or governments of one area must ensure that their cost structures are lower than alternative competing areas in order to attract capital investment. This ultimately depresses global wages and degrades working conditions.

This global neoliberal framework demands a loosening of social, political and economic regulation in order to allow capital greater mobility across national boundaries. Deregulation has affected all nations regardless of their level of economic development over the past quarter of a century. The decline of the state therefore undermined 'autocentric' development processes. States recast themselves as 'constituent elements of an integral world production system' over which they have little control (Robinson 2004: 16).

William Robinson's (2004: 139) declinist position is best labelled 'weak' or a qualified one, because he observes that states have performed important roles as agents of globalization through promoting this adjust-ment to the new requirements of capital accumulation. Over the past quarter of a century, governments of all political shades have been 'regu-lating for deregulation'. The regulatory 'core' has shifted to the powerful 'supranational institutions' that include the WTO, the IMF and the World Bank, along with regional forums such as NAFTA, APEC and the EU. These institutions act as a lubricant allowing capital to operate more freely across the globe. The World Bank and the IMF also act as discipli-nary instruments for securing the integration of poorer countries into the global system (Bello 2003). These bodies remain formally linked to states, but not all states possess equal capacity to influence these institu-tions (as Chapter 6 demonstrated).

This qualified 'declinist' argument predicts the disappearance of a *specific* form of state structure – the postwar welfare state and develop-mental state. This is being replaced with another form of state that will-ingly defers to supranational governance while setting in place the necessary support for transnational capital accumulation. Thus, the state has not declined – it has merely metamorphosized into a 'neoliberal state' which according to William Robinson (2004: 124–5) serves to:

- apply appropriate fiscal and monetary policies to maintain macro-economic stability;
- supply the infrastructural resources that facilitate globalized trade (air and seaports, communications networks, educational systems and so on); and
- guarantee social stability through 'direct coercion and ideological apparatuses'.

Held and McGrew (2002) also present a weak version of the declinist thesis through referring to the 'layering' of governance in the contempo-rary world, whereby supranational institutions are imposed on national levels of state authority (see also Brawley 2003; ILO 2004: 119; Yarborough and Yarborough 1994). What distinguishes these more qualified arguments from the bolder predictions of the absolute decline of the state is that the weaker arguments view the state as 'reconfigured' rather than redundant (Rapley 2004: 77; see also Meiksins Wood 1999: 8–12).

Critics of declinism have pointed to the ongoing functions that states continue to perform in the new millennium. Despite the employment of multinational forces in various conflicts, states continue to assert their monopoly over the means of violence. Transnational corporations do not possess armies, even though they might rely on such forces or exert undue pressure on states to protect their interests. Furthermore, the focus on 'asymmetrical wars' (such as the so-called 'war on terror') emphasizes the legitimacy that states have over the means of violence. Throughout modern history, many states have had to contend with guerrilla forces and national liberation movements. Yet, these movements (except anarchist ones) have only challenged particular states or the legitimacy of specific governments rather than the state itself (Guerin 1970).

Apart from its monopoly on violence and its infrastructural support for global capitalism, the state also continues to perform a crucial role in restricting the movement of people between one territory and another (Roy 2004: 72). This is one key difference between the end of the nineteenth century and the new millennium. In the earlier stage, only a handful of states (such as Russia) possessed passport systems. Many contemporary commentators have noted the irony that capital has never been freer from, and labour more restricted by, national boundaries.

Another criticism of declinism emerges from commentators who point to the central role that states continue to perform in the process of development. These critics refuse to swallow the neoliberal claim that states are less efficient allocators of goods than markets. For example, Chang and Grabel (2004), Johnson (1995) and Weiss (1998) have all argued that the developmental experience of NICs could not have occurred without a strong state that mobilized and harnessed social forces towards targeted goals. Others have pointed out that once firms sink costs in a specific country then this constrains their mobility (McGrath-Champ 2006: 180). In this way, location still matters in a more globally fluid world.

Fukuyama (2004: 163) has even expressed concern that neoliberalism helped generate some of the problems of 'failed states' that emerged in the 1990s. Indeed, he predicts that one of the key issues facing the global community in the foreseeable future is precisely 'state-building'. This task was neglected in the 1990s as the triumphal march of neoliberalism placed priority on freeing markets. One consequence of neglecting the state – especially in Sub-Saharan Africa and former socialist republics – was the growing problems of governance, lawlessness and the breakdown of administrative competence. Failed states can be understood as a form of 'blowback' occasioned by the policy excesses of neoliberalism (Johnson 2002).

Marxist critics of declinism point out that the 'combined and uneven development' that characterizes capitalist reproduction demands precisely the possibility of movement and mobility and hence unevenness. Marxists and dependency theorists have never accepted that the core–periphery relationship was geographically determined, rather than socially and politically structured. Wallerstein (2004: 24) argues that only a 'multiplicity of states within the overall division of labour assures this possibility'. If wages and working conditions were equalized across the world – either through upward or downward levelling – capitalism would be faced with the same dilemma it began to face in the more regulated early postwar era. From this vantage point, equality and full employment remain utopian dreams under neoliberal global capitalism (see Jameson 2004).

Mapping Globalization

Given the ubiquity of the concept of globalization, it is tempting to accept Kay's (2003: 310) conclusion that it has 'acquired too many meanings, and too much emotional force, to be useful'. Yet, as Francis (2002: 91) notes, the development process has become 'inseparable' from globalization (see also Pieterse 2004: 118). All meanings of globalization examined so far suggest some relationship to inequality and this last section of the chapter focuses on two related questions: first, what distinguishes the current process of globalization from previous developmental processes, and, secondly, has globalization reduced or heightened inequality?

Using these two sets of questions, different writers can be positioned within the four quadrants of the figure in Box 8.2. Numerous classificatory

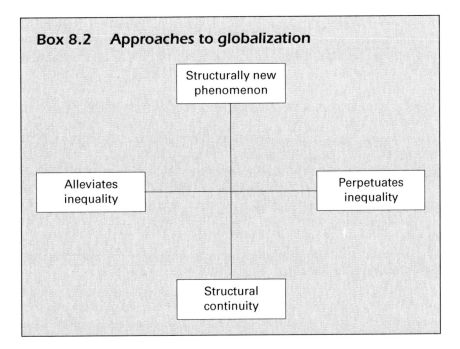

Box 8.2   Approaches to globalization

Structurally new phenomenon

Alleviates inequality

Perpetuates inequality

Structural continuity

schemes have been designed to organize the vast globalization literature and no claim is advanced here that this grid is superior. It has been developed for the purposes of adding clarity to the central concern of this book – global inequality.

The horizontal axis indicates the extent to which commentators believe that the process of globalization has reduced or exacerbated inequalities. On the western side of the figure sit numerous neoliberal institutions and commentators, such as the IMF and the WTO, who adopt the stance that free markets spread wealth. This position is also taken by commentators such as Friedman (2006), Kay (2003), Lal (2004: Ch. 5), Norberg (2003) and Wolf (2005). It is also possible to argue that globalization initially heightens inequality in the interests of accelerated economic growth, before more robust and stable economic conditions bring about greater equality (Kuznets 1952). Such a stance would be located closer to the middle of the western side of the diagram, as globalization and equality would be positively correlated *in the longer run*. This has always been a core belief in modernization theory.

It might also be possible to argue that globalization causes inequality on some dimensions but not others. For instance, it is necessary to determine whether commentators are referring to inequality between nations or within specific nations. Inequality could also refer to gender relations, ethnic relations or any number of sociological categories, particularly considering that there is no area of academic inquiry that has not had the conceptual torch of globalization shone on it from football to religion. It is possible to argue that globalization has resulted in the heightening of some forms of inequality and the lessening of others. For instance, it is possible to argue that, on average, globalization has reduced gender inequality while increasing class inequalities. However, 'on average' does not offer much comfort to all groups of women.

A good example of a position that sits at the centre of the horizontal axis would be the United Nations Development Programme (UNDP 1997: Chapter 4) which argued that 'globalization has its winners and its losers', while maintaining 'inequality is not inherent in globalization'. Soros (2004: 94) shares this optimistic belief in the potential of globalization, claiming that its benefits outweigh its costs 'in the sense that the increased wealth produced by globalization could be used to make up for the inequities and other shortcomings of globalization and there would still be some extra wealth left over'. The UN Millennium Project (UNMP 2005a) also places faith in the potential of more open global markets to unleash growth in poorer countries while at the same time recognizing its negative impacts, 'including brain drain, environmental degradation, capital flight, and terms-of-trade decline'. This medium position tends to view globalization as a double-edged sword (see also Frieden 2006).

Commentators who link globalization with growing inequality are located on the eastern side of the figure. The UN *Report on the World Social Situation* (UN Department of Economic and Social Affairs 2005: 5) concluded that the 'costs and benefits of globalization are not equally shared among countries and peoples'. Comeliau (2002: 84) also insists that 'it is no longer possible to ignore the problem of the relationship between the spread of capitalist modernity and the sharpening of inequalities'. Identifying the same modern 'paradox' as Marx – namely the existence of want among privilege – he pointed out that the global system 'is capable of the most extraordinary technological achievements, and therefore of unprecedented growth in output, yet it cannot organize itself in such a way that its own products are available to all members of society' (Comeliau 2002: 89). The key question in studying global inequality is 'whether positive changes and negative changes are separable from each other, or whether they are two sides of a single tendency' (Comeliau 2002: 11).

After examining a variety of methodologies that measure world income distribution, Wade (2001b) also concluded that the weight of evidence contradicts the neoliberal claim that inequalities have narrowed over the past few decades. He identifies a number of trends that have increased global inequality: higher rates of growth within wealthier countries; higher rates of population growth in poorer countries; sluggish growth in Africa and parts of rural Asia; widening rural–urban inequalities and output rates in China and India; technological change; financial liberalization; and the tendency for the products of poorer countries to fall relative to those of wealthier countries. He argues that 'global inequality is widening' and that globalization is not 'moving the world in the right direction' (Wade 2004: 16). The 'state declinists' examined in the previous section who claim that the erosion of state powers leaves citizens more exposed to the winds of global inequalities also belong to this eastern side of the diagram.

The vertical axis refers to the structural properties of globalization. Is the world a qualitatively different place now that global relations pervade societies? This vertical axis bears some resemblance to Giddens' (1999) single-axis classification, which places 'global radicals' at one end and 'global sceptics' at the other. In our model, Giddens' global sceptics – who don't believe that globalization is a fundamentally new phenomenon and who believe that recent changes have exacerbated inequality – would appear in the south-eastern quadrant of the figure. Global radicals – who belief that cultural, political and economic changes are so profound that they represent a radical change in the world – would appear on the northern half of the figure and either on the western or eastern half, depending on whether this fundamental shift has dampened or stoked the fires of inequality. Held and McGrew (2002) present a similar single-axis scale, where globalists would be in the northern half and sceptics in the southern half.

Commentators such as Ohmae (2000) belong in the northern half of the diagram, as do other proponents of capitalist-driven globalization, such as Friedman (2000). William Robinson's (2004: 2) 'global capitalism' thesis would be located in the north-eastern quadrant. It argues that the world has entered 'a new stage in the evolving world capitalist system' and represents 'an epochal shift in the history of world capitalism'. However, because this transformation remains within the parameters of capitalist development (not a rupture or discontinuity *per se*), Robinson would be positioned closer to the centre of the figure (see Box 8.3). His description of globalization as 'qualitatively new' places him closer to the global radicals than the global sceptics. On the other hand, William Robinson (2004: 168) shares with the global sceptics a concern that globalization has exacerbated inequalities, and this reinforces his position in the north-eastern quadrant of the diagram: 'Expanding poverty; inequality, marginality; and deprivation are the dark underside of the global capitalist cornucopia so celebrated by the transnational elite.'

Those positioned in the southern half of the figure question whether the world has fundamentally changed and imply that the dynamics driving social relations remain unaltered. The fundamental question that has to be answered in identifying writers along this vertical axis is whether – in Wallerstein's (2002: 238) words – we are dealing with 'cyclical rhythms' or 'secular trends'.

This argument can take the form of strong statements that globalization is a figment of commentators' imaginations. George (2004: 11) defines globalization as an ideological cover for 'the latest stage of world capitalism and the political framework that helps it thrive', while Broad (1995: 20) argues that history demonstrates that 'globalization is nothing new'. Other global sceptics on this far southern end of the diagram have argued that the scale and scope of global transactions in the current epoch are no greater than they were during the decades prior to the First World War (Hirst and Thompson 1996; Weiss 1998). There are also sceptics who point out that globalization itself is not the cause of depressed wages and worsening conditions. The reduction of labour costs is inherent in capitalist production, and globalization is merely an epiphenomenon of this 'iron law' (Hobsbawm 2000, 128–9; see also Rosenberg 2000; Tabb 1997).

Commentators closer to the middle of the diagram (but still in the southern half) state that an understanding of global inequality must retain explanatory concepts such as capitalism and imperialism. While this argument does not necessarily deny that profound social change has

Box 8.3   Robinson on quantitative and qualitative shifts in the world capitalist system

Robinson's 'theory of global capitalism' retains the historical flavour of world systems analysis. His principal theoretical innovation has been to decentre the state from the analysis of the political economy of globalization. Globalization represents the fourth epoch of the world capitalist system:

• *First, or mercantilist, epoch (1492–1789)*
Capitalism emerged in the fifteenth century out of the 'cocoon' of feudalism. The conquest of the Americas accelerated primitive capital accumulation.

• *Second, or competitive, epoch (1789–1900)*
This era witnessed the rise of the modern industrial bourgeoisie and the dominance of industrial capital. It also consolidated the modern nation-state.

• *Third, or monopoly, epoch (1900–1970)*
This era saw the establishment of a 'single world market' structured by a system of nation-states. The rise of finance capital also occurred and the intensified competition between imperialist powers led to global warfare. During the twentieth century, the challenge of a socialist alternative emerged.

• *Fourth, or globalization, epoch (1970 to the present)*
We are currently in the early stages of this new epoch of globalization. The key characteristics of this epoch remain 'emergent' but are all transnational – transnational production, transnational capitalists, and the transnational state – as well as the technological symbols of the microchip and the computer and the proclamation by the transnational ruling class of the end of socialism.

Reflecting on the distinctions between his model and world systems analysis, he argues that the latter offers a different definition of capitalism, one closer to the Weberian definition of capitalism as market-oriented activity, rather than the capital-labour relationship: The distinction, he argues, 'is not mere semantics and is relevant to the discussion of globalization. The former position implies that globalization can only be a quantitative intensification of a 500-year old process, whereas the latter allows for quantitative change to give way under globalization to qualitative change, with important implications for macro-social analysis'

Source: summarized from William Robinson (2004: 8–10).

occurred, it stresses that new conceptual frameworks are not needed to understand these changes. Dicken (2003), for instance, suggests that the differences between the late-nineteenth century globalization and the contemporary one are merely about a 'deepening' of integrative trends. Rapley (2004: 84) phrases it differently: he acknowledges that globalization's pedigree can be traced to the origins of capitalism, but the last few decades have witnessed 'a new chapter in that history'.

The complexity of this structural dimension can be illustrated if we take the example of world-systems analysis. Wallerstein (1974) observed as early as the 1970s that the world capitalist system was undergoing a process of transformation that signalled the beginning of a post-*pax Americana* era and the growing importance of multinational corporations (see Chapter 5). This change, like all earlier transformations, was still only a *stage* in the development of the capitalist international division of labour. Thus Wallerstein (2004: 84) would be located in the southern half of the diagram. His belief that the gap between core and periphery has become 'greater than ever' during the last two decades of the twentieth century would help locate him in the south-eastern quadrant.

This stance is also supported by the ILO (2004: 37), which notes that the 'strong initial economic base, abundance of capital and skill, and technological leadership' possessed by the wealthier countries ensured that they exploited the benefits of globalization, along with a small number of NICs. Drawing a similar picture to that presented by the UN Millennium Project, the ILO (2004: 38) are at pains to point out that under globalization 'the rest' remain:

> trapped in a vicious circle of interlocking handicaps including poverty and illiteracy, civil strife, geographical disadvantages, poor governance . . . inflexible economies largely dependent on a single commodity . . . burdened by high external debt and hit hard by the continuing decline in the price of primary commodities . . . compounded by continuing agricultural protectionism in the industrialized countries.

To conclude, the 'globalization debate' can often appear as if academic specialists are arguing over how many angels can dance on the head of a pin. As Pieterse (2004: 37) notes – staking his claim to the north-eastern quadrant of our diagram – there must be some uniqueness to the contemporary phase of globalization. Denying structural change is the theoretical equivalent of development studies sticking its head in the sand: 'Equating capitalism = imperialism = globalization = neoliberal globalization creates a transhistorical soup in which nothing essentially changes over, well, two to five hundred years.'

So, this review of the way that globalization is defined in recent literature might appear to add weight to Rodrik's (2000: 298) understandable lament that it has become 'a topic about which it is futile to have a rational conversation'. However, the same claim can apply to other concepts, such as 'development', as the concluding chapter will show. Disagreement does not necessarily signify confusion. A more charitable interpretation of the 'globalization debate' would be to acknowledge that events and processes at the end of the twentieth century raised unique developmental challenges for the new millennium and this manifested itself in a blossoming of different perspectives. Or, to modify Hegel's metaphor, Minerva's owl began its flight only in the gathering dusk of the old millennium. Can we therefore expect certainty at the dawn of the new millennium?

Chapter 9

Modernity, Development and their Discontents

Throughout this book, most approaches to development have assumed that the poorer countries can emulate the earlier developmental 'prototypes' and follow the path to modern development experienced by western Europe, the USA and the NICs. Despite the theoretical and political controversies encountered along the way, it has been difficult to avoid comparisons with modern western development. In both modernization theory and dependency theory, rich countries figure prominently either as prototypes to emulate or as the obstacles to that emulation. Furthermore, both Cold War superpowers were engaged in an ideological battle to demonstrate the supremacy of their form of modernity. Rarely did postwar developmental models question modernity itself, with its emphasis on industrialization, modern economic growth, urbanization, rational economic calculation, growth in rates of Gross National Product, economies of scale and higher levels of material consumption.

While development and progress had become dominant themes in western thought by the late-eighteenth century, they were never without their discontents. Romantics, anarchists and anti-urbanists have all accompanied modern developmental progress. Many European explorers encountering Pacific Islands, such as James Cook and Bruni d'Entrecasteaux, agreed with the philosopher Jean-Jacques Rousseau that it was questionable whether humans were not freer and more content as 'noble savages' rather than enslaved by modern conventions and socially produced inequalities. There are many contemporary discontents who continue to challenge the dominant development project, sometimes with radical solutions to address poverty and inequality. These alternative development approaches can be grouped under the labels 'environment', 'women' and 'postdevelopment', although there is much overlap and the labels can be loosely fitting.

Environmental Challenges

The environment and modernity

The history of economic development has always involved 'the development of more intensive ways of exploiting the natural environment' (Wilkinson 1973: 90). Thus, one of the most persistent themes of discontent with development has come from environmental concerns. Originally, environmentalism took the form of an aesthetic distaste at the consequences of urbanization and industrialization, which scarred the earth's surface as its reach extended. Urban environmental fears also took the form of observations that modernity adversely impacted on the health of the population, especially through deforming working-class children. This became an offical concern when they were unfit to fight imperialist wars. Every generation over the past 200 years has recognized environmental degradation as an issue, although the form that environmental problems have assumed and the way concern is expressed has changed over time. The one constant feature in this history of environmentalism has been its marginalization by more powerful economic and political forces. Many contemporary environmental social movements focus on this link between power, knowledge and action in an effort to draw attention to the urgency of taking precautionary measures to save the earth's biosphere.

Recent environmental concerns have focused on the pressures that human activities exert on the ecology of the planet. These warnings have come more from scientific prediction than aesthetic concern. Environmentalism poses serious questions to the development project. As Woodhouse (2002: 136, 156) notes, today 'environmental issues affect virtually all aspects of development policy'. What is at stake is nothing less than a 'reappraisal of the relationship between humanity and nature'. Ethically, environmentalism questions the *desirability* of every nation emulating the western prototype. It asks whether the planet could cope with global levels of industrialization and consumption that the richer countires currently experience. Perhaps both modernization theory and dependency theory have been fighting over how best to operate the same unsustainable model. Because contemporary environmentalists challenge dominant neoliberal development theory and practice, it is first necessary to outline the defence of the neoliberal approach to environmental concerns.

The environment and neoliberalism

Many of the commentators who argue that neoliberal globalization reduces inequality also argue that the process of capitalist economic growth has encouraged environmental sustainability. By emulating the industrial forerunners, the poorer countries will eventually have the physical and intellectual resources to take up the challenge of reversing environmental degradation. In their competition with other firms, capitalist enterprises must constantly search for more productive and more efficient methods of production. This means that those who use fewer resources to produce goods and services are more profitable. Competitive capitalism is therefore good for the environment.

Neoliberals claim that the WTO also encourages environmental sustainability by breaking down barriers to global trade. They argue that free trade allows countries to concentrate on producing goods in which they have a comparative advantage and this maximizes output from a given input of resources. The WTO (2004) has claimed that trade liberalization can produce a 'win–win situation' not only in terms of development but also in terms of the environment. For example, government subsidization for unproductive farming leads to higher rates of pesticide and herbicide use. As a corollary, neoliberals argue that trade restrictions by the EU and USA are irrational, inequitable and environmentally suboptimal.

From finite inputs to endangered species, neoliberals claim that resources are best protected when the market assigns a value to them that reflects their social respect. Nature, in other words, is best treated as a commodity. Criticizing government legislation to protect endangered species, Moran (2000) argues that:

> restraint to trade in endangered species has done a great deal to prevent the use and hence harvesting and protection of wild animals. The rhino and elephant are dangerous creatures that destroy

village crops unless their ownership is vested and the villagers can harvest them and otherwise gain, for example by protecting them for tourism. Similarly such issues are present in Australia where we foolishly prevent the export of parrots and other wildlife which transforms them into vermin competing for fodder and water rather than the incubator of a new farming industry.

According to Norberg (2003: 225–6), poverty restrains the environmental options available to poorer countries. Raising living standards is the imperative that should drive environmental policy under such circumstances and only once economic growth is sustainable can countries turn to environmental problems such as air quality and effluent emissions. This stance has also been adopted by Lomborg (2003: 5–6):

London air has never been cleaner since medieval times. . . . You will notice that whilst decreasing air pollution is true for all developed countries it is not true for Beijing or Bangkok. There, things are actually getting worse and worse. But it is not very surprising either. That's exactly what we saw in London. Basically, if you don't have industry, you don't have any pollution, but you don't have any money either. So, you say, cool, when I get industrialized, I can start buying food for my kids, give them an education, maybe buy some stuff for myself, and so never mind, I cough. That was the trade-off that Londoners and many of the rest of us made, and it's only once you get sufficiently rich . . . per person, you start saying, Ah, now it would be nice to cough a little less.

This is the developmental sequence drawn by neoliberals: economic growth first, then poverty alleviation, then environmental protection. In other words, when the poor get wealthier, they can afford to take better care of the environment.

Critics of the neoliberal approach claim that prioritizing economic growth at all costs will destroy the very basis of life (Lowe 2004). For instance, the UN Millennium Project (UNMP 2005a: 64, 90) warns that the 'oft-heard argument – that the poor should wait until their incomes have risen before investing in better management of the environment – is misplaced [because] in many parts of the developing world environmental degradation already places a binding constraint on development'. This is consistent with the MDG logic that environmentally sustainable practices must be a constituent part of development programmes rather than being seen as an end result. Pointing out that environmental sustainability was one of the MDGs, Kofi Annan (2002: 2) also emphasized that 'it is also a prerequisite for reaching all of them'.

Box 9.1   Darfur, conflict and environmental degradation

In the early years of the new millennium conflict erupted in the region of Darfur in Sudan. A global humanitarian effort concentrated on finding a solution to what many commentators have called a genocidal campaign where Black African farmers have been terrorized, their villages and livelihood destroyed, women raped and millions of inhabitants forced into displacement camps. Hundreds of thousands of Darfurians have been killed.

The origins of the war are complex and have been superimposed onto a civil war that has raged on and off since Sudan's independence from Britain in 1956. The Darfur region has always remained marginalized from the centre of Sudanese power and when rebel groups formed against the central government in 2003, this provoked the Government of Sudan to arm a Arab militia, or *janjawid*, which are accused of committing the atrocities mentioned above.

Underlying the conflict is the delicate nature of natural resource management, which has deteriorated to the point where long-standing ethnic rivalries – previously managed through traditional conflict resolution mechanisms – have turned into a vicious form of modern warfare in a region awash with modern weaponry. The northern part of the region is dominated by Arab nomadic pastoralists while the southern part is home to more sedentary African agricultural farmers, who harvest millet, sorghum, watermelons, groundnuts, sesame and gum Arabic. Traditionally, negotiations have allowed the nomadic population to graze on communal lands as they moved through the settled southern areas during their periodic migration.

However, a series of climatic, ecological, agricultural, demographic, technological and administrative circumstances has changed the socioeconomic relations between these different groups of land users. First, since independence the population of Darfur has increased from 1 million to 6 million, placing addition pressure on the delicate ecosystem. Second, since

→

While many neoliberals argue that the free market ultimately leads to improved environmental quality, critics point to the uneven impact of the market on different social groups, arguing that it promotes a heightening of local, national and international dimensions of ecological inequality (UNDP 2003: 88). They remain sceptical about the chances of finding a global solution to environmental and social problems within the existing confines of a neoliberal framework. For instance, if the wealthiest 20 per cent of the globe presently consume approximately 80 per cent of the world's non-renewable resources, then reducing this inequality through emulation assumes that there are sufficient resources to allow the other 80 per cent to catch up. This form of globalization will place additional

→

the 1960s, the Sahelian region which Darfur forms part of has suffered a long dry spell often with severe drought conditions. Third, farmers have tried to cope with these conditions through increasing their acreage of crops and other risk avoidance practices such as building up their own animal stocks (mainly sheep and goats). Fourth, during the 1970s, the central government also encouraged increased production of cash crops for market export as the country struggled under higher debt burdens and structural adjustment programmes. Fifth, these changes have adversely affected the ability of the nomadic population to graze their animals as more land is fenced in for agriculture and more land used for farmers' animals. Sixth, because of the severity of the drought in the north, more nomadic pastoralists are migrating south adding to land competition. Contributing environmental factors such as deforestation, depleted soils and desertification have led to a vicious circle of ecological degradation, lowered carrying capacity of the land and growing land-use conflict. They have also moved tribal groups further away from the previously more sustainable mixed land-use practices involving trees, crop-rotation and pastoral land for grazing.

As a 2004 conference held by the Africa Program of the University for Peace (2006: 13, 22) stated, 'there is an indisputable connexion between the conflict in Darfur and environmental depletion', and there is an 'essential need to address the root cause of the problem – competition over dwindling resources'. This conclusion was also reached in a report from Physicians for Human Rights (2006: 54), which concluded that: 'To succeed, any political solution must address the historical marginalization of Darfur as well as the intensifying competition for scarce resources'.

Each year, millions of people are killed in environmental and resource-based conflicts. However, these conflicts not only affect countries with poor natural endowments. Those with the most highly prized resources, such as Nigerian and Sudanese oil, or Congolese diamonds and coltan, often experience the most intense and debilitating conflict.

stress on the already degraded environment and depleted resources (ILO 2004: 108). It has been estimated that emulation would require the resources of four planet earths. Over half of the greenhouse gases emitted today are produced by the 16 per cent of the world's population living in the richer countries (UNDP 2003: 130). One quarter emanate from the USA (Woodhouse 2002: 150).

At the 2002 World Summit on Sustainable Development in Johannesburg, Kofi Annan (2002: 2) pointed out that the process of development as practised since the end of the Second World War has been kind to the wealthy few but mean to the poor majority. He warned that this road 'to prosperity that ravages the environment and leaves a majority of humankind behind in squalor will soon prove to be a dead-end road for everyone'. Global wealth and poverty, he seemed to be suggesting, have been twin consequences of the dominant developmental project. Others have argued that the environmental crisis in the high-income countries is the result of being 'developed to death' while the environmental crisis in the low-income countries is due more to distorted development, extreme poverty and landlessness (Shanmugaratnam 1989: 13; Trainer 1994; UNDP 2003: 88 and 123) – a combination of the 'desperation of the poor and the heedlessness of the rich' (Sachs and Reid 2006). Economic development that fails to take consideration of the sustainability of natural resources tends to impact more on the poor (see Box 9.1). For example, unsustainable rates of deforestation can potentially boost rates of national economic growth while destroying local communities and livelihoods. Forestry products earn poorer countries some US$54 billion annually, and over 90 per cent of the world's extreme poor rely on forests for their part of their survival (World Bank 2006).

The environment and globalization

Critics of neoliberalism have also stressed the unequal global power relations between large transnational businesses and farmers in poorer countries. For example, Shiva (2001: 118–20; 2003) describes how leading global food companies such as Monsanto sign agreements with seed companies to control crop production. This narrows the choice of seeds available to farmers and increasingly draws them into global production chains. In effect, farmers are becoming 'bio-serfs' of these 'seed-lords'. Biodiversity is threatened by the monopolization of seed varieties and patents by global corporations. India used to have 200,000 varieties of rice, the USA had 7000 apple varieties, peasants in the Andes grew 3000 varieties of potatoes, and Papua New Guinea had as many as 5000 varieties of sweet potatoes. In place of such diversity, global corporations are creating 'a global monoculture pushing millions of species to extinction and creating new health problems in the midst of overproduction as manipulated foods and reduced diversity create nutritional insecurity' (Shiva 2001: 121).

The choices consumers make in local supermarkets have global consequences (Blackwell and Seabrook 1993: 86). When food chains become more global and the link between consumers and the producers of goods more distant, buyers become less aware of the social and environmental impact of production and distribution systems. This creates a widening feedback loop between our actions and the consequences of our actions. An example of a tight feedback loop is a self-sufficient village where its inhabitants experience change directly, are able to link it to their actions, grasp the dimensions of problems and then respond to further change. However, the more impersonal and expansive nature of globalization alters this feedback loop. The further away an individual stands from the consequences of their action, the greater is the feeling of detachment from the problem. Consequently, actors experience a sense that the pace of change is beyond their control, or that they are powerless to intervene.

Rist (1999: 186) has also argued that 'market induced globalization mystifies the process of production, and hinders environmental consciousness':

> Whereas an economy based upon local resources makes people imme-diately sensitive to any deterioration in their environment, and in most cases eager to preserve it, the market makes it possible to take resources from one region, to consume them in another region, and to dispose of the waste in yet another. Everything undertaken in the name of expanding international trade allows production to be dissociated from consumption and consumption from disposal. This spares the consumer–polluter from realizing that he is involved in using up resources and accumulating waste, as the trade circuit obscures what is actually taking place. Transnational companies favour this dilution of responsibility, operating as they do in many different places at once and constantly splitting creation from destruction of resources.

Dyball (2005) also points out that global food chains increase the envi-ronmental costs of transportation and distribution. Approximately 77 per cent of the energy costs associated with food commodity chains is incurred through transportation, distribution, packaging and processing. This proportion of costs increases as global production and distribution networks thicken (see Ryan and Durning 1997; Woodward 2002: 2–3).

This issue of taking the full costs of production and distribution into consideration is also reflected in waste disposal. It is economically cheaper to ship waste to a poorer country than to dispose of it in richer countries. This is because developing countries such as India do not calculate the full ecological costs of waste disposal. International trade in waste is good business and increases the GNP of poorer countries. Yet, this exercise in neoliberal globalization takes global inequalities to a new level: 'If pollution and waste migrate to the South under "free trade" and the knowledge, biological diversity and wealth created from it are travel-ling north . . . the inevitable outcome of globalization must be environ-mental apartheid' (Shiva 2000: 115).

Most environmentalists state that the responsibility for fixing envi-ronmental problems must rest with the developmental prototypes that generated the mess in the first place: 'If we believe that people should contribute to fixing something in proportion to their responsibility for breaking it, then the developed nations owe it to the rest of the world to fix the problem with the atmosphere' (Singer 2002: 37–8; see also Singer and Gregg 2004: Ch. 5; UNDP 2003: 124; UNMP 2005a: 230). Indeed, this responsibility has been officially acknowledged by the rich countries ever since the 1992 Rio Summit (Woodhouse 2002: 148).

Many environmentalists also argue that there are negative environmental consequences associated with undermining state sovereignty. Legally binding measures on TNCs are necessary to ensure respect for the environment. Yet, the adoption of trade liberalization policies reflect the opposite trend, whereby governments are surrendering the control they previously exercised over territory and markets. This loosening of local and national political feedback loops through loss of government control represents additional risks to the environment. As Roy (2004: 14–5) warns, the 'further away geographically decisions are taken, the more scope you have for incredible injustice'.

Other environmentalists adopt a different stance, arguing that *global* institutions must be strengthened to ensure that they are accountable to everyone, rather than to corporate shareholders. Hamilton (2001) states that both national and international responses are necessary for environmentally sustainable practices. It would be a mistake, he claims, to dismantle global institutions or become more autarchic. What is needed is the democratization of these institutions 'so that instead of being the agents of market ideology, they reflect the diversity of interests of ordinary people in developing and developed countries'. While national environmental policies end at national borders, environmental problems spill across them (Cocks 2003: Chapter 1; UNDP 2003: 130).

Like the other challenges to mainstream development analysed later in this chapter, environmental critics argue that the problem of development must be approached from a new angle. They agree with Einstein that it is 'impossible to solve today's problems by thinking the way we thought when we created the problems'. The concept of environmental sustainability alerts people to the greatest inequality that the current generation can indulge in – the intergenerational dimension of inequality that passes onto future generations a less habitable planet than the one the present generation inherited.

Feminist Challenges

The heightened global awareness of the environmental impact of development practices has influenced the policies and principles of many political movements. In the twenty-first century, the debate over the environment usually revolves round the 'shade' of green that one professes (Blainey 2002). Most people, as Trainer (1998: 4) notes, have a green tinge. Although 'green' parties have won seats in many national parliaments, environmentalism is an amorphous form of politics that has moved beyond single-issue campaigns while attempting to avoid the hierarchical organizational structures that characterized the mass political parties of the twentieth century.

In this sense, environmentalism shares many similarities with feminism. Few commentators publicly oppose gender equity even though globally women continue to experience higher levels of poverty and discrimination. Like environmentalism, gender politics has permeated all layers of the political process over the past few decades and has begun to alter developmental practices. This section on the relationship between feminism and development begins by examining one strand of feminism – ecofeminism – which focuses on the link between environmentally unsustainable development and women's marginalization.

Ecofeminism

Ecofeminists begin with the claim that the environment is a feminist issue and that knowledge is not gender-neutral (Warren 1987). As the expression 'mother earth' suggests, many cultures have imbued nature with 'feminine' attributes along with caring, cooperation and nurturing (Merchant 1982: 1–2). On the other hand, phenomena such as science, reason and competition are often characterized as 'masculine'. Modernity framed progress as a struggle between civilization and the forces of nature. Thus, from an ecofeminist perspective, environmental degradation of the earth can be viewed as a consequence of patriarchal structures that treat the planet as inert matter to be endlessly manipulated for ever-expanding human ends. The combination of production for profit, the ideology of progress and scientific advancement combined to alter modern relationships with the physical environment from one of harmony to one of domination. Ecofeminists view modernity as an extension of patriarchal relations and consider science and technology to be a reflection of male-centred control over the social and physical world (Shiva 1989).

The environmental destruction which postwar development has visited on the earth has, according to ecofeminists, affected the sphere of women's lives to a greater extent than men's. Women continue to work more closely with the natural environment through their greater participation in tasks such as crop cultivation, water-gathering and animal husbandry (Elliott 2004: 125–6; Shiva 1989: 43). As a consequence, they are more directly attuned to the negative impacts that science and technology impose on the environment. It is therefore understandable that women, especially in the less industrialized world, have been at the forefront of many environmental protests (Hunt 2004: 252; Roy 2004). Many researchers have noted that there are 'real gender differences in experiences of nature and responsibility for the environment that derived not from biology but from social constructions of gender that varied with class, race, and place' (Peet 1999: 189). Any sustainable solution to development, ecofeminists conclude, must take into consideration women's environmental knowledge, as 'they live it more directly' (Calvert and Calvert 2003: 240).

As the following sections will show, ecofeminism is only one of many strands of feminist theory and it has been criticized on various grounds. First, it has been accused of 'essentialism', by tending to homogenize women's experiences across time and space and assuming a fixed, romanticized relationship between women and nature (Sutton 2004: 108–9). Secondly, it tends to neglect other social dimensions that divide women, such as class, ethnicity and household status (Hunt 2004: 254; Jackson 1993). Once the nature of the association between women and the environment is unpacked and examined in specific contexts, any universal relationship disappears. Jackson (1993) points out that in many non-western cultures 'men are associated with nature' and there is a danger of western feminism falling into an ethnocentric trap of reading the world through the eyes of western environmental traditions.

Ecofeminism, like other feminist challenges, is a relatively new departure for development theory and practice. Until the 1970s development studies – like most other social sciences – remained 'gender blind'. By the early twenty-first century, gender had assumed a more prominent place in development theory and practice. On the one hand, some commentators argue that this gender focus is 'revolutionizing' development theory (Hettne 1995: 193). Others label it 'gender mainstreaming', whereby developmental policy and practice takes into consideration the impact of women. On the other hand, others claim that 'women-centred initiatives have on the whole remained relatively marginal in global governance' (Scholte 2000). This leaves open the issue of whether women continue to participate in male-oriented projects (co-option) or whether their equal participation will result in a radically new orientation for development. As Chapter 7 showed, the Millennium Project is conscious of the need to incorporate gender as an integral part of the the MDGs. The following section describes how gender arrived on the development agenda.

Modernization and the invisible women

Until the 1970s, the social sciences tended to ignore women as agents of social change. This applied as much to the study of high-income countries as to poor countries (Baxter 2000; Bulbeck 1988: 104; Ramamurthy 2000: 241). When women did merit academic attention, it was usually within the sociological subdiscipline of 'family studies', indicating where a male-dominated establishment consigned women. It is hardly surprising then that women remained marginalized subjects within postwar development studies (see Box 9.2). Most development theory and practice was 'concerned with changing what men do and little consideration has been given to either involving women in the development process or the impact of male-dominated development programmes on the lives of women' (Thomas 1986: 1).

Modernization theorists predicted that the modernizing process would emancipate women from their traditional roles. This would entail the emergence of a more egalitarian family structure in which all

---

Box 9.2   Men behaving modern

During the 1960s and 1970s, Inkeles and his colleagues (1976; Inkeles and Smith 1993), set out to examine attitudinal change in the modernizing world. Great care was taken to ensure that the 6000 respondents were as representative as possible of the process of modernization, choosing individuals and countries that would allow the researchers to identify 'points on a presumed continuum of exposure to modernizing influences'. Yet, to paraphrase Inkeles, the research was about 'making men modern' – every respondent was male.

Like most sociological research of the period, there was an inbuilt assumption that the attitudes of the common man (Inkeles 1976: 323) could be generalized to represent broader social attitudes and values. Women's status was considered to be 'derived' from their 'kinship attachments' to men (Blake 1976: 305). Inkeles did inquire, incidentally, into whether 'the opinions of a man's wife or young son merit serious consideration when important public issues are being discussed' – daughters presumably held no such views on these public issues (Inkeles 1966: 155). This shed light on how modernization affected men's attitudes towards women and whether 'the liberating influence of the forces making for modernization would act on men's attitudes and incline them to accord to women status and rights more nearly equal to those enjoyed by men' (Inkeles 1976: 338). However, it tells us little about the views women held. As Handelman notes, 'scholars, Third World governments, and Western development agencies appeared strangely oblivious to women's role in the modernization process' (see also Kothari 2002: 40).

members would participate more widely in the family's functions (see Chapter 5). The demand for equality within this model of development would become more pronounced once the economy had successfully negotiated its journey to maturity. At this stage, concern for redistribution would take precedence over production and growth. Women could then expect to challenge existing power relations. Thus, in the same way that poorer societies would inevitably 'catch up' with the modernizing prototypes, women would also inevitably catch up with men as soon as the requisite levels of development had been achieved. Male status, in other words, was the goal to which women could aspire.

This 'derived' status (Blake 1976: 305) that women possessed obscured the issue of whether women performed distinct roles in the developmental process that affected their outlook and their life-chances in unique ways. Women's distinct relationship to the natural environment (theorized from a materialist, spiritual or essentialist perspective) has already shown the possible differential impact of gender on development.

Modernization theory also tended to downplay the role that colonization had performed in shaping the 'traditional' role of women. In many cases, colonial administrators transformed or reinforced patriarchal relationships through imposing an assumption that the public world of politics was a man's affair (Bulbeck 1988: 101). Furthermore, the introduction of large-scale capitalist agriculture into colonial societies often undermined women's economic status. As Peet (1999: 180) points out, modernization was far from gender-neutral because this process was 'supervised by colonial authorities imbued with Western notions of the sexual division of labor, [and] placed new technologies under the control of men, thereby marginalizing women, reducing their status, and undercutting their power and income'.

Boserup's (1970) *Women's Role in Economic Development* examined how modernization effected significant changes in gender relations: first, it alienated women from their traditional productive roles; secondly, it diminished their social status; thirdly, it reinforced their dependency; fourthly, it offered a vision of emancipation based on a future stage of modernity; and fifthly, it made certain unsupported assumptions about relations between men and women that made women's role in the development process invisible (see also Kothari 2002: 40). More structuralist approaches went further than demanding that women be considered in development programmes and argued that gender relations helped shape the form that social change assumed (see Ramamurthy 2000: 243–5). In her study of the intrusion of multinational agribusiness into Senegal during the 1970s, Mackintosh (1989: 37) brought to the fore the interrelationships between class, gender, farming practices and household relations. She warned that it was impossible to 'understand the making of a

---

Box 9.3   Feminism and development methodology

Once feminists began to examine the relationship between gender and development, this not only brought to the surface inequalities of power, status and resources. It also questioned some of the methodologies that underpinned the measurement of development.

- First, individual households have usually been taken as the principle unit of analysis for measuring poverty and inequality. However, one methodological disadvantage of this measure is that it doesn't capture the distribution of resources within the household (Mackintosh 1989).
- Secondly, many activities that are carried out by women often go unreported due to the fact that these tasks are considered outside the category of work or are considered part of women's natural responsibility. As Pearson (2002: 386) notes: 'In the rural sectors of many low income countries both men and women often report to census enumerators and researchers that women do not do any productive agricultural work, or they are just involved as family helpers or they carry out only domestic work.' As a result, women are often labelled dependents, when in fact they carry out a significant proportion of the tasks that ensure the ongoing functioning of the household unit.
- Thirdly, women contribute most of the unpaid work tasks within a household (Waring 1989: Ch. 3). If these tasks were translated into monetary value, then they would contribute significantly to GNP figures. Studies in various poorer countries have revealed that often the majority of income in poor households is generated outside the formal labour market and most of this is contributed by women (Hunt 2004: 255).
- Fourthly, the stereotype of a household headed by a male breadwinner sits uneasily with evidence that 35 per cent of Third World households in poorer countries are headed by women (Panayiotopolous 2001: 199).

For these reasons, feminists have questioned the masculinist assumptions underpinning much development theory and practice.

---

class without understanding how male–female relations change in the process, since those changes are integral to the way classes are structured and reproduced – and experienced'.

During the 1970s, many of these gender-related issues began to reach the offices of international development organizations. The year 1975 was designated the 'international year of women' and international institutions pledged the following decade to promote 'the advancement of women'. As a result, a number of high-profile UN conferences have since focused attention on the role of women in the development process (Mexico City 1975, Copenhagen 1980, Nairobi 1985, and Beijing 1995). Out of the early conferences, the world was given the following summary of the state of gender inequality: 'women make up half the world's population, perform two-thirds of the world's working hours, receive one-tenth of the world's income and own only one-hundredth of the world's property' (Abbott et al. 2005: 82).

However, development brought mixed blessings for gender equality. This applies to the wealthier nations as well as the poorer nations. In the wealthier nations, it appears that after some considerable gains during the 1960s and 1970s, gender equality has stalled (Summers 2003). The achievement of formal legal equality coexisting with the persistence of income and status inequality has been labelled the 'glass ceiling'. Poorer countries present other problems for gender equality. The absence of legal equality can aggravate the injustices faced by women across cultures in poorer countries (Handelman 2003: 116). For instance, despite their crucial role in farming worldwide, women own on average under 2 per cent of land, and in some countries (such as Nepal, India and Thailand) this proportion drops to one per cent. Less than one in ten dollars of credit is allocated to women (ILO 2004: 48, 90). Within the 15–24 age category, women in poorer countries have a literacy rate of 60 per cent, 20 percentage points less than men. In some Indian states, literacy rates for women are less than 10 per cent (UNDP 2003: 86; for Africa see Commission for Africa 2005: 62–3).

Furthermore, medical technology does not necessarily reduce inequalities or injustices. Despite medical advances, modern medicine has failed to make a significant impact on the prevalence of neonatal diseases in many poorer countries (Calvert and Calvert 2003). Many couples hoping for the birth of a boy now have the capacity to use ultrasound technology to terminate their pregnancy if the scan disappoints those hopes. As noted in Chapter 2, it has been estimated that gender discrimination has resulted in some 100 million missing women in Asia.

In only 7 countries do women account for 30 per cent or more parliamentarians (UNDP 2003: 86). However, they have achieved the highest political office in many poor nations, such as India, Pakistan, Bangladesh, Sri Lanka, the Philippines, Indonesia, Nicaragua and Chile (Handelman 2003: 134), although what is notable about many of these cases is the fact that – like most men – they often derive their power from their elite status and their familial associations. This suggests that gender inequality is correlated in complex ways with other variables, such as class, family, status, race and ethnicity.

Women and globalization

Gender inequality preceded modernity. Indeed, modernization theory predicts that modernity will bring an end to various dimensions of gender inequality associated with traditional social relations. Supporters of global free trade have also argued that the contemporary process of globalization will have an ameliorating effect on gender inequality. According to Norberg (2003: 43–4), the spread of market relations breaks down traditional barriers to women's emancipation:

> One of the traditions challenged by globalization is the long-standing subjugation of women. Through cultural contacts and the interchange of ideas, new hopes and ideals are disseminated. . . . When women begin making their own decisions about their consumer behaviour or their employment, they become more insistent in demanding equal liberty and power in other fields.

Sen (2001: 201) has also observed that there has been a marked decline in fertility rates in Bangladesh as women have been incorporated into public life through paid work and participative development projects (see also Sachs 2005: 10–14). Other commentators more critical of globalization have also acknowledged that there have been marked reductions in the gender gap in fields as diverse as education, employment and health. By the end of the twentieth century, global enrolment in secondary education covered almost two-thirds of girls. The participation of women in the formal labour market increased by an extra 11 per cent between 1973 and 1990 as technological change and capital mobility promoted global industrial restructuring. Scholte (2000: 254) calculates that 'global capitalism has increased women's opportunities for paid employment; global governance has introduced a number of legal and institutional initiatives to promote the status of women; and global civil society has provided increased means to mobilize for gender equity' (see also ILO 2004: 48).

These claims resonate with the underlying themes of modernization theory. Handelman (2003: 140) also acknowledges that there is a positive relationship between gender equality and other indicators of development, such as length of formal education, literacy, rates of urbanization and industrialization. However, he rejects any simple causation, arguing that 'modernization affects women's status positively over the long run, but often has adverse effects in the short-to-medium terms' (Handelman 2003: 121). This gendered version of Kuznet's U-curve might suggest that the pessimism of dependency theory holds in the shorter term, while the optimism of modernization theory carries more weight in the longer term – an argument also consistent with Etzioni-Halevy's (1980) synthetic theoretical approach to development theories (see Chapter 5).

Many of the negative trends that globalized employment opportunities have imposed on women are often concentrated in specific industry sectors. The 'new international division of labour' was based on more foot-loose capitalist enterprises seeking to reduce its labour costs through moving to regions with cheaper and less militant workers (see Chapter 8). The export processing zones and new industrial districts that emerged in poorer countries as a result of global industrial restructuring were often associated with labour-intensive assembly operations where there was an abundant supply of labour, especially women workers (Ramamurthy 2000: 251). From the Asian electronics industry in the late 1970s to Mexican clothing assembly plants, women have increased their participation in the paid workforce. Within higher-income countries that were exporting manufacturing jobs, new 'feminized', or 'pink-collar', sectors have expanded that offer women opportunities, especially in the so-called service sectors (retailing, cleaning and data processing). However, the abundant supply of labour in these fields tends to depress wages (Rowbottom 1992).

These trends associated with the new international division of labour suggest that women 'are central to economic change and that Third World industrialization would not be possible without the exploitation of women as cheap workers' (Panayiotopoulos 2003: 198). Claims of women's 'marginality' carried more weight before the expansion of global industrialization, but they have been challenged by what the ILO (2004: 120) has labelled the 'global feminization' of work. The UN's 2005 *Report on the World Social Situation* (2005: 4) concluded that the growing numbers of women in paid work 'masks the deterioration in the terms and conditions of employment, as women tend to secure jobs with lower pay'. For instance, at the turn of the new millennium, Russian women earned on average only half the male wage (UNDP 2003: 65).

The reduction of state support for health, education and basic food subsidies that has accompanied neoliberal globalization affected women more than men (ILO 2004: 47). IMF-imposed structural adjustment programmes demanded cuts to social services which have also adversely impacted on women. This is due to the fact that they are disproportionately represented as workers in the worst-affected sectors, such as nursing, health care and teaching. Not only have women absorbed more of the 'double burden' of paid work and domestic work, but they have done so through moving into the lowest-paid sectors of the labour market while experiencing reduced state assistance.

Taking a sceptical view, Mies (1994: 110–15) has argued that the growing trend among international development agencies to 'invest in women' is primarily an attempt to lower global labour costs through increasing the exploitability of women and instilling greater discipline into the labour force. She has labelled this global phenomenon the 'housewifization' of capitalist development (Mies 1987). According to Mies, housewifization functions to ensure the material conditions of global capital accumulation (see also Broad 1995: 26–7).

The transformation of the global economy over the past 30 years has raised awareness of the gendering of work patterns. It is difficult to untangle the dynamics of economic development from the transformation of gender relations (Mackintosh 1989). The social roles women perform often lead to specific forms of organization, participation and resistance and, as the following section shows, even 'pose questions about the purpose and direction of development' (Johnson 1992: 172). While modernization theory predicted that women's emancipation would be an outcome of successful development, commentators such as Sen (2001: 203) consider women's participation in social, political and economic life as a constituent part of the process of development (see also UNDP 2003: 85). Indeed, Sen argues that nothing 'is as important today in the political economy of development as an adequate recognition of political, economic and social participation and leadership of women'.

Some forms of gender analysis have gone beyond reassessing the role of women in development. They have opened up other theoretical issues associated with development, such as the power to define reality (regimes of truth), and how this affects practical issues concerning exclusion and inclusion, as well as empowerment and disempowerment.

Postdevelopmental Challenges

Environmental and women's movements have been far from monolithic, but it is possible to summarize their impact on development studies as a deepening critique of its theory and practice. Originally, they questioned the absence in development practice of any concern for the impact on the environment and on women. However, over the past two decades these concerns have generated a strand of critical thinking that has questioned the very process of development itself. Combined with approaches that analyse development from the perspective of marginalized (or subaltern) peoples, this has led to what Kothari (2002: 39) has called a 'methodological revisionism that enables a wholesale critique of Western structures of knowledge and power'.

From an original aim of adding more variables into the development equation, feminist and environmental movements have become highly suspicion of the values embedded within the equation. Many of these critics draw on postmodernism. At first glance, postmodernism would appear to offer little to the poorer countries whose historical trajectories differ so markedly from the 'modern' wealthier countries (Rosenau 1992, 152). However, as Escobar (1995: 116) explains: 'Rejecting grand revolutionary struggles as authoritarian, and seeking instead to grant individuals maximum power to determine their environment, radical postmodernists typically look for popular struggles in grassroots politics and activism centered on social movements such as women's and environmental groups.' During the 1990s, a radical 'postdevelopment' movement issued a powerful challenge to the development project. Given this genealogy, postdevelopmentalism can be appreciated by examining the deepening critique that feminism produced of development theory and practice.

Gender and postdevelopment

From the 1980s onwards a growing number of feminists began to view development as a postwar narrative of patriarchal capitalism and questioned the liberating potential that modernization brought in its wake. This critique led many feminists to deepen their critique of the very nature of development and the idea of progress (see Ramamurthy 2000: 248–9).

Furthermore, international women's conferences were questioning the possibility of a unified women's voice. They began to recognize that women from different classes could experience their gendered existence from different vantage points. In addition, women from diverse cultural backgrounds and historical experiences could have different understandings of 'liberation' (Bulbeck 1988). A more self-critical awareness emerged among many feminists that their demands reflected the vantage point of those in wealthier nations and could be interpreted as 'eurocentric'. In other words, the meaning that women attached to development in the wealthier nations might be meaningless from the perspective of women whose countries had experienced colonial encounters (Pettman 1992).

Many feminists therefore refused to take for granted any natural basis for women's solidarity or at least refused *a priori* to consider this to be the underlying basis of women's oppression. As Handelman (2003: 127, 136) notes, 'because the developing world encompasses so wide a variety of cultural traditions, and because social change has impinged so differently on the various social classes and sectors within individual nations, there can be no simple generalizations about the way in which modernization has influenced the political status of Third World women'. Cultural context and the heterogeneity of experience gained more attention.

This recognition of diverse experiences has methodological implications for the way postdevelopment feminists examine gender. They reject the idea that the western experience is a prototype that postcolonial women can follow. They are also wary of broad concepts that cluster women or other subject groups. Therefore, concepts such as class, ethnicity and even gender itself need to be analysed from the perspective of the culture in which they are embedded. Postdevelopment writers also question claims about the generalizability of research and the transferability of findings from one setting to other social and historical circumstances. This scepticism over 'grand narratives' and grand theory narrows the choice of research tools to more microsociological methods, such as individual case studies, ethnographies or the deconstruction of discourses imposed on, or created within, cultural settings (see Crotty 1998: Ch. 8; Saunders 2002).

Drawing on critiques of the western portrayal of the 'oriental subject' by writers such as Said (1979), postdevelopment feminists are aware that many western writers have created a monolithic 'Third World woman' as an object to examine, diagnose, test and cure. In this manner, poverty and want in poorer nations becomes a 'problem' that western experts can monitor and manage (Berger 1993: 270; Kothari 2002: 47). A more multifaceted approach to the experience of women's oppression involves acknowledging that western observers invariably imposed their ethnocentric intellectual categories onto non-western circumstances. As Escobar (1995: 203) warned:

> To be sure, Eurocentered historical materialism and feminisms provide us with illuminating views of the conversion of nature and women into objects of work and production; to this extent they are extremely important. At the same time, however, an effort should be made to understand social life in the Third World (and in the West) through frameworks that do not rely solely on these intellectual achievements.

Mies (1994: 108) took this critique further, arguing that the very concepts of development and growth are biological metaphors designed to make a violent, oppressive, exploitative, inequitable process appear natural and inevitable.

Postmodern and postdevelopment feminisms might not have changed the world so far, but they have prompted a higher level of critical reflection among development theorists and practitioners. They have also problematized western scientific knowledge and have attempted to provide more space for marginalized voices. In this way, they challenge taken-for-granted assumptions about development practices and raise questions about the relationship between what we know and the exercise of power. As Kothari (2002: 50) notes, even though modernization principles remain dominant in the early twenty-first century, 'there is now a growing body of intellectual resources, debate and people within the discipline with the potential to decentre masculinist and colonial thinking'.

Postdevelopment and postmodernism

The very idea of 'stages' of development is problematic for postdevelopmentalism – bearing as it does all the hallmarks of linear progress. Postdevelopment analysis begins with the postmodern rejection of 'grand narratives' – explanations of social change that claim to account for the driving force behind history and which therefore possess the answers to the problems of global poverty and inequality. For postmodernists, this type of reasoning has characterized western thinking since the Enlightenment and has treated the notion of 'progress' as unproblematic (Lyotard 1991; Richard 1993: 463).

Despite the controversies that this book has discussed so far (between the sociological classics, between postwar modernization and dependency theorists, or between analysts of globalization) postdevelopmentalists would classify most of them as variations of modernism. Controversies within this modernist discourse serve to mask their underlying unity. The discursive framework of development, with its underlying assumption of inevitable progress, has remained fundamentally unchallenged. According to postdevelopmental writers, development-as-a-paradigm is a 'regime of truth' used by the powerful to ensure global compliance for an inequitable socioeconomic system.

Postdevelopment theorists have also been among the strongest opponents of the 'collective noun' dilemma in development studies and they provide a powerful critique of the language of postwar development studies (see Chapter 3). According to Escobar (1995: 6), the western world after the Second World War began looking upon 'poverty and backwardness as a new domain of thought and experience, namely development'. Development studies subsequently emerged as a discipline that has been implicated in a 'discursive formation' linking dominant forms of thought to specific techniques and practices of power. Escobar (1995: 10) summarizes this position by approaching development:

> as a historically singular experience, the creation of a domain of thought and action, by analyzing the characteristics and interrelations

of the three axes that define it: the forms of knowledge that refer to it and through which it comes into being and is elaborated into objects, concepts, theories, and the like; the system of power that regulates its practice; and the forms of subjectivity fostered by this discourse, those through which people come to recognize themselves as developed or underdeveloped.

Mark Berger (1993: 260) also argues that since the end of the Second World War 'more information and knowledge have been extracted from various parts of the globe and filtered through an array of intellectual and policy processes dominated by the so-called "First World", the effect of which has been to contribute to the managing of the "Third World".' Development studies, in other words, is principally a postwar grand narrative of 'global poverty', which in turn is a 'myth, a construct and an invention' of western civilization (Rahnema 1997b: 158; see also Rahnema 1992). In the case of postwar development, the stories constructed have all revolved around identifying a problem (what the poor 'lack'), which then allows the west to manage the task of removing the obstacles that lie in the path of advancement towards the western ideal (see Box 9.4).

Postdevelopment has also been associated with 'subaltern studies'. Subaltern studies was a term appropriated from the Italian Marxist Antonio Gramsci by a group of Indian historians in the early 1980s seeking to reinterpret the history of Indian workers and peasants in a manner that avoided assuming that the colonizers and the Indian elite were the only makers of history (Chakrabatry 1990: 101–2). As the research evolved, these historians began to look more warily on the very concept of 'history', in the same way that postdevelopment thinkers began to deconstruct 'development'. According to Chakrabarty, history, like development, is implicated in relationships of oppression and subordination. As we noted in Chapter 3, the discipline of history helped to generate the nationalist lore needed to legitimate the modern nation-state. As a consequence, subaltern studies 'could only be written with a critical eye on this point, that is by producing histories that contested the "nation's" homogenising claims on the people's diverse pasts' (Chakrabarty 1990: 104–5).

Like postmodernism and postdevelopmentalism, this awareness of the misuses of homogenizing and generalizing perspectives meant that microsociological studies and ethnographies were the most appropriate methodological tools for deconstructing 'history' and giving voice to the marginalized. For Escobar (1995: 19), there is no use in 'searching for grand alternative models or strategies'. Instead, researchers should focus on the 'investigation of alternative representations and practices in

---

Box 9.4   Development and scientific language

All disciplines evolve, and at any particular time a specific paradigm tends to dominate the way in which practitioners approach their subject matter (Kuhn 1970).

Postwar development theories have been criticized by postdevelopment writers for creating a new language of domination that not only limits the way the investigator approaches the subject, but also marginalizes the people that it proclaims to be the benefactors – the world's poor. Drawing on Foucault, postdevelopment writers point to how the marginalized can internalize this discipline and treat its findings as truth. However, such disciplines adorn themselves with the mystique of scientific investigation in order to disseminate 'powerful truths' and identify problems and justify intervention (Escobar 1995: 20). Language is always implicated in power relations.

A recent example of this use of technical language can be found in Jeffrey Sachs's (2005) book *The End of Poverty*. Chapter 7 has already pointed out how Sachs (and the UN Millennium Project) retains the flavour of the prototype/emulator model by viewing development as a 'ladder', up which all countries climb. In Chapter 4 of *The End of Poverty*, Sachs argues that development economics 'needs an overhaul in order to be much more like modern medicine'. Impoverished countries are seen as sick patients, in need of a cure. 'Crisis-ridden countries' (or 'patients') need to undertake a 'differential diagnosis' – a 'physical exam' – which then suggests an 'appropriate treatment regimen' (see also Freedman 2005: 19).

Critiques of 'regimes of power' – especially the role of scientific language and expertise – have a long history. Albert Einstein (1998: 2) warned that we 'should be on our guard not to overestimate science and scientific methods when it is a question of human problems: and we should not assume that experts are the only ones who have a right to express themselves on questions affecting the organization of society'.

---

concrete local settings, particularly as they exist in contexts of hybridization, collective action, and political mobilization'.

Postdevelopment theorists argue that development as it is currently practised often does more harm than good; at least to the communities it purports to benefit. In the same way that 'aid' could be reinterpreted as advancing the interests of the donors (Hayter 1971; Kothari 2002: 38–9), the development community has been accused by both postdevelopment theorists and right-wing think tanks of living off a 'development industry'. Solving the problem of development would cut off the livelihood of development practitioners (Escobar 1995: 46–7).

Finally, drawing logical inferences from this approach, postdevelopment provides an interesting twist to the assessment of development practice over the past half century. If development is reinterpreted as a discursive framework that has upheld relations of exploitation, then by the very criteria postdevelopment uses, development has been an outstanding success . . . for those whose interests it serves. This is explicitly acknowledged by Escobar (1995: 47) when he observes that 'development has been successful to the extent that it has been able to integrate, manage, and control countries and populations in increasingly detailed and encompassing ways'. The west has been able to manage 'sustainable' forms of underdevelopment, in the sense that this condition was needed for the west to maintain its dominance. It is possible to conclude that development has been a failure only if the 'innocent' claim is accepted that development was intended to alleviate poverty and reduce inequality. From a postmodern or postdevelopment angle, no narrative is ever innocent – not even postdevelopment, which explicitly tries to link its own intellectual activity with those whose story has been silenced by western discourse.

Critiques of postdevelopment

Despite its deconstruction of the language of development, its efforts to uncover its western imperialistic undertones and its willingness to listen to the diversity of voices that have been subsumed under the 'rest', critics of postdevelopment have claimed that the approach appeals largely to privileged western intellectuals. It has remained marginal in the anticolonial or postcolonial environment. Some critics view it as the latest western fad, colonizing and decontextualizing subaltern voices (Peet 1999). Simon During (1990: 96) suggested that its failure to penetrate beyond a few 'whites and diasporic Indian intellectuals' is due to the fact that the so-called postcolonial condition is not experienced in the same way within the richer and the poorer countries, despite the impact of global mass migration.

Writers depicted as 'modernist' have questioned the pessimistic portrait that postdevelopment draws of the Enlightenment. For example, Sachs (2005: 252) believes that technological, scientific and medical progress, rising living standards and a decline in the proportion of people living in extreme poverty 'has been real and sustained'. The 'claim of progress is correct as long as it is not taken to be a claim of perfection'. There is a reality to progress and while no one has denied that it is perfect, it remains a valid aspiration that the world community should aim for. He interprets the Enlightenment commitment to reason not as a 'denial of the unreasonable side of human nature, but rather a belief that despite human irrationality and passions, human reason can still be harnessed through science, nonviolent action, and historical reflection to solve basic problems of social organization and to improve human welfare'.

Others have criticized postdevelopment approaches for offering little in the way of practical guidance to reducing poverty and overcoming oppression. Its conclusions tend to be vague calls for further deconstruction of the language of oppression. Peet (1999: 193) notes that it hesitates to offer any concrete action: 'studies that cry out for some proposal of what to do in desperate situations suddenly end where they should propose, or call (safely) for "further research"'. As a consequence, postdevelopment writers have been accused of failing to provide an adequate political or policy response to poverty and inequality. For example, Escobar (1995: 203–4) suggests that to 'accede to postdevelopment, communities need to experiment with alternative productive strategies and, simultaneously practise semiotic resistance to capital's and modernity's restructuring of nature and society'. However, critics question whether semiotic resistance will ever escape from university classrooms. One example of alternative strategies identified by Escobar (1995: 99–100) involves returning to more autarchic production systems. This original dependency solution is still favoured by many environmentalists as the most practical hope for an ecologically sustainable future and the US Marxist David Harvey's (2000) dream of a near-future utopian society is clearly based on more autarchic communities.

Rapley (2002: 116) has also criticized postdevelopment for this failure to adequately address solutions to global inequality. Acknowledging that it positions itself with the poor, he worries that 'radical postmodernism may not offer them a practical means to lift themselves from their poverty'. However, he also acknowledges that postdevelopment has performed a positive role through challenging some long-held assumptions concerning the nature of development: 'if postdevelopment theory fails to provide answers to the pressing needs of today's third world, it remains useful for the questions it raises' (see also Kiely 1998: 10–21; Ramamurthy 2000: 253). 'Salutary broadsides' can often draw attention to directions previously ignored. Many argue that this critique adds vitality to development studies, particularly when the assumptions of modernization theory continue to hold sway within mainstream policy circles and international financial institutions (Kothari 2002: 50; Power 2003: 105; Sylvester 1999).

Postdevelopment thinkers can argue that they are wary of offering 'solutions' and repeating the errors of arrogant western developmental experts. They can also argue that no global solution is available – only local democratically derived responses to particular issues. After all, this was how Marx and Engels (1969: 92–3) responded to utopian socialists who conjured up blueprints for the future: such solutions were mere 'castles in the air'. Under these conditions, Kothari (2002: 51) admits that 'we do not yet know what a decolonized, demasculinized development will actually look like'. Even if postdevelopment hasn't offered a path to a more egalitarian future, it has served to make practitioners and theorists question the taken-for-grantedness of concepts such as 'progress', which remains 'a blinker deeply set within collective cognition' (Shanin 1995).

There is one political trend that many postdevelopment thinkers have come to view with hope of global liberating potential – the World Social Forum (also called the 'Porte Allegre movement' after the venue that hosted a large gathering of diverse social movements from across the world in 2001). This loose formation of grass roots organizations – embracing environmentalists, feminists, socialists, ethnic minorities, anarchists, and other discontents or anti-systemic movements – has captured the attention of a growing number of commentators in the early twenty-first century and has been hailed as the first serious post-Cold War contender for an organizing focus against global corporate capitalism. A short history of these anti-systemic movements will complete this survey of challenges to mainstream development.

The Globalization of New Social Movements

The first three sections of this chapter examined a range of theoretical, cultural and political critiques that not only challenged the practice of development, but also the concept of development itself. These concerns have grown over the past three decades. However, as the environmentalist challenge shows, modernity has always had its discontents. Throughout this history of modernity, voices have persistently been raised against the inequalities that coincided with progress. Supporters of progress often justified these inequalities with reassuring forecasts that inequality was a necessary phase before greater equality emerged. Inequality was one of the 'growing pains' of development.

During the 1960s, issues surrounding poverty and wealth drew the attention of sociologists to the rise of new social movements in the more affluent countries. Despite unprecedented levels of economic growth, affluent states 'rediscovered' poverty within their midst. Various movements, ranging from women's liberation groups to racial and ethnic groups, began to also demand an end to discriminatory practices that maintained specific dimensions of inequality. These movements implicitly questioned the optimistic claims made by modernization theorists that modernity brought meritocratic award structures in its wake (McClelland 1961).

At the same time, new social movements arose associated with affluence. Inglehart (1971) argued that the basis of politics in affluent countries was changing. He claimed that the emerging 'post-industrial' society would reveal new attitudinal cleavages based on the attachment to 'material' or 'postmaterial' values. His research revealed that people who grew up in the first half of the twentieth century held a more materialist orientation compared with those who grew up in the more affluent age of the 1950s and 1960s. According to Inglehart, the old materialist politics was primarily about the fulfilment of material needs and the conflict between clearly identifiable social groups over the resources to fulfil these needs. This materialist approach encouraged a class-centred approach to politics.

Both Inglehart (1971) and Rostow (1960: 11) argued that the likelihood of new political values emerging would be enhanced once basic material needs were satisfied. These alternative values found a constituency among the more affluent, better-educated, baby-boomer generation that began to reach political maturity during the 1960s. This generation found the old politics of class less relevant to their everyday experience and were searching for a 'new politics' that corresponded with this attitudinal shift. This 'new politics' is a label attached to a range of social movements that has emerged since the late 1960s, including student movements, civil rights movements, women's movements, ethnic rights groups, peace movements and environment movements. Papadakis (1991) argued that the new politics has made an impact in three interrelated areas: a range of 'single issues'; the mobilization of new political constituencies, or identity politics; and new political methods, procedures and forms of organization. This new politics has never coalesced into a stable political ideology. It tends to be organizationally decentralized, preferring grass roots mobilization over expert representation, and tends to form loose coalitions around specific issues.

According to Touraine (1985), these new social movements are not merely interested in the redistribution of social production (or materialist goals). They are engaged in issues surrounding the very control of our lives, including culture, work, participation, organization and quality of life. In other words, they represent a fundamental (or postmaterialist) challenge to our way of life, our morality and the way we experience and express truths. They also sow doubts about the sustainability of the cultural and productive trends that both modernization theory and classical Marxism took for granted. What is at stake is nothing more that the legitimacy of our life-world, or our 'cultural totality'. According to one estimate, these civil society organizations and non-government organizations have mushroomed throughout the world from around 1500 in number in the mid-1950s to some 25,000 by the beginning of the twenty-first century (ILO 2004: 125).

After the Cold War, these new social movements coalesced around the 'anti-globalization movement', although the global links they formed lent themselves to the qualification that they are opposed to *corporately controlled* globalization and the ideology of neoliberal globalization. The broad philosophy of this new global social movement also appeals to postmaterialist values and it rejects the neoliberal claim that there is no alternative to market-oriented development. Indeed, the slogan it has adopted is that 'another world is possible' (George 2004), and they assert that multiple coexisting futures are available (Kingsnorth 2003).

As globalization became more ubiquitous during the 1990s, the 'new politics' became more dispersed, linking political and social movements across the world. As Escobar (1995: 215) observed:

> a relatively coherent body of work has emerged which highlights the role of grassroots movements, local knowledge, and popular power in transforming development. The authors representing this trend state that they are interested not in development alternatives but in alternatives to development, that is, the rejection of the entire paradigm altogether. In spite of significant differences, the members of this group share certain preoccupations and interests: an interest in local culture and knowledge; a critical stance with respect to established scientific discourses; and the defense and promotion of localized, pluralistic grassroots movements.

This movement achieved worldwide notoriety and acclaim after a WTO meeting in Seattle in late 1999. The confrontations between police and the diverse range of 'anti-globalization' groups attracted global media attention by forcing the closure of Seattle's central business district and the postponement of the WTO event. The economist Deepak Lal (2004: 3) was lost to explain how the 'benign process' of globalization could 'inflame the passions' of the kaleidoscopic crowd (which included, he claims, a 'phalanx of bare-breasted women' wielding a sign 'Vegan Dykes against the WTO'). One lasting consequence of the 'Battle of Seattle' was that the role of supranational institutions such as the WTO and the IMF came under more critical scrutiny. Subsequent IFI conferences rallied anti-globalization protesters and by 2001 these groups began holding their own forums under the umbrella of the World Social Forum. Referring to Fukuyama's predictions, Bendana (2001) suggested that the Battle of Seattle signalled the restart of a 'positive history' and the end of the end of history.

The new social movements associated with the World Social Forum have become adept at employing the technologies and techniques that facilitated greater capital mobility, using them for their alternative ends. Klein (2001) has documented how various new social movements have targeted global corporations through associating their most precious asset – the brand name – with unethical practices such as environmental destruction, worker exploitation and urban alienation. Robinson (2004: 146) claims that these 'media-oriented protests represented but the visible tip of a dramatic upsurge in transnationally networked grass-roots resistance movements in countries around the world and the making of a common critical (counter-hegemonic) consciousness and political practice'.

The philosophy behind the World Social Forum reflects many of the theoretical developments that have questioned the 'juggernaut' of globalization (Goodman and Ranald 2000):

> We are diverse – women and men, adults and youth, indigenous peoples, rural and urban, workers and unemployed, homeless, the elderly, students, migrants, professionals, peoples of every creed, color and sexual orientation. The expression of this diversity is our strength and the basis of our unity. We are a global solidarity movement, united in our determination to fight against the concentration of wealth, the proliferation of poverty and inequalities, and the destruction of our earth.   (World Social Forum 2002: 1)

Emphasizing the benefits of political decentralization and local participatory direct action, supporters of the World Social Forum view this new social movement as an alternative transnational force that challenges the practices of global capitalist expansion. It pits a counter-hegemonic globalization-from-below against the dominant globalization-from-above (Ramonet 2004: 29–31). Its supporters view it as a practical illustration that 'another world is possible' if enough people reject the environmentally destructive, undemocratic, competitive, militaristic nature of western power relations and their global extension (George 2004). Their analysis suggests that the path of globalizing capitalist modernity will not lead to greater equality through spreading prosperity, but towards planetary chaos once the 'limits of growth' are overshot (Meadows et al. 2005: ch. 1). This resistance by anti-globalization movements to neoliberal globalization has also brought the issue of a more interventionist state back into the developmental equation as a means of protecting the vulnerable from global market forces. This is rather ironic considering the detractors of the anti-globalization movement often accuse it of harbouring dangerous anarchist tendencies.

Critics regard this networked movement as the latest of a long line of anarchic Luddite fads that modernity inevitably spawns. According to Krugman (2001) the emergence of this movement presents a grave danger to the aspirations of the world's poor. Even though the movement might express well-meaning indignation when confronted with poverty, their naïve solutions would prove disastrous. Referring to anti-corporate demonstrators, he states that the 'people outside the fence, whatever their intentions, are doing their best to make the poor even poorer'. By attacking the 'goose that lays the golden egg', these new social movements are in effect not challenging global inequality and poverty but prolonging it. Easterly (2002: xiii) also accuses anti-globalization movements of abandoning the 'quest' for development. In effect, new social movements in the rich world are accused of attempting to block poorer countries from undertaking the same path that led to their own stage of prosperity and that allows them the freedoms to voice their concerns about the state of global inequality.

Other critics claim that environmental groups restrict the ability of poor nations to exploit the very resources that will enable them to develop. If poverty causes environmental degradation, then economic growth is the best means of alleviating this problem, and liberalism and free trade is the most effective means of achieving sustainable economic growth (Landes 2002: 516; Lomberg 2001; Norberg 2003). Having effectively climbed the ladder of development and fed on its successes, these postmaterialist anti-globalization activists have forgotten the grave consequences of basic-resource poverty. They have erected the equivalent of a developmental 'glass ceiling' that allows the poorer nations to see the wealth that can be generated by the free market while prohibiting the poor from accessing the means of achieving progress and prosperity. In other words, these social movements perpetuate global inequality through ensuring that the poorer countries never get to emulate the wealthier forerunners.

The movement is also often charged with 'protectionism' by its opponents (Norberg 2003). The withdrawal from the global market experienced during the interwar era resulted in the rise of virulent forms of nationalism that led to fascism. Market-oriented globalization fosters intercultural communication, the exchange of goods, democratic governance and international understanding (Friedman 2000). Some critics of global social movements claim that it is no coincidence that the nationalistic far right often appears as its strange bedfellow. Any effort that impedes individual aspirations invariably leads to authoritarian politics. For a similar reason, some critics have labelled environmentalism as the 'emotional sister of fascism' (McGuinness 1990). It is intent on imposing its austere environmental future on an unwilling majority that aspires to higher levels of consumption.

The breadth and heterogeneity of the World Social Forum also lends itself to the charge that its message is 'incoherent'. Echoing many of the critiques against postdevelopment, Kay (2003: 324) claimed that it clearly proclaims its opposition to modern capitalism without presenting an alternative vision. Sachs (2005: 357) also criticized the movement for dismissing 'the possibilities of capitalism with a human face, in which the remarkable power of trade and investment can be harnessed while acknowledging and addressing limitations through compensatory collective actions'. Singer (2002: 63) has also warned that more is needed than 'repeated rituals of street theatre' in order to solve the very real economic problems facing the planet.

Many of these critiques can, in turn, be accused of caricaturizing the anti-globalization movement. Tabb (2000) has stressed that anti-globalization protesters 'are not against rules governing the global economy'. On the contrary, they demand an alternative set of rules capable of bringing 'rapacious capital' to heel. He calls for 'stronger laws' that reflect the 'values endorsed by the vast majority of the world's citizens' (see also Bello 2003; ILO 2004: 126). As Wallerstein (2004: 86–7; 2003) also notes, the World Social Forum is keenly aware that the world economy has entered a period of systemic crisis and the political options advocated by the movement are more realistic than 'business as usual'. This political contest involves the hearts and minds of the global community.

Furthermore, the overriding sentiment expressed by the World Social Forum is that global equality cannot be achieved through resource-extensive capitalist development. The only economic growth worth considering is environmentally sustainable development even if this means – to paraphrase Gandhi – that the rich will have to live more simply, so that the poor may simply live. It is also inaccurate to label the anti-globalization movement a rich-world phenomenon. Many groups associated with the anti-globalization movement are based in poorer countries and many reject large-scale capitalist development projects, such as the anti-dam movement in India (Roy 2002, 2004).

Sen (2001a: 11) acknowledges that these new social movements can perform an important role in challenging the way development is conceived. He argues that to dismiss 'the doubts that the protestors raise would be the wrong response' because doubt and reflection always have a place in critical analysis – even if it does not coincide with dominant understandings of the truth – and it forces people to look at uncomfortable evidence. In the same way that environmentalists have brought questions concerning humanity's relationship with nature to the fore, new social movements have done the same with marginalization, poverty and inequality (UNDP 2003: 140).

There are also sympathetic commentators who warn that the dominant forces of global capitalism are intent on co-opting sections of the new social movements. By the beginning of the twenty-first century, the neoliberal 'triumphalism' of the 1990s was more subdued and was replaced with a tone of 'compromise, dialogue, and compassion' (William Robinson 2004: 171). The neoliberal World Economic Forum began inviting NGOs to their elite global colloquia. The UN also established a 'global compact' that brought together TNCs in the spirit of 'corporate responsibility, sustainability and philanthropy'. While some non-government organizations saw this as nothing more than 'greenwash', other civil society organizations have accepted roles on UN advisory committees. The UN Millennium Project and other MDG-promoters believe that NGOs are important agents in delivering the MDGs. The UNDP (2003: 23) has identified three roles: as participants in project design; as service providers; and as government watchdogs.

This link between state organizations and NGOs will continue to be a contentious issue. The earlier environmental and feminist sections of this chapter have already introduced this issue of co-option. Co-option can be read either as a Machiavellian attempt by global elites to accommodate change without altering the structure of power, or it can be seen as a manifestation of the success and growing influence of alternative social movements. This issue of co-option – whether in the form of 'mainstreaming gender', choosing between different shades of green, or between reform and revolution – has a history as old as liberal democracy itself. It will be revisited again in the following chapter where the value of participation in development projects is explored.

Chapter 10

Development, Politics and Participation

Democratization: Power to the People

Decentralization: Rolling Down the State

Participation: the New Orthodoxy

It has been apparent throughout this book that there is a strong link between the distribution of power and the establishment and maintenance of structures of inequality and poverty. This chapter examines various aspects of these unequal power relations through the conceptual lens of politics. This involves looking at the struggles that have taken place on 'macro' and 'micro' levels to bring 'power to the people'. They involve democratization, decentralization and participation.

Democratization: Power to the People

Our enquiry into democratization begins by returning to the theme of colonialism and the argument made in Chapter 4 that the colonial experience had a strong influence on contemporary politics in poorer countries. Colonialism interacted with existing indigenous social and political structures to produce a variety of legacies that can be observed in contemporary political practice and power distribution. Although colonialism was a common experience for almost all poorer countries it occurred at different times, encountered different social and political organizations, was undertaken by different imperialist countries and took place in different geographical circumstances.

There are several lessons relating to political inequality that can be drawn from the diverse colonial encounters. First, colonialism involved imposing systems of pronounced political inequality both between nations and within them. The colonial power dominated the subjugated

colony and the internal order of the colony involved political stratification with colonizers at the apex and indigenous populations at the base.
Decision-making powers resided at the apex with occasional concessions
to emerging middle classes but not to the masses. Secondly, order was
maintained by the threat or actual utilization of violence by the colonial
state using its own forces and even some recruited from the indigenous
population. Thirdly, local political leaders could be co-opted or overthrown. In Latin America it was the latter strategy which prevailed. In
many British colonial possessions, co-option of local leaders was practised as an efficient management alternative, and in some cases, such as
in Fiji, 'traditional' patterns of leadership could be partly invented
(Lawson 1991). The objective in all cases was to maintain colonial hegemony. Fourthly, pathways to political independence could be more or
less violent – from bloody wars of independence in Latin America to
entirely peaceful transitions in Papua New Guinea (see Box 4.2). Fifthly,
colonial policy did not simply act upon existing elements of cultural and
political structures. There was reciprocal interaction. Some patterns of
indigenous politics, such as leadership styles and strategies, survived or
mutated through the colonial times, while others were forged in them or
were the result of anti-colonial struggles. Sixthly, despite the rhetoric of
freedom and liberation evident in anti-colonial struggles, the reality
could be one in which the reimposition of pronounced political inequality was evident. New elites grasped power from departing elites or some
ethnic groups asserted domination over others. In such circumstances
there was an unfortunate and undesirable continuity: the poor and disadvantaged retained their deprived status, excluded from the exercise of
effective political power.

As noted in Chapter 4, decolonization was on the global agenda at the
end of the Second World War. If some colonial powers believed that the
status quo could be restored in their colonial possessions they were
mistaken. A combination of factors indicated that the colonies would
sooner, rather than later, break free from the formal political control of
their European and American masters. Whichever path was taken the
resulting destination was the same – political independence. The nation-
alists were also influenced and emboldened by the newly formed United
Nations, which was espousing human rights, equal rights and freedom.

There was also a demonstration effect from countries which had
started the decolonization juggernaut rolling. The example of India
'echoed through Africa' (Hunter 1962: 38). Although India's independence was granted in 1947 it actually represented the culmination of a
long process originating in the first quarter of the nineteenth century
when liberal ideas made their first appearance on the subcontinent and
culminating with the Gandhi-inspired mass movement of the 1920s and

1930s (Gupta 1995). The Philippines provided another model for independence-seeking countries to follow. At the end of the nineteenth century in the Philippines, the USA had followed up their defeat of the Spanish colonizers with a brutal colonization of their own (Wolff 1960). Once control had been established over the archipelago, the inexperienced imperialists gave early indication of intentions for Philippine independence 'as soon as a stable government can be established therein' (*Jones Law* of 1916, as quoted in Agoncillo and Guerrero 1973: 345). Political socialization was provided in a democratically elected legislature populated by members of the Philippine elite, and when the Second World War broke out only currency and foreign relations remained in American hands. Full independence came swiftly after the war, in 1946, with the USA keen to display to the world its 'showcase of democracy' in Asia (Karnow 1989).

India and the Philippines were soon emulated by countries throughout Africa and Asia. Within 15 years of the end of the Second World War, most African countries had achieved independence. It was a similar story in south-east Asia where political leaders seized independence, sometimes by force, after 1945. In the island territories of the Caribbean and South Pacific there was a later and more gradual move to independence. There were a few early starters, for example Jamaica and Trinidad and Tobago in 1962, but for most Caribbean countries independence came in the 1970s. This was when decolonization arrived in the South Pacific commencing with Fiji in 1970 and Papua New Guinea in 1975 and then carrying on to microstates such as Kiribati and Tuvalu.

Decolonization seemed to represent the removal of political inequity between nations. Modernization theorists generally assumed this to be the case and also claimed a clear association between capitalism and democracy. They argued that capitalism produced wealth which would 'trickle down' to the wider population, help build a stabilizing middle class and produce social changes favourable to democracy. The liberal democracy of the West would be reproduced and consolidated across the developing world. Traditional forms of authority, such as those deriving from ethnic identity, would succumb to modernization and the creation of orderly mass political participation.

This golden vision was not, however, being reflected in reality. Many leaders in developing countries began to speak out against continued inequities in the relations between rich and poor nations and alleged that old-style colonialism had been replaced with a new and closely related phenomenon – neocolonialism. Thus, using ideas that were later adopted by dependency theory, Nkwame Nkrumah (the first Prime Minister of Ghana) observed that while independence had provided 'the outward trappings of international sovereignty', the reality was that the new states' economic systems and 'political policy' were still being 'directed from outside' (as quoted in Smith 2003). Similarly, Julius Nyerere (the first President of Tanzania) remarked that his country had 'attained neither economic power nor economic independence' (as quoted in Smith 2003). His country was still shackled by powerful Western nations.

The dependency theorists encountered in Chapter 5 provided a more structural analysis when pointing to international political economy as the culprit. In political terms, their analysis emphasized the subjugation of peripheral country populations by domestic elites who were themselves the junior agents of the metropolitan bourgeoisie who ruled the world from the boardrooms of New York, London and other rich-country capitals. While some of the basic principles of this mode of analysis remain of considerable relevance when considering the activities and influence of multinational corporations and the power of IFIs, one should take care in assuming total political domination by external organizations. As O'Brien (1991: 161) warned, 'the manipulations of the dependent are not to be underestimated'. Thus, the bargaining power of some African patrimonial leaders has been described as 'formidable', using 'dependency as a carefully maintained resource' to extract income from metropolitan powers often for the benefit of ruling élites. Similarly in Asia, the US government's relationship with the authoritarian President Marcos has been likened to 'waltzing with a dictator', the latter determining the steps which the US government dutifully followed (Bonner 1987).

If there was dissatisfaction with an unequal world order among poorer countries, was there better news for the populations from political developments taking place within their territorial boundaries? The new democratic institutions were often found to be shallow-rooted, a matter which had become apparent in Latin America a century earlier. The general trend was towards authoritarian rule – what Pinkney (2003) has described as 'the eclipse of democracy' – and was manifest in the suspension of parliaments, military coups, the imprisonment of opposition leaders, human rights abuses and muzzling of the media. The democratic rights that had, at independence, been given 'to the people' were all too quickly being taken away from them. In Africa, 'politics came to involve competition among a small and fractured elite for control over a dwindling state pie' (Chazan et al. 1988: 62). In Asia, there emerged a pattern of state-led economic development involving either authoritarian control or quasi-democracies where opposition parties existed but were too weak to win. In general, states were seen to be weak and governments often incapable of providing adequate services to their constituents. Myrdal (1977: 150) wrote of 'soft states' in which 'governments require extraordinarily little of their citizens'. Huntington (1968: 2) asserted that developing countries had 'a shortage of political community and of effective, authoritative, legitimate government' and, somewhat ominously, that the 'most important political distinction among countries concerns not their form of government but their degree of government' (Huntington 1968: 1). Effectiveness of the political system was the important consideration. Thus, an effective democracy was more like an effective authoritarian system than a weak developing country state.

During the 1970s and 1980s, military intervention in the politics of poor countries became 'a depressingly regular occurrence' (Smith 2003: 173). Coups were commonplace and military uniforms were increasingly to be seen in the offices of government – from cabinet rooms to provincial administrations. Statistical comparisons of these phenomena aimed at identifying the underlying causes of the military colonization of government proved inconclusive. However, political scientists were not short of explanatory theories. One group advanced the notion that coups occurred where the social mobility associated with modernization put an intolerable burden on the new democratic institutions for dealing with conflict (Huntington 1968). They were not up to the task as they were insufficiently institutionalized. This allowed or encouraged militaries to intervene invariably on the grounds of saving the country from mismanagement at the hands of its civilian politicians. An alternative perspective was that countries with 'low political culture' were particularly vulnerable to military coups. Thus, Finer (1962: 1) argued that 'where public attachment to civilian institutions is weak or non-existent, military intervention in politics will find wide scope'. Social class is sometimes used as an explanatory device. For example, a coup may be mounted in defence of middle-class interests, especially if officers are members of that class (Nun 1967 and 1986). Alternatively, a coup may provide opportunities for the upward mobility of military officers through a process of embourgeoisement (Smith 2003). A final perspective on military intervention in politics takes the view that organizational characteristics, rather than the socioeconomic or political context, are the crucial variable. The military is well-organized with a clear chain of command. Its officers are trained in a variety of disciplines and will use this professional competence 'to defend the state against forces that would undermine its integrity' (Smith 2003: 189).

A handful of electoral democracies survived throughout authoritarian times from the 1960s to the 1980s. In other cases the 'eclipse of democracy' was brief or was manifest in milder forms of authoritarianism. But by the late 1970s across vast swathes of the poorer world it was apparent that democracy was an endangered species. What little power the people had acquired in the postcolonial transitions to democracy had been taken away and, to rub salt into the wound, in many cases there had been little material progress. In some instances populations were becoming worse off. Only in the developmental east Asian states such as South Korea and Taiwan had levels of welfare improved considerably under authoritarian rule. But in the 1980s, the political pendulum started to swing back towards democratization. Using another metaphor, 'the third wave' of democratization began to break across the poorer world (Huntington 1991) (see Box 10.1).

Power was returning to the people. In the Philippines, massive 'people power' demonstrations in 1985 marked the beginning of the end for President Ferdinand Marcos. In Latin America, military rulers began

Box 10.1   The 'three waves' of democratization

According to Huntington (1991: 15–16) 'a wave of democratization is a group of transitions from non-democratic to democratic regimes that occur within a specified period of time and that significantly outnumber transitions in the opposite direction during that period of time'. In some cases, full democratization – for Huntington this is essentially clean elections – is not attained but the wave may result in partial democratization or liberalization. The first two waves have been followed by reverse waves leading to non-democratic forms of government.

- *The First Wave* started at the beginning of the nineteenth century and lasted until about 1930.
- *The First Reverse Wave* from 1926 to 1942 involved the rise of fascism in Europe.
- *The Second Wave* commenced at the end of the Second World War in 1945 and lasted until 1960s.
- *The Second Reverse Wave* involved the failure of democratic consolidation especially in the developing world but also in some countries of southern Europe.
- *The Third Wave* began in southern Europe in 1974 and spread to poorer countries in the 1980s

Huntington (1991) identified five factors to account for this global empowerment: legitimacy problems of authoritarian governments; rising expectations especially by the middle classes; liberalization in the Roman Catholic Church; advocacy of democracy by multilateral organizations and the USA; and the demonstration effect of democratizing nations in a world of globalized communication. The optimistic conclusion is that globalization is the handmaiden of democratization but detailed examination of specific country cases reveals that factors and actors such as social classes, civil society and the nature of the state may also be of considerable significance (Grugel 2002).

retreating to the barracks. By 1989, the wave started to have an impact in Central and Eastern Europe and in Africa so that by the 1990s countries across the poorer world including the Middle East were embracing electoral democracy or at least taking steps towards it.

But has the 'third wave' actually empowered people in developing countries? Are the voices of the poor listened to and acted upon? Have women been able to aggregate and articulate policy demands? Is ethnicity no longer a basis for discrimination? In short, are we witnessing sustained progress towards political equality across the poorer world? If we take the narrow view, one adopted by Huntington, then we may simply look to see if elections are being held. If this is so, then democratization has taken place and presumably the benefits deriving from it will trickle down to the population at large just like neoliberal theories of development predict. But voting in elections is an inadequate single measure of a healthy democracy, and if employed can lead to the 'fallacy of electoralism' (Schmitter and Karl 1991). Elections may be characterized by unfair competition with a ruling party dominating resources and writing the rules of the game. Elected elites may not represent or articulate the interests of the poor and disadvantaged. Family dynasties sometimes control political office such as in the Philippines where between 60 and 100 families are alleged 'to dominate and influence the process of selection of the country's elective and appointive government positions' (Gutierrez et al. 1992: 4; see also Gutierrez 1994). The electorate itself may view voting in a way alien to the western theories of liberal democracy. For example, a survey of Cambodian citizens revealed that while they were keen to participate in elections, they saw voting as fulfilling their 'civic duty' rather than as an opportunity to pass judgment on public policy or 'to change the direction of their country' (Asia Foundation 2003: 10). There may also be cheating, intimidation and manipulation in elections. In some cases, authoritarian rulers have tried to rehabilitate themselves through elections but then annul the results if the outcome is not to their liking. In Burma (Myanmar) the military government called an election in 1990 expecting their candidates to win but the opposition National League for Democracy (NLD) led by Aung San Suu Kyi captured 87.7 per cent of the seats. The military refused to transfer power and 'reverted to terrorizing the political opposition' (Alamgir 1997: 345). And even where there has been a record of uninterrupted elections, as in Papua New Guinea, candidates can be elected to office with a mere 5 per cent of the votes cast and evidence of bad governance is clearly manifested in corruption, poor service delivery and the inability to impose the rule of law (Dinnen 2001; Reilly 1999). Box 10.2 provides further evidence of the incomplete coverage of the Third Wave of democratisation with the example of China, the world's most populous state.

Box 10.2 How the third wave of democratization bypassed China

While China has impressed the world with its record of sustained economic growth, Huntington's (1991) third wave of democratization appears to have rolled on by. The political regime has remained resolutely authoritarian. The Chinese Communist Party (CCP) has retained its exclusive dominance of politics and has eschewed the use of democratic elections for choosing people to fill government offices. The CCP has made one exception to this rule at the lowest level in the political hierarchy, the village. Elections for village committees started as an autonomous development in two Guanxi counties in 1980–1. After examining this development, the CCP backed these village committees and both urged and organized their extension nationwide on the grounds that they were perfect vehicles for the exercise of grassroots democracy.

Another perhaps more pressing reason was the CCP's belief in the need to restore order and governing structure to rural areas to get the population to follow state directives. Today, each of China's one million villages directly elects its village committee every three years. Quite how representative they are and what authority they actually have are still debatable matters. Research in the late 1990s suggested that only about 10 per cent of villages had genuinely competitive elections and that under 50 per cent of the rural population thought their committee had been elected. The CCP and higher administrative levels most often have strong influence on who is elected and what they actually do. But according to some observers, there are 'tantalising signs' that the era of voter indifference is being challenged by the gradual emergence of an 'ideological marketplace' supportive of democratization and that villagers are becoming 'complex voters' 'very aware of their political environment' (Kennedy 2002: 482; O'Brien and Li 2000: 488). Also notable is the reported increase in rural unrest as villagers take action against forced eviction, corruption and abusive CCP cadres.

The official response to the lack of democratization has traditionally been that the people are not ready for it. However, there have been promises, such as that to visiting UK Prime Minister Tony Blair, that village elections will be extended upwards to township level in the next few years (BBC 2005). While we monitor whether this happens we might also ponder on whether any countries have succeeded in introducing democracy from the bottom up. Most analysts look to the democratizing effects of a growing middle class. Such a class has certainly grown in both size and prosperity in China but it has been characterized as elitist and unsupportive of multi-party elections for the nation's leaders (Unger 2006). The state's policies of raising middle-class salaries has secured their allegiance to the status quo, making the middle class 'a bulwark of the current regime' (Unger 2006: 31). The third wave will not be making a big splash in China in the near future.

If elections represent an unreliable indicator of the health of democracy, what other elements need to be present? While UNDP (2002: 36) acknowledges that there 'is no unambiguous, uncontroversial measure', it does list a number of indicators that can be employed to monitor the progress of democratization. These include 'objective indicators' which are both election-related, such as voter turnout and seats in parliament held by women, and extra-electoral, such as trade union membership and number of NGOs. A much longer list of 'subjective indicators' incorporates measures of freedom of expression, open media, constraints of the chief executive, transparency, legal impartiality, corruption and bureaucratic quality. The interest of the UNDP in promoting and monitoring these indicators of democracy derives from its vision of human development that is inseparable from the application of democratic principles.

While advocating that societies can be 'differently democratic', and do not have to follow some standardized liberal democratic template, one feature that is held to be necessary is 'a vibrant civil society' (UNDP 2002: 55). For example, Gill (2000: 241) asserts that 'civil society forces are intrinsic to the process of democratic transition' because the elite's creation of democratic structures needs to be complemented by 'a culture of public involvement'. These views were also consistent with Inkeles' approach to 'making men modern' (see Chapter 5). But there is some disagreement in defining what civil society actually is. It certainly comprises organizations that are neither government nor business, but which ones? Most definitions would include NGOs that provide services, emergency relief or advocacy on behalf of the poor and disadvantaged. Labour unions, religious organizations, community groups and the media are also on most lists. But there are also 'traditional' groups whose boundaries are more blurred and which 'fade into the larger society at one extreme and non-state forms of political authority on the other' (Ottaway 2005: 126). For example, in Afghanistan, there are non-state community councils (*jirgas* and *shuras*), normally comprising male elders, which meet to resolve problems and conflicts as they arise (Kakar 2005: 10). But what does such a disparate collection of organizations contribute to democratization and enhanced political equality? From a liberal democratic perspective civil society puts limits on state power, provides an arena for citizen participation, promotes the development of democratic values, provides the means to aggregate and articulate interests, and 'lowers the burden and demands placed on the state' (Diamond 1994; Grugel 2002: 94). But, from a structuralist perspective, civil society is primarily about struggles with the state to overcome unequal power relations. It has been most effectively demonstrated in 'people power' movements from Manila and Jakarta to T'bilisi and Kiev which have led to the overthrow of authoritarian rule.

The experience of civil society has varied across the poorer world not only between countries but also within countries at different times. For example, in South Africa civil society played a major part in ending apartheid and was expected to 'gather momentum that would overwhelm the new state, but it has so far been kept in check' (Pinkney 2003: 106). In some conflict-torn African countries, the cycle of violence has had drastic consequences for both 'modern' and 'traditional' forms of civil society (see University for Peace 2006). For many democratizing societies the achievement of the transition may be followed by a decline in the effectiveness of civil society in promoting greater popular participation and political equity. 'Movement fatigue', the expansion of 'political society', co-option by the democratic state or declining external assistance are among the reasons given for the decline (Grugel 2002; Schmitter and O'Donnell 1986). The task of democratization is thus left unfinished as other social forces and constructs assert themselves. These might include class, gender hierarchies, ethnicity and sectoral economic interests (Grugel 2002).

Democratization in the poorer countries is characteristically incomplete. Democracies need to be 'consolidated' but many remain in an 'unconsolidated' form thus allowing the perpetuation of political inequality (Schmitter 1995: 16). Consolidation occurs when democracy is 'the only game in town' and when no other alternative political arrangements are deemed acceptable (Linz 1990: 156). More specifically, consolidation has occurred *behaviourally* when no 'significant' groups are trying to overthrow democracy or secede; *attitudinally* when the majority of citizens regard democratic forms to be the best way to govern collective life; and *constitutionally* when the formal laws and rules are seen as the legitimate way to resolve conflict (Linz and Stepan 1996). But there is 'no clear and unambiguous criterion' for determining when a regime is consolidated or unconsolidated, although attempting to measure whether political inequality is declining could provide some guidance as to whether consolidation is occurring (Gill 2000: 235). Furthermore, there appear to be relatively few cases where it is agreed that consolidation has taken place. For example, Pinkney (2003) lists Uruguay followed, with less enthusiastic endorsement, by Argentina, Chile, South Africa and 'perhaps' Ghana. He also refers to the possible disqualification of most of the rest of the poorer world, pausing only to admit India and Costa Rica – and Bangladesh at a pinch. Whether or not one agrees with his list, it does draw attention to the widely held view that democratic consolidation is rare and points to the fact that inequity in the distribution of political power is still a prominent feature of poor countries. This explains the urgent and considerable task to engage in 'deepening democracy by tackling democratic deficits' (UNDP 2002: 63).

This exercise in deepening democracy involves a wide variety of initiatives (UNDP 2002). A few of the many possibilities for action are set out below. Promoting public accountability is regarded as a high priority and may involve increasing demands for information, transparency and participation by civil society organizations or the creation of formal structures such as Human Rights Commissions or Electoral Commissions, which if given the adequate resources and authority can ensure that fine words in constitutions and laws are actually realized in practice.

The judicial system in poorer countries is frequently seen as exemplifying arbitrariness, corruption and state violence rather than presiding over the rule of law. The UNDP (2002: 66) observes that 'judicial systems often seem more diligent in prosecuting crimes committed by poor people than crimes against them'. In Brazil there is a long history of extrajudicial killing perpetrated by police and associated death squads. The Pastoral Land Commission recorded 1730 'politically motivated killings' between 1964 and 1992 of peasants, rural workers, trade union leaders, religious workers and human rights lawyers. Only 30 were brought to trial and 18 convicted (UNDP 2002: 66). Human Rights Watch (2006: 168) reports that little has changed and that 'police violence is one of Brazil's most systemic, widespread and longstanding human rights concerns, disproportionately affecting the country's poorest and most vulnerable populations'.

Gender is another area of democratization in which continued action is necessary to redress the often profound inequalities and biases that permeate the distribution of power in society. Chapter 9 pointed out that women are underrepresented in the legislatures and political parties of poorer countries. But in some cases quotas have been introduced to ensure greater female representation. In India, a constitutional amendment in 1993 opened the way for one-third of seats in local governments to be reserved for women while in 1997 the South African Development Community (SADC) agreed that by 2005 at least 30 per cent of positions in political and decision-making structures should be occupied by women (Kandawasvika-Nhundu 2003). Although there has been some progress in all SADC countries – with South Africa and Mozambique achieving the target – in most SADC parliaments the percentage of women representatives remains below 10 per cent (SADC Parliamentary Forum 1999). Quotas for women are just the beginning and are 'no substitute for raising awareness, increasing political education, mobilizing citizens and removing procedural obstacles to women getting nominated and elected' (UNDP 2002: 70).

This section has charted the long, winding and frequently bumpy road to democracy and political equality. As we have seen, the destination –

consolidated democracy – has by no means been reached, and there are numerous democratic deficits apparent across the globe. But there is a powerful coalition of intellectual and institutional forces, including the United Nations, which argues for persisting in promoting democracy as 'it is an essential component of the process of development', with countries not needing to be judged 'fit for democracy' but rather becoming 'fit through democracy' (Sen 2001: Chapter 6).

Decentralization: Rolling Down the State

One of the most popular initiatives for reducing democratic deficits has been decentralization involving the delegation of decision-making authority from central governments to political bodies in provinces, municipalities, communes and other subnational territories. Although back in the early 1980s Conyers (1983) had labelled decentralization 'the latest fashion in development administration', it was not until the 1990s that the decentralization bandwagon really began to roll. By the end of the decade the World Bank (1999: 107) declared that 'countries everywhere – large and small, rich and poor – are devolving political, fiscal, and administrative powers to subnational tiers'. The policy has a large cast of admirers ranging from disadvantaged rural populations through to international financial institutions. All have great expectations that territorial decentralization can bring about positive changes such as deepened democracy and improved service delivery, although many are also aware of the obstacles that have to be overcome to make decentralization a success (see Crook and Manor 1994; Turner 1999a; World Bank 2005b).

Stakeholders' enthusiasm for decentralization is backed by theory. Liberal democratic theory stretching back to John Stuart Mill sees both national and local benefits deriving from democratic decentralization. These include political education in the meaning and practice of democracy; training in political leadership; political stability through the trust generated in democratic structures and processes; political equality through citizen participation in the political process; accountability to the citizenry; and responsiveness to the people's demands (Smith 1985). Economists have also given their blessing to democratic decentralization on three major grounds (Ford 2000). First, local government offers allocative efficiency as decisions on public expenditure are made by government which is close to the people and thus more likely to reflect the real needs and demands of the population. Secondly, the 'competitiveness' and hence innovation of government will be encouraged and should result in greater fulfilment of the citizens' wishes. Thirdly, 'people

Box 10.3   The great expectations of decentralization

The potential gains from decentralization have been categorized by Smith (1993) as the nine 'major expectations'.

(1)   Specific local needs can be more easily addressed by responsive local officials than remote central government bureaucrats.

(2)   The poor are more directly engaged in local politics which should facilitate an increased flow of better-directed resources to poverty alleviation.

(3)   Service delivery is improved because the population in a subnational territory has good access to known and approachable local officials, especially those who they have elected into office.

(4)   Resistance to change can be more easily overcome by local officials who can generate support for development initiatives especially where the results can be seen to be of value by local populations.

(5)   This should also assist in the mobilization of local resources such as finance, labour and knowledge which are thought to have 'efficiency value'.

(6)   Some services can be produced more cheaply with local resources than through standardized central approaches.

(7)   A further efficiency gain is derived from improved coordination of development activities through 'an integrated spatial focus, which ideally eliminates wasteful duplication and maximizes the benefits of cooperation' (Turner 1999a: 10).

(8)   Even central government benefits from decentralization through 'decongestion' as functions are delegated to subnational governments which now concentrate on policy and monitoring activities, and the red-tape of centralized bureaucracy ideally becomes a memory of the past.

(9)   National unity and political stability are enhanced by decentralizing significant decision-making as communities are empowered to look after many of their own affairs rather than rely on or be dominated by central government towards whom they may feel resentment.

Source: B. Smith (1993).

are more willing to pay for services that respond to their priorities, especially if they have been involved in the decision-making process for the delivery of these services' (ibid., 6). The potential benefits deriving from decentralization are impressive and are set out in Box 10.3.

The most important benefit of decentralization from the perspective of political equality is increased participation. It should be manifested in a variety of ways. Of greatest importance is accountability. This can be through the ballot box when citizens elect their local representatives, or it can be attendance at open council meetings. Making information on council decisions and activities publicly available is a further expression of accountability. There may be citizen complaints procedures and special offices such as ombudsmen to deal with them. Surveys of citizen satisfaction, consultation with NGOs, and mayoral reports are all further examples of how participation can be harnessed to ensure accountability. The incorporation of civil society organizations onto councils or planning bodies is another aspect of empowerment as these organizations and individuals can represent the specific interests of the poor and disadvantaged. But, as noted in the previous chapter, NGOs can also be co-opted by the state to strengthen the state. For example, they work as 'strategic partners' with ministries, fill gaps in service delivery, aggregate and channel moderate political demands, and assist the executive circumventing the legislature (Clarke 1998). They are frequently drawn into the 'alms bazaar', becoming dependent on the financial flows of donors, the implementers of the latter's policies and projects (Hulme and Edwards 1997; Smillie 1995).

There has been some concern, however, that there has been differential empowerment of organizations with those who have traditionally represented the poor being less favoured (Jeppesen 2002). One of the tests of Bolivia's decentralization policy is whether public expenditure is reflecting local preferences and the distribution of population. A World Bank study believes this has happened, with local governments showing quite different expenditure patterns from central government (Faguet 2001). In particular, local governments have directed funding to education, urban development, water and sanitation, and 'possibly' health. Decentralization has also provided far more equitable distribution of funds across the nation as distinct from the highly skewed pattern prevailing under centralized government.

In the cases of decentralization so far presented there have been local victories in the war against 'democratic deficits'. However, even in these experiences there may be substantial room for improvement and whether poverty has been seriously tackled through decentralization remains open to doubt. There are other countries where the introduction of democratic decentralized government has produced very disappointing results, and the promised benefits have simply not accrued to the citizenry. Turner (1999a) has listed seven 'problems and obstacles' which can derail the decentralization train, slow its progress or send it off on a branch line away from the intended destination. These include the encouragement of parochialism; function-shedding by central government without the necessary funds and with little interest in what happens; the maintenance of central control through regulation and funding; the assumption of political office by self-interested elites; unpopularity with decentralization

Box 10.4   Decentralization in practice – the Philippines and Bolivia

A few examples will demonstrate how such benefits can be realized in practice.

In the Philippines after the authoritarian regime of President Marcos had been overthrown, in large part by a 'people power' movement, the new government set about embedding democratic principles deep into the national polity through decentralization (Turner 1999b). The *1991 Local Government Code* provided for popularly elected councils at every subnational level – province, city, municipality and *barangay* (community). Furthermore, NGOs were to make up 25 per cent of the members of the local development council which had responsibilities for planning and monitoring development. Also legislated was a 'process whereby the registered voters of a local government unit may directly propose, enact or amend any ordinance' (Philippines 1991, Book 1, Title 9, Ch. 2, Sect. 120). A power of recall of local officials through citizens' petitions also made it into the Code. Substantial functions were delegated to the local government units by the central government including health, agriculture, public works, social welfare, and environment and natural resources. The matching funding for these new functions was also guaranteed and the subnational government's share of the 'internal revenue allotment' doubled from 20 to 40 per cent. There is even an annual awards event in which local governments are recognized for their innovations and achievements in providing services to their constituents and enhancing participatory governance (Brillantes 2003).

Bolivia has a history of centralized government, with minimal participation of the local citizenry in that government. Local government existed 'at best in name, as an honorary and ceremonial institution devoid of administrative capability and starved for funds'. The practice of electing municipal mayors was only introduced in 1942 and then lasted for only 5 years. The population had to wait until 1987 before they could once again vote in municipal elections, this event marking the start of the country's experiment with decentralized government (Burki et al. 1999). The major changes came in 1994 with the 'popular participation law' that incorporated all national territory within 311 municipalities, 198 of which were new; doubled the share of municipalities in national tax revenues from 10 to 20 per cent; gave municipalities the 'exclusive authority to impose vehicle and property taxes' (Burki et al. 1999: 13–14); transferred many physical assets, such as schools, hospitals and some roads, to municipal control; allocated responsibilities for maintenance of these assets to municipalities with added duties for construction. The participation of civil society has also been a key feature of Bolivian decentralization and led to the growth in the number of civil society organizations and their participation in local government. They are prominent in oversight committees (*Comités de Vigilancia*) which monitor the expenditure of 'popular participation funds' and propose new projects. They can move beyond monitoring to halt disbursements from the central government if they believe that money is being stolen or misused.

plans among affected populations and civil servants; inadequate capacity to undertake decentralized functions efficiently and effectively; and the continued exclusion of the poor and disadvantaged from influencing the decisions which affect their welfare.

The problems elaborated above have plagued decentralization in Africa. Top-down control has most often been retained. Thus, Wunsch (2001: 278) characterizes local-level planning as 'merely going through the motions' and a variety of 'recentralization'. Budgeting suffers from poor capacity, complex processes and central recapture of control over local budget resources and choices. In personnel management Wunsch (2001: 281) generally found that 'local elected officials felt they had inadequate managerial authority over such personnel'. Crook (2003: 79), in reviewing the connection between poverty reduction and decentralization in Africa, notes that even where there has been greater citizen participation it has not led to 'policies that are more responsive to the poor – or indeed, to citizens generally'. Tanzania's local government system is seen by many citizens as a means of securing compliance to the wishes of the ruling party. In Nigeria, local government has been used by military rulers to install political 'bosses' and agencies for the distribution of patronage. In Kenya, 'representation of the poor is weak' and heads of District Development Committees are able to act undemocratically (Crook 2003: 81). Crook (2003: 82) further argues that 'local government representation of disadvantaged groups in Africa is not part of popular discourse'. The dominant political game is run by central government and involves the creation of dependent local elites who lack accountability to local populations.

There are other examples of poorly performing or stalled decentralization experiments. For example, devolution in Russia has been described as 'the regionalization of autocracy' (Hutchcroft 201: 47) while Bangladesh's history of decentralization experiments until the late 1990s has been characterized by 'creating systems that strengthen national government patronage networks over rural élites', resulting in government service provision remaining at 'exceptionally low levels' (Hulme and Siddiquee 1999: 41). However, it has also spurred the growth of NGOs to provide the missing services and to engage the poor and disadvantaged, assisting them in overcoming poverty and deprivation. Such participatory practices are often closely interlinked with territorial decentralization and are the topic of the next section.

Participation: the New Orthodoxy

Getting people, especially poor people, to be involved in the planning and implementation of their own development is not a new developmental

initiative. Historical searches show the origins of participatory development in the twilight of colonialism in the form of two institutions which
were introduced then but were taken up with greater vigour by successor
independent governments. These institutions or movements are *community development* and *cooperatives*. Both were state-driven, oriented to
the diffusion of capitalism, and sought to extend the control of 'modern'
governments over 'traditional' populations in order to engineer the
latter's transformation into modernity.

A project in the Etawah district of Uttar Pradesh in India in the late
1940s is generally seen as the starting point for postcolonial community
development. The project was based on 'the mobilization of villagers by
a multi-purpose village-level worker to increase agricultural output and
improve rural infrastructure, largely through self-help efforts' (Hulme
and Turner 1990: 187). The apparent success of this project eventually
led to an ambitious government plan to cover all India with the
Community Development Program (CDP). Village-level workers (VLWs)
were trained in community mobilization techniques and sent to rural
posts across the country to act as catalysts in the transformation of
village society and economy. The popularity of CDP was, however, short-
lived and much of the 'voluntary' labour was in fact coerced from the
ranks of the poor to undertake projects which mainly benefited local
élites.

The history of the cooperative movement in developing countries
bears a close resemblance to community development. Many cooperative
experiences commenced in the colonial era and mainly in British possessions where the colonizers believed they could build modern capitalist
economic organizations using traditional cooperative arrangements. In
addition, operating cooperatives would socialize rural populations into
the ways of liberal democracy. After independence the cooperative star
remained undimmed as political regimes of all types embraced the institution as a foundation for rural development. By the 1960s and 1970s
cooperatives were under fire, being seen as subject to mismanagement
and political manipulation, and as inefficient producers of goods and
services, dominated by local élites and of little benefit to the poor
(Apthorpe 1970; Fals Borda 1969).

The experience of community development led to reflection on the
nature, purpose and supposed benefits of participatory development. In
Latin America, Freire (1972) advocated adult literacy classes with a
difference. They challenged the structure of oppression and exploitation
under which landless and powerless peasants lived. By analysing their
own situation the peasantry would be engaging in 'conscientization',
which would encourage them to take political action to improve their
situation. Needless to say, authoritarian rulers (and even democratically

elected ones) were unenthusiastic about the prospects for such radical participation in development. They were also wary of newly formed *comunidades eclesiales de bases* (Basic Christian Communities – BCCs), which mushroomed in number during the 1970s and 1980s. The BCCs also used participation to challenge the status quo. They comprised mostly poor people who came together in small groups to 'combine consciousness-raising, bible study, worship, mutual help and political action in defense of their rights' (Berryman 1984: 27).

Academics were also considering participation and the lessons to be drawn from the community development and cooperative experiences. First, participation was of a weak variety. People participated according to government instructions, and these seldom incorporated listening to the people, especially the poor and disadvantaged. Secondly, the approaches had been standardized, organized by bureaucracies in a top-down manner. Thirdly, little or no attention was paid to differences between target groups and their situations, especially the local power structure. The question of why poor people should participate in these introduced institutions was rarely investigated or treated seriously.

Using these and other lessons, alternative approaches to participatory development began to appear during the 1970s. Korten (1980: 497) identified a 'learning process approach' in which 'villagers and programme personnel shared their knowledge and resources to create a programme which achieved a fit between needs and capacities of the beneficiaries and those of the outsiders who were providing assistance'. Rondinelli (1983) stressed the need for the intended beneficiaries of development projects to be included in both planning and management in his 'adaptive approach to development administration'. Johnston and Clark (1982: 173) argued that the rural poor will 'invest active participation only in an organization that is responsive to most intensely felt needs'. People should be viewed as 'problem-solving agents capable of acquiring increased competence and confidence' (Johnston and Clark 1982: 270). A technique known as Rapid Rural Appraisal (RRA) emerged in the late 1970s as a method of participatory enquiry into rural economy and society and involving 'semi-structured interviewing, methods for team interactions, transects, sketch mapping, and flow, decision-tree and causal diagramming' (Chambers 1993: 98). Following criticism that it was being conducted by outsiders in order to extract information, RRA evolved into PRA (Participatory Rural Appraisal). PRA was supposedly more experiential and action-based than RRA, more enabling and empowering, and more popular. Through PRA poor people could define what sort of development they wanted and become empowered through its methods.

During the 1980s, this academic interest in participation and the experiments in participatory approaches began to be examined by the IFIs, bilateral aid agencies and the family of United Nations organizations. They were seeking new directions as old methods of development were not producing the anticipated benefits while aid-receiving governments were increasingly being seen as a significant part of the problem of development. Participation had now been 'discovered' by the mainstream and was being enthusiastically embraced, so much so that by the mid-1990s it had become an orthodoxy. In its *Participation Sourcebook*, the World Bank (1996: ix) acknowledged the centrality of participation in development and defined it as 'a process through which stakeholders influence and share control over development initiatives and the decisions and resources which affect them'. Participation increasingly became a common and even compulsory feature of donor-funded development projects. Participation was also incorporated into the World Bank's poverty reduction strategies (PRSP), which became mandatory Bank requirements for many poorer countries (Brown 2004; World Bank 2000).

Complementary changes in development thinking contributed to the rise of participatory development as an integral component of strategies to address poverty and inequality. The disillusionment with earlier development practice had led to the increasing role of NGOs in development. They were seen to embody a variety of organizational virtues – flexible, honest, committed, responsive, skilled, oriented to poverty alleviation, effective and participatory (Turner and Hulme 1997). In 1970 international NGOs spent US$3.64 billion on development aid while by 1999 the sum had risen to US$12.4 billion (Clarke and Thomas 2006: 416). They seemed to appeal to most stakeholders. On the one hand the neoliberal agenda of development adopted by the IFIs supported NGOs as market-based actors who were contributing to the privatization of service delivery and hence to the improved effectiveness and efficiency which allegedly accompanied market-based interventions. For those pushing for strengthening civil society and building social capital as essential elements of democratic development, NGOs were also to be encouraged. The newly fashionable notion of governance (see Box 10.5), and the perceived need to improve it, provided yet another boost to NGOs and participation in general. Policies were being evaluated against their contribution to improving governance, and one of the measures was the existence of participatory processes.

No sooner had participatory development been absorbed into the mainstream of development practice, than it came under critical fire from a range of actors who had reached the conclusion that poor people were not being empowered, whatever the IFIs were saying. Some authors noted that participation was a fuzzy concept and that there were different types

Box 10.5   The rise of governance

The concept of governance rose to prominence in the 1990s in the after-math of the collapse of the Berlin Wall when international development agencies turned their attention to reformulating frameworks of government in recipient countries – although governance is much more than government. In the broadest sense, governance can be defined as 'the exercise of political, economic and administrative authority to manage a nation's affairs. It is the complex mechanisms, processes, relationships and institutions through which citizens and groups articulate their interests, exercise their rights and obligations and mediate their differences' (UNDP 1997: 9). Initially, the adjective 'good' was attached to governance indicating the desired enabling environment for a prosperous capitalist future. Components of such good governance included improved public sector management, enhanced accountability of public officials, a robust legal framework, and information availability and transparency (Asian Development Bank 1999; World Bank 1992).

The UNDP has been one of the keenest proponents of governance through 'democratic governance'. This approach has tied governance to the achievement of sustainable human development and, more recently, the attainment of the MDGs, especially the eradication of poverty. In pursuit of these goals, the UNDP sees itself as responding to the requests and needs of poorer countries in a variety of governance activities including parliamentary development, electoral systems and processes, justice and human rights, e-governance and access to information, decentralization and local governance and development, and public administration and anti-corruption. Gender is seen as an issue which cross-cuts all of the above.

of participation, some of which were definitely not empowering. These were weak strains that might merely involve consultation as the provision of information as distinct from strong forms in which the community took initiatives for collective action and remained in control even where outside assistance was required (Agarwal 2001; Pretty 1995). Sometimes the classifications emphasized the distinction between participation as the *means* to accomplish project aims and an *end*, 'where the community sets up a process to control its own development' (McGee 2002: 104).

From within PRA came a declaration of the importance of 'self-critical epistemological awareness' (Chambers 1997: 32). An example of this awareness could include continuing concern that simplistic views of community and its members' motivations are still prevalent in PRA practice. They hark back to anthropological models in which community relations were portrayed as harmonious with reciprocity providing the social cement to bind communities together. Subsequent anthropological studies have uncovered quite different patterns of power relations which may be inaccessible or difficult to locate using PRA methodology. Thus, which community members undertake the assessment and how willing they are to speak will have a profound influence on what results are obtained and what initiatives are subsequently taken from the participatory analysis.

Some of the most severe critiques of the discourse surrounding participation are postdevelopment writers (see Chapter 9) who see PRA and its methodological kin as part of 'the poisonous gift' of development (Rahnema 1997a: 381). In this postdevelopment literature, current practices of participation are simply a part of the destructive force which has been unleashed upon cultures and communities across the poorer world. Such participation is a 'myth' acting a 'Trojan horse', a political practice which has been made politically palatable to the ruling classes and its institutions (Rahmena 1992: 167). By contrast, the desired postdevelopment future is a world of small, autonomous communities which build on their cultural legacy and select judiciously from advances in technology. Power differences will not be eliminated but they will be significantly reduced in this 'bottom-up aesthetic order' (Rahnema 1997a: 399; Rahnema and Bawtree 1997). Power, or rather the lack of it, is the crucial variable for those who classify participatory development as 'the new tyranny' characterized by 'the illegitimate and/or unjust uses of power' (Cooke and Kothari 2001: 14). The poor are manipulated and cannot be empowered using current participatory practices, notably PRA. The power which is alleged to accrue to the poor is 'delusional' and the whole industry of participatory development 'should consider closing itself down' (Cooke 2004: 42).

But efforts to promote participatory development not only persist but appear to have been strengthened. The debate on theory and practice has also moved on from, on the one hand, a narrow focus on projects and, on the other, allegations of tyrannical PRA practices. Much current thinking is concerned with linking participation to wider structures of inequality and processes of social change (Hickey and Mohan 2004). For example, why is participation often difficult for poor and disadvantaged groups in the first place? To answer this we must put political analysis in participation, rather than dealing with participation simply as a technocratic exercise. Thus, Gaventa (2004) noted the separation of social and political aspects of development policy and practice and how that produced adverse consequences for those in need. But they and others see constructive possibilities in combining the two in the concept and practice of 'citizenship participation'. Such potential is demonstrated in the training handbook for India's *Panchayati Raj* institutions (PRIs), the village-level organizations of governance (Jain and Polman 2003). In this book a template on how to organize and implement a People's Planning Campaign shows how villagers can mobilize and articulate their preferences to influence the PRI. They can thus influence socioeconomic development through political action.

The bringing together of citizenship and participation is a difficult business, not least because both concepts are contested in theory and practice. But 'social citizenship' is seen by some 'to bridge the gap between citizen and the state by recasting citizenship as practiced rather than as given' (Cornwall and Gaventa 2006: 408). That is, the agency of citizens is given emphasis, making them into 'makers and shapers' rather than 'users and choosers' (Cornwall and Gaventa 2006: 409). They enter the political arena where they have the right of participation and contribute to decisions which affect their lives. These are not simply choices about how to implement the village's latest development project but also about underlying structures of inequality involving social justice and entitlement. More nuanced understanding of local power relations is essential if the promises of social citizenship are to be achieved. For example, mainstream participatory approaches aimed at producing transparent decision-making in Ghana were resisted by women who regarded it as reducing 'their opportunities for formal politicking through male elders' (Hickey and Mohan 2004: 14; Waddington and Mohan 2004). This may, however, be less of a new approach and more the practice of good social science research techniques which are then used to inform development practice.

While these 'new approaches' to participation appear to offer openings for the expression of voice by poor and marginalized populations and while such voices may actually be heard and acted upon, there are many obstacles. The cooperation of bureaucracy is essential, especially the support of powerful advocates from the upper levels. All too often people in poorer countries see their governments and bureaucratic representatives as distant, disinterested and corrupt (see, for example, Narayan et al. 2000). The capacity for citizens to organize is also vital, and not only for the establishment of an organization but also to make it sustainable, goal-driven and able to change. There are opponents of participation who see it as a threat to their power, status and economic standing. Lethargy, exhaustion or disillusionment also affect attitudes to and energies for participation. Overcoming the democratic deficits provides a major challenge for the citizens of poorer countries who have often seen the postcolonial promises of empowerment unfulfilled. However, with the convergence of democratization, decentralization and participation there is still hope of bringing power to the people.

Chapter 11

Conclusion: the Ends of Development and the End of Inequality

Competing Definitions of Development

This book has dealt with two contentious concepts – development and inequality – and has shown that developmental debates invariably lead to the question of inequality. This concluding chapter reviews different approaches to development and emphasizes two key points made throughout the book: that contemporary approaches to development have deep historical roots; and that the meaning we attach to the 'ends of development' will determine the weight attached to the importance of contemporary global inequalities.

The history of the theory and practice of development shows development as a multifaceted process. One of the strengths of modernization theory lies in recognizing the complex interconnections between cultural, economic, political and technological change. However, the previous chapter highlighted another level of complexity; those who design and those who participate in the process often possess different understandings of development.

For example, top-down 'creators' of developmental projects (governments, engineers, aid and development NGOs, the IMF, the World Bank) and grass roots, community-level 'users' of the projects often possess different visions of the ends of development, as well as proposing different means of achieving these ends. The history of development reveals many cases where this has resulted in clashes where more often than not local communities lose out. In India, for example, the technocratic dreams of the state and the World Bank to promote development through constructing power-generating dams was met by resistance from small-scale farmers whose lands were to be flooded (Roy 2002). This Indian example leads to the question: what is development all about? As Tucker (1977: 64) notes, while it might appear commonsensical to view development as 'the improvement of the individual lives of the great mass of people', state elites have often seen the world through different lenses.

Regardless of how sharply development is defined, it will invariably encounter competing definitions. On these grounds, this book resisted the temptation of beginning with a fixed definition of development as this would have limited its ability to explore the different meanings of development as they emerged within specific historical contexts. When the results of developmental processes are being assessed, there must be an appreciation of how the tensions between competing visions are resolved. As the Indian example suggests, development must be approached with the following questions in mind: 'development for whom?', 'development for what?', 'who wins?', 'who loses?', 'what's introduced?', 'what's lost?' (see Wallerstein 1994: 4). These questions enable researchers to reflect more critically on their operational concepts.

Has Development Failed?

To illustrate these points, the following section reviews a variety of responses to Kothari and Minogue's (2002: 2) evaluation that 'there has been a failure of the postwar development project'. Throughout the book, there have been many examples to add weight to this claim and an equivalent weight contesting it.

The case for development

The case for development can be mounted on many grounds. First, as Chapter 7 pointed out, progressively since the end of the Second World War, a smaller proportion of the world's population has been living in poverty. On aggregate, life expectancy has increased significantly, people are healthier and better educated, possess more leisure, suffer fewer accidents, eat more and enjoy more amenities (Lomborg 2001). According to Norberg (2005), the rich are getting richer, but this is less important than the fact that the poor are also getting richer at a faster pace than the rich. If this assessment is correct, then the developmental gap is narrowing.

Second, the growth in world productive capacity has been impressive. This applies to manufacturing, agriculture and services. International commerce has also grown substantially, networking economies and calling into question the rationality of national borders. Neoliberals argue that it is no coincidence that most of the poorest countries tend to have the weakest links to the global economy. From this perspective, market-led development has been an unqualified success, even if it has wrenched governments and workers in some sectors out of their rent-seeking security.

Third, as the previous chapter pointed out, by the beginning of the new millennium there are more countries practising electoral democracy than ever before. Again, many of the poorest countries – those that have failed to bridge the development gap – are controlled by authoritarian regimes that have closed their country from the global market. This adds support to the claim that open markets enhance the prospects for democratic reform.

Fourth, perhaps it is unfair to measure the success of development on the limited timeframe of the past 60 years. As Chapters 4 and 5 showed, the shadow of the Cold War hung over the poorer countries up until 1990. The geopolitical interests of the Cold Warriors distorted development, bending it according to the strategic interests of competing superpowers. The first 45 years of the development project can be interpreted as a 'false start'. This argument is consistent with Fukuyama's version on modernization theory (see Chapter 6) as well as Friedman's (2000: xi) claim at the turn of the millennium that 'the world is ten years old'. Rhetorically speaking, how long did it take the west to climb the ladder of development? Development takes time.

Fifth, the IMF have admitted that many of the structural adjustment programmes that they imposed on indebted countries over the past 20 years have not borne their expected fruit. However, they claim that the problem lies not with the developmental path offered, but the failure of governments to swallow the medicine needed to boost a healthier economic constitution. If governments in poorer countries had met the conditions requested, then development would have had greater success. From this perspective, the problem of postwar development involves the lack of political will in poorer countries or poor governance rather than the dominant developmental model on offer.

Sixth, from another angle Sachs also believes that the poor results from developmental decades are not grounds for pessimism (see Chapter 7). He lays more blame at the door of IFIs and wealthier countries for failing to meet their obligations to the poor. The Millennium Development Goals are also based on a qualified positive reading of the past 60 years. Many countries did succeed in climbing the ladder of development. The Asian NICs demonstrate that development leads to higher human development, and over the past decade countries such as China, India and Bangladesh have experienced impressive levels of economic growth and increased levels of per capita income. Now that the world possesses more wealth than ever before, the richer countries can help lift the poorest onto the first rung of the ladder. While development cannot be considered an unqualified success, it has shown a path to better life-chances for hundreds of millions of people who would otherwise have experienced extreme poverty.

Seventh, optimists also claim that many of the social, environmental and economic problems that modernity introduces in its wake are short-term consequences of stepping onto the ladder of development. Chapter 9 described how optimists have adopted an environmental version of Kuznets' U-curve to explain environmental degradation. If societies never began the process of modern economic growth, then it is true that humanity would live in a more pristine environment. However, higher levels of air and water pollution are a necessary consequence of modern growth. At early stages of development people have little time to dwell on environmental destruction. As growth generates higher levels of wealth, people can then turn their attention to improving their physical surroundings. Drawing on the experience of the western prototypes, it is possible to deduce that the environmentally degraded state of the contemporary cities in poorer countries will gradually abate.

Each of these arguments presents development as a qualified success on the grounds that it has delivered significant improvements in human development. Other commentators disagree with this verdict, but the variety of political positions adopted by different optimists makes this a powerful argument.

There are also positions that judge development to be a success even though the authors question whether human development has improved significantly. For example, from a postdevelopment perspective, it is possible to judge development a success because it was never primarily intended to 'develop' the poorer countries. Development was defined by and organized by the 'west' as a means of retaining its hold over the 'rest'. Through 'discovering' the problem of mass poverty, the more powerful countries were able to forge policy tools to manage and control the poorer countries. Mark Berger (1993: 266) claims that the 'rest' 'has been created and understood primarily in terms of the failure of the (poorer countries) to become idealized versions of the industrialized democracies of North America and Western Europe'. This prototype/emulator model enabled the wealthier countries to control the agenda of social change so that it served the interests of powerful classes. Institutions such as the IMF are still able to attach 'conditionality' to poorer countries. From this perspective, the development project has enjoyed immeasurable success as a form of international socioeconomic control.

Another version of this argument is mounted by Marxist commentators who argue that the development project was principally about securing the ongoing conditions for capital accumulation and the expansion of capitalist relations on a world scale. As discussed in Chapter 8, the earlier postwar combination of fiscal 'pump-priming' and state-centred modernization served capital well until the profit squeeze of the early 1970s. Globalization, neoliberalism, the erosion of state sovereignty and the rise of supranational institutions (what W. Robinson has called the 'transnational class structure') overcame the limitations to accumulation inherent within the earlier version of the development project. It modified the motor of development to ensure the ongoing expansion of capitalist relations. If the development project is conceived in these terms, then it has cleared the path for capital accumulation to prevail in the face of a succession of political and social movements that challenged its power.

Rose-tinted glasses are not needed to view the development project as success. It depends on the way in which the project is understood, the way the motives of actors are interpreted and the timeframe the observer chooses.

The case against development

This book has also presented compelling data indicating a growing divide between the richer and poorer countries, as well as inequality within countries and global inequalities between people. These inequalities question the success of the development project. The very need to set Millennium Development Goals is testimony to the failure of development. Furthermore, the UN Millennium Project and the World Bank have both released warnings that, five years into the MDGs, many countries are 'off-target'. While optimists point to rising standards of living in the medium-income countries, detractors point to various regions (such as Sub-Saharan Africa, some former communist countries, parts of the Middle East and East Asia and the Pacific) that are falling further behind (see Chapter 7).

The road to development has not been as smooth as modernization theorists predicted. As early as the 1960s, dependency theorists criticized their predictions as an ideological screen that hid the exploitation of the poorer countries by the wealthier countries. From the dependency perspective, development was always a doomed project, condemned to fail as long as the economic bonds that tie the poorer countries to the richer countries remained secured. Wade (2004) argues that the gap between the rich who mainly reside in the North and the poor who largely live in the South 'is a structural divide, not just a matter of a lag in the South's catch-up'. This more structural explanation for the failure of the development project contrasts with the answer that modernization theory gave for lack of success – the failure of poorer countries to transform their traditional norms and attitudes, institutions, economy and political processes along modern lines.

The anti-globalization movement, examined in Chapter 9, also rejects the dominant development project in the twenty-first century. The multi-faceted nature of the World Social Forum reveals the breadth of challenges that confront neoliberal visions of global development in the new millennium. While many components of the Forum are suspicious of the MDGs, both the anti-globalization movement and the MDG framework operate on the assumption that neoliberal policies have led to developmental crises. By proclaiming that another world is possible, the World Social Forum implicitly rejects the neoliberal developmental vision as short-sighted and socially harmful. The diversity that constitutes the anti-globalization movement is based on people who have gained little from market-oriented development policies over the past few decades. Women's groups, environmental groups, ethnic minorities and indigenous populations, and workers' movements are just some of the groups who claim that the way that globalization has unfolded has disempowered groups whose collective interests conflict with market expansion. This forms the basis of a wide range of protests and struggles across the globe: anti-dam protests, struggles against the privatization of essential services (water, education, health), campaigns for fair trade and a debt moratorium, calls for corporation transparency in dealing with governments, struggles for minimum labour standards and protests against environmental degradation, biodiversity loss and habitat destruction. Each of these campaigns illustrates the failure of development conceived of as the universalization of well-being.

The environmental movement has mounted one of the most powerful challenges against the development project. As Chapter 9 showed, it presents a warning that societies must become more conscious of the impact that human behaviour has on the biosphere. It also poses a direct challenge to the ways in which progress has been conceived. The environmental movement is often portrayed as a romantic reaction to progress and development. However, its strongest challenge comes through its appraisal of scientific evidence and prediction, sowing doubt on the ability of the planet to sustain high levels of economic growth. If development studies as a discipline has focused on *underdevelopment* over the past 60 years, the environmental movement has emphasized *overdevelopment*. Both these developmental distortions point to the failure of development as sustainable, equitable, balanced growth.

Disillusionment with development, in terms of narrowing the gap between richer and poorer countries, has led some commentators to reassess the value of colonialism and empire. This critique of the development project was discussed in Chapters 4 and 6. Lal, d'Sousa, Windschuttle and Ferguson have all recently reinterpreted the era of European colonial tutelage as a far more secure, efficient and productive world than the one that emerged in the wake of postwar colonial liberation. Ignatieff (2003: 123) has also defended the 'empire-lite' version led by the USA through pointing to the barren results of postwar hopes for international peace and development:

> The moral premises of anti-imperialist struggles in this century – all peoples should be equal, and all peoples should rule themselves – are not wrong. But history is not a morality tale. The age of empire ought to have been succeeded by an age of independent, equal and self-governing nation states. In reality, it has been succeeded by an age of ethnic cleansing and state failure. This is the context in which the empire has made its return.

This scenario of 'state failure' that Ignatieff addresses became a more prominent international concern after the end of the Cold War. The departure from the world scene of socialist states ended another era in the development project – symbolized in the failure of alternative forms of development. As Chapter 5 pointed out, in the aftermath of the Second World War many poorer countries were enthralled by the ability of the USSR to concentrate its energies on state planning, lift its rates of economic growth and establish new industrial sectors. Even after Khrushchev's denunciation of Stalin in 1956, other non-capitalist paths of development offered alternatives to gauge mainstream development against: for instance, the Chinese path, the Cuban model, the Chilean path, African socialism or the Sandinista model. There is no space in this book to explore the fate of these models except to say that the assessment of their strengths is as controversial as the assessment of mainstream development. Pro-market analysts celebrate their demise and claim that the real task of development can begin, while socialists mourn the constraints that ensured the demise of alternative models.

The point here is that there are very different political persuasions arguing that the development project has been a failure. As the previous section showed, being on the 'left' or 'right' of the political spectrum provides insufficient information to predict any authors' verdict on the development project. In part, this is due to different authors having such different understandings of what constitutes development. It is also partly due to development being a balancing act between costs and benefits, militating against any 'blanket pessimism or optimism' (Kiely 1998: 141, 145).

A Summary of Developmental Visions

As pointed out throughout the book, the idea of development means different things to different people (Kothari 2002: 11–12). Clark (2002: 22–4) has identified 30 ways in which the concept has been used – from the general, to the economic, the sociocultural, the social and political, through to human and sustainability definitions (not to mention 'under-development'). As development studies itself developed, knowledge did not progress in a uniform or linear direction. A better metaphor for the development of development thinking might be the branching and thickening of a tree of knowledge, constantly pruned by critical gardeners.

Then again, the field of development studies abounds with metaphors used to describe and explain development. Even development itself is a metaphor (Berger 1985a; Mies 1994: 108; Wallerstein 1994), and therefore metaphors can end up piling on top of each other . . . metaphorically speaking. One of the most difficult tasks in writing about competing definitions of development is to avoid mixing these metaphors. With an acute awareness of the problems of employing metaphors, but at a loss to know how to avoid them (see Molotch 2005: 69), this concluding section of the book assesses some of the dominant metaphors in development studies.

Development as growth and abundance

'Development as growth' was one of the earliest and most resilient shoots from the development tree – indeed, it is difficult to imagine development without it, given the connection between the two metaphors (Rist 1999: 214–16). As Chapters 2 and 3 pointed out, raising the total sum of production and services has remained a key goal for development practitioners. No politician with a sense of self-survival would question the need for ongoing economic development. Contemporary neoliberals view economic growth as the precondition for overcoming the problems that beset the world, from environmental degradation to employment generation, and from gender equality to extreme poverty.

Yet, some areas of the world have found sustainable growth difficult to achieve. In *Guns, Germs and Steel*, Jared Diamond (1997: 14) recounted walking along a beach with a New Guinean politician who inquired: 'Why is it that you white people developed so much cargo and brought it to New Guinea, but we black people had little cargo of our own?' In development studies this comparative question of national differences and national inequalities has remained as important as – if not more important than – the technical issue of stimulating economic growth. Growing global consciousness merely intensifies the sense of deprivation among economically, socially and politically marginalized groups. One important political consequence of this discontent has been the emergence of the challenges to neoliberal globalization that were described in Chapter 9.

As Gurr (1971), Davies (1962) and more recently Rapley (2004: 2) have emphasized, economic growth can only alleviate so much poverty, because raised expectations open up vistas of material improvement. Philosophers examine these as 'adaptive preferences' – what you want changes with what you already have. Where these aspirations are blocked, discontent can multiply. Deprivation and poverty are therefore both relative and absolute terms. For instance, the material abundance enjoyed by richer countries over the postwar era has not brought a commensurate growth in happiness – merely the disease of 'affluenza' (Hamilton and Denniss 2005). Environmentally speaking, there are limits to growth but, psychologically speaking, 'development as more' is the Promethean myth within the human condition (Wallerstein 1994: 5).

The neoliberal approach to development outlined in Chapter 6 highlights the narrowness of the 'development as growth' vision. Neoliberalism promises to unleash economic growth and thereby reduce poverty, generate wealth, expand employment and entrepreneurial opportunities. However, critics of neoliberalism have accused supporters of this developmental model of helping to widen the gap between the rich and the poor, both within and between countries. According to Rapley (2004: 148), neoliberalism engineered a successful 'growth regime' at the expense of a progressive 'distributional regime'.

The promise of 'potential plenty' should not be dismissed simply as a 'false hope' (Hayek 1944: 95) but as a developmental opportunity. For example, the Millennium Development Goals rest on two foundations of growth (see Chapter 7). First, the capacity of the richer countries to generate surplus wealth continues to expand (see Sachs 2005). A key development question is how this wealth should to be used. Secondly, apart from the early industrializers, the accumulated experience from different cultural contexts suggests that economic growth can reduce poverty. The broader vision is, again, growth for what? and for whom?

Development as sustainability

The most powerful challenge to 'development as growth' has emerged from the concept of *sustainable development*. Chapter 9 began by pointing to the hold that progress has had on the modern consciousness and how this has led to the expectation of perpetual material improvement. The prototype/emulator model that has dominated development thinking since the Second World War encouraged poorer countries to envisage their future as the replication of European and US paths to modern economic growth. Metaphors for development, such as stages of growth and ladders of development, suggested a linear model of development. Julian Simon confidently predicted in the 1970s that within a century all of humanity would be able to experience Western living standards (quoted in Lomborg 2001). Lowe (2005: 8), on the other hand, argues that this belief in unlimited growth has been 'the fundamental myth of modern society'.

While modern capitalism has succeeded in generating unprecedented growth and while this has the potential to increase life expectancy, improve health, eradicate hunger and heighten standards of living, one of the greatest challenges to development thinking is whether the underlying principle of 'development as growth' – defined by Marx (1976) as 'accumulate! accumulate!' – is sustainable. Generating sustained growth has been the greatest success of capitalism, but this success might be overshadowed by its adverse consequences (Christian 1992: 27–8).

By the early 1970s, this model of 'development as growth' was challenged by environmental critiques that questioned whether the planet's resource base was adequate to sustain the industrial/petroleum/chemical paradigm of development (Meadows et al. 1972). This debate over the future supply of nonrenewable resources continues today, as Chapter 9 illustrated. However, it has been compounded by other scientific concerns about the impact of our dominant mode of development upon the environment.

Environmental issues remain shrouded in scientific and political controversy. Despite this, in the new millennium there is a growing awareness that the end of global inequality cannot be guaranteed through lifting all countries to the current material status of the wealthiest countries. According to Meadows et al. (2005: xv), the challenge for the future involves meeting the twin goals of increasing the level of consumption of the world's poorest while simultaneously minimizing humanity's ecological footprint. Implicit in this challenge is a convergence or equalization of global living standards – lowering average consumption in the wealthier world while raising consumption in the poorer world.

The modern understanding of the relationship between humanity and nature has almost turned full circle over the past 200 years (Malouf 1998). As Chapter 4 noted, the premodern position tended to see humanity at the mercy of natural and supernatural forces. Modernity offered the hope that human intellect and innovation was capable of controlling nature and widening the scope of human well-being. In the early twenty-first century, there is greater foreboding that our socio-economic behaviour can lead to damaging environmental and ecological consequences that threaten the security of human tenure on the planet, along with those we share it with.

The consequences of our social and economic behaviour are now incalculably complex and require more precautionary measures (Beck 1994). As the world becomes more globally interconnected, the problems to be faced become more political than scientific. This fraught relationship between sustainability and the politics of development has been summed up by Stephen Jay Gould (2002): while scientific analysis can reveal 'many wonderful and disturbing things', it cannot help us when it comes to matters of the regulation of social behaviour. These matters of social policy are beyond the realm of science and belong more to the realm of ethics and politics.

Development as security

If progress is portrayed as the growing dominance of humanity over the forces of nature, then 'security' is also an important component of development. Throughout the book, security has been analysed on individual, national and global levels.

Many commentators, from T. H. Marshall (1977) onward, have linked progress to a deepening sense of personal security. For example, on the eve of the Second World War, as Britain struggled out of the 1930s Depression, Laski (1937: 51) proclaimed that 'without economic security, liberty is not worth having'. This sentiment characterized the postwar vision of the welfare state (see Chapter 4). From a very different philosophical position, Hayek (1944: 124–5) also defined postwar social trends as a further erosion of individual liberty and the encroachment of state-guaranteed security. The 1948 Universal Declaration of Human Rights emphasized the social conditions needed for this security: 'Everyone has the right to a standard of living adequate for the health and well-being of himself and of his family, including food, clothing, housing and medical care and necessary social services, and the right to security in the event of unemployment, sickness, disability, widowhood, old age or other lack of livelihood.' Drawing a link between 'development as growth' and 'development as security', George (2004: 141) has affirmed that if this remained an aspiration at the end of the Second World War, the world is now wealthy enough to deliver on the promise.

At a more macro-analytical level, development has often been justified by governments as a national imperative. As pointed out throughout the book, leaders of the richer countries have often recognized that the security of their states could never be assured if their isolated islands of wealth remained surrounded by a sea of extreme poverty. Furthermore, as Myrdal (1977: 6) complained, in the midst of the Cold War, many development reports were 'justified by their contribution to the security of the United States or Western countries' (see also Fukuyama 2006: 120).

Yet, there was also an understandable desire among newly independent countries to promote development as a means of protecting their hard-won sovereignty through adopting policies that encouraged self-reliance – or at least a shift away from reliance on primary commodities with fluctuating export prices and insecure markets (for Papua New Guinea, see Turner 1990: 187). A more diversified, balanced economic structure appeared to offer better national security. Postwar developmental schemes in the newly independent countries were often framed as nation-building projects (Kiely 1998: 62). The ability of the Soviet Union to withstand militarily the threat of Nazi Germany provided a historical illustration of how industrial development underpinned national security.

After the 1970s, the rise of neoliberalism and the debt crisis trimmed the sails of these nation-building development schemes, but more recently the recognition that failed states affect global security has led to a renewed emphasis on 'state building' (Fukuyama 2004). The post-Cold War era has failed to bring a 'peace dividend' to many parts of the world, including the wealthier regions, as armed conflict, ethnic tensions and transnational migration replace the nuclear threat as major sources of global insecurity. Neoliberal state building begins with the premise that development rests on good governance because that provides an environment conducive for economic growth. This includes respect for human rights, respect for private property, transparency in government dealings with companies, and rule of law.

However, economic development does not always correlate with a growing sense of security. As Kay (2004: 372) points out, the highly developed USA has experienced widening inequalities and deeper poverty, increased levels of crime, an expanding prison population and more people retreating within gated communities. Wherever the 'security' industry is growing, this appears to be positively correlated with a growing sense of personal and community insecurity.

Chapter 9 examined security from another angle. Is it possible to have security without social justice? Environmental commentators have warned of the impact that transnational–controlled food commodity chains are having on 'food security' of the poor (Shiva 2001). The global social movements challenging neoliberal globalization have also questioned the right of the rich to security in a world where over a billion people live on less than US$1 a day. The UN Millennium Project (UNMP 2005a: 10) reiterates this claim that it is in the enlightened self-interest of the wealthier countries to alleviate global poverty in order to 'safeguard peace and security'.

Development as illusion

Discontent with development has grown over time – among those who consider it a failure, those who believe that it is at an impasse, as well as amongst environmentalists. Chapter 9 showed that there are many contemporary commentators who consider development illusory. Gray (2004) considers progress to be the great illusion of our age and dismisses development as a fraudulent mission statement for 'purposeless change'. This challenges the core belief of the development project, which has always understood development as 'directional change' (McMichael 2000: 3). The recent history outlined in this book also suggests that it would be imprudent to base faith on the assertion that through time human well-being improves as knowledge expands.

As Chapter 9 also pointed out, another version of the 'development as illusion' thesis has been adopted by postdevelopmentalists. During the past two centuries, the concept of development could motivate altruistic works as well as justify appalling repression. On occasions, the two could be combined in a style of authoritarian development that claimed that 'you can't have omelettes without breaking eggs' – a phrase attributed to Joseph Chamberlain as well as Joseph Stalin (Ferguson 2004: 221). The illusory nature of development only becomes clear after eggs are cracked without omelettes appearing. Too often, developmental programmes have dismantled pre-existing socioeconomic structures without delivering the benefits of modernity. Postdevelopmentalists claim that the abstract nature of the concept of development, with its tendency to universalize experience, always contained an anti-democratic and anti-participatory logic. One of the problems facing postdevelopment approaches, however, concerns what to fill in the place vacated by the illusion (see Escobar 1995: 223–6).

A more qualified version of the 'development as illusion' thesis is offered by Chakrabarty (1990: 108), who also rejects the possibility that modern capitalist growth can deliver universal development:

What if modernity was structurally based on the twin phenomena of mass consumerism and mass poverty, those two relatively recent developments in human history? What if poverty and unequal consumption of resources were precisely the conditions that made it possible for some of us to have institutions that promote 'free' enquiry and debate?

This structuralist hypothesis recalls the paradox of modernity noted in Chapter 1, and links the benefits of modernity with its costs. This possibility was also addressed by the more structural approach of dependency theory (see Chapter 5), which focused on the expropriation of the surplus of peripheral countries to boost the development of the core countries. If the world system continues to be premised on such global inequalities, then the illusion of development is the modern 'opiate of the poor'.

Development as lodestar

Throughout this book the vision of development as a lodestar has been a consistent theme (see Wallerstein 1994). Since its inception, the field of development studies has promoted targets set according to bright lights in the distance. Chapter 4 referred to this tendency as the prototype/emulator model. The development of poorer countries was charted along a previously explored course. This implied that overcoming national inequalities involved a process of 'catching up' with earlier nations, or 'following their footsteps' or 'climbing rungs' on the development ladder. This not only suggested that models could be transferred across space and time, but also that successful development would involve a high degree of global homogenization.

Modernization theory most explicitly looked towards this lodestar. However, the origins of this vision could be found in Marx's claim that the more developed countries presented the less developed ones with an image of their own destiny (although the longer this metaphor is pondered, the more puzzling it becomes – surely we see ourselves and what's behind us in a mirror, not our future selves!). From a modernization perspective, Lerner employed a similar analogy, comparing the developed world to a mirror into which the less developed gazed. During the early postwar era, the lodestar analogy was reinforced through the strong role assigned to state planning (Galbraith 1962). Planning by its very nature demands an ideal vision on the time-horizon. This penchant for planning was driven to extremes by the Soviet model for development.

As Chapter 6 noted, the star of state planning faded with the rise of neoliberalism. An older metaphor returned to explain the development process – the workings of the 'invisible hand' of the market. The combined effect of decisions made by countless rationally calculating individuals was seen as the foundations for freeing up entrepreneurship and modernizing the economy. However, even neoliberalism could be interpreted as treating development as a lodestar shining in the form of certain prototypes – such as the Asian NICs – that had previously followed the correct, market-oriented path to growth by 'getting the fundamentals right' and avoiding the temptation of too much state intervention (World Bank 1993). This neoliberal model, championed by IFIs, has encountered growing criticism over the past decade. The fruits of its policy have proved disappointing and the voices of its victims have grown louder (see Chapters 6, 8 and 9).

The Millennium Development Goals also signal a more explicit return to the loadstar metaphor for development. As Chapter 7 pointed out, these are goal-driven targets according to which currently available resources are to be mobilized. The Millennium Project has explicitly criticized the IMF for failing to look up from the ground of existing constraints, rather than focusing on the horizon.

The lodestar metaphor therefore still retains a qualified hold on development studies. This qualification involves recognizing that development is a voyage rather than a destination. The value of this qualification has been enhanced over the past few decades as it has become increasingly clear that the so-called 'developed countries' are also 'transitional' in the sense that they continue to evolve within a globally networked system of production, distribution and consumption. There has been a growing consciousness that development problems and challenges have become increasingly global in the twenty-first century.

Development as freedom

The lodestar metaphor is predicated on the Enlightenment concept of progress, which predicted the expansion of human freedom – from both natural elements and from ignorance. Freedom, therefore, was posited as an endpoint of progress. 'Development as modernization' adopted this notion of freedom as a goal towards which all societies strove. Within this model, freedom appeared as a dependent variable or a consequence of structural transformations in social and economic relations.

As Chapter 6 pointed out, Fukuyama retained this vision of development, interpreting the end of the Cold War as a victory for political and economic liberty. The path to freedom was assured now that liberalism had defeated its ideological foes. Along with neoliberal interpretations of development, Fukuyama reasserted the Enlightenment optimism that this path to political freedom was tied to the adoption of liberal economic policies. This thread of thought from the Enlightenment through to the new millennium has remained the dominant approach to understanding human freedom – emancipation through growth (Pieterse 2004: 70).

There have always been dissenting voices. World-systems analysts questioned whether participation in the modern world economy necessarily enhanced the prospects of national or individual freedom or, alternatively, whether it linked peripheral nations into stronger ties of dependency. By the 1970s, after reviewing postwar struggles for political freedom and national independence, Wertheim (1974) also questioned whether the conception of freedom as a consequence of progressive development had ever been valid. Without rejecting progress, he suggested that it was more appropriate to view emancipation as a series of ascending waves, a view also developed by Huntington (see Chapter 10).

Increasingly over the past few decades, commentators have begun to question whether freedom is a dependent variable of the development process. This more sceptical approach has focused on the *quality* of growth (Sen 2001b: 126). For example, the Millennium Development Goals emphasize participation in development programmes by those it intends to benefit. Freedom therefore becomes a condition for development as well as an end in itself. As Sen (2001b: 53, see also 281) argues, 'people have to be seen . . . as being actively involved – given the opportunity – in shaping their own destiny, and not just as passive recipients of the fruits of cunning development programs'.

In Chapter 2, Sen's (2001b: 3–4) approach was described as one way of collapsing the distance between the *means* and *ends* of development: 'If freedom is what development advances, then there is a major argument for concentrating on that overarching objective, rather than on some particular means, or some specially chosen list of instruments.' From this perspective, the development project is intrinsically bound with freedom. Political liberty, adequate economic infrastructure, equal opportunities, fair laws and 'protective security' are all instrumental components of the process of development (Sen 2001: 38). Freedom, in this sense, is constitutive of development, rather than an endpoint – a 'primary means' and a 'principal end' of development (Sen 2001b: 36, 287–8).

Sen (2001b: 144) also acknowledges that this approach to development bears a resemblance to the 'quality of life' and the 'human development' approaches discussed in Chapters 2 and 3. It also corresponds closely with the emphasis that the MDGs place on the interlinkages between health and literacy, which are seen as important not merely as means to higher levels of economic development but as substantial freedoms in their own right that liberate individuals and broaden opportunities (Sen 2001b: 36). Sen's 'capability deprivation' approach also sheds light on the significance of the global inequalities associated with the marginalization examined in Chapter 8, because the condition of relative poverty 'in a rich country can be a great capability handicap, even when one's absolute income is high in terms of world standards' (Sen 2001: 87–9). Poverty varies with social context as well as within the different communities and families that constitute an individual's lifeworld.

If capabilities are context-dependent, this reinforces the point that inequalities are a central concern for development theory and practice. Indeed, Sen (2001b: 267) argues that the issues of inequality and public goods are the 'big challenges' that capitalism faces in the new millennium.

Development and the End to Inequality

If freedom was understood from the Enlightenment onwards as an endpoint of progress and development, the same has been true for the end of inequality. Marx, for instance, argued that class inequalities would gradually disappear after the proletariat dismantled the structure of capitalist relations and remodelled the world after its own, more egalitarian, image. Postwar modernization theory also approached the end of inequality as an endpoint. The inequalities between the wealthier countries and the poorer countries would lessen as the latter worked their way through predefined stages of economic development.

An important assumption built into modernization theory was that each country could reach the level of development achieved by wealthier countries. However, dependency theory challenged this vision of equality through emulation. It approached inequality as a relationship between the weak and the strong. The principal claim of this structuralist approach is that the 'wealth of some nations' (Caldwell 1977) is predicated on the extraction of the wealth of others. This relationship diminishes the capacity of others to undertake development. From dependency theory through to the Millennium Project, many development theorists and practitioners have made the observation that balanced development is thwarted by inequalities perpetrated by the richer countries on the poorer countries.

The debate on globalization, assessed in Chapter 8, has highlighted another form of inequality central to development theories – inequalities between peoples. The stance different commentators adopt on this relationship between globalization and inequality depends greatly on how neoliberalism is understood. Neoliberal sympathizers assess manifestations of global inequality from a perspective of overall growth and development:

If everyone is coming to be better off what does it matter that the improvement comes faster for some than for others. Surely the important thing is for everyone to be as well off as possible, not whether one group is better off than another. Only those who consider wealth a greater problem than poverty can find a problem in some becoming millionaires while others grow wealthier from their own starting point.   (Norberg 2003: 54)

Critics of neoliberalism identify narrowing inequality gaps as an important means to development. Sen's capability approach falls within this category. High levels of inequality curtail the ability of the poor to fully participate in social life, from markets to politics. From a more structuralist perspective, Myrdal (1989: 16) argued against a vision of development that foresaw merely the distribution of more money to the poor to help them rise above some predetermined poverty line. Development required 'fundamental changes in the conditions under which they are living and working'. This transformation demanded a focus on the simultaneous goals of 'greater equality and increased productivity'. The quality of growth was paramount in any judgement of the success of development.

The neoliberal wager on growth also draws little support from environmental critics who question the capacity of the earth to sustain the resource-intensive lifestyles enjoyed in the wealthier countries. The environmental critique, as this book has stressed, also implicitly calls for an end to inequality through redistributing the share of global resources to the poor while reducing the share of the rich. This would involve placing a heavier, much more visible, regulatory hand on the market mechanism than neoliberals recommend. W. Robinson (2004: 177) also claims that a 'measure of transnational social governance' is needed to counterbalance the liberalizing impact of WTO policies as a means of redistributing wealth towards the world's marginalized.

At present, the economic integration that neoliberal policies produce sits uneasily with growing social polarization. Even if there are improvements among the world's poorest, this would not necessarily promote global stability, as better conditions often raise expectations and awareness of new possibilities, including a fairer world (Rapley 2004) and mean that 'the poor of the world are better able to consider their position and to take action, rather than spend all their time and strength keeping body and soul together for another day' (Hobsbawm 2000: 164). Once levels of inequality are perceived to be too wide, this can provoke social conflict and weaken social cohesion (ILO 2004: 56).

In this sense, inequality is closely related to feelings of security and to perceptions of enlightened self-interest. If the poor lack security over their means of existence, then the wealthy cannot feel secure in their comfort (Fukuyama 2006: 141). The form of globalization that has facilitated higher standards of living has also globalized the risks to that lifestyle, not only from environmental limitations but also from the marginalized. Todaro's (1990: 605) comments, written at the end of the Cold War, still remain pertinent in the new millennium: as rich and poor countries 'share an increasingly common destiny', it is time for the world to 'realize that a more equitable international order is not just possible, it is essential'.

Enlightened self-interest is not the only motivation for challenging global inequality. As the Millennium Development Goals starkly illustrate, it is morally unacceptable to ignore the fate of the extreme poor, especially once their plight has registered in the minds of the wealthy and the globally connected. Even if the claim is accepted that the MDGs are too ambitious, it does not necessarily follow that they should be abandoned. Individuals spend their lives aspiring to goals that they might never attain, but that does not make their lives any less worthwhile. If the Enlightenment concept of progress revealed anything, it was that humanity is not a slave to fate. In the contemporary world, where meeting the basic annual needs of the world's poorest would cost the equivalent of Europe's consumption of perfume (Ramonet 2004: 127), it is difficult to argue that humanity does not possess the means to challenge global inequality.

Marx (1973: 146) quipped that all great world-historic facts appear twice: 'the first time as tragedy, the second time as farce'. Pessimists, looking back on the last six decades of development practice, would argue that the next few decades will bear all the hallmarks of the farcical. Then, again, Marx (1983: 160) also claimed that humankind 'always sets itself only such tasks as it can solve'. Optimists would look upon the next few decades of development practice as an example of a realistic challenge for humankind.

References

Abbott, P. et al. (2005), *An Introduction to Sociology: Feminist Perspectives* (London: Routledge).

Agarwal, B. (2001), 'Participatory exclusions, community forestry, and gender: an analysis for South Asia and a conceptual framework', *World Development*, 29(10): 1623–48.

Agoncillo, T. and Guerrero, M. (1973), *History of the Filipino People* (Quezon City: R. P. Garcia Publishing).

Alavi, H. and Shanin, T. (eds) (1982), *An Introduction to the Sociology of 'Developing Societies'* (Basingstoke: Macmillan).

Ali, T. (2002), *The Clash of Fundamentalisms* (London: Verso Press).

Alkire, S. (2002), *Valuing Freedoms: Sen's Capability Approach and Poverty Reduction* (Oxford: Oxford University Press).

Almagir, J. (1997) 'Against the current: the survival of authoritarianism in Burma', *Pacific Affairs*, 70(3): 333–50.

Ambrose, S. (1979), *Rise to Globalism: American Foreign Policy, 1938–1976* (London: Penguin).

Amin, S. (1974), *Accumulation on a World Scale: A Critique of the Theory of Underdevelopment* (New York: Monthly Review Press).

Amin, S. (1981), *The Future of Maoism* (New York: Monthly Review Press).

Amin, S. (1985), *Delinking* (New York: Monthly Review Press).

Anderson, B. (1991), *Imagined Communities* (London: Verso Press).

Annan, K. (2002), 'Address to the World Summit on Sustainable Development', Johannesburg, 2 September, http://www.un.org/events/wssd/statements/sgE.htm

Annan, K. (2005a), 'An aspiration to a larger freedom', *Financial Times*, London, 21 March.

Annan, B. (2005b), www.un.org/largerfreedom/sgreport-21Mar)S-oped.pdf, p. 2.

Apter, D. (1967), *The Politics of Modernization* (Chicago: University of Chicago Press).

Apthorpe, R. (ed.) (1970), *Rural Cooperatives and Planned Change in Africa* (Geneva: UNRISD).

Arnold, G. (1993), *The End of the Third World* (New York: St Martin's Press).

Arrighi, G., Hopkins, T. K. and Wallerstan, I. (1989), *Anti-Systemic Movements* (London: Verso Press).

Asia Foundation (2003), *Democracy in Cambodia – 2003: A Survey of the Cambodian Electorate* (Phnom Penh: Asia Foundation).

Asian Development Bank (1999), *Governance: Sound Development Management* (Manila: Asian Development Bank).

Asian Times Online (2005), 7 April.

Avineri, S. (1976), 'Karl Marx on colonialism and modernization', in M. Howard and J. King (eds), *The Economics of Marx* (London: Penguin).

Babbie, E. (1983), *The Practice of Social Research* (Belmont, CA: Wadsworth Publishing).

Bali, M. (2002), 'Promoting safe lifestyle in Somaliland', *Somaliland Alternative Newsletter*, Occasional Papers no. 3, September.

Banfield, E. (1958), *The Moral Basis of a Backward Society* (New York: Free Press).

Baran, P. (1970), 'On the political economy of backwardness', in R. Rhodes (ed.), *Imperialism and Underdevelopment* (New York: Monthly Review Press), pp. 285–301.

Baran, P. (1973), *The Political Economy of Growth* (London: Penguin).

Bark, D. L. (1986), *The Red Orchestra: Instruments of Soviet Policy in Latin America and the Caribbean* (Stanford, CA: Hoover Institution Press).

Barnet, R. and Cavanagh, J. (1995), *Global Dreams: Imperial Corporations and the New World Order* (New York: Touchstone).

Barrientos, A., Gorman, M. and Heslop, A. (2003), 'Old age poverty in developing countries: contributions and dependence in later life', *World Development*, 31(3): 555–70.

Bates, R. (2006), 'Ethnicity and development', in D. A. Clark (ed.), *The Elgar Companion to Development Studies* (Cheltenham: Edward Elgar).

Bauer, P. (1976), *Dissent on Development* (Cambridge, MA: Harvard University Press).

Bauer, P. (1981), *Equality: The Third World and Economic Delusion* (Cambridge, MA: Harvard University Press).

Bauman, Z. (2000), *Liquid Modernity* (Cambridge: Polity Press).

Baxter, J. (2000), 'Gender inequality in Australian society', in J. Najman and J. Western (eds), *A Sociology of Australian Society* (Melbourne: Macmillan).

Bayart, J.-F. (1991), 'Finishing with the idea of the Third World: the concept of the political trajectory', in J. Manor (ed.), *Rethinking Third World Politics* (London: Longman), pp. 51–71.

BBC (2005), 'China village democracy skin deep', accesed 10 May. http://news.bbc.co.uk/2/hi/asia-pacific/4319954.stm

BBC News (2004), 'Mbeki seeks urgent UN reform', accessed 19 August, http://news.bbc.co.uk/1/hi/world/africa/3580338.stm

Beck, U. (1994), *Risk Society* (Cambridge: Polity Press).

Beeson, M. (2004), 'Southeast Asia', in A. Payne (ed.), *The New Regional Politics of Development* (Basingstoke: Palgrave Macmillan).

Bello, W. (2003), 'The meaning of Cancun', accessed from http://www.nadir.org/nadir/initiativ/agp/free/wto/news/0918meaning_of_cancun.htm.

Bendana, A. (2001), 'From Seattle to September 11', text of remarks to Jubilee South and International Initiative on Corruption and Governance, 26 November, Seattle, http://transcend.org/al_ben.htm

Berger, M. (1993), 'The end of the Third World', in *Third World Quarterly*, 15(2).

Berger, M. (2004), 'After the Third World: history, destiny and the fate of Third-Worldism', *Third World Quarterly*, 25(1), February.

Berger, P. (1977), *Pyramids of Sacrifice: Political Ethics and Social Change* (London: Penguin).

Berger, P. (1985a), 'Speaking to the Third World', in P. Berger and M. Novak, *Essays on Development and Democracy* (Washington, DC: American Enterprise Institute for Public Policy Research).

Berger, P. (1985b), 'Underdevelopment revisited', in P. Berger and M. Novak, *Essays on Development and Democracy* (Washington, DC: American Enterprise Institute for Public Policy Research).

Bergesen, A. (1980), 'From utilitarianism to globology: the shift from the individual to the world as a whole as the primordial unit of analysis', in A. Bergesen (ed.), *Studies of the Modern World-system* (New York: Sage).

Bergesen, A. (1990), 'Turning world-systems theory on its head', in *Theory, Culture and Society*, vol. 7.

Berryman, P. (1984), 'Basic Christian communities and the future of Latin America', *Monthly Review*, 36 (July–August): 27–40.

Betts, R. (ed.) (1972), *The Scramble for Africa: Causes and Dimensions of Empire* (Lexington, MA: D. C. Heath).

Bevan, P. (2004), 'Exploring the structured dynamics of chronic poverty', *WeD Working Paper*, no. 6, University of Bath, UK.

Bhagwati, J. (2004), *In Defense of Globalization* (Oxford: Oxford University Press).

Bibby, A. (2003), 'For universal development of the post', paper presented to the 1st Uni-Postal World Congress, Geneva, 4–5 November 2003, http://www.andrewbibby.com/pdf/Universal%20Development%20of% 20the%20Post%20E.pdf

Black, G. (1984), *Garrison Guatemala* (London: Zed Books).

Blackburn, R. (ed.) (1991), *After the Fall: The Failure of Communism and the Future of Socialism* (London: Verso Press).

Blackwell, T. and J. Seabrook (1993), *The Revolt against Change: Towards a Conserving Radicalism* (London: Vintage).

Blainey, G. (2002), *This Land is All Horizon* (Sydney: ABC Books).

Blake, J. (1976), 'The changing status of women in developed countries', in C. Black (ed.), *Comparative Modernization: A Reader* (New York: Free Press).

Bock, K. (1979), 'Theories of progress, development, evolution', in T. Bottomore and R. Nisbet (eds), *A History of Sociological Analysis* (London: Heinemann).

Bonner, R. (1987), *Waltzing with a Dictator: The Marcoses and the Making of American Policy* (New York: Times Books).

Booth, D. (1985), 'Marxism and development sociology: interpreting the impasse', *World Development*, 13(7): 761–87.

Boserup, E. (1970), *Women's Role in Economic Development* (New York: St Martin's Press).

Braudel, F. (1985), *Ecrits sur Histoire* (Paris: Flammarion).

Brawley, M. (2003), *The Politics of Globalization: Gaining Perspective, Assessing Consequences* (Ontario: Broadview Press).

Brecher, J. and Costello, T. (1994), *Global Village or Global Pillage: Economic Reconstruction from the Bottom Up* (Boston, MA: South End Press).

Breman, J. (1996), *Footloose Labour: Working in India's Informal Economy* (Cambridge: Cambridge University Press).

Brenner, R. (1982), 'The origins of capitalist development: a critique of neo-Smithian Marxism', in H. Alavi and T. Shanin (eds), *An Introduction to the Sociology of 'Developing Societies'* (Basingstoke: Macmillan).

Brenner, R. (1998), 'The economics of global turbulence: a special report on the world economy, 1950–1998', *New Left Review*, 229.

Breslin, S. (2004), 'Northeast Asia', in A. Payne (ed.), *The New Regional Politics of Development* (Basingstoke: Palgrave Macmillan).

Brewer, A. (1989), *Marxist Theories of Imperialism: A Critical Survey* (London: Routledge).

Brillantes, A. (2003), *Innovations and Excellence: Understanding Local Governments in the Philippines* (Quezon City: Center for Local and Regional Governance, University of the Philippines).

Broad, D. (1995), 'Globalization versus labor', *Monthly Review*, December.

Bromley, S. (2004), The Middle East', in A. Payne (ed.), *The New Regional Politics of Development* (Basingstoke: Palgrave Macmillan).

Brown, D. (2004), 'Participation in poverty reduction strategies: democracy strengthened or democracy undermined', in S. Hickey and G. Mohan (eds), *Participation: From Tyranny to Transformation* (London: Zed Books), pp. 237–51.

Browne, J. (1995), *Charles Darwin Voyaging* (London: Jonathan Cape).

Buckman, G. (2005), *Global Trade: Past Mistakes, Future Choices* (London: Zed Books).

Bukharin, N. (1976), *Imperialism and the World Economy* (London: The Merlin Press).

Bulbeck, C. (1988), *One World Women's Movement* (London: Pluto Press).

Burke, P. (1980), *Sociology and History* (London: George Allen & Unwin).

Burki, S., Perry, G. and Dillinger, W. (1999), *Beyond the Center: Decentralizing the State* (Washington, DC: World Bank).

Caldwell, M. (1977), *The Wealth of Some Nations* (London: Zed Books).

Callinicos, A. (1991), *The Revenge of History: Marxism and the Eastern European Revolutions* (Cambridge: Polity Press).

Calvert, S. and Calvert, P. (2003), *Politics and Society in the Third World* (London: Prentice Hall).

Cammack, P. (2002), 'Neoliberalism, the World Bank and the new politics of development', in U. Kothari and M. Minogue (eds), *Development Theory and Practice: Critical Perspectives* (Basingstoke: Palgrave Macmillan).

Carr, E. H. (1976a), *The Bolshevik Revolution*, Volume 1 (London: Penguin).

Carr, E. H. (1976b), *The Bolshevik Revolution*, Volume 3 (London: Penguin).

Castells, M. (1991), *The Informational City* (Oxford: Blackwell).

Castells, M. (1998), *The Information Age: Economy, Society and Culture*, 3 vols (Malden, MA: Blackwell).

Castro, F. (1985), *How Latin America's and the Third World's Unpayable Debt Can and Should Be Cancelled and the Pressing Need for a New International Economic Order* (La Habana: Editora Politica).

Chakrabatry, D. (1990), 'Trafficking in history and theory: subaltern studies', in K. Ruthven (ed.), *Beyond the Disciplines: The New Humanities*, Australian Academy of the Humanities Symposium, Occasional Paper no. 13, pp. 101–8.

Chambers, Robert (1983) *Rural Development: Putting the Last First* (London: Longman).

Chambers, Robert (1997), *Whose Reality Counts? Putting the First Last* (London: Intermediate Technology Publications).

Chan, S. and Qingyang, G. (2006), 'Investment in China migrates inland', *Far Eastern Economic Review*, 169(4): 52–5.

Chang, H.-J. and Grabel, I. (2004), *Reclaiming Development: An Alternative Economic Policy Manual* (London: Zed Books).

Chase Dunn, C. (1980), 'Socialist states in the world capitalist system', *Social Problems*, 27.

Chase Dunn, C. (1999), 'Globalization: a world-systems perspective', *Journal of World-Systems Research*, vol. 2.

Chazan, N., Mortimer, R., Ravenhill, J. and Rothchild, D. (1988), *Politics and Society in Contemporary Africa* (Basingstoke: Macmillan).

Chenery, H., Ahluwalia, M., Bell, C., Duloy, J. and Jolly, R. (1974), *Redistribution with Growth: Policies to Improve Income Distribution in Developing Countries in the Context of Economic Growth* (Oxford: Oxford University Press for the World Bank and IDS).

Christian, D. (1992), '*Perestroika* and World History', *Australian Journal of Slavonic and Eastern European Studies*, 6(1).

Clark, D. A. (2002), *Visions of Development: A Study of Human Values* (Cheltenham: Edward Elgar).

Clark, D. A. (2006), 'Capability approach', in D. A. Clark (ed.), *The Elgar Companion to Development Studies* (Cheltenham: Edward Elgar).

Clark, D. A. and Qizilbash, M. (2003), 'Core poverty and extreme vulnerability in South Africa', paper presented at the conference on *Staying Poor: Chronic Poverty and Development Policy*, IDPM, University of Manchester, 7–9 April 2005. Available online at http://www.chronicpoverty.org/pdfs/conferencepapers/Clark.pdf (accessed 2 November 2005).

Clarke, G. (1998), *The Politics of NGOs in South-East Asia* (London: Routledge).

Clarke, G. and Thomas, A. (2006), 'Nongovernmental organizations, civil society, and development governance', in A. Huque and H. Zafarullah (eds), *International Development Governance* (Boca Raton: CRC), pp. 415–428.

Clemens, M., Kenny, C. and Moss, T. (2004), 'The trouble with the MDGs: confronting expectations of aid and development success', Centre for Global Development Working Paper no. 40, May, Washington, DC.

Cockett, R. (1994), *Thinking the Unthinkable: Think-Tanks and the Economic Counter-Revolution, 1931–1983* (London: HarperCollins).

Cocks, D. (2003), *Deep Futures: Our Prospects for Survival* (Sydney: University of New South Wales Press).

Cohn, T. H. (2005) *Global Political Economy: Theory and Practice* (New York: Pearson).

Comeliau, C. (2002), *The Impasse of Modernity: Debating the Future of the Global Market Economy* (London: Zed Press).

Commission for Africa (2005), *Our Common Interest: An Argument* (London: Penguin).

Connell, R.W. (1977), *Ruling Class, Ruling Culture* (Cambridge: Cambridge University Press).

Constantini, P. (2001), 'What's wrong with the WTO? A guide to where the mines are buried', http://www.speakeasy.org/~peterc/wtow/, November.

Conyers, D. (1983), 'Decentralisation: the latest fashion in development administration', *Public Administration and Development*, 3(2): 97–109.

Cooke, B. (2004), 'Rules of thumb for participatory change agents', in S. Hickey and G. Mohan (eds), *Participation: From Tyranny to Transformation* (London: Zed Books), pp. 42–55.

Cooke, B. and Kothari, U. (2001), 'The case for participation as tyranny', in B. Cooke and U. Kothari (eds), *Participation: The New Tyranny* (London: Zed Books), pp. 1–15.

Cornwall, A. and Gaventa, J. (2006) 'Participation in governance', in A. Huque and H. Zafarullah (eds), *International Development Governance* (Boca Raton: CRC), pp. 405–14.

Coser, L. (1971), *Masters of Sociological Thought: Ideas in Historical and Social Context* (New York: Harcourt Brace Jovanovich).

Cowen, T. (2002), *Creative Destruction: How Globalization is Changing the World's Cultures* (Princeton, NJ: Princeton University Press).

CPRC (2004), *The Chronic Poverty Report 2004/5*, Chronic Poverty Research Centre, University of Manchester, UK. http://www.chronicpoverty.org

Craib, I. (1984), *Modern Social Theory: From Parsons to Habermas* (New York: Wheatsheaf Books).

Crook, R. (2003), 'Decentralisation and poverty reduction in Africa: the politics of central–local relations', *Public Administration and Development*, 23(1): 77–88.

Crook, R. and Manor, J. (1994), *Enhancing Participation and Institutional Performance: Democratic Decentralisation in West Africa and South Asia* (London: Overseas Development Administration).

Crook, S., Waters, M. and Pakulski, J. (1992), *Postmodernization: Change in Advanced Society* (London: Sage).

Crotty, M. (1998), *The Foundations of Social Research: Meaning and Perspective in the Research Process* (Sydney: Allen & Unwin).

Davies, J. (1962), 'Towards a theory of revolution', *American Sociological Review*, 27.

Davis, M. (2006), *Planet of Slums* (London: Verso Press).

Dercon, S. (2006), 'Poverty measurement', in D. A. Clark (ed.), *The Elgar Companion to Development Studies* (Cheltenham: Edward Elgar).

Derrida, J. (1994), *Specters of Marx: The State of the Debt, the Work of Mourning, and the New International* (London: Routledge).

Desai, V. and Potter, R. B. (2002) *The Companion to Development Studies* (London: Edward Arnold).

de Soto, H. (1999), *The Mystery of Capital: Why Capitalism Triumphs in the West and Fails Everywhere Else* (London: Black Swan).

d'Sousa, D. (2002), 'Two cheers for colonialism', *The Chronicle of Higher Education*, 10 May.

Diamond, J. (1997), *Guns, Germs, and Steel: The Fate of Human Societies* (New York: W. W. Norton).

Diamond, L. (1994), 'Rethinking civil society towards democratic consolidation', *Journal of Democracy*, 5(3): 5–17.

Dicken, P. (2003), *Global Shift: Transforming the World Economy* (London: Paul Chapman).

Dinnen, S. (2001), *Law and Order in a Weak State: Crime and Politics in Papua New Guinea* (Honolulu and Bathurst: University of Hawaii Press and Crawford House).

Donaldson, P. (1973), *World's Apart: The Economic Gulf Between Nations* (London: Penguin).

Donaldson, P. (1988 [1973]), *Economics of the Real World* (London: Penguin).

Dower, N. (2006), 'Rawls, John (1921–2002)', in D. A. Clark (ed.), *The Elgar Companion to Development Studies* (Cheltenham: Edward Elgar).

Doyal, L. and Gough, I. (1991), *A Theory of Human Need* (Basingstoke: Macmillan).

During, S. (1990), 'Post-colonialism', in K. Ruthven (ed.), *Beyond the Disciplines: The New Humanities*, Australian Academy of the Humanities Symposium, Occasional paper no. 13, pp. 88–100.

Durkheim, E. (1915), *The Elementary Forms of the Religious Life* (New York: Free Press).

Durkheim, E. (1965), *The Division of Labour in Society* (New York: The Free Press).

Dyball, R. (2005), 'Understanding obesogenic environments from the perspective of human ecology', *Proceedings of the 2nd State of Australian Cities Conference*, Brisbane, November–December.

Eagleton, T. (2004), *After Theory* (London: Penguin).

Easterly, W. (2002), *The Elusive Quest for Growth* (Cambridge, MA: MIT Press).

Easterly, W. (2005), 'A modest proposal', *The Washington Post*, March 13.

Easterly, W. (2006) *The White Man's Burden: Why the West's Efforts to Aid the Rest Have Done So Much Ill and So Little Good* (New York: Penguin).

The Economist (2006) 'A survey of China', 25 March, pp. 3–20.

Einstein, A. (1998), 'Why socialism?', *Monthly Review*, May, http://www.monthlyreview.org//598einst.htm.

Eisenstadt, S.N. (1973), 'The problem of modernisation and development in sociological analysis', in *Tradition, Change and Modernity* (New York: John Wiley), pp. 3–21.

Elias, N. (1982), *The Civilizing Process* (Oxford: Blackwell).

Elliott, L. (2004), *The Global Politics of the Environment* (Basingstoke: Palgrave Macmillan).

Ellwood, W. (2000), *The No-Nonsense Guide to Globalization* (London: Verso Press).

Elworthy, S. and Rogers, P. (2001), 'The United States, Europe and the majority world after 11 September', *Oxford Research Group Briefing Papers*, September 2001.

Emmanuel, A. (1972), *Unequal Exchange: A Study of the Imperialism of Trade* (New York: Monthly Review Books).

Erb, S. and Harriss-White, B. (2002) *Outcast from Social Welfare: Adult Disability, Incapacity and Development in Rural South Asia* (Bangalore: Books for Change).

Escobar, A. (1995), *Encountering Development: The Making and Unmaking of the Third World* (Princeton, NJ: Princeton University Press).

Escobar, A. (2004), 'Beyond the Third World: imperial globality, global coloniality and anti-globalisation social movements', *Third World Quarterly*, 25(1), February.

Etzioni-Halevy, E. (1981), *Social Change: The Advent and Maturity of Modernity* (London: Routledge and Kegan Paul).

Faguet, J.-P. (2001), 'Does decentralisation increase responsiveness to local needs? Evidence from Bolivia', *Policy Research Working Paper* no. 2516 (Washington, DC: World Bank).

Falk, J. and Camilieri, J. (1992), *The End of Sovereignty? The Politics of a Shrinking and Fragmenting World* (Aldershot: Edward Elgar).

Fals Borda, O. (1969) *Cooperatives and Rural Development in Latin America* (Geneva: UNRISD).

Far Eastern Economic Review (2003), 9 January.

Ferguson, N. (2003), *Empire: How Britain Made the Modern World* (London: Penguin).

Ferguson, N. (2004), *Collosus: The Rise and Fall of the American Empire* (London: Penguin).

Focus on the Global South (2005), www.focusweb.org

Finer, S. (1962), *The Man on Horseback: The Role of the Military in Politics* (London: Pall Mall Press).

Ford, J. (2000), 'Rationale for decentralization', in J. Litvack and J. Seddon (eds), *Decentralization Briefing Notes* (Washington, DC: World Bank Institute), pp. 6–8.

Foucault, M. (2000), *Ethics* (London: Penguin).

Francis, P. (2002), 'Social capital, civil society and social exclusion', in U. Kothari and M. Minogue (eds), *Development Theory and Practice: Critical Perspectives* (Basingstoke: Palgrave Macmillan).

Frank, A. G. (1969), *Sociology of Development and Underdevelopment of Sociology* (Stockholm: Zenit).

Frank, A. G. (1970), 'The development of underdevelopment', in R. Rhodes (ed.), *Imperialism and Underdevelopment* (New York: Monthly Review Press), pp. 4–17.

Frank, A. G. (1971), *Capitalism and Underdevelopment in Latin America* (London: Penguin).

Frank, A. G. (1974), *Lumpenbourgeiosie/Lumpendevelopment: Dependence, Class, and Politics in Latin America* (New York: Monthly Review Press).

Frank, A. G. (1984), *Critique and Anti-Critique: Essays on Dependence and Reformism* (London: Macmillan).

Freedman, L. (2005), 'Achieving the MDGs: health systems as core social institutions', *Development*, 48(1), March.

Freire, P. (1972), *Pedagogy of the Oppressed* (Harmondsworth: Penguin).

Friedan, J. A. (2006), *Global Capitalism: Its Fall and Rise in the Twentieth Century* (New York: W. W. Norton).

Friedman, M. and Friedman, R. (1980), *Free to Choose – A Personal Statement* (London: Secker and Warburg).

Friedman, T. (2000), *The Lexus and the Olive Tree* (New York: Harper Collins).

Friedman, T. (2006), *The World is Flat* (New York: Farrer, Straus & Giroux).

Frum, D. and Perle, R. (2003), *An End to Evil* (New York: Random House).

Fukuyama, F. (1989), 'The end of history?', *The National Interest*, Summer.

Fukuyama, F. (1992), *The End of History and the Last Man* (New York: The Free Press).

Fukuyama, F. (2001), 'History beyond the end', *The Australian*, 9 October; also published in the *Guardian*, 11 October 2001.

Fukuyama, F. (2002), 'Has history restarted since September 11?', 19th John Bonython Lecture, *CIS Occasional Paper no. 81* (Melbourne: Centre for Independent Studies); also at http://www.cis.org.au/Events/JBL/JBL02.htm.

Fukuyama, F. (2004), *State Building: Governance and World Order in the Twenty-First Century* (London: Profile Books).

Fukuyama, F. (2006), *After the NeoCons* (London: Profile Books).

Gaay Fortman, B. de (2006), 'Human rights,' in D. A. Clark (ed.), *The Elgar Companion to Development Studies* (Cheltenham: Edward Elgar).

Galbriath, J. K. (1962), *Economic Development in Perspective* (New York: Fawcett Publications).

Galbraith, J. K. (1987), *The Nature of Mass Poverty* (London: Penguin).

Galeano, E. (1988), *Century of the Wind* (New York: Pantheon Books).

Game, A. and Metcalfe, A. (2003), *The First-Year Experience* (Sydney: Federation Press).

Gaventa, J. (2004), 'Towards participatory governance: assessing the transformative possibilities', in S. Hickey and G. Mohan (eds), *Participation: From Tyranny to Transformation* (London: Zed Books), pp. 25–41.

George, S. (1990), *A Fate Worse than Debt* (London: Penguin).

George, S. (2001), 'The global citizens movement: a new actor for a new politics', paper presented at the conference on 'Reshaping Globalization', Budapest, October 2001.

George, S. (2004), *Another World is Possible if . . .* (London: Verso Books).

George, S. and Sabelli, F. (1994), *Faith and Credit: The World Bank's Secular Empire* (London: Penguin).

Germani, G. (ed.) (1973), *Modernization, Urbanization, and the Urban Crisis* (Boston, MA: Little, Brown).

Gerschenkron, A. (1962), *Economic Backwardness in Historical Perspective* (Cambridge, MA: Belknap Press).

Giddens, A. (1978), *Capitalism and Modern Social Theory* (Cambridge: Cambridge University Press).

Giddens, A. (1984), *The Constitution of Society* (London: Policy Press).

Giddens, A. (1997), 'The scope of sociology', in A. Giddens (ed.), *Sociology: Introductory Readings* (Cambridge: Polity Press).

Giddens, A. (1999), *Runaway World: How Globalisation is Reshaping Our Lives* (London: Profile Books).

Gill, G. (2000), *The Dynamics of Democratization: Elites, Civil Society and the Transition Process* (Basingstoke: Macmillan).

Gleick, J. (1999), *Faster: The Acceleration of Just about Everything* (London: Abacus).

Golding, P. and Middleton, S. (1982), *Images of Welfare* (Oxford: Martin Robinson).

Goldthorpe, J. (1996), *The Sociology of Post-Colonial Society* (Cambridge: Cambridge University Press).

Goodman, J. and Ranald, P. (2000), *Stopping the Juggernaut: Public Interest versus the Multilateral Agreement on Investment* (Sydney: Pluto Press).

Gordon, D., Nandy, S., Pantazis, C., Pemberton, S. and Townsend, P. (2003), *The Distribution of Child Poverty in the Developing World* (Bristol: University of Bristol).

Gordon, J. S. (1992), 'Numbers Game', *Forbes*, 9 October.

Gould, S.J. (2002), *Rocks of Ages* (London: Vintage Books).

Government of Malawi (2002) *Malawi Poverty Reduction Strategy Paper*.

Gray, J. (2004), *Heresies: Against Progress and Other Illusions* (London: Granta Books).

Green, M. (2002), 'Social development: issues and approaches', in U. Kothari and M. Minogue (eds), *Development Theory and Practice: Critical Perspectives* (Basingstoke: Palgrave Macmillan).

Greig, A. (1995), *The Stuff Dreams are Made Of* (Melbourne: Melbourne University Press).

Greig, A. (2002), 'The struggle for outwork reform in the clothing industry', *Journal of Australian Political Economy*, 49 (June).

Greig, A. et al. (2003), *Inequality in Australia* (Cambridge: Cambridge University Press).

Griffin, J., Nelson, H. and Firth, S. (1979), *Papua New Guinea: A Political History* (London: Heinemann).

Grugel, J. (2002), *Democratization: A Critical Introduction* (Basingstoke: Palgrave Macmillan).

Guardian On-line (2005), 'Bolton throws UN Summit into chaos', 26 August.

Guerin, D. (1970), *Anarchism* (New York: Monthly Review Press).

Gurr, T. (1971), *Why Men Rebel* (Princeton, NJ: Princeton University Press).

Gutierrez, E. (1994) *The Ties that Bind: A Guide to Family, Business and Other Interests in the Ninth House of Representatives* (Metro Manila: Philippine Center for Investigative Journalism and Institute for Popular Democracy).

Gutierrez, E., Torrente, I. and Narca, N. (1992), *All in the Family: A Study of Elites and Power Relations in the Philippines* (Quezon City: Institute for Popular Democracy).

Habermas, J. (1971), *Towards a Rational Society* (London: Heineman).

Haigh, G. (2003), 'Elititis', *Australian Book Review*, September 2003.

Hall, C. (2005), 'Writing histories of difference: new histories of nation and empire', The Allan Martin Lecture, 2005 (Canberra: Pandanus Books).

Hall, S. (1996), 'The rest and the west: discourse and power', in S. Hall, D. Held, D. Hubert and K. Thompson (eds), *Modernity: An Introduction to Modern Societies* (Malden, MA: Blackwell).

Hamilton, C. (1994), *The Mystic Economist* (Canberra: Willow Park Press).

Hamilton, C. (2001), 'Globalisation', in C. Sheil (ed.), *Globalisation: Australian Impacts* (Sydney: University of New South Wales Press).

Hamilton, C. (2003), *Growth Fetish* (Sydney: Allen & Unwin).

Hamilton, C. and Denniss, R. (2005), *Affluenza* (Sydney: Allen & Unwin).

Handelman, H. (2003), *The Challenge of Third World Development* (Englewood Cliffs, NJ: Prentice Hall).

Harcourt, W. (2005), 'The millennium development goals: a missed opportunity?', *Development*, 48(1).

Harding, N. (1983), *Lenin's Political Thought: Theory and Practice in the Democratic and Socialist Revolutions*, 2 vols (London: Macmillan).

Hardt, M. and Negri, A. (2001), *Empire* (Cambridge, MA: Harvard University Press).

Harman, C. (1996), 'Globalisation: a critique of a new orthodoxy', *International Socialism*, 73 (December).

Harries, O. (2003), *Benign or Imperial? Reflections on American Hegemony* (Sydney: ABC Books).

Harrigan, J., Wang, C. and Hamed, E. (2006) 'The economic and political determinants of IMF and World Bank lending in the Middle East and North Africa', *World Development*, 34(2): 247–70.

Harris, N. (1987), *The End of the Third World* (London: Penguin).

Harrison, G. (2004), 'Sub-Saharan Africa', in A. Payne (ed.), *The New Regional Politics of Development* (Basingstoke: Palgrave Macmillan).

Harrison, L. and Huntington, S. (2000), *Culture Matters: How Values Shape Human Progress* (New York: Basic Books).

Harriss-White, B. (2002), 'Development and the intermediate classes', in V. Desai and R. B. Potter (eds), *The Companion to Development Studies* (London: Edward Arnold), pp. 175–9.

Harvey, D. (1989), *The Condition of Postmodernity: An Enquiry into the Origins of Cultural Change* (Oxford: Basil Blackwell).

Harvey, D. (2000), *Spaces of Hope* (Berkeley: University of California Press).

Hayek, F. A. (1944), *The Road to Serfdom* (Sydney: Dymock's Book Arcade).

Hayter, T. (1971), *Aid as Imperialism* (London: Penguin).

Held, D. and McGrew, A. (2002), *Globalization/Anti-Globalization* (Cambridge: Polity Press).

HelpAge International (1999), *The Ageing and Development Report* (London: Earthscan).

Hertz, N. (2002), *The Silent Takeover: Global Capitalism and the Death of Democracy* (London: Arrow Books).

Hertz, N. (2004), *IOU: The Debt Threat and Why We Must Defuse It* (London: Fourth Estate).

Hettne, B. (1995), *Development Theory and the Three Worlds* (Harlow: Longman).

Hickey, S. and Mohan, G. (2004), 'From tyranny to transformation?', in S. Hickey and G. Mohan (eds), *Participation: From Tyranny to Transformation* (London: Zed Books), pp. 3–24.

Himmelfarb, G. (1991), *Poverty and Compassion: The Moral Imagination of the Late Victorians* (New York: Alfred A. Knopf).

Hindess, B. and Hirst, P. (1975), *Pre-Capitalist Modes of Production* (London: Routledge and Kegan Paul).

Hirschman, A. (1981), *Essays in Trespassing: Economics to Politics and Beyond* (New Haven, CT: Yale University Press).

Hirst, P. and Thompson, G. (1996), *Globalisation in Question* (Cambridge: Polity Press).

Hobsbawm, E. (1987), *The Age of Empire, 1875–1914* (New York: Pantheon Books).

Hobsbawm, E. (1994), *Age of Extremes: The Short Twentieth Century, 1914–1991* (London: Michael Joseph).

Hobsbawm, E. (2000), *The New Century* (London: Abacus).

Hogan, T. (2002), 'Globalisation: experiences and explanations', in P. Beilharz and T. Hogan (eds), *Social Self, Global Culture: An Introduction to Sociological Ideas* (Melbourne: Oxford University Press).

Holton, R. (2000), 'Globalization's cultural consequences', *Annals*, AAPSS, July.

Hoogvelt, A. (1978), *The Sociology of Developing Societies* (Basingstoke: Macmillan).

Hoogvelt, A. (1997), *Globalisation and the Postcolonial World: The New Political Economy of Development* (Basingstoke: Macmillan).

Horowitz, D. (1967), *From Yalta to Vietnam: American Foreign Policy in the Cold War* (London: Penguin).

Horowitz, I. L. (ed.) (1974), *The Rise and Fall of Project Camelot* (Cambridge: MIT Press).

Horrocks, C. (1999), *Baudrillard and the Millennium* (Cambridge: Icon Books).

Hull, T. H. and Hull, V. J. (1992), 'Dimensions of population and development', *Briefing Paper No. 26*, Australian Development Studies Network, Australian National University, Canberra.

Hulme, D. (2004), 'Thinking small and the understanding of poverty: Maymana and Mofizul's Story', *Journal of Human Development*, 5(2): 161–76.

Hulme, D. and Edwards, M. (1997), 'NGOs, states and donors: an overview', in D. Hulme and M. Edwards (eds), *NGOs, States and Donors: Too Close for Comfort* (Basingstoke: Macmillan), pp. 3–21.

Hulme, D. and Siddiquee, N. (1999) 'Decentralization in Bangladesh: promises, performance and policies', in M. Turner (ed.) *Central–Local Relations in Asia–Pacific: Convergence or Divergence?* (Basingstoke: Macmillan), pp. 19–47.

Hulme, D. and Toye, J. (2006), 'The case for cross-disciplinary social science research on poverty, inequality and well-being', *Journal of Development Studies*, forthcoming.

Hulme, D. and M. Turner (1990), *Sociology and Development: Theories, Policies and Practices* (New York: Harvester Wheatsheaf).

Human Rights Watch (2006), *World Report 2006* (New York: Human Rights Watch).

Hunt, J. (2004), 'Gender and development', in D. Kingsbury, J. Remenyi, J. McKay and J. Hunt, *Key Issues in Development* (Basingstoke: Palgrave Macmillan).

Hunter, G. (1962), *The New Societies of Tropical Africa: A Selective Study* (London: Oxford University Press).

Huntington, S. (1968), *Political Order in Changing Societies* (New Haven, CT: Yale University Press).

Huntington, S. (1991), *The Third Wave: Democratization in the Late Twentieth Century* (Norman: University of Oklahoma Press).

Huntington, S. (1993), 'The Clash of Civilizations', *Foreign Affairs*, Summer.

Huntington, S. (2004), *Who Are We? The Challenges to America's National Identity* (New York: Simon & Schuster).

Hutchcroft, P. (2001) 'Centralization and decentralization in administration and politics: assessing territorial dimensions of authority and power', *Governance: An International Journal of Policy and Administration*, 14(1): 25–53.

Huws, U. (2000), 'The making of a cybertariat: virtual work in a real world', in L. Panitch and C. Leys (eds), *The Global Proletariat: Socialist Register 2001* (London: Merlin Press).

Huxley, A. (1958), *The Human Situation* (St Albans: Triad Panther).

Ignatieff, M. (2003), *Empire Lite* (London: Vintage Books).

Immerman, R. (1982), *The CIA in Guatemala* (Austin: University of Texas Press).

ICIDI (Independent Commission on International Development Issues) (1980), *North–South: A Programme for Survival* (London: Pan Books).

Inglehart, R. (1971), 'The silent revolution in Europe: intergenerational change in post-industrial societies', *American Political Science Review*, 65.

Inkeles, A. (1966), 'The modernization of man', in M. Weiner (ed.), *Modernization: The Dynamics of Growth* (Washington, DC: Voice of America Forum Lectures).

Inkeles, A. (1976), 'A model of the modern man: theoretical and methodological issues', in C. Black (ed.), *Comparative Modernization: A Reader* (New York: Free Press).

Inkeles, A. and Smith, D. (1993), 'Becoming modern', in M. A. Seligson and J. T. Passe Smith (eds), *Development and Underdevelopment* (Boulder, CO: Lynne Rienner Publishers).

Institute of Development Studies (2006), 'The power of labeling in development practice', *IDS Policy Briefing*, no. 28, April.

International Labour Organisation (2004), *A Fair Globalization? Creating Opportunities for All* (Geneva: World Commission on the Social Dimensions of Globalization, ILO).

International Monetary Fund (1998), *The IMF and the Poor*, IMF Fiscal Affairs Department (Washington, DC: IMF).

International Monetary Fund (2006), 'Transcript of the World Economic Outlook Press Briefing', April 19, http://www.imf.org/external/np/tr/2006/tr060419.ttm

Jackson, C. (1993), 'Women/nature or gender/history? A critique of ecofeminist "development"', *Journal of Peasant Studies*, 20(3): April.

Jain, S. and Polman, W. (2003), *A Handbook for Trainers on Participatory Local Development*, 2nd edn (Bangkok: FAO).

Jameson, F. (2004), 'Politics of Utopia', *New Left Review*, January/February.

Jawara, F. and A. Kwa (2003), *Behind the Scenes at the WTO: The Real World of International Trade Negotiations* (London: Zed Books).

Jeppesen, A. (2002), 'Reading the Bolivian landscape of exclusion and inclusion: the Law of Popular Participation', in N. Webster and L. Engberg-Pendersen (eds), *In the Name of the Poor: Contesting Political Space for Poverty Reduction* (London: Zed Books).

Johnson, C. (1995), *Japan: Who Governs? The Rise of the Developmental State* (New York: W. W. Norton).

Johnson, C. (2002), *Blowback* (New York: Time Warner Books).

Johnson, H. (1992), 'Women's empowerment and public action: experiences from Latin America', in M. Wuyts, M. Macintosh and T. Hewitt (eds), *Development Policy and Public Action* (Oxford: Oxford University Press).

Johnston, B. and Clark, W. (1982), *Redesigning Rural Development: A Strategic Perspective* (Baltimore: Johns Hopkins University Press).

Jolly, L. (2000), 'Aborigines and Torres Strait Islanders in Australian Society', in J. Najman and J. Western (eds), *A Sociology of Australian Society*, 3rd edn (Melbourne: Macmillan).

Jordan, J. (1999), 'The end of chaos? Global markets in the information era', 16th Annual John Bonython Lecture, www.cis.org.au/JBL99.html

Kakar, P. (2005), 'Fine-tuning the NSP: discussions of problems and solutions with facilitating partners', Working Paper Series, Afghanistan Research and Evaluation Unit, Kabul.

Kanbur, R. (2002), 'Economics, social science and development', *World Development*, 30(3): 477–86.

Kandawasvika-Nhundu, R. (2003), 'Implementation of quotas: experiences of the SADC Parliamentary Forum', paper presented at the International Institute for Democracy and Electoral Assistance(IDEA)/Electoral Institute of Southern Africa (WISA)/South African Development Community (SADC), Parliamentary Forum Conference, Pretoria, South Africa, 11–12 November.

Kaplinsky, R. (2005), *Globalization, Poverty and Inequality* (Cambridge: Polity Press).

Karnow, S. (1989), *In Our Image: America's Empire in the Philippines* (New York: Random House).

Kasper, W. (2006), 'Make poverty history: tackle corruption' (Sydney: Centre for Independent Studies, Issue Analysis, no. 67).

Kay, G. (1975), *Development and Underdevelopment: A Marxist Analysis* (Basingstoke: Macmillan).

Kay, J. (2004), *The Truth about Markets: Why some Countries are Rich but Most Remain Poor* (London: Penguin).

Kennedy, J. (2002), 'The face of "grssroots democracy" in rural China: real versus cosmetic elections', *Asian Survey*, 42(3): 456–82.

Kiely, R. (1995), *Sociology and Development: The Impasse and Beyond* (London: UCL Press).

Kiely, R. (1998), *Industrialization and Development: A Comparative Analysis* (London: UCL Press).

Kiernan, V. (1972), *The Lords of Human Kind: European Attitudes to the Outside World in the Imperial Age* (London: Penguin).

Kingsnorth, P. (2003), *One No, Many Yeses: The Journey to the Heart of the Global Resistance Movement* (London: Free Press).

Kirkpatrick, J. (1979), 'Dictatorships and double standards', *Commentary*, November.

Klasen, S. (2006), 'Missing women', in D. A. Clark (ed.), *The Elgar Companion to Development Studies* (Cheltenham: Edward Elgar).

Klein, N. (2001), *No Logo* (London: Flamingo).

Kolko, G. (1988), *Confronting the Third World: United States Foreign Policy, 1945–1980* (New York: Pantheon Books).

Korany, B. (1994), 'End of history, or its continuation and accentuation? The global South and new transformation literature', in *Third World Quarterly*, 15(1).

Korten, D. (1980) 'Community organization and rural development: a learning process approach', *Public Administration Review*, 40(5): 480–511.

Kothari, U. (2002), 'Feminist and postcolonial challenges to development', in U. Kothari and M. Minogue (eds), *Development Theory and Practice: Critical Perspectives* (Basingstoke: Palgrave).

Kothari, U. and Minogue, M. (2002), 'Critical perspectives on development: an introduction', in U. Kothari and M. Minogue (eds), *Development Theory and Practice: Critical Perspectives* (Basingstoke: Palgrave).

Krol, L. and L. Goldman (2005), 'The world's billionaires', accessed 3 October 2005, http://www.forbes.com/billionaires/

Krugman, P. (2001), 'Reckonings: hears and minds', *New York Times*, 22 April.

Kuhn, T. S. (1970), *The Structure of Scientific Revolutions* (Chicago: University of Chicago Press).

Kumar, K. (1993), *From Post-Industrial to Post-Modern Society: New Theories of the Contemporary World* (Oxford: Blackwell).

Kuznets, S. (1952), 'Economic growth and income inequality', *American Economic Review*, March, 5(1).

Lal, D. (2004), *In Praise of Empire: Globalization and Order* (Basingstoke: Palgrave).

Landes, D. (2002), *The Wealth and Poverty of Nations* (London: Abacus Books).

Larrain, J. (1989), *Theories of Development: Capitalism, Colonialism and Dependency* (Cambridge: Polity Press).

Lash, S. and Urry, J. (1994), *Economies of Signs and Space* (London: Sage).

Laski, H. (1937), *Liberty in the Modern State* (London: Penguin).

Lawson, S. (1991), *The Failure of Democratic Politics in Fiji* (Oxford: Clarendon Press).

Le Feber, W. (1983), *Inevitable Revolutions: The United States in Central America* (New York: W. W. Norton).

Lehman, G. (2003), 'Telling us true', in R. Manne (ed.), *Whitewash: On Keith Windschuttle's Fabrication of Aboriginal History* (Melbourne: Black).

Lenin, V. I. (1970), *Imperialism: The Highest Stage of Capitalism* (Moscow: Progress Publishers).

Lerner, D. (1972), 'Modernization: social aspects', in D. Sills (ed.), *International Encyclopedia of the Social Sciences*, vol. 9 (New York: Collier Macmillan).

Letwin, W. (1983), *Against Equality* (London: Macmillan).

Lewis, W. A. (1969), *The Principles of Economic Planning* (London: Unwin University Books).

Leys, C. (2004), 'The rise and fall of development theory', in M. Edelman and A. Haugerud (eds), *The Anthropology of Development and Globalisation* (Oxford: Blackwell), pp. 109–25.

Liebman, M. (1975), *Leninism under Lenin* (London: Jonathan Cape).

Lines, W. (1992), *Taming the Great South Land* (Sydney: Allen & Unwin).

Linz, J. (1990), 'Transitions to democracy', *Washington Quarterly*, 13(3).

Linz, J. and Stepan, A. (1996), *Problems of Democratic Transition and Consolidation: South Europe, South America and Post-Communist Europe* (Baltimore, MD: Johns Hopkins University Press).

Lipietz, A. (1987), *Miracles and Mirages: The Crisis of Global Fordism* (London: Verso Books).

Lipietz, A. (1988), 'New tendencies in the international division of labour: regimes of accumulation and modes of regulation', in A. J. Scott and M. Storper (eds), *Production, Work, Territory: The Geographical Anatomy of Industrial Capitalism* (Boston, MA: Unwin Hyman).

Lister, R. (2004), *Poverty* (Cambridge: Polity Press).

Little, S. (2004), *Design and Determination: The Role of Technology in Redressing Regional Inequities in the Development Process* (Aldershot: Ashgate).

Lomberg, B. (2001), *The Skeptical Environmentalist: Measuring the Real State of the World* (Cambridge: Cambridge University Press).

Lomborg, B. (2003), 'How do we prioritize our resources?', *The IPA Review*, 55(4), December.

Lowe, I. (2004), *Dissent*, Summer 2003–4.

Lowe, I. (2005), *The Big Fix: Radical Solutions to Australia's Environmental Crisis* (Melbourne: Black).

Lummis, C. D. (1992), 'Equality', in W. Sachs (ed.), *The Development Dictionary* (London: Zed Press).

Lyotard, J.-F. (1991), *The Postmodern Explained to Children* (Sydney: Power Publications).

Mabogunje, A. (1980), *The Development Process: A Spatial Perspective* (London: Hutchinson).

Mackintosh, M. (1989), *Gender, Class and Rural Transition: Agribusiness and the Food Crisis in Senegal* (London: Zed Books).

Malouf, D. (1998), *A Spirit of Play* (Sydney: ABC Books).

Mandel, E. (1980), *The Second Slump* (London: Verso Press).

Margolis, J. (2000), *A Brief History of Tomorrow: The Future Past and Present* (London: Bloomsbury).

Marrakhesh Action Plan for Statistics (2004), 'Better data for better results: an action plan for improving development statistics', http://unstats.un.org/unsd/statcom/doc04/marrakhesh.phf

Marshall, T. H. (1977), *Class, Citizenship and Social Development* (Chicago: University of Chicago Press).

Martin, H.-P. and H. Schumann (1997), *The Global Trap: Globalization and the Assault on Democracy and Prosperity* (London: Zed Books).

Marx, K. (1967), *Capital*, vol. 3 (New York: International Publishers).

Marx, K. (1973), 'The Eighteenth Brumaire of Louis Bonaparte', in *Surveys from Exile* (London: Penguin).

Marx, K. (1976), *Capital*, vol. 1 (London: Penguin).

Marx, K. (1982), 'Pathways of social development: a brief against supra-historical theory', in H. Alavi and T. Shanin (eds), *An Introduction to the Sociology of 'Developing Societies'* (Basingstoke: Macmillan).

Marx, K. (1983), 'A contribution to the critique of political economy', in *The Portable Karl Marx* (London: Penguin).

Marx, K. and Engels, F. (1969), *Manifesto of the Communist Party* (Moscow: Progress Publishers).

Marx, K. and Engels, F. (1976), *The German Ideology* (Moscow: Progress Publishers).

Mattera, P. (1986), *Off the Books* (London: Pluto Press).

May, R. (1997), 'East Sepik Province, 1976–1992', in R. May and A. Regan (eds), *Political Decentralisation in a New State: The Experience of Provincial Government in Papua New Guinea* (Bathurst: Crawford House), pp. 228–61.

McClelland, D. (1961), *The Achieving Society* (Princeton, NJ: D. van Nostrand).

McCormick, P. (2002), 'Internet access in Africa: a critical review of public policy pssues', *Comparative Studies of South Asia, Africa and the Middle East*, 22 (1–2).

McGee, R. (2004), 'Constructing poverty trends in Uganda: a multidisciplinary perspective', *Development and Change*, 35(3): 499–523.

McGrath-Champ, S. (2006), 'A spatial perspective on international work and management', in M. Hearn and G. Michelson (eds), *Rethinking Work: Time, Space and Discourse* (Cambridge: Cambridge University Press).

McGuinness, P. P. (1990), *McGuinness: Collected Thoughts* (Melbourne: Schwartz & Wilkinson).

McMichael, P. (2000), *Development and Change: A Global Perspective* (Thousand Oaks, CA: Pine Forge Press).

McMurtry, J. (1978), *The Structure of Marx's World-View* (Princeton, NJ: Princeton University Press).

Meadows, D. *et al.* (1972), *The Limits to Growth* (New York: Signet Books).

Meadows, D. *et al.* (2005), *Limits to Growth: The 30-Year Update* (London: Earthscan).

Mehrotra, S. (2006), 'Child poverty', in D. A. Clark (ed.), *The Elgar Companion to Development Studies* (Cheltenham: Edward Elgar).

Meiksins Wood, E. (1999), 'Unhappy families: global capitalism in a world of nation-states', *Monthly Review*, 51(3), July–August.

Melotti, U. (1981), *Marx and the Third World* (London: Macmillan).

Mennell, S. (1985), *All Manners of Food* (Urbana: University of Illinois Press).

Menshikov, S. (1999), 'Russian capitalism today', *Monthly Review*, 51(3), July–August.

Merchant, C. (1982), *The Death of Nature: Women, Ecology and the Scientific Revolution* (London: Wildwood House).

Mies, M. (1987), *Patriarchy and Accumulation on a World Scale* (London: Zed Books).

Mies, M. (1994), ' "Gender" and Global Capitalism', in L. Sklair (ed.), *Capitalism and Development* (London: Routledge).

Mill, J. S. (1859 [1974]), *On Liberty* (Harmondsworth: Penguin).

Miller, D. (1992), 'Equality and inequality', in W. Outhwaite and T. Bottomore (eds), *The Blackwell Dictionary of Twentieth-Century Social Thought* (Oxford: Blackwell), pp. 200–2.

Mills, C.W. (1973), *The Sociological Imagination* (London: Penguin).

Minogue, M. (2002), 'Power to the people: good governance and the reshaping of the state', in U. Kothari and M. Minogue (eds), *Development Theory and Practice: Critical Perspectives* (Basingstoke: Palgrave).

Mittelman, J. (1988), *Out from Underdevelopment* (London: Macmillan).

Molotch, H. (2005), *Where Stuff Comes From* (New York: Routledge).

Mooney, G. (2000), 'Class and social policy', in G. Lewis, S. Gewirtz and J. Clarke (eds), *Rethinking Social Policy* (London: Sage).

Moran, A. (2000) 'Globalisation and the Environment', accessed 27 October 2000, http://www.ipa.org.au/Speechesandsubmssns/amglobenv. html

Morawetz, D. (1977), *Twenty-Five Years of Economic Development: 1950–1975* (Washington, DC: World Bank).

Morley, M. (2002), *Washington, Somoza, and the Sandinistas* (Cambridge: Cambridge University Press).

Moussa, P. (1962), *The Underprivileged Nations* (London: Sidgwick & Jackson).

Muni, S. D. (1979), 'The Third World: concept and controversy', *Third World Quarterly*, 1 (3).

Murray, C. (1984), *Losing Ground: American Social Policy, 1950–1980* (New York: Basic Books).

Murray, C. (2001), *Underclass + 10* (London: Insitute for the Study of Civil Society).

Myrdal, G. (1951), 'The trend towards economic planning', *Manchester School of Economic and Social Studies*, 29, January.

Myrdal, G. (1977), *Asian Drama: An Inquiry into the Poverty of Nations* (London: Penguin).

Myrdal, G. (1989), 'The equality issue in world development', *American Economic Review*, 79(6).

Naipaul, S. (1988), 'The illusion of the Third World', in S. Naipaul, *An Unfinished Journey* (London: Abacus).

Narayan, D., Chambers, R., Shah, M. and Petesch, P. (2000) *Voices of the Poor: Crying out for Change* (Washington, DC: World Bank).

Narayan, D. with Patel, R., Schafft, K., Rademacher, A. and Koch-Schulte, S. (2000), *Voices of the Poor: Can Anyone Hear Us?* (Oxford: Oxford University Press for the World Bank).

New Internationalist (2001), 'Shrink it or sink it', no. 334, May.

New Internationalist (2006), 'Worldbeaters: Hernando de Soto', no. 389, May.

Nolan, B. and Whelan, C. T. (1996) *Resources, Deprivation and Poverty* (Oxford: Clarendon Press).

Norberg, J. (2003), *In Defense of Global Capitalism* (Washington, DC: CATO Institute).

Norberg, J. (2005), 'The wealth of generations: capitalism and the belief in the future', 22nd John Bonython Lecture, Sydney, accessed 11 October, http://www.cis.org.au/Events/JBL/JBL05.htm

Nordstrom, H. and Vaughan, S. (1999), *Trade and the Environment*, WTO Special Studies 4, Geneva, WTO.

Nove, A. (1964), *Was Stalin Really Necessary?* (London: George Allen & Unwin).

Nove, A. (1980), *An Economic History of the USSR* (London: Penguin).

Nun, J. (1967), 'The middle-class military coup', in C. Véliz (ed.), *The Politics of Conformity in Latin America* (Oxford: Oxford University Press), pp. 66–118.

Nun, J. (1986), 'The middle-class military coup revisited', in A. Lowenthal and J. Fitch (eds), *Armies and Politics in Latin America* (New York: Holmes and Meier), pp. 59–95.

Nussbaum, M. C. (2000), *Women and Human Development: The Capabilities Approach* (Cambridge: Cambridge University Press).

O'Brien, K. and Li, L. (2000), 'Accommodating "democracy" in a one-party state: introducing village elections in China', *The China Quarterly*, 162: 465–89.

O'Connor, A. (2001), *Poverty Knowledge: Social Science, Social Policy, and the Poor in Twentieth-Century US History* (Princeton, NJ: Princeton University Press).

Ohmae, K. (2000), 'A world no longer round: the new frontier is shifting fundamental life assumptions', *The Australian*, 26 July.

Olsen, M. (1982), *The Rise and Decline of Nations* (New Haven, CT: Yale University Press).

Orwell, G. (1962 [1946]), 'Politics and the English language', in *Inside the Whale and Other Essays* (London: Penguin).

Ottaway, M. (2005), 'Civil society', in P. Burnell and V. Randall (eds), *Politics in the Developing World* (Oxford: Oxford University Press), pp. 120–35.

Paluzzi, J. and Farmer, P. (2005), 'The wrong question', *Development*, 48(1): March.

Panayiotopoulos, P. (2001), 'The global textile industry: an engendered protectionism', in P. Panyiotopoulos and G. Capps (ed.), *World Development: An Introduction* (London: Pluto Press).

Panitch, L. and Gindin, S. (2004), in L. Panitch and C. Leys (eds), *The Imperial Challenge: The Socialist Register 2004* (Monmouth: Merlin Press).

Papadakis, E. (1991), 'Does the new politics have a future?', in F. G. Castles (ed.), *Australia Compared: People, Policies and Politics* (Sydney: Allen & Unwin).

Parson, T. (1964), *The Social System* (New York: Free Press).

Passe-Smith, J. T. (1993), 'The persistence of the gap: taking stock of economic growth in the post-World War Two era', in M. A. Seligson and J. T. Passé-Smith (eds), *Development and Underdevelopment: The Political Economy of Inequality* (Boulder, CO: Lynne Rienner).

Patnaik, P. (1999), 'Capitalism in Asia at the end of the Millennium', *Monthly Review*, 51(3), July–August.

Payer, C. (1974), *The Debt Trap: The IMF and the Third World* (London: Penguin).

Payne, A. (2005), *The Global Politics of Unequal Development* (Basingstoke: Palgrave Macmillan).

Payne, R. and Nasser, J. (2006), *Politics and Culture in the Developing World: The Impact of Globalization* (New York: Pearson Longman).

Pearson, R. (2002), 'Rethinking gender matters in development', in T. Allen and A. Thomas (eds), *Poverty and Development into the 21st Century* (Oxford: Oxford University Press).

Peck, J. (2001), *Workfare States* (New York: Guildford Press).

Peet, R. (1999), *Theories of Development* (New York: Guilford Press).

Petras, J. (1996), 'The process of globalization: the role of the state and multinational corporations', *Links*, 7 (July–October).

Petras, J. and H. Veltmeyer (1999), 'Latin America at the end of the Millennium', *Monthly Review*, 51(3), July–August.

Pettman, J. (1992), *Living in the Margins* (Sydney: Allen & Unwin).

Philippines, Republic of the (1991) *Republic Act 7160: The Local Government Code of 1991*, Manila.

Phillips, N. (2004), 'The Americas', in A. Payne (ed.), *The New Regional Politics of Development* (Basingstoke: Palgrave Macmillan).

Physicians for Human Rights (2006), *Darfur – Assault on Survival: A Call for Security, Justice, and Restitution* (Cambridge, MA: Physicians for Human Rights).

Pieterse, J. N. (2004), *Globalization or Empire?* (London: Routledge).

Pinkney, R. (2003), *Democracy in the Third World*, 2nd edn (Boulder, CO: Lynne Rienner).

Pinter, H. (2006), 'Art, truth and politics', in B. Eno *et al.*, *Not One More Death* (London: Verso).

Piore, M. and Sabel, C. (1984), *The Second Industrial Divide* (New York: Basic Books).

Pogge, T. (2002), *World Poverty and Human Rights: Cosmopolitan Responsibilities and Reform* (Cambridge: Polity Press).

Power, M. (2003), *Rethinking Development Geographies* (London: Routledge).

Preobrazhensky, E. (1967), *The New Economics* (Oxford: Clarendon Press).

Preston, P. W. (1996), *Development Theory: An Introduction* (Oxford: Blackwell).

Pretty, J. (1995), 'Participatory learning for sustainable agriculture', *World Development*, 23(8): 1247–63.

Price, G. (2003), 'Economic growth in a cross-section of non-industrial countries: does colonial heritage matter for Africa', *Review of Development Economics*, 7(3).

Probert, B. (1993), 'Globalization, economic restructuring and the state' in S. Bell and B. Head (eds), *State, Economy and Public Policy in Australia* (Melbourne: Oxford University Press).

Prosterman, R. (2005), 'The UN's empty plan for poverty', *Far Eastern Economic Review*, April, 43–5.

Putnis, P. (2001), 'Popular discourses and images of poverty and welfare in the news media', in R. Fincher and P. Saunders (eds), *Creating Unequal Futures: Rethinking Poverty, Inequality and Disadvantage* (Sydney: Allen & Unwin, 2001).

Qizilbash, M. (2002), 'Development, common foes and shared values', *Review of Political Economy*, 14(4): 463–80.

Rahmen, A. N. S. H. (2000), 'In quest of quality education for the excluded', paper presented at the International Special Education Congress, University of Manchester, 24–8 July.

Rahnema, M. (1991), *Global Poverty: A Pauperizing Myth* (Montreal, Intercultural).

Rahnema, M. (1992), 'Participation', in W. Sachs (ed.) *The Development Dictionary: A Guide to Knowledge as Power* (London: Zed Books).

Rahnema, M. (1997a), 'Afterword: towards post-development – searching for signposts, a new language and new paradigms', in M. Rahnema and V. Bawtree (eds), *The Post-Development Reader* (London: Zed Books), pp. 377–403.

Rahnema, M. (1997b), 'Poverty', in W. Sachs (ed.), *The Development Dictionary: A Guide to Knowledge as Power* (London: Zed Books).

Rahnema, M. and Bawtree, V. (eds) (1997), *The Post-Development Reader* (London: Zed Books).

Ramamurthy, P. (2000), 'Indexing alternatives: feminist development studies and global political economy', *Feminist Theory*, 1(2).

Ramonet, I. (2004), *Wars of the 21st Century: New Threats*, New Fears (Melbourne: Ocean Press).

Ranis, G. (1997), 'The World Bank near the turn of the century', in R. Culpepper, A. Berry and F. Stewart (eds), *Global Development Fifty Years after Bretton Woods* (New York: St Martin's Press).

Rapley, J. (2002), *Understanding Development: Theory and Practice in the Third World* (Boulder, CO: Lynne Rienner).

Rapley, J. (2004), *Globalization and Inequality: Neoliberalism's Downward Spiral* (Boulder, CO: Lynne Rienner).

Ravallion, M. (2001), 'Growth, inequality and poverty: looking beyond averages', *World Development* 29(11): 1803–15.

Rawls, J. (1971), *A Theory of Justice* (Oxford: Clarendon Press).

Reddy, S. and Pogge, T. (2003), 'How not to count the poor', available online at www.socialanalysis.org/ (forthcoming in S. Anand and J. Stiglitz (eds), *Measuring Global Poverty*, Oxford: Oxford University Press).

Reich, R. (1992), *The Work of Nations* (New York: Vintage).

Reilly, B. (1999) 'Party politics in Papua New Guinea: a deviant case?', *Pacific Affairs*, 72(2): 225–40.

Reynolds, H. (1989), *Dispossession* (Sydney: Allen & Unwin).

Rhodes, R. (ed.) (1970), *Imperialism and Underdevelopment* (New York: Monthly Review Press).

Richard, N. (1993), 'Postmodernism and periphery', in T. Docherty (ed.), *Postmodernism: A Reader* (New York: Harvester Wheatsheaf).

Rigby, H. (1977), 'Stalinism and the mono-organizational society', in R. Tucker (ed.), *Stalinism: Essays in Historical Interpretation* (New York: W. W. Norton).

Rist, G. (1999), *The History of Development: From Western Origins to Global Faith* (London: Zed Books).

Ritzer, G. (1993), *The McDonaldization of Society* (Thousand Oaks, CA: Pine Forge Press).

Robertson, R. (1990), 'Mapping the global condition: globalization as the central concept', in M. Featherstone (ed.), *Global Culture* (London: Sage).

Robertson, R. (1992), *Globalization: Social Theory and Global Culture* (London: Sage).

Robinson, N. (2004), 'The post-Soviet space', in A. Payne (ed.), *The New Regional Politics of Development* (Basingstoke: Palgrave Macmillan).

Robinson, W. (2004), *A Theory of Global Capitalism* (Baltimore, MD: Johns Hopkins University Press).

Rodney, W. (1972), *How Europe Underdeveloped Africa* (London: Bogle-L'Ouverture Publications).

Rodrik, D. (2000), 'Has globalization gone too far?', in J. Timmons Roberts and A. Hite (eds), *From Modernization to Globalization: Perspectives on Development and Social Change* (Oxford: Blackwell).

Rondinelli, D. (1982), *Development Projects as Policy Experiments: An Adaptive Approach to Development Administration* (London: Methuen).

Rosenau, P. M. (1992), *Post-Modernism and the Social Sciences: Insights, Inroads, and Intrusions* (Princeton, NJ: Princeton University Press).

Rosenberg, J. (2000), *The Follies of Globalisation Theory* (London: Verso).

Ross, A. (ed.) (1997), *No Sweat: Fashion, Free Trade and the Rights of Garment Workers* (London: Verso Press).

Rostow, W.W. (1960), *The Stages of Economic Growth: A Non-Communist Manifesto* (Cambridge: Cambridge University Press).

Rowbottom, S. (1993), *Homeworkers Worldwide* (London: Merlin).

Rowntree, B. S. (1901), *Poverty: A Study of Town Life* (London: Macmillan).

Roxborough, I. (1979), *Theories of Underdevelopment* (London: Macmillan).

Roy, A. (2002), *The Algebra of Infinite Justice* (London: Famingo).

Roy, A. (2004), *The Chequebook and the Cruise-Missile* (London: Harper Perennial).

Rubel, M. (1969), 'The relationship of Bolshevism to Marxism', in R. Pipes (ed.), *Revolutionary Russia: A Symposium* (New York: Anchor Books).

Ruigrok, W. and R. van Tulder (1995), *The Logic of International Restructuring* (London).

Ryan, J. and Durning, A. T. (1997), *Stuff: The Secret Life of Things* (Seattle: Northwest Environment Watch).

Sachs, J. (2005), *The End of Poverty: How We Can Make it Happen in our Lifetime* (London: Penguin).

Sachs, J. (2006), 'Foreign aid skeptics thrive on pessimism', *Los Angeles Times*, 7 May.

Sachs, J. and Reid, W. (2006), 'Investments toward sustainable development', *Science*, 312(19).

SADC Parliamentary Forum (1999) SADC Parliamentary Forum Website http://www.sadcpf.org/index.php?disp=profilehome, accessed 9 March 2006.

Sadasivam, B. (2005), 'Wooing the MDG-Skeptics', in *Development*, 48(1), March.

Said, E. (1979), *Orientalism* (New York: Vintage).

Said, E. (1994), *Imperialism and Culture* (London: Vintage).

Sanderson, S. K. (2005), 'World-systems analysis after thirty years: should it rest in peace?', *International Journal of Comparative Sociology*, 46(3).

Saul, J. S. and Leys, C. (1999), 'Sub-Saharan Africa in global capitalism', *Monthly Review*, 51(3), July–August.

Saunders, K. (ed.) (2002), *Feminist Post-Development Thought: Rethinking Modernity, Post-Colonialism and Representation* (London: Zed Books).

Saunders, P. (2005), *The Poverty Wars* (Sydney: University of New South Wales Press).

Savage, M. (2000), *Class Analysis and Social Transformation* (London: Open University Press).

Schlesinger, S. and Kinger, S. (1982), *Bitter Fruit: The Untold Story of the American Coup in Guatemala* (London: Sinclair Brown).

Schmitter, P. (1995), 'Transitology: the science and art of democratization', in J. Tulchin and B. Romero (eds), *The Consolidation of Democracy in Latin America* (Boulder, CO: Lynne Rienner).

Schmitter, P. and Karl, T. (1991), 'What democracy is . . . and is not', *Journal of Democracy*, 2(3): 75–88.

Schmitter, P. and O'Donnell, G. (1986), *Transformations from Authoritarian Rule: Tentative Conclusions from Uncertain Democracies* (Baltimore, MD: Johns Hopkins University Press).

Scholte, J. A. (2000), *Globalization: A Critical Introduction* (Basingstoke: Palgrave Macmillan).

Schumpeter, J. (1975), *Capitalism, Socialism and Democracy* (New York: Harper).

Scott, J. (1998), *Seeing like a State: How Certain Schemes to Improve the Human Condition Have Failed* (New Haven, CT: Yale University Press).

Sen, A. K. (1981), *Poverty and Famines: An Essay on Entitlements and Deprivation* (Oxford: Oxford University Press).

Sen, A. K. (1984), *Resources, Values and Development* (Oxford: Basil Blackwell).

Sen, A. K. (1990a), 'Development as capability expansion', in K. Griffin and J. Knight (eds), *Human Development and the International Development Strategy for the 1990s* (London: Macmillan), pp. 41–58.

Sen, A. K. (1990b), 'More than 100 million women are missing', *New York Review of Books*, 20 December.

Sen, A. K. (1992), *Inequality Re-examined* (Oxford: Clarendon Press).

Sen, A. K. (1993), 'Capability and well-being', in M. C. Nussbaum and A. Sen (eds), *The Quality of Life* (Oxford: Clarendon Press), pp. 30–53.

Sen, A. K. (2001a), 'Global Doubts as Global Solutions', Alfred Deakin Lecture, ABC Radio National, Melbourne, accessed 15 May, http://www.abc.net.au/rn/deakin/stories/s296978.htm.

Sen, A. K. (2001b), *Development as Freedom* (Oxford: Oxford University Press).

Sen, A. K. (2005), 'Human rights and capabilities', *Journal of Human Development*, 6(2): 151–66.

Sen, A. K. (2006a), 'The man without a plan', *Foreign Affairs*, March/April.

Sen, A. K. (2006b), 'Human Development Index' in D. A. Clark (ed.), *The Elgar Companion to Development Studies* (Cheltenham: Edward Elgar).

Shachtman (1962), *The Bureaucratic Revolution: The Rise of the Stalinist State* (New York: The Donald Press).

Shahidullah, S. (1996), 'The Third World after the Cold War: global imperatives and local peculiarities', *Journal of Developing Societies*, XII (June).

Shanin, T. (ed.) (1984), *Marx and the Russian Road: Marx and 'the Peripheries' of Capitalism* (London: Routledge and Kegan Paul).

Shanin, T. (1995), 'The Idea of Progress', accessed November, http://www.msses.ru/shanin/idea.html.

Shanmugaratnam, N. (1989), 'Development and environment: a view from the South', *Race and Class*, 30(3).

Shetty, S. (2005), 'The Millennium Campaign: getting governments to keep their promises', *Development*, 48(1), March.

Shiva, V. (1989), *Staying Alive: Women, Ecology and Development* (London: Zed Books).

Shiva, V. (2001), 'The world on the edge', in W. Hutton and A. Giddens (eds), *On the Edge: Living with Global Capitalism* (London: Vintage Books).

Shiva, V. (2003), 'Food democracy versus food dictatorship: the politics of genetically modified food', *Z Magazine*, April.

Sikora, J. (2004), 'Global inequality: moral obligations of wealthy nations? Attitudes in 26 countries in 1999/2000', in M. Evans and J. Kelley (eds), *Australian Economy and Society 2002* (Sydney: The Federation Press).

Simmel, G. (1964), *The Sociology of Georg Simmel* (New York: Free Press).

Singer, P. (2002), *One World: The Ethics of Globalisation* (Melbourne: Text Press).

Singer, P. and Gregg, T. (2004), *How Ethical is Australia? An Examination of Australia's Record as a Global Citizen* (Melbourne: Black).

SIPRI (2006), *SIPRI Yearbook 2006: Armaments, Disarmament and International Security* (Stockholm: Stockholm International Peace Research Institute).

Sklair, L. (2001), *The Transnational Capitalist Class* (Oxford: Blackwell).

Smart, B. (1993), *Postmodernity* (London: Routledge).

Smillie, I. (1995) *The Alms Bazaar* (London: IT Publications).

Smith, A. (1983), *State and Nation in the Third World* (London: Wheatsheaf).

Smith, B. (1985) *Decentralization: The Territorial Dimension of the State* (London: George Allen & Unwin).

Smith, B. (1993) *Choices in the Design of Decentralisation* (London: Commonwealth Secretariat).

Smith, B. (1996), *Understanding Third World Politics* (Basingstoke: Macmillan).

Smith, B. (2003), *Understanding Third World Politics: Theories of Political Change and Development*, 2nd edn (Basingstoke: Palgrave Macmillan).

So, A. (1990), *Social Change and Development: Modernization, Dependency, and World-Systems Analysis* (London: Sage).

Soja, E. (1989), *Post-Modern Geographies* (London: Verso Press).

Soros, G. (2004), *The Bubble of American Supremacy* (London: Pheonix).

Spencer, H. (1982), *Man versus the State* (Indianapolis: Liberty Classics).

Spulber, N. (1964), *Soviet Strategies for Economic Growth* (Bloomington: Indiana University Press).

Stewart, F. (1985), *Planning to Meet Basic Needs* (Basingstoke: Macmillan).

Stewart F. (2006), 'Basic needs approach', in D. A. Clark (ed.), *The Elgar Companion to Development Studies* (Cheltenham: Edward Elgar).

Stiglitz, J. (2002), *Globalization and its Discontents* (London: Penguin).

Streeten, P. P., Burki, S.J., Haq, M. ul, Hicks, N. and Stewart, F. (1981), *First Things First: Meeting Basic Human Needs in Developing Countries* (New York: Oxford University Press).

Stretton, H. (1987), *Political Essays* (Melbourne: Georgian House).

Summers, A. (2003), *The End of Equality* (Sydney: Random House).

Sundaram, K. and Tendulkar, S. (2003) 'NAS-NSS estimates of private consumption for poverty estimation', *Economic and Political Weekly*, 25 January 2003.

Sutor, K. (2000), *In Defence of Globalisation* (Sydney: University of New South Wales Press).

Sutton, P.W. (2004), *Nature, Environment and Society* (Basingstoke: Palgrave Macmillan).

Sylvester, C. (1999), 'Development studies and postcolonial studies: disparate tales of the "Third World"', *Third World Quarterly*, 20(4).

Tabb, W. (1997), 'Globalization is *an* issue, the power of capital is *the* issue', *Monthly Review*, 49(2).

Tabb, W. (2000), 'After Seattle: understanding the politics of globalization', *Monthly Review*, 51(10), March.

Tabb, W. (2001) *The Amoral Elephant* (New York: Monthly Review Press).

Tabb, W. (2004), *Economic Governance in the Age of Globalization* (New York: Colombia University Press).

Tanner, L. (1999), *Open Australia* (Sydney: Pluto Press).

Tanzer, M. (1995), 'Globalizing the economy: the influence of the International Monetary Fund and the World Bank', *Monthly Review*, 47(4), September.

Tawney, R. H. (1931), *Equality* (London: G. Allen & Unwin).

Thomas, H. (2003), *Rivers of Gold* (London: Weidenfeld & Nicolson).

Thomas, P. (1986), 'Women and development: a two-edged sword', in Australian Council for Overseas Aid, *Development in the Pacific: What Women Say*, Development Dossier no. 18.

Thompson, E. (1993), *Fair Enough: Egalitarianism in Australia* (Sydney: University of New South Wales Press).

Todaro, M. (1980), *Economics for a Developing World* (London: Longman).

Todaro, M. (1990), *Economic Development in the Third World* (London: Longman).

Toit, A. du, (2005), 'Poverty measurement blues: some reflections on the space for understanding "chronic" and "structural" poverty in South Africa', *CPRC Working Paper no. 55*, Chronic Poverty Research Centre,

University of Manchester, UK. Available online at http://www.chronicpoverty.org/pdfs/55duToit.pdf, accessed 3 November 2005.

Toulmin, S. (1990), *Cosmopolis* (Chicago: University of Chicago Press).

Touraine, A. (1985), 'An introduction to the study of new social movements', *Social Research*, 52(4).

Townsend, P. (1979), *Poverty in the United Kingdom: A Survey of Household Resources and Standards of Living* (Penguin: Harmondsworth).

Townsend, P. (2002), 'Poverty, social exclusion and social polarisation: the need to construct an international welfare stage', in P. Townsend and D. Gordon (eds), *World Poverty* (Bristol: Policy Press), pp. 3–24.

Trainer, T. (1994), *Developed to Death: Rethinking Third World Development* (London: Merlin Press).

Trainer, T. (1998), *Saving the Environment* (Sydney: University of New South Wales Press).

Trotsky, L. (1959), *The Russian Revolution* (New York: Doubleday Anchor).

Trotsky, L. (1980), *The Revolution Betrayed: What is the Soviet Union and Where is it Going?* (New York: Pathfinder Press).

Tucker, R. (1977), *The Inequality of Nations* (New York: Basic Books).

Turner, M. (1990) *Papua New Guinea: The Challenge of Independence* (London: Penguin).

Turner, M. (1999a) 'Central–local relations: themes and issues', in M.Turner (ed.), *Central–Local Relations in Asia-Pacific: Convergence or Divergence?* (Basingstoke: Macmillan), pp. 1–18.

Turner, M. (1999b) 'Philippines: from centralism to localism', in M. Turner (ed.), *Central–Local Relations in Asia-Pacific: Convergence or Divergence?* (Basingstoke: Macmillan), pp. 97–122.

Turner, M. and Hulme, D. (1997) *Governance, Administration and Development: Making the State Work* (Basingstoke: Macmillan).

Unger, J. (2006), 'China's conservative middle class', *Far Eastern Economic Review*, 169(3): 27–31.

UN Department of Economic and Social Affairs (2005), *Report on the World Social Situation 2005: The Inequality Predicament* (New York: United Nations).

UN Development Programme (1992), *Human Development Report 1992* (New York: Oxford University Press).

UN Development Programme (1995), *Human Development Report 1995: International Cooperation at a Crossroads – Aid, Trade and Security in an Unequal World* (New York: Oxford University Press).

UN Development Programme (1997), *Reconceptualising Governance* (New York: UNDP).

UN Development Programme (1997), *Human Development Report 1997: Eradicating Poverty* (New York: Oxford University Press).

UN Development Programme (2000), *Human Development Report 2000: Human Rights and Human Development* (New York: Oxford University Press).

UN Development Programme (2002), *Human Development Report 2002: Deepening Democracy in a Fragmented World* (New York: Oxford University Press).

UN Development Programme (2003), *Human Development Report 2003: Millennium Development Goals: A Compact Among Nations to End Human Poverty* (New York: Oxford University Press).

UN Development Programme (2004a), *South Africa Human Development Report: The Challenge of Sustainable Development* (Oxford: Oxford University Press).

UN Development Programme (2004b) *Human Development Report 2004* (Oxford: Oxford University Press).

UN Development Programme (2005), *Human Development Report 2005* (New York: United Nations).

UN Habitat (2004), *The State of the World's Cities 2004/2005* (London: Earthscan).

UNHCR (2005), *2004 Global Refugee Trends: Overview of Refugee Populations, New Arrivals, Durable Solutions, Asylum Seekers, Stateless and other Persons of Concern to the UNHCR*, 17 June (Geneva: UNHCR).

United Nations Information Service (2004), 'United Nations Drug Office Reports Major Increase in Opium Cultivation in Afghanistan', www.unis.unvienna.org/unis/pressrels/2004/unisnar867.htm

UN Millennium Project (2005a), *Investing in Development: A Practical Plan to Achieve the Millennium Development Goals* (New York: United Nations).

UN Millennium Project (2005b), *The Millennium Development Goals Report 2005* (New York: United Nations).

University for Peace (2006), *Environmental Degradation as a Source of Conflict in Darfur* (Addis Ababa: University of Peace Africa Program).

Valenzuela, J. S. and Valenzuela, A. (1978), 'Modernization and dependency: alternative perspectives in the study of Latin American development', in *Comparative Politics* 10(4).

Vandemoortele, J. (2005), 'Ambition is Golden: Meeting the MDGs', *Development* 48(1), March.

Van de Walle, N. (2005), *Overcoming Stagnation in Aid-Dependent Countries* (Washington, DC: Centre for Global Development).

van Krieken, R. *et al.* (2000), *Sociology: Themes and Perspectives* (Melbourne: Longman).

Wachtel, H. (1986), *The Money Mandarins: The Making of a New Supranational Economic Order* (New York: Pantheon Books).

Waddington, M. and Mohan, G. (2004), 'Failing forward: going beyond PRA and imposed forms of participation', in S. Hickey and G. Mohan (eds), *Participation: From Tyranny to Transformation* (London: Zed Books), pp. 219–34.

Wade, R. (2001a), 'US hegemony and the World Bank', *New Left Review*, 7.

Wade, R. (2001b), 'Winners and losers', in *The Economist*, 26 April 2001.

Wade, R. (2004), 'Is Globalisation Reducing Poverty and Inequality?', *World Development*, 32(4).

Wade, R. (2006), 'Choking the South', *New Left Review*, March/April.

Walicki, A. (1979), *A History of Russian Thought from the Enlightenment to Marxism* (Stanford, CA: Stanford University Press).

Wallerstein, I. (1974), 'The rise and future demise of the world capitalist system', *Comparative Studies in Society and History*, 16(4), September.

Wallerstein, I. (1976), *The Modern World-System*, vol. I: *Capitalist Agriculture and the Origins of the European World-Economy in the Sixteenth Century* (London: Academic Press).

Wallerstein, I. (1980), *The Modern World-System*, vol. 2: *Mercantilism and the Consolidation of the European World-Economy* (London: Academic Press).

Wallerstein, I. (1982), 'The rise and future demise of the world capitalist system: concepts for comparative analysis', in H. Alavi and T. Shamin (eds), *An Introduction to the Sociology of 'Developing Societies'* (Basingstoke: Macmillan).

Wallerstein, I. (1994), 'Development: lodestar or illusion', in L. Sklair (ed.), *Capitalism and Development* (London: Routledge).

Wallerstein, I. (2002), *The Decline of American Power* (New York: The New Press).

Wallerstein, I. (2003), 'Entering global anarchy', *New Left Review*, 22, July–August.

Wallerstein, I. (2004), *World-Systems Analysis: An Introduction* (Durham, NC: Duke University Press).

Waring, M. (1989), *Counting for Nothing: What Men Value and what Women are Worth* (Wellington: Allen & Unwin).

Warren, K. (1987), 'Feminism and ecology: making connections', *Environmental Ethics* vol. 9.

Weaver, J. and M. Berger (1984), 'The Marxist critique of dependency theory: an introduction', in C. Wilber (ed.), *The Political Economy of Development and Underdevelopment* (New York: Random House).

Weber, E. (1976), *Peasants into Frenchmen: The Modernization of Rural France, 1870–1914* (Stanford, CA: Stanford University Press).

Weber, M. (1947), *The Theory of Social and Economic Organization* (New York: Free Press).

Weber, M. (1978), *The Protestant Ethic and the Spirit of Capitalism* (London: Allen & Unwin).

Webster, A. (1984), *Introduction to the Sociology of Development* (Basingstoke: Macmillan).

Weiss, L. (1998), *The Myth of the Powerless State: Governing the Economy in a Global Era* (Cambridge: Polity Press).

Wertheim, W.F. (1974), 'The rising waves of emancipation – from counterpoint towards revolution', in E. de Kadt and G. Williams (ed.), *Sociology and Development* (London: Tavistock).

White, H. (2006), 'Millennium Development Goals', in D. A. Clark (ed.), *The Elgar Companion to Development Studies* (Cheltenham: Edward Elgar).

Wilkinson, R. (1973), *Poverty and Progress* (London: Methuen).

Williams, E. (1987), *Capitalism and Slavery* (London: André Deutsch).

Williams, R. (1983), *Towards 2000* (London: Chatto & Windus).

Williamson, J. (1994), *The Political Economy of Policy Reform* (Washington, DC: Institute for Policy Reform).

Wilson, F. and Ramphela, R. (1989), *Uprooting Poverty: The South African Challenge* (New York: W. W. Norton).

Windschuttle, K. (2000), 'Rewriting the history of the British Empire', in *New Criterion*, 18(9), May.

Wolf, M. (2005), *Why Globalization Works* (New Haven, CT: Yale University Press).

Wolff, L. (1960), *Little Brown Brother: How the United States Purchased and Pacified the Philippines* (Singapore: Oxford University Press).

Wood, G. (2003), 'Staying secure, staying poor: the "Faustian Bargain" ', *World Development*, 31(3): 455–71.

Woodall, P. (2000), 'The new economy: falling through the net?', *The Economist*, 23 September.

Woodhouse, P. (2002), 'Development policies and environmental agendas', in U. Kothari and M. Minogue (eds), *Development Theory and Practice: Critical Perspectives* (Basingstoke: Palgrave Macmillan).

Woodward, L. (ed.) (2002), 'Eating oil', summary version of the report *Eating Oil: Food Supply in a Changing Climate*, produced by Sustain and Elm Tree Research Centre, Newbury, January.

Working Group on the WTO/MAI (1999), *The Citizen's Guide to the World Trade Organisation*, http://www.citizen.org/documents/wto-book.pdf

World Bank (2006), 'Forests and forestry', http://web.worldbank.org/ WBSITE/EXTERNAL/TOPICS/EXTARD/EXTFORESTS/0,menuPK:98 5797~pagePK:149018~piPK:149093~theSitePK:985785,00.html

World Bank (1989), *World Development Report* (New York: Oxford University Press).

World Bank (1992), *Governance and Development* (Washington, DC: World Bank).

World Bank (1993), *The East Asian Miracle: Economic Growth and Public Policy* (New York: Oxford University Press).

World Bank (1996), *The World Bank Participation Sourcebook* (Washington, DC: World Bank).

World Bank (1999), *World Development Report 1999/2000* (New York: Oxford University Press).

World Bank (2000a), *PRSP Sourcebook* (Washington, DC: World Bank).

World Bank (2000b), *World Development Report 2000/01: Attacking Poverty* (Oxford: Oxford University Press).

World Bank (2001), *Globalization, Growth and Poverty: Building an Inclusive World Economy* (Washington, DC: World Bank Policy Research Report, May).

World Bank (2003), *World Development Report 2004* (Oxford: Oxford University Press).

World Bank (2005a), *East Asia Decentralizes: Making Local Governments Work* (Washington, DC: World Bank).

World Bank (2005b), *World Development Report 2006: Equity and Development* (Oxford: Oxford University Press).

World Social Forum (2002a), 'Call of Social Movements', http://forumsocialmundial.org.br/eng/portoalegrefinal_english.asp

World Trade Organization (2004), *Brief History of the Trade and Environment Debate* (Genva: WTO).

World Trade Organization (2002b), 'The WTO . . . in Brief', http://www.wto.org/english/thewto_e/whatis_e/inbrief_e/inbr00_e.htm

Worsely, P. (1973), *The Third World* (London: Weidenfeld & Nicolson).

Worsley, P. (1979), 'How many worlds', *Third World Quarterly*, 1(2), April.

Wright, H. (ed.) (1976), *The 'New Imperialism': Analysis of Late Nineteenth-Century Expansion* (Lexington: D. C. Heath).

Wright, R. (2005), *A Short History of Progress* (Melbourne: Text Publising).

Wunsch, J. (2001), 'Decentralization, local governance and "recentralization" in Africa', *Public Administration and Development*, 21(4): 277–88.

Wyatt, A. (2004), 'South Asia', in A. Payne (ed.), *The New Regional Politics of Development* (Basingstoke: Palgrave Macmillan).

Yarborough, B. V. and Yarborough, R. M. (1994), 'Regulation and layered governance', *Journal of International Affairs*, 48(1).

Yates, M. (2004), *Naming the System: Inequality and Work in the Global System* (New York: Monthly Review Press).

Yeo, R. and Moore, K. (2003), 'Including disabled people in poverty reduction work: "nothing about us, without us" ', *World Development*, 31(3): 571–90.

Zizek, S. (2004), *Welcome to the Desert of the Real* (London: Verso Press).

Index